David Toews Was Here
1870–1947

David Toews Was Here

1870–1947

by

Helmut Harder

CMBC Publications
Winnipeg, Manitoba
2002

CMBC Publications
600 Shaftesbury Blvd.
Winnipeg, Manitoba R3P 0M4

Photos, unless otherwise identified, are from the
Toews Family Collection
Map on page 8 is reproduced by permission
from *Mennonite Historical Atlas* (Courtesy: Springfield Publishers)

Cover: Roberta Fast
Cartography: Christopher Werner

National Library of Canada Cataloguing in Publication Data
Harder, Helmut, 1934–
 David Toews Was Here, 1870–1947

 Includes bibliographical references.
 ISBN: 0-920718-74-4

1. Toews, David, 1870–1947. 2. Mennonites—Canada—Clergy—Biography.
3. Rosthern Region (Sask.)—Biography. I. Title.

BX8143.T645H37   2002   289.7'092   C2002-910582-X

Copyright ©2002
Canadian Mennonite University

Printed in Canada
by
Christian Press
Winnipeg, Manitoba

Contents

The publisher acknowledges, with thanks:

· the Gerhard Lohrenz Publishing Fund for a generous subsidy;
· Mennonite Foundation Canada, the Mennonite Historical Society of Saskatchewan, and members of the Toews family for raising financial support for this writing project;
· Archives staff, Toews family members, and others for making key documents available.

Acknowledgements

This biography was not written in isolation but was, from beginning to end, a project undertaken in community. While it is substantially the work of one writer, many persons contributed in various ways to its formation.

My conversation with three daughters of David and Margarete Toews provided initial inspiration and orientation for the writing project. Louise (Toews) and Blake Friesen shared memories and resources from their personal collection of family letters and photos. Elsie (Toews) Hooge (now deceased) and Anna (Toews) and Sylvester Funk reflected freely on the dynamics of the Toews household. I also gained much from a timely afternoon visit with Miss Kaethe Hooge (now deceased), a close family friend and long-time secretary for Toews. These relatives and friends provided a living connection with David Toews.

Many others who contributed to this project are hereby gratefully acknowledged:

- staff of the Mennonite Heritage Centre Archives, especially former director Ken Reddig and current director Alfred Redekopp;
- members of the Heritage Committee of Mennonite Church Canada;
- manuscript readers: Lawrence Klippenstein, Henry Paetkau, Ted Regehr, Janet Thiessen, Leo Driedger, and especially Verner Friesen who gave key assistance on details regarding the life of David Toews;
- Jake Wiens and Edward Enns for translation work.

A final word of acknowledgement goes to Irma, my supportive life-partner. She provided the lone audience when I emerged from my writing desk to recount aloud the stories, both joyful and troublesome, that comprised the life of David Toews. She was always ready to listen and to offer words of encouragement. Before the manuscript was given to the editor, she scrutinized the entire text for readability and style.

While I am most grateful for all who gave support and advice, I take full responsibility for what has been written. I pray that the story contained between these covers will inspire the reader as it has the writer.

Helmut Harder
Easter Monday
April 1, 2002

Foreword

The David Toews story has been waiting a long time to be told. Nearly two generations have come and gone since that untiring father, husband and grandfather, teacher, minister, churchman and con-ference leader was still among us. It is more than a half century since he laboured to lead his people toward goals which he felt were so worthy that giving his life to them was not too much and doing less was too little.

Toews arrived on the Canadian Mennonite scene in his early twenties, unobtrusively and unsure of where all this might lead. Steadily he made his way to centre stage, accepting each part of the way as something God was asking him to do and hoping to do what he should.

His arrival in Gretna in 1893 after an eventful trek, that had taken him from Lysanderhöhe on the Volga in central Russia to Kansas in the United States, turned out to be only a prelude to a much longer journey. It would include all those family, community, national, and even international ministries which placed him in the forefront of Canadian Mennonite church and community life right up to 1947 when he went to his reward.

Mennonites of western Canada faced many challenges in the half century of his involvements which are chronicled and analyzed in this volume. In the 1890s they were still newcomers in this region of the country—indeed they were still arriving from southern Russia. Leaders were emerging in the fields of education, pastoral work, intercongregational organization, and joint ministries across the Canada-United States border. But there were numerous gaps in the Mennonite frontier communities of Manitoba and Saskatchewan that needed to be filled. David Toews helped significantly to do just that. How he did so, what moved him to try, and with what effect, is what this book is all about.

It was Heinrich Ewert of Gretna, just then launching a career of real import for Mennonites in Canada, who brought David to Manitoba and mentored him there for a time. They became close friends and soon worked together in committees, though not always seeing eye to eye as time went on. In Saskatchewan Toews helped to found Rosthern Junior College. There he was soon one of a number of ministers serving the Rosenorter Mennonitengemeinde which was founded not long after he moved to Saskatchewan.

Toews played a key role in the administration and visioning of the Conference of Mennonites in Canada which came into being in 1902. The Conference would bring together Manitoba and Saskatchewan Mennonites with a goal of working together. Later congregations from other provinces chose to be part of this venture.

Toews had colleagues within the Conference as well as on the Canadian Mennonite Board of Colonization. Always a significant number of people looked to him for a word of encouragement or a signal on how all their projects could move ahead: the *Gemeinden* were helped to grow, the Junior College survived, the immigration of Mennonites from Soviet Russia did happen, the *Reiseschuld* (transportation debt) was paid off (yes, with some debts written off in the end), and the Conference managed to fulfil its mandate with significant success.

His family experiences remain central to this story, even with all the rest that is said here. David's wife, Margarete, could say—as did her husband at Bergthal when no one arrived for the service—"Margarete was here." She would repeat that for as long as she shared the entire, almost unimaginable, load of responsibilities that fell on their shoulders before their work was done. The children were there also—never out of his thoughts, if not always in his presence.

Toews was not perfect, as a story of significant achievement and successes sometimes is made to sound. No doubt some of his acquaintances and colleagues might have written this book somewhat differently; even this recorded version may get varying interpretations.

But the story stands on its own. Toews was there—at the turn of the century, in the teens, the twenties, thirties and forties—among all in the Canadian Mennonite experience of those years. It is important to know about it and to ponder what it means to us who followed.

This "life and times of . . . ," if you like, remains a clear reminder of what strong commitment, total dedication, endless hard work, and unwavering faithfulness to God can give to others as a result. David Toews was here, and for that we can be thankful.

Lawrence Klippenstein
Retired Archivist
Mennonite Heritage Centre
Winnipeg, Manitoba

Preface

The title for this book has its origin in a story often told about David Toews.[*] Four miles east of Rosthern, where Toews resided for most of his working years, was the settlement of Bergthal. Toews was one of the itinerant preachers who took his turn serving the local Mennonite group that congregated in the local schoolhouse there for worship. In the wintertime it was not uncommon for Sunday services to be cancelled when the temperature became unbearably cold and the snow made roads impassable.

On one particularly frigid Sunday morning—the temperature was said to have been 30 degrees below zero—the person in charge of stoking the stove early Sunday morning predicted that the preacher scheduled to come from Rosthern would not show up. So he left the place unheated and wrote on the blackboard: "There will be no service because the minister can't come." Meanwhile, David Toews had decided to brave the cold weather and walk the four miles to the Bergthal school. When he pushed open the door of the school house, he found the place empty. Seeing the announcement on the blackboard, he picked up the chalk and added four words: "DAVID TOEWS WAS HERE." Since no one had come for the service, he stepped out into the cold morning air and trudged back to Rosthern. The next morning teacher and pupils found his message.

This simple story provides a foretaste of the character of David Toews. He made every effort to fulfil his obligation that Sunday morning. Very likely he comforted himself during the long walk home with the thought that at least *he* had done what *he* could, even if he happened to show up at a non-event. There's a German phrase that makes reference to his kind of person: "Er stellte seinen Mann." That is to say, "He was present to the situation with his entire being." One of his unpublished biographers says of Toews: "He would rather be than appear to be." ("Er wollte lieber sein als scheinen.") It is in this sense that "David Toews was here."

---

[*] For one version of the story, see Cornelius J. Dyck, "David Toews, 1870–1947," chapter in *Twelve Becoming: Biographies of Mennonite Disciples from the Sixteenth to the Twentieth Century* (Newton: Faith and Life Press, 1973), 54.

1
Lysanderhöhe
1870–1880

On the ninth of February in the year 1870, a son was born to Jacob and Anna (Wiebe) Toews. The birth occurred in Lysanderhöhe, a village in the Mennonite settlement, Am Trakt, in the Russian province of Samara.[1] The parents called their son David, a name not found in the recent lineage of either the Toews or the Wiebe families, but the name of a well-known shepherd boy who became king of Old Testament Israel. David was the fifth of eight surviving children of Jacob and Anna Toews.[2] Eight additional children were born to them, all of whom died in infancy. In that day families were large and the rate of infant mortality was high. Humanly speaking, David was fortunate to have been given the gift of life.

Genealogical Roots
David Toews was born in eastern Russia, but his genealogical heritage reached back to Prussia and even further back to the Nether-lands. Being of Anabaptist-Mennonite religious persuasion, David's forebears on both the paternal and maternal side were a persecuted minority in their Dutch homeland. When the situation there became unbearable, perhaps by the end of the sixteenth century, they moved eastward to Prussia to quieter and friendlier surroundings. There, in the delta of the Vistula River south of the city of Danzig, they found land upon which to sustain their large families. Actually, it was swampland that needed reclaiming, but this was no deterrent as they had learned the art of building and maintaining dikes in their former homeland.

Our information about the Toews genealogy begins with David's great-grandfather on the paternal side.[3] He was born in 1785 or 1786, and lived in the village of Hochzeit near the city of Danzig. Hochzeit was located in the Danziger Werder, a low-lying island about 30 kilometres in length. The island was one of many that had been converted into fertile farmland. Once the dikes were built, it took constant vigilance to retain and repair the high walls so the waters would not again flood their lands. There the hard-working Mennonite farmers built their villages and pursued their agrarian way of life.

At the time great-grandfather Toews was a young man, an additional destructive force threatened to destroy the dikes. When General Napoleon of France led his army in an invasion of Prussia between 1806 and 1813, one of his tactics was to destroy the dikes outside the city of Danzig in order to flood the area and make the city dysfunctional. Consequently, the Napoleonic invasion had a debilitating effect upon the economic life of the Mennonites. It took at least two decades to recover from this setback. By the time the elder Toews died at the ripe old age of 84 years, he had faced many challenges, both environmentally and politically.

David's grandfather, whose name was Jacob Toews, was born during the time of Napoleon's invasions. He grew up in the village of Hochzeit. However, when he married in 1833, Jacob and his spouse established a home in the nearby village of Wotslaf. Grandfather Jacob Toews was not only a farmer but was also one of the ministers in the local Mennonite church.

One of grandfather Jacob Toews' sons was also named Jacob. This Jacob, the father of David, was born in 1838 and grew into adulthood in his parental village of Wotslaf. In later years he recalled how, from earliest times, he seemed to have had a special awareness of God's presence in his life. He remembered how, as a four-year-old, he was once rescued from drowning after falling into one of the drainage canals while crossing it on a narrow bridge. He took this as a sign that God had preserved him for some special future purpose. He also remembered how, on the occasion of his Christian baptism at the age of 16, he was overwhelmed by "the sacredness of this holy experience."[4] The special yet undefined purpose for which God had designated him seemed to be confirmed again in this holy moment.

At the age of 20, Jacob Toews and two friends set out on a month-long adventurous trip to visit relatives in the Molotschna colony in Ukraine. Several of his uncles and their families had moved there around 1840. The three made their trip by *troika*, a sturdy wagon pulled by three horses. They left in the spring of 1858 with plans to return in the fall, but they ended up spending the winter in the newly established colony, Am Trakt. There Jacob got a preview of the place to which he and his family would migrate some ten years later.

When Jacob arrived back in Prussia from his journey to Molotschna, he found to his dismay that his mother had died during his absence. While he mourned her loss deeply, the event brought him to the realization that it was time to consider establishing his own home. Jacob found a mate whom he liked and who appeared willing to enter into marriage with him. Her name was Anna Wiebe, the daughter of a widow.

Anna (Wiebe) Toews (at left), mother of David Toews, and her mother. Photo: Fred R. Belk, *The Great Trek*

In accordance with the customs of the day, Jacob informed his father of his intentions, who then approached Anna's mother to ask if her daughter might become Jacob's wife. Permission was granted and the wedding took place in March of 1860.

Jacob and Anna Toews were a good team. Anna was a resourceful and devoted homemaker; Jacob was an industrious farmer and also took a keen interest in spiritual matters. They took charge of the well-established family farm. Together they built an economically stable and spiritually pious home. Jacob's widowed father lived with them as well. In the spring of 1862 the elder Toews was able to make a journey to Molotschna, like his son had done earlier, where he enjoyed a reunion with two of his brothers. Two years after his return in 1864, grandfather Jacob Toews died of pneumonia. His death left a vacancy in the church where he had served as minister. That same year the congregation conducted elections to fill the ministerial position now vacant. Jacob Toews, son of the deceased Jacob, was elected from among the list of nominees. This succession of ministers, from generation to generation, was destined to continue into the next generation as well, in the person of David, Jacob and Anna's son.

Religious Roots

The religious roots of the Toews family reached back into the soil of Anabaptist and Mennonite history. The so-called Anabaptists had their beginning in the left wing of the Reformation in sixteenth-century Europe.[5] This movement originated in two regions of western Europe, the first in the 1520s in Switzerland and South Germany, the second somewhat later, in the 1530s, in the Netherlands and in North Germany. The adherents of this movement were called Anabaptists ("re-baptizers") because they discounted the legitimacy of infant baptism and rather baptized adults on the basis of a personal and mature confession of their faith. The Anabaptists endured much persecution for their radical stance. Menno Simons, a former Catholic priest, converted to the movement in 1536, and distinguished himself as a widely influential pastoral leader and prolific writer on behalf of the persecuted Anabaptists. The name "Mennist," derived from Menno Simons, replaced the term Anabaptist in the latter part of the sixteenth century. Eventually the term "Mennonite Church" persisted as the most common denominational term for this Christian body of believers.

In the context of the sixteenth-century Reformation in Europe, the Anabaptist movement forged a unique understanding of the Christian faith. Its adherents distinguished themselves from the dominant and traditional Catholic Church of the Middle Ages and also from the churches of the Protestant Reformation.[6] Besides adult baptism, the Anabaptists and their Mennonite successors held to the separation of church and state, non-participation in war, an emphasis on following Jesus in discipleship (*Nachfolge*), and the inseparability of grace and works. For their radical beliefs, they were severely persecuted and put to death in considerable numbers. Consequently, they often moved from one region to another in search of a safe haven under a tolerant civil government. This was the religious milieu that cradled David Toews and nurtured his identity.

For the Sake of Peace

When Catherine the Great came to power in Russia in 1762, she had an interest in settling her crown lands with industrious settlers skilled in agriculture. In 1786, her invitation reached the ears of the Mennonite citizens in Prussia. This offer of free land and freedom from military conscription appealed to many, especially the poor and the landless. At that time, the Mennonites sent two representatives, Jacob Hoeppner and Johann Bartsch, to investigate the "promised land." It was a difficult journey, but the two men came back to West Prussia with favourable reports of what they had seen and of what they had been promised.

In the fall of 1788, 225 families left for their new homeland.[7] It was a difficult journey which they did not complete until the following spring. When they finally did arrive at their destination, they were not given the land originally promised. Rather, they ended up in what became the Chortitza Colony along the Dniepr River. Despite difficult beginnings, others followed. Between 1793 and 1797, an additional 118 families joined those already there. They were driven mainly by the fear of what might happen politically if and when, as was being planned, Danzig would be annexed to Prussia in the early 1790s. The uncertainties of Russia were preferable to the heavy political hand of Prussia. Besides, in Russia the settlers had been assured certain exemptions and privileges. This included a parcel of free land for each family, religious toleration, exemption from military service and certain civil service, liberty to establish their own schools and their own language, freedom to establish political and economic institutions as necessary, the right to forbid the erection of taverns in their region, and the right to produce their own beverages. This all sounded very positive.

A second wave of immigrants began in the summer of 1803 with the departure of 162 families.[8] By 1820, this had amounted to 600 families with 400 more following by 1840. Most of the latter settled south of Chortitza in a colony called Molotschna. By 1840 the population of the Molotschna colony was about 10,000 inhabitants spread throughout 46 villages. These immigrants brought more material possessions with them than the earlier Chortitza group since by then they had established themselves quite well in Prussia.

The new Prussian constitution of 1850 produced another wave of interest in immigration to Russia. It was becoming increasingly clearer that the Mennonites were losing any assurance of exemption from military service on religious grounds. But by now the land in the colonies of Chortitza and Molotschna had all been assigned. This meant prospective immigrants had to look elsewhere for settlement possibilities. After extensive negotiations between the Prussian Mennonites and the Russian government, permission was granted to open a settlement in the province of Samara, a considerable distance northeast of the two colonies already established. This time the Mennonite settlers were assured of exemption from military service for a 20-year period. The Russian embassy required each family to pay a sum of money as guarantee that they would not become a burden to the Russian government.

Jacob and Anna Too

In light of the difficult situation in Prussia, Jacob and Anna Toews also faced a decision. Should they stay in Prussia and hope that things

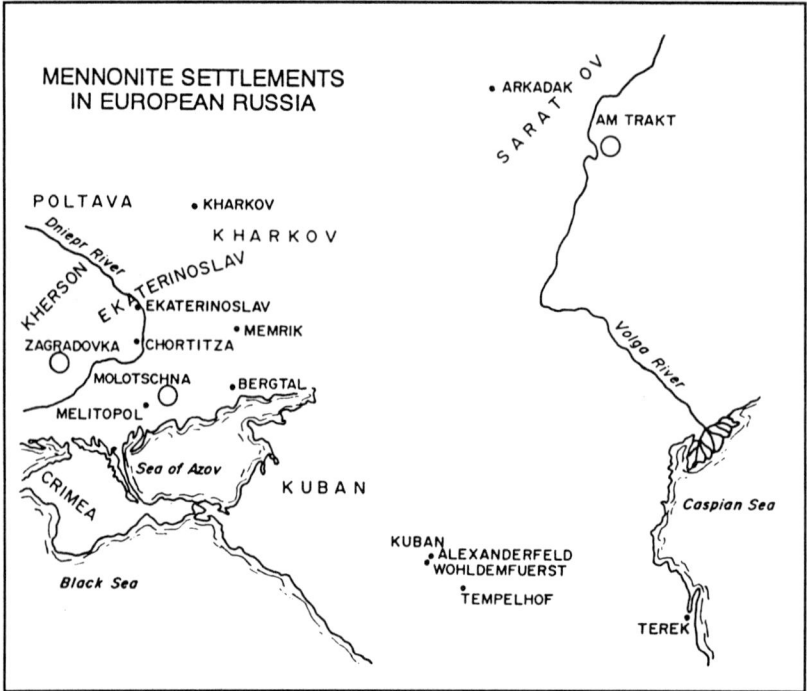

MENNONITE SETTLEMENTS
IN EUROPEAN RUSSIA

would get better? Or should they leave? It did not take Jacob long to decide. By the year 1868, the young couple already had four children: Jacob born in 1861, Heinrich in 1862, Johannes in 1865, and Cornelius in 1868. Given the shortage of land, a growing family of boys, and the threat of military conscription, Prussia was no longer a place to call home. He must take his family elsewhere. He would take his chances on Russia where, at least for the next while, exemption from military service and the freedom to practise their faith in their own way, was guaranteed. So Jacob and Anna sold their property and planned their move to Russia. This was no small sacrifice as it meant uprooting the family and leaving community and church obligations behind. There was some comfort in the fact that he knew where he was going, having visited the Am Trakt settlement some ten years earlier.

Prophetic Stirrings

For Jacob Toews, the move to Russia was motivated not only by pacifist convictions but also by prophetic fervour. Along with other Mennonites at the time, he had come under the influence of the writings of Heinrich Jung-Stilling of Germany. Jung-Stilling (1740–1817) was a physician and scholar in the pietistic tradition who took a keen interest in prophetic biblical interpretation.[9] He expounded ideas known as millennialism or chiliasm, with their emphasis on a coming time of tribulation followed by a thousand-year reign of peace and ending with the final coming again of Jesus Christ. In his view, Russia would play a crucial role in these prophetic events. While a professor at Kaiserslautern between 1777 and 1787, Jung-Stilling had come in contact with Mennonites in the area. His writings showed the influence of their life and thought, in particular their aspirations for a peaceable kingdom.[10] Jacob Toews found himself drawn to the ideas of chiliasm.[11] He was not alone in this. Many of the ministers and lay people in his congregational circle were caught up in discussions of prophecy concerning the future. Some, including Jacob Toews, believed that the move to Russia would bring them more centrally into the vortex of millennial events. Perhaps their journey would lead them to a place of refuge where they would await the eventual return of Christ.

To Lysanderhöhe

While it was one thing to be driven by ideology and theology, it was quite another to face the practical implications. It was no simple matter to break up a family household with its economic and social base and to make a new beginning in another country. David's parents, grandparents, and great-grandparents had lived in the Vistula Delta for generations within a community of like-minded adherents to the Mennonite faith. To leave all things behind, despite the recollection of difficult times, must have evoked feelings of confusion. And what must it have been like to make preparations and engage on a journey with four small sons in tow? Nevertheless, in the summer of 1869 Jacob and Anna Toews sold their farm and many of their possessions, packed their essential earthly belongings into travelling chests, pocketed their money, and headed for the Am Trakt settlement.

Earlier travellers usually had made the journey from Prussia to Russia by horse and wagon. The Toews family went by train from Danzig via St. Petersburg to Nizhni Novgorod. From there they made their way down the Volga River by steamship. At the city of Zaratov near the Am Trakt colony, they disembarked and completed the last part of the journey by horse and wagon. In his report of the trip Jacob said that the last part had been the most difficult, even though it was the shortest distance.[12] The heat was intense and the roads were unbearably dusty, yet the family arrived in good spirits and in good health.

Lysanderhöhe was one of the ten villages of the newly established Mennonite settlement, Am Trakt, which lay in the province of Samara in the eastern portion of European Russia. Not far away was the Volga River which flowed southward on its way to the Caspian Sea. Am Trakt, meaning literally, "stretch or tract of land," lay along an important trade route, the so-called "Salz-Trakt," used to bring salt from the Elton Sea to the interior provinces of eastern Russia.[13] The settlement had been established in 1853 under the direction of Klaas Epp, Sr., and Johann

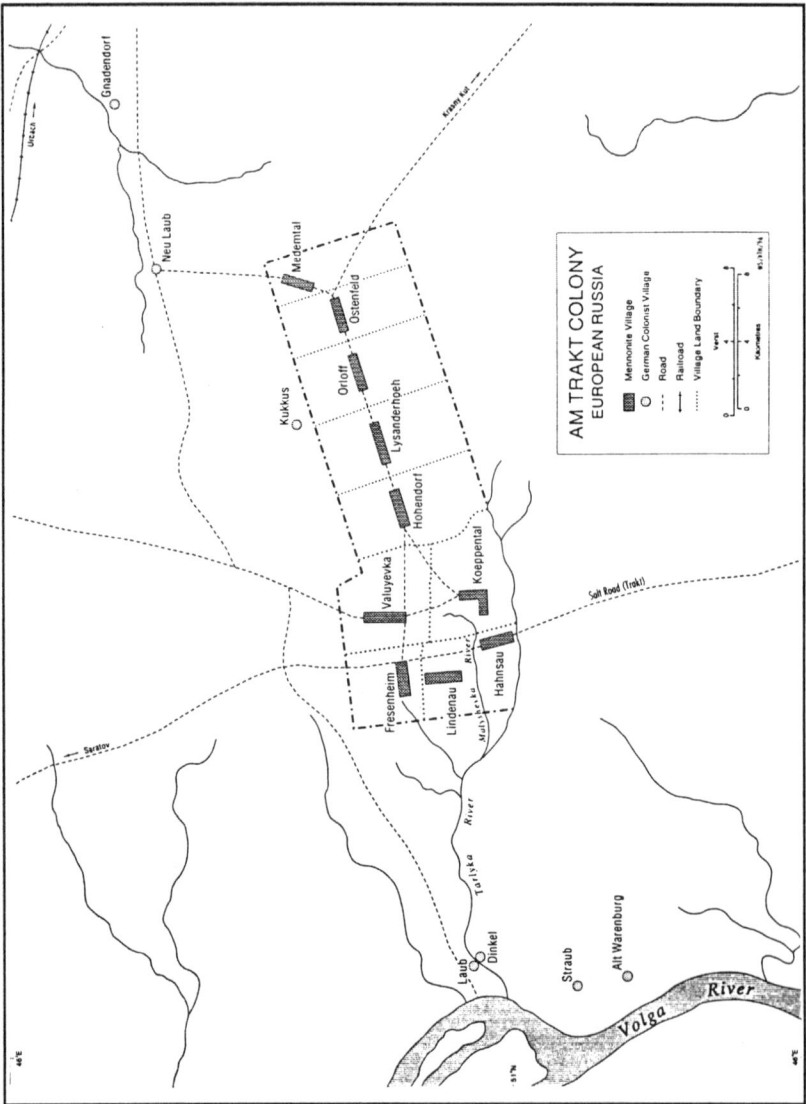

AM TRAKT COLONY
EUROPEAN RUSSIA

■ Mennonite Village
○ German Colonist Village
Road
Railroad
Village Land Boundary

Wall. Since its beginning, migrants from Mennonite villages in Prussia had populated the area. Lysanderhöhe was the sixth village to be established in the settlement. It was begun in 1864 and completed in 1870, the year David Toews was born.[14] Jacob and Anna purchased a plot of land adjacent to the village of Lysanderhöhe and built a home along the main street of the village.[15] It was a comfortable and relatively spacious home, reflecting the fact that Jacob had brought enough material possessions with him to ensure a good start in his new homeland. In this village and in this house, David Toews first saw the light of day.

There was a marked contrast between the prosperous community they had left behind and the poor conditions they found in this new settlement. The soil was hard and arid. They dug wells in search of water, and sometimes had to dig in several places before they were successful. But excellent farming skills, a cooperative community spirit, and sheer hard work brought a relative degree of success after some time. Yet life was always a bitter-sweet mixture of fortune and misfortune. This was felt particularly keenly in the area of child-bearing. After David, who was the fifth surviving son in the family, three surviving sisters were added to the family: Catherine in 1871, Louise in 1875, and Anna in 1877. The births of the eight surviving children were interspersed with an additional eight children who died in infancy.

By the time David was ready for school, the level of cultural and educational life in the settlement was respectable. In elementary school David had good teachers, notably one Wilhelm Penner. The children had access to good books and music. We know little of David's childhood

The house in Lysanderhöhe where David Toews was born. Photo: J. Dyck & W.E. Surukin, *Am Trakt*

and elementary school years. One biographer guessed that young David would have had a hard time complying with the stringent demands of a minister-father.[16] Another surmised that his strict upbringing would have honed him well for later tasks in life for which self-discipline was required.[17] Whatever the situation, David seemed to have had a relatively carefree childhood.

For Jacob Toews, there were other less tangible benefits that came with the move to Russia. What pleased him particularly was the interest in spiritual matters among some in the settlement. He could continue the discussions on prophecy that he had enjoyed back in the Prussian homeland. Jacob spoke in later life of the "delightful time which we spent with those people" and of the "deeply spiritual life" which he found there.[18] He also appreciated the discussions on the Scriptures with the emphasis on "signs of the times." Later in life, when Jacob reflected on this time, he wrote: "And though our views regarding the coming of the Lord have changed, nevertheless I say, we are grateful to our Lord, and should be even more so, that we have had this experience."[19]

No Abiding Place

It soon became apparent that for Jacob and Anna, Lysanderhöhe offered no abiding place. During the 1860s and 1870s the Russian government began to remove some special privileges under which the Mennonites had come to Russia. These included the guarantee of free use of the German language, the right to establish private schools, and exemption from military service. Now the government introduced legislation calling for compulsory military service. It had given the Mennonites six years, until 1880, to decide what they would do about the new regulations. Many, including Jacob Toews, wanted no part of this, not even if there was an arrangement for alternate service. Even to comply with its requirement, such as participation in a reforestation program in lieu of military service, was in a sense to recognize the government's jurisdiction over the life of young Mennonite men. For the elder Toews this amounted to an unacceptable complicity of which he wanted no part.

Being the kind of person he was, Jacob Toews responded proactively to these developments. He was motivated by two factors: a desire to protect the traditional Mennonite religious way of life and respect for the more recent prophetic voices concerning the end times. Perhaps it was time to move on again. But where to go? According to prophetic interpretation among his ministerial colleagues, emigration to North America was out of the question. There was a strong conviction that "Russia had an important place to fill for the church of the latter days."[20] If anything, the prophetic finger pointed toward the east, not to North

America in the west, as the place where the Lord expected to meet his faithful flock. What this meant was not yet clear. Meanwhile it was a matter of exploring options and awaiting a direction.

To inform themselves and to decide on next steps, Toews and others made several trips to Molotschna to share their thinking and ponder the future with like-minded apocalyptically-oriented leaders. They came back from one of these trips with the news that a small group of Mennonites had decided to move to the region of the Caucasus where it seemed that they would be granted religious freedom. It was becoming ever clearer that somewhere in the east the faithful would be led to a "place of refuge" where they should expect the Lord himself to appear.[21]

In 1879, Toews and three companions were delegated to go to St. Petersburg where they hoped to meet with Russian officials who could help them out of their dilemma.[22] Either they would have to gain a concession on military service or they would need to be assigned a place where they could practise their convictions without compromise. The delegation had an audience with Governor General von Kaufmann of Turkestan who happened to be in the city on business. He promised them a safe haven, abundant land, and exemption from military service if they came to his region. The delegation returned from St. Petersburg with no clear sense of direction. Jacob Toews wrote of these as agonizing times:

> Oh! Those were most solemn and serious days. But finally, the influence of those of our surrounding community, who believed that Revelation 12:14 seemed to indicate that Russia had a service to render for the church of the latter times, was the deciding factor for our final decision. We decided to emigrate to Asia.[23]

Two of their men were promptly sent to Turkestan to spy out the land of which the Governor General had spoken. They came back with a positive report. This tipped the scales in favour of an eastward migration to this Asian land of promise.

It is in this setting that David Toews was nurtured as a child. One can well imagine that from moments of earliest consciousness he would have imbibed an atmosphere of unsettledness. There would be the stories of the Prussian homeland the parents had recently left. And there would be the conversations about moving on. In those early years, David probably had little idea that the major reason Jacob and Anna had risked life and home to move to Russia was to protect their children, in particular their sons, from the evils of military involvement. Undoubtedly, the experiences that awaited David in his teenage years would bring new insights and questions about the values of the religious and social milieu in which his life was taking shape.

2
Turkestan
1880–1884

If the first ten years of David Toews' life, encompassing infancy and early childhood, constituted the initial chapter of his existence, then the subsequent four years, spanning later childhood and early adolescence, formed the second phase of his development. Both chapters had a geographical orientation, although the second environmental context was very different from the first. For the first ten years, David was oriented to a small village in an emerging Mennonite colony. For the next four years his home would become a moving caravan of pilgrims in search of a place of refuge in some distant land to the east. The journey on which Jacob Toews had determined to embark, with wife and children and mother-in-law in tow, is referred to in Mennonite history as the "Great Trek." For the contingent of which David was a part, the trek began in the summer of 1880 and ended in the spring of 1884. What an expansive experience for a young lad emerging out of childhood into the time of youth!

Place of Refuge

Immigration was in the air in the 1870s. Beginning in 1873, many Mennonites left for United States and Canada. If one must leave Russia, this would have been the logical direction to go. Immigrants to America had the prospect of specific destinations and even the likelihood of assistance from their Swiss Mennonite co-religionists, some of whom were well established in America. But David's father, along with many others from the Am Trakt colony and some from the Molotschna colony to the southwest, had other ideas. By now they were convinced that God was directing them eastward to a place where they would meet the Lord Jesus upon his return, a place where in the meantime they would be able to live in peace and without obligation to serve secular military powers. Their minds were made up despite the fact that theirs was a minority view, that they did not have absolute assurance of non-military privilege, and that the land on which they hoped to settle needed yet to be found. While some were moving to America in search of land, with the hope of relief from poverty, this was not the Toews' motivation for leaving. They enjoyed a relatively comfortable home, and the economic conditions held some promise. But all this didn't seem to matter. According to prophetic interpretation, Am Trakt was at best a safe haven from which to set forth in search of another home.[1] The real destination would be shown them. Eventually about 600 Mennonite millennialists made the trek eastward in search of their place of refuge. Jacob and Anna Toews and their children were among them.

Among those who exerted influence on the Am Trakt residents was Klaas Epp, Jr.[2] He was a farmer in Hahnsau, the original village of the settlement. In 1853, his father, Klaas Epp, Sr., together with a travelling companion, Johann Wall, had been in charge of finding and founding the Am Trakt colony. Now, some 25 years later, his oldest son, Klaas, Jr., had become a convincing interpreter of prophecies and a dynamic preacher of the millennialist perspective. In 1880, at the age of 42, he became the chief organizer and leader of the great trek.

Drawn to the ideas propounded by Klaas, Jr., Jacob Toews struggled with the question of what all this meant practically. His emphasis was more on exemption from military service than on a date and place for meeting the Lord.[3] In his memoirs, written in the 1920s during his retirement years in Aberdeen, Idaho, Toews mused about the difficulty of deciding whether or not to join the journey eastward. There was the experience in St. Petersburg where, after some discouraging contacts initially, things seemed to be falling into place. Officials there gave the delegation assurances that they would find a welcome in Turkestan. But then there was the pull westward, especially from acquaintances in the Molotschna colony to the southwest. Letters also came from relatives and friends in Prussia who were preparing to move to America. They urged Toews to move there as well. Toews was quite undecided about what to do. Later in life, he remembered this as "a time of earnest consideration and waiting on the Lord for guidance and light from above which way we should choose."[4] He admitted that he had been swayed by "the influence of those of our surrounding community who believed that Revelation 12:14 seemed to indicate that Russia had a service to render for the church of the latter times as the deciding factor for our final decision."[5] This text from the last book of the Bible stated: "But the woman was given the two wings of the great eagle, so that she could fly from the serpent into the wilderness, to her place where she is nourished for a time, and times, and half a time." This verse provided the clue that he should seek a place of refuge in a "wilderness" where the faithful would be strengthened by the Lord before a time of tribulation, the "time, and times, and half a time." Toews felt the pressure to make a decision, which he did, but not without a great deal of soul-searching and some second thoughts. Even after the conviction came that God was opening the door to Asia, Toews could not shake a deep trepidation. He wrote: "Our future seemed dark and uncertain, bearing in mind that we were depending only on a verbal promise of the officials."[6]

The Trek Began

Preparations for the journey required a great deal of planning and work. The farm was sold and contents of the house and farmyard auctioned off. Sturdy covered wagons were built for the trip. Strong horses were selected and in some cases purchased specifically for this purpose. They were needed for pulling the wagons as well as for riding by the boys. Wagons were arranged as living quarters, with places for storing food, clothing, bedding, and the necessary cooking gear. Pots and pans dangled from the exterior of the wagons. Each family and each wagon had an assigned place in the caravan.

Participants in the great trek left in five stages. The first group departed in July of 1880 and the last group in August of 1881. Four of the wagon trains left from Am Trakt and one from Molotschna. The first caravan of ten families and 17 wagons proceeded from the original Am Trakt village of Hahnsau, the home village of Klaas Epp, Jr. Franz Bartsch, leader of the first wagon, wrote a careful account of the entire trip.[7] His "Foreword" to the 1907 edition contains this disconcerting sentence on the reason for his account:

> I want to remind [our congregations] and us of a devastating example in our history to prevent us from committing the same errors, of interpreting Scripture capriciously and arbitrarily in order to justify and reinforce preconceived notions and opinions, and of accepting uncritically the emergence of self-appointed and self-aggrandizing leaders.[8]

As it turned out, the great trek proved to be a very difficult journey, one that David Toews rarely if ever mentioned in later years.

Jacob and Anna, their children, and Anna's mother were in the second group which departed on August 13, 1880 from Medemtal, the most easterly village of the settlement.[9] Belk indicates there were 13 families with 30 wagons;[10] Toews remembers 23.[11] The business leader was Heinrich Jantzen, a devoted follower of Klaas Epp, Jr. Jacob Toews and teacher J.K. Penner served as ministers to the group. Toews usually led the morning and evening worship services which were conducted in the centre of the wagon circle. The services consisted of a hymn, Scripture reading, and prayer.[12] It was Toews' duty to keep the visionary purpose of the trip before the travellers. Anna Toews, his faithful supporter, was skilful in caring for people who were ill along the way.

The wagon train must have been quite a sight as it snaked its way along. From beginning to end, the assortment of horse-drawn wagons and carts, interspersed with groups of children and young people walking alongside and between them, extended for over a kilometre. The group moved eastward by way of Uralsk, Orenburg, and Orsk, travelling about 45 kilometres on a good travel day, and much less on rainy days or when obstacles such as rivers and mountains impeded the journey. For the first several weeks progress was slow as recent excessive rains had made the trail quite muddy. After a while there were mountains to cross and rivers to ford. At Orsk they crossed the Ural River. There they pointed their horses southward toward Kazalinsk just east of the Aral Sea where the caravan entered the Russian protectorate of Turkestan. During the latter part of this stretch the entourage passed through the Kara Kum Desert. When the horses and wagons strayed from the packed road they faced the challenge of ploughing their way through soft sand. And all the while, Jacob, who had embarked on the journey with a heavy heart and with uncertain mind, faced the task of beginning and ending each day with a word of hope and vision.

The small children found caravan life hard, and mothers had to take care of their little ones under these unaccustomed transient circumstances. It is one thing to be sick and to attend to the sick; it is quite another to do so while bumping along day after day on rough roads. No doubt the older children turned the whole thing into something of an adventure. As a ten-year-old, David probably took things in stride. He would not have shared his father's anxieties. There were new experiences along the way. We can imagine that the first sight of camels in the desert region would have evoked wide-eyed wonder in David and his travelling companions.

In a lengthy historical novel entitled, *Our Asian Journey* (1997), the American Mennonite writer, Dallas Wiebe, builds his story of the great trek in part on Jacob Toews' memoirs and employs Jacob and Anna as his main characters.[13] Wiebe gives them the names, Joseph and Sarah. Their son, David, takes his place in the novel as Benjamin. While Wiebe's novel fictionalizes the great trek, he provides some imaginable insight into what may well have transpired along the way. The boys would have become quite skilled in throwing rocks at local village dogs when they nipped at the horses' heels. The teen-agers, joined by some of the older children, would have walked behind the wagons from time to time where they could mislead each other into such experiments as walking barefoot. In the desert the children would have jumped from the moving wagons to gather souvenirs such as skull bones. When the caravan stopped for the evening, the young people would gather firewood for the night fire. Some of the boys would dig the hole for the "excuse me," novelist Wiebe's euphemism for the improvised toilet.

In the course of the journey, David would have been entrusted with riding the horses from time to time, giving them a break from pulling the wagons. At the end of the day when the caravan stopped for the night, the boys would take the horses to a nearby stream or river for a drink. Then the horses were put out to pasture, with ropes long enough to permit them to find sufficient feed. It was important that they received good care, since without good horses there would be no trek. At one point, Wiebe's central character, Joseph, recounts an interchange with his son, Benjamin.[14] "This morning I did not conduct myself in a Christian manner," he admitted. The young men, which included Benjamin, were again racing the horses on the way back from the river where they had taken them to drink. Joseph suspected that it was his son, Benjamin, who once again was "one of the instigators." So he dealt with the misdemeanour. "When they returned this morning, at full gallop, I took Benjamin behind the door of our quarters and told him he had a perverse spirit, that he was full of stirs and foolish thoughts," recounted Joseph. He went on: "I reminded him that he was not mindful of his elders and that he lacks the spirit of understanding. I told him that he does not drink from the fountain of wisdom. . . . I told him to stop the folly. I told him I was most angry with him." Then the author added this note: "Later I saw Sarah [Anna] wagging a finger at him while he stood and laughed." Was this a fair caricature of David Toews as an emerging teenager?

A Difficult Winter

On November 27, after about 16 weeks en route and with winter approaching, the weary travellers settled in at Kaplan Bek near Tashkent. Governor General von Kaufmann, on whose invitation they were relying for military exemption and the offer of land, had arranged winter homes for them there. The first group had already arrived at Kaplan Bek. The Toews group joined them, and soon the third group arrived as well. The plan was to wait there while the men inspected the surrounding area for available settlement possibilities. The trip had been difficult for each of the groups, particularly marked by the deaths of children and by sickness among the elderly. Fortunately the Toews family was in reasonably good health, with the exception of David's Grandmother Wiebe who found the trip physically very difficult. Everyone looked forward to a time of rest and the restoration of hope. A school was built so the children could continue their education.

But the winter brought an epidemic of typhoid fever. Almost every family in Kaplan Bek was affected. Twelve members of the second wagon train died, including the oldest sons of wagon master Heinrich Jantzen. The sickness continued into the spring and summer. Taking all the wagon trains into account, it is estimated that between 50 and 80 persons, 15 to 20 percent of the total great trek Mennonite population, died of the epidemic.[15] Miraculously, the Toews family was spared.

The coming of spring brought with it further unsettledness. The group had counted on finding land somewhere in the Tashkent area. But then in mid-March came the news from St. Petersburg that Tsar Alexander II had been assassinated. This was worrisome, since he, together with Governor von Kaufmann, had given the assurance that for at least 15 years their young men would be protected from the military draft. It was known that the tsar's son, already crowned as Alexander III, would not be as gracious. This was born out when General Kaufmann suddenly became ambivalent in his attitude toward the wanderers. To make matters worse, Kaufmann became ill and died in mid-May. To Jacob Toews came the words, "Put not your trust in princes," and he resolved to trust God more fervently.[16] But many began to feel that Turkestan might not be the place of refuge they were looking for after all.

At Kaplan Bek the entire group split into two contingents. Some travelled 230 kilometres north-eastward to the Aulie Ata area to accept an offer of land there. The others, including the Toews family, decided to head for Samarkand, some 500 kilometres to the southwest. This second group was following the voice of Klaas Epp who now believed the place of refuge to lie in the Bukhara region south of Samarkand. On July 28, after a series of delays, the contingent of 153 persons, 48 wagons, and 81 horses set out.[17] The temperature was sweltering hot; the air was dry and dusty. But before they could leave the Tashkent area, departure was again delayed because yet another person—the twelfth in Tashkent—had died and needed to be afforded a decent funeral and burial. Always it meant that places of mourning were left behind, never to be revisited again.

The trip to Samarkand was marked by roads that were rutted and stony, rivers that needed either to be forded or crossed by ferry, and hot dusty desert areas. The children received constant warnings of dangerous tigers in the reeds along the way. But the pilgrims were driven by the hope for land and protection against military conscription for their young men. After an arduous journey they eventually arrived in Samarkand.[18]

The plan was to press on beyond Samarkand into Bukhara, located in a region beyond the Russian border and ruled by a khan. However, the group was delayed for two weeks before facing the second leg of the trip to Bukhara. Activities included repairing wagons, gathering supplies, attending to the sick, and burying one of their elderly members. Mean-

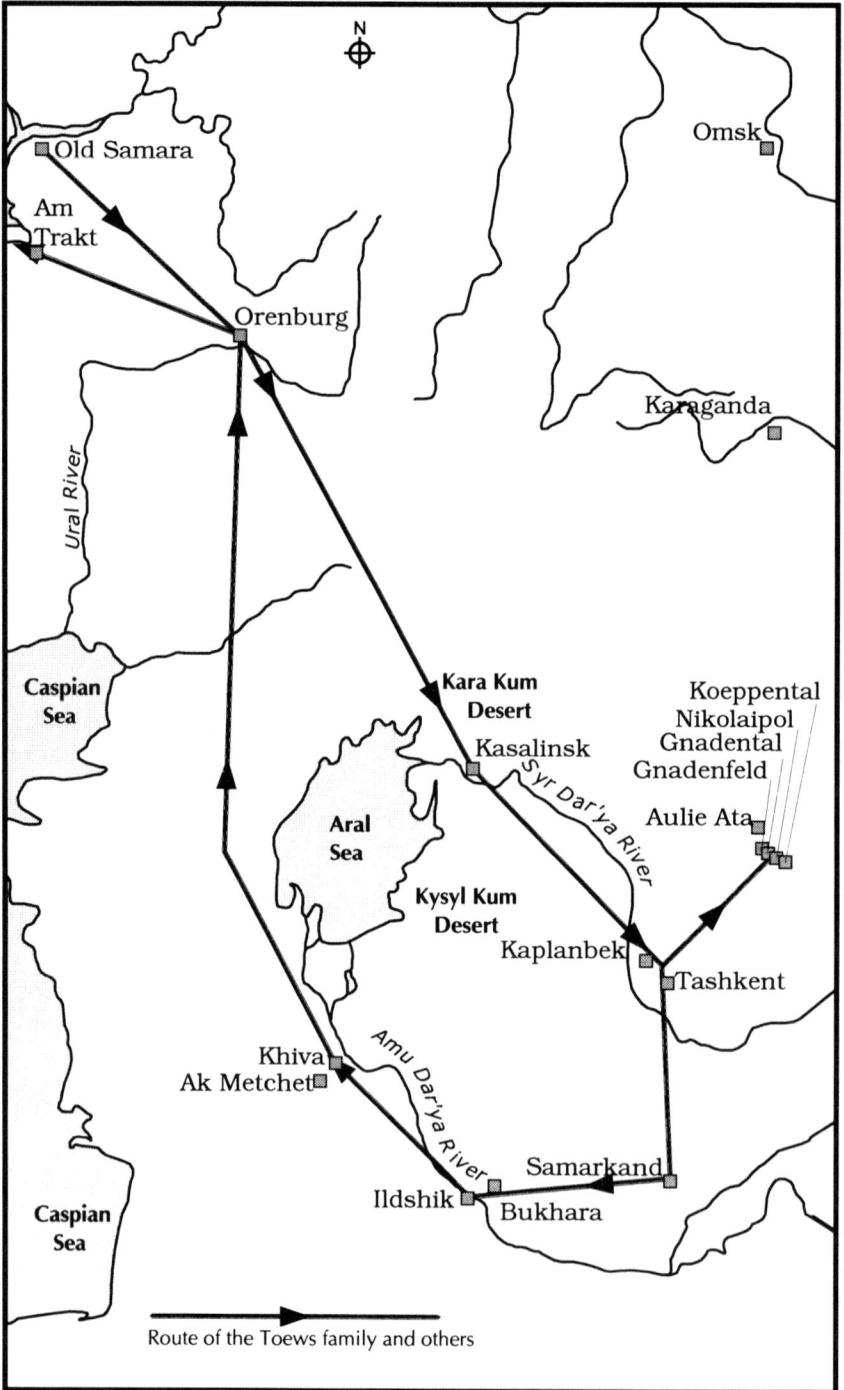

N

Old Samara

Omsk

Am
Trakt

Orenburg

Karaganda

Ural River

Kara Kum
Desert

Koeppental
Nikolaipol
Gnadental
Gnadenfeld

Caspian
Sea

Kasalinsk

Syr Dar'ya River

Aral
Sea

Aulie Ata

Kysyl Kum
Desert

Kaplanbek

Tashkent

Amu Dar'ya River

Khiva
Ak Metchet

Samarkand

Caspian
Sea

Ildshik

Bukhara

Route of the Toews family and others

Map: Christopher Werner

while, the children enjoyed the pleasant city with its parks and pools. Then it was time to move on again.

Another two weeks of travel, and the group arrived in Bukhara where they hoped they would find a safe haven. However, the officials of the area thought differently and drove them back across the border into Russia proper. Eventually, they were allowed to settle temporarily in a neutral area between the border and Bukhara. They named the place Ebenezer, meaning, "We have arrived here with the help of the Lord."

The Second Winter

At Ebenezer the group began to lay plans for a village and to make preparations for winter. For the Toews family this proved to be a worrisome time because David's mother became critically ill with digestive problems. Thankfully she was spared even while others met their death through the same diarrhetic illness. One of these was Anna Wiebe, David's maternal grandmother. At 66 years of age, she found the trip very strenuous. Once she had contracted the illness, she did not have the physical stamina to withstand its onslaughts. In his recollections, Jacob Toews wrote of the distress that his mother-in-law's agony caused the family. She would cry constantly: "If I could only be in a warm room," and "Ach, it is so dark, so very dark!"[19] At such times, he must have had second thoughts about the whole undertaking. At the beginning of October of 1881 she died. Jacob interpreted these events as a severe conflict with Satan. Yet he claimed that, even in such times, he was confident that the gracious hand of God was caring for them.[20]

They planned to stay at Ebenezer for the winter of 1881–1882, even to claim this as their place of refuge. But such ideas were thwarted when local officials, bolstered by an aggressive military, ordered the "Russian" pilgrims to return to their homeland. This necessitated a retreat to Zerabulak inside the Russian border. Also some of the prophetic pundits began to reconsider their theological predictions. Perhaps this was the place the tribulation would occur, whereas the actual place of refuge might be somewhere else.[21] In any case, the plan now was to stay in Zerabulak for the winter. They were helped by cooperative local Muslims.

For the Toews family, several memorable events occurred at Zerabulak. One was the marriage of David's older brother Heinrich to Anna Wiebe, the daughter of a widow on the trek. The ceremony took place in a local mosque, where the group was also permitted to hold its church services and congregational meetings. Father Jacob, who performed the service, chose as his text John 14:27: "Peace I leave with you, my peace I give to you: not as the world giveth, give I unto you. Let not your heart be troubled, neither let it be afraid."[22]

David Seriously Ill

A second unforgettable event was the serious illness of young David. Along with other children and adults, he became severely stricken with smallpox. Everyone was thankful that the plague passed over in a short while. Later, Jacob Toews would write of this in his diary:

> A faithful God who had cared for us on our long journey held his hand over us. We were not spared from times of sorrow and affliction. Sickness came and on frequent occasions we wended our way to the graves of our beloved ones. Even in these times of deep sorrow we still received a blessing through the assurance which we had of the forgiveness of sins through the blood of Jesus Christ and the hope of eternal life when we die.[23]

It is indeed remarkable and amazing that Toews could write this way, given not only the physical troubles that constantly beset the travellers but also the internal dissension that plagued the group. As physical difficulties became more and more difficult, with rough terrain, bad weather, illness, and fatigue, interest in millennialism waned. The travellers' attention turned to immediate survival. Where discussions of prophecy did occur, moderating voices challenged Klaas Epp's interpretation of the Bible. A small Mennonite Brethren group on the trek had its own theological perspective on church life, including adherence to immersion as the mode of baptism. The larger contingent of *kirchliche* (Church) Mennonites, being part of the traditional original Mennonite church in Russia, brought their conservative perspective to the debate. With the loss of their original chiliastic zeal, the group was losing its sense of unity and of a common goal.[24]

The trekkers at Zerabulak were now in a no-man's land. They had been ejected from Bukhara, and in Russia they were threatened by military conscription. After spending the winter in Zerabulak, a decision was made to explore the possibility of moving to Khiva.[25] This city lay in a Russian protectorate to the northwest. The region had a degree of sovereignty under a ruling khan. Inspired by the continuing visions of Klaas Epp, Jr., a delegation made the 600-mile trip to Khiva which paved the way for the others. By the end of August 1882, the caravan was on its way with those who were still on Epp's side. This included the Toews family, but Jacob Toews' devotion was not to last long.

Shortly before starting out for Khiva, an unusual incident occurred in the Toews home. In the summer of 1882 a young German by the name of Johann Drake moved in with the family.[26] He had fled his home in western Russia to escape the military draft. It happened that Jacob had quite a sum of money in the house since he was the treasurer of the

Zerabulak group. The family awoke one morning to find that Drake was missing, along with one of Toews' fine horses and a sizeable amount of cash taken from a locked dresser drawer in the living room. Upon inquiry, someone had spotted Drake heading for Tashkent. There was great concern for both Drake and the money, but worries were alleviated when, a week later, Jacob Toews received a letter from a repentant Johann in Tashkent. He explained that he had been distraught over a failed love affair, and this had confused his thinking and caused him to commit the rash act of stealing. Could he return and make things right? Meanwhile he had sold Toews' horse in Tashkent and spent some of the money. Even though the group had questions about Drake's story, they decided to forgive him and reinstate him into their community. This event shows the magnanimous spirit of Jacob and Anna Toews. Surely the incident impressed David as a model for treatment of someone who commits a transgression. Meanwhile the group had more important matters of concern, namely the journey itself.

The caravan set out for Khiva at the end of August 1882. It must have been quite a spectacle, with about 150 people, some 50 wagons, 80 horses, 10 carts, and about 140 camels.[27] Since the trek through the desert would be formidable, the group hired about 50 uniformed soldiers to escort them through Bukhara territory. The soldiers helped repair roads and bridges along the way and guided them through the dangerous desert and quicksand areas. On this trip it was the bandits in the hills, not the threat of tigers, that struck fear in the adults and the children. The trip involved a 12-day stretch of cross-country travel, then a three-day sojourn through the Kara Kul desert. Once the desert had been traversed, the entire group floated down the Amu Daria River on rented flat-bottom boats 140 feet in length.[28]

In mid-October the group arrived at Lausan in the Khiva area. There they negotiated with the governor for a place to settle. Klaas Epp was convinced that they had reached their place of refuge. Not all agreed, mainly because of the poor conditions of the land and because of uncertainty as to whether the territory might pass into the hands of Russia in the near future. There was also some anxiety because of the unfriendliness of the local people. Yet they had little choice at this point but to build a settlement for protection against the coming winter. Fears about their safety were justified when one of the group, Heinrich Abrams, was murdered at the hands of Turkoman bandits.[29]

Because of the dangerous conditions, about two-thirds of the colonists relocated closer to the city of Khiva south of Lausan. In this move they followed Klaas Epp with his convictions that this new location, Ak Metchet, was surely their place of refuge. In the new location, Epp became extremely fanatical in his views, causing even his most faithful followers to question their loyalty to him.

Abandoning the Trek

Meanwhile, those who had remained in Lausan had had enough. Led by the sentiments of Jacob Toews and others, they made plans to migrate to America. There, they hoped, they could temper their millennial views and protect their stance of nonresistance.[30] Through exchange of letters with Mennonite relatives in Beatrice, Nebraska, and Newton, Kansas, they received assurance of financial aid to assist them in their journey westward. In America an "Aid Committee for the Needy Brethren in Khiva" was formed to make the migration financially possible. Throughout the four-year adventure, American Mennonites had been kept informed of the trek through articles in *Der Christlicher Bundesbote* and through correspondence.

So it happened that in the spring of 1884 the Lausan group, now consisting of 23 families, broke up its settlement, had its last worship service, and prepared for the 12,000-mile journey to America.[31] The Toews family was among them. After eight more weeks of difficult travel they reached Orenburg. The trip was once more dotted with episodes of childbirths and infant deaths and of tedious labour as the wagons were pulled through desert sands and through muddy river beds. At one point a little boy fell beneath the wheels of a wagon. His ribs were broken and his arms bruised. Fortunately he recovered from the accident. Eventually the group reached Orenburg where they remained for two months to arrange for passports. During this time some of the immigrants, including the Toews family, made a side trip back to their former Am Trakt homestead. One can only imagine the stories about the recent past and sentiments about the future that were shared during these visits!

On to America

After a long wait, some of the migrants obtained their passports, though others did not. The first group left on August 10, 1884. The train took them to Bremen, Germany, where they were put on board the *Ems*, a large passenger ship of the North German Lloyd Line. The second group, which included the Jacob Toews family and the family of son Heinrich Toews, obtained their passports about a month later, and soon thereafter were on their way by train as well. At Bremen they boarded the *Fulda* for the nine-day voyage to New York, arriving on October 4. But the trip ended with another tragedy. This time it struck the Toews family. Maria Toews, the 14-month-old daughter of David's brother, Heinrich, and his wife Anna, had come in contact with smallpox during their last days in Russia. On the trip she became deathly sick and died just as they were approaching New York harbour. She was buried on Ellis Island.[32]

As the ship docked in New York harbour, the disappointed Mennonite millennialists were met by a small delegation from Kansas and Nebraska. These compassionate co-religionists helped their kinfolk board the train and complete the last part of their incredible journey. They travelled westward by way of Niagara Falls and Chicago. After a stopover in Beatrice, Nebraska, to visit acquaintances, they continued on to Newton, Kansas, where they were welcomed by Kansas Mennonites.

Lasting Impact

What was the effect of the Asian journey on Jacob Toews? As far as prophecy and chiliasm were concerned, it appears that he saw in the trek an opportunity to test his interpretation of biblical prophecy rather than to confirm something held as an absolute conviction. He did not embark on the trek with absolute confidence that it was the right direction to take. His basic reason for going eastward had more to do with finding a place free of military obligation to the state than finding a place of refuge from tribulation. At the same time, he found spiritual sustenance in the company of those who were exploring new prophetic interpretations of the Scriptures. It seems that in the end he did not find it difficult to break with Epp and go a different direction. Later in life, Jacob Toews spent more time musing quietly about the affair and continuing to ponder its spiritual significance than second-guessing his involvement.

What does one make of this search for a "place of refuge" where the faithful gather for protection against the storms of history and staunchly await the coming again of the Lord? What does one make of Jacob Toews' willingness to endanger his family for the sake of this vision? A word of wisdom comes from the pen of Rev. Jacob H. Janzen.[33] "We do not know," he admitted, "why it had to come to this wide detour from the Marienburger Delta by way of Zaratov, Orenburg, Tashkent, Bukhara, Khiva, and then back again to Bremen and New York to Newton, Kansas." Yet Janzen could see the four-year journey as a "miraculous pilgrimage of faith through which God achieved his goal with his children." When one looks at the way things ended up, "a miracle is suggested by the fact that the Toewses, despite all the sacrifices that this way demanded, were still able to acquire a small farm near Newton on which to re-establish themselves and restore their lost fortunes." Admittedly, they did not arrive at their goal as originally envisioned. Instead, they continued "on the way," even if in a different direction, by becoming engaged in the ministry of a congregation in Newton. And the small farm east of Newton became in its own way a "place of refuge."

In a review of Belk's, *The Great Trek of the Russian Mennonites to Central Asia 1880–1884,* referred to above, Waldemar Janzen has proposed that the great trek was determined less by the chiliasm of Klaas Epp than by the search for a place where Mennonite principles of nonresistance could be taught and practised.[34] Janzen writes that at most, Epp's chiliasm

> performed a triggering function, determined certain decisions concerning the timing and the geography, and added its accents of fervor and hope, as well as excess and blindness, to a migration which was in many ways paradigmatic of Mennonite migrations through the centuries; a migration of a group of practical and pious people who—though not averse to comfort and affluence—were ready to bring great sacrifices as they searched for a place of refuge where a life of obedience to God could be lived.[35]

The sentiments and actions of Jacob Toews, revealed during four years on the journey, seem to support the thesis put forward by Janzen.

What of David Toews? One wonders what lasting effect the experience had on the young lad at this impressionable age. One biographer of David Toews surmised that with the four-year experience of the trek and the trip to America, David was certainly no "spoiled brat."[36] He had learned to look out for himself, to make do with what was available, and to be resourceful in facing challenges and troubles.[37] It appears that David must have taken the trek in stride as a kind of adventure. Yes, he had bounced around on horses and wagons. He had suffered an attack of smallpox along the way. Active and curious lad that he was, he had evoked disciplinary admonishment from mother and father from time to time. And he certainly would have had moments of anxiety as he endured the storms and stresses of caravan life along with struggling and often disheartened adults. But from all appearances the experience did not affect him negatively. For him the sojourn had amounted to an interesting escapade, but not something that would warp or determine his psyche. He was ready to get on with the rest of his life.

On a more profound level, another biographer and friend of David Toews in later years, Rev. Jacob H. Janzen, musing on the question of the lasting impact of the trek on David, wrote as follows:

> The ten-year-old David of that time understood nothing of what drove his parents and the entire contingent into the beyond, yet in his heart he already carried the old German longing for a place to call home-turf (*Scholle*), and he never allowed this longing to die out, not even when he had already become a teacher respected by everyone. It was exactly

this longing that gave him a love for his agrarian people, the people he served and serves with his gifts, and prepared his heart for the work which he should do to rescue a people ripped from its foundation and its earth for the sake of its faith.[38]

It may well be that David's Asian adventure planted in his being a longing for land. Certainly he will have gained the impression through interaction with the company he kept those four years that one may need to go to great lengths in pursuit of "place." It could be that the venture whetted his appetite for his own land and for a settled agrarian life where he could enjoy fine horses and a place of refuge. As it turned out, the dominant note in the life of David Toews was not about finding his own turf but about finding land for others. And the theme of pilgrimage, which he tasted in those early years, was a prominent motif in his own life, albeit in a revised form. He was destined to criss-cross America and to cross the ocean more than once in pursuit of a "place of refuge" for a suffering people who had left their homeland behind.

3

Kansas
1884–1893

A decade before the Toews family arrived in Newton, Kansas, Mennonites from Prussia and Russia had begun to settle there.[1] They were of the same ethnic background as the family of Jacob Toews and had come to Kansas for some of the same reasons that he first moved from Prussia to Russia, then decided to join the trek to Turkestan. Since 1772, when the Polish governors were replaced by German rulers who incorporated the Mennonite settlements into the Kingdom of Prussia, immigration was on the minds of these pacifists.[2] A considerable number of Mennonite families scurried southward to Russia, with migrations beginning in 1789 and not ending until about 1870. By the end of that time some, who already had lived in Russia for a good while, were thinking of moving on to America.

Meanwhile in Prussia, the pressure to comply with military demands had kept mounting. Consequently, it came down to a choice between integration into society or migration to a place where freedom of conscience could be guaranteed. Many sought to endure the pressure to conform to the ideals of the state with the hope that things would improve for them, but this was not to be. In 1874 alone, some 600 families had migrated from Russia to Nebraska and Kansas. In about 1876 a handful of families left the Mennonite village of Heubuden in Prussia, and found their way to some farmland east of the town of Newton in Kansas.[3] They came with two typical aspirations: to protect their nonresistant principles and to find good farmland. It was this community, with barely ten years of experience in a new country, that welcomed Jacob and Anna Toews and their children when they arrived in 1884. When the American Mennonites heard about the 20 families that had abandoned the trek to Central Asia and desired to come to America, they had set up "aid committees" to assist them. Two men in Newton, Peter Claassen and Bernhard Regier, were members of the Newton aid committee and helped the Jacob Toews family get settled east of town.

By the time the family arrived in 1884, the ground had already been laid for educational and religious institutions.[4] One of the first churches organized by the German-speaking immigrants in 1875 was the Halstead

Mennonite Church. When Prussian Mennonites began to arrive in Kansas in 1876, they founded churches at Emmaus, Elbing, as well as First Mennonite Church of Newton, Kansas. The Kansas Mennonite educational efforts began with parochial schools that promoted the German language and the Bible but these were soon replaced by the public education system. Secondary schools were established, patterned after the *Zentralschulen* in Russia. In 1882, Halstead Seminary began offering collegiate education, a forerunner to college education. This was the setting in which the Toews family arrived in 1884 and in which David Toews entered the third phase of his personal development, what we might call his "Kansas chapter."

Farmer and Elder

Jacob and Anna Toews, now in their mid-forties, had spent a considerable portion of their first 24 years of married life either moving or discussing the prospect of moving. Now, after an exhausting four-year journey, they were ready to settle down. The Mennonite community in Newton helped them find a small farm east of town where they proceeded to make a home for themselves and plant their crops. It is remarkable that the parents had not only the energy but also the financial means to begin again in this way.

Jacob Toews had barely settled his family into their new home when he was drawn into the leadership circle of First Mennonite Church in Newton. This in itself was remarkable, given the negative sentiments some Mennonites held about the foolishness of the Asian trekkers. Historian John D. Thiesen remarks that "there is no record of any questioning Jacob Toews regarding his theology."[5] In the same year the Toews family arrived in Kansas, Jacob was elected as a minister in the congregation and in 1886, after a year and a half of taking his turn behind the pulpit on Sunday mornings, he was elected as *Ältester* (elder, leading minister). This meant that besides taking his turn in the pulpit on Sunday mornings, he was responsible for serving communion, instructing candidates for baptism, and conducting baptism. The ordination service was held August 15, 1886. Apparently this had been no easy decision for Jacob Toews, but he was willing to serve to the best of his abilities.

Toews' tenure as elder of First Mennonite Church saw a number of controversies. Later in life his older children recalled that "father, under difficult circumstances, was elected to the office of elder" and that it took a great deal of patience and wisdom to provide leadership to the congregation. But he "received the necessary strength to carry on in faithful service, and remained true to his Lord and was not moved to bitterness in spite of the many difficulties and reproaches which beset his

David Toews' parents, Jacob
(1838–1922) and Anna (d.
1924). Jacob served as
Ältester of First Mennonite
Church in Newton, Kansas,
for over 30 years until his
retirement in 1917. Photo:
MHC Archives

way."[6] The difficulties referred to included several problems that plagued
First Mennonite Church in the early decades of its existence.[7] One
example was the question whether church members were permitted to
belong to secret societies such as the Masonic Lodge, or even to social
organizations such as the Newton Athletics Club or political parties such
as the Farmers' Alliance. In the first two decades of the twentieth
century, the liberal-fundamentalist controversies as well as debate over
questions of war and nonresistance arose in the congregation.

Elder Toews served First Mennonite Church faithfully for 30 years
until his retirement in 1917. Visitors to the church in Newton can view
the left front stained-glass window dedicated to his memory. Upon
retiring, he and Anna made one last sojourn. They sold almost everything
they owned in Kansas and moved to Aberdeen, Idaho. There they lived
close to their two sons, Henry and John, who had moved there earlier. In
1920, Jacob and Anna celebrated their 60th wedding anniversary in
Aberdeen. According to Dallas Wiebe's historical novel, Jacob spent his
last years doing a lot of thinking about the circuitous route his life had
taken. This is evident in his memoirs as well.[8] Jacob died on January 2,
1922 at age 84. This left Anna a widow until her death on April 17,
1924, at the age of 86. In her last years, Anna Toews participated in a
small way in another trek: the immigration of Mennonites in the 1920s.
When she heard from David, her son, that the Russian Mennonites were
in need of clothing, she took part in the relief effort by knitting many

pairs of stockings for the immigrants. In the Rosthern community, where David lived by then, the story of Anna Toews' knitting project apparently evoked "quite a little sensation."[9]

Learning English

For David, the year 1884 was momentous. He was 14 years of age, a time young people typically begin to realize that they are, or will shortly need to become, accountable for their own decisions. Since his parents had established a home base in America, he probably sensed that the temporary nature of the family's existence was behind them. This would have given David a sense of confidence that he could begin to think about his own aspirations in long-range terms. Meanwhile, one immediate task needed attention. If he was to live meaningfully in this new country, he must learn its language. Barely settled in his new homeland, he turned his attention to schooling. His parents enrolled him in the local elementary school where his first task was to learn some English. This was not difficult for someone of his age and ability. The greater challenge was "squaring off" with the other older children on the schoolyard. Children often test the edges of their own temptation to dominance by teasing one another at the point of their social peculiarities. David had two strikes against him in this regard, at least in the eyes of his peers. They laughed at his awkward use of the English language and they laughed at him for having to sit in a classroom with children much younger and smaller than he was. The story is told, perhaps by David himself in later years, of how the school children taunted him with:

> Dutchman, Dutchman, belly full of straw,
> Can say nothing but Ja, Ja, Ja.[10]

David's tendency was to answer such provocations with his fists. His self-defensive emotions and skills had been honed on the trek where one learned to look out for oneself. The situation was strained by the fact that, even while he was beyond the years of his classmates, he was not yet at their level in language skills or American social ways. But no one was too concerned as David was used to adversity, and at heart he had a likeable personality. Besides, the experiences he had accumulated in life thus far advanced him somewhat beyond his age in wisdom and in understanding.

As soon as the school year ended and vacation began, David pursued his passion of farming.[11] He was not needed on the small family farm so he was hired by a neighbour, Bernhard Regier. This was a bonus for David as Regier was a good farmer and a caring person. There David could foster his love for horses and pursue his agrarian dream. His experience on the Asian journey had taught him much about the nature and physical characteristics of horses. His yen for farming remained with him for many years to come. He appeared to have the ambitions of an ordinary person. Even in later years, when he would move among persons of high rank, he never sought their level of life. He tended to feel most at home with the common folk and with earthy concerns.

Student at Halstead

Neither David's elementary schoolyard problems nor his agrarian ambitions lasted very long. After a year in elementary school and a summer or two as a farm-hand, he got on with serious and focused learning. Both his parents and his employer urged him to continue with further study. His parents provided moral encouragement; farmer Regier advanced him the money to make this possible. In the fall of 1885, after a year of elementary school attendance, David entered Halstead Seminary, a *Fortbildungsschule* (school of continuing education), in the town of Halstead, Kansas. The school had its beginning in 1883 in the Mennonite settlement of Alexanderwohl in the town of Emmatal, 12 miles north of Newton. After one year in Emmatal, the school relocated to a larger facility in Halstead and eventually became known as the Halstead Seminary. When David Toews enrolled, the school was beginning its third year of operation.[12] Halstead Seminary was not a "seminary" in the sense in which we use the term. It was what today might be called a high school except that its specific purpose was to prepare teachers for the "common schools," that is, for elementary schools in both the private and public spheres. As well, the school prepared students for college entrance by offering liberal art courses. Mennonites saw the need to conduct their own schools of this kind so that teachers would have facility in teaching the German language and the Mennonite faith alongside the state-required program.

The first teacher and principal of the *Fortbildungsschule* at Emmatal, and then also at Halstead, was Heinrich H. Ewert.[13] Ewert (1855–1934), who was born in the Vistula Delta in West Prussia, was the eldest in a large family of 12 children. When in the late 1860s Prussia increased and broadened its military commitment by joining the North German Federation, and indicated to the Mennonites that even they would not be exempted from military service, Heinrich's father decided to emigrate to the United States. Thus in 1874 the Ewert family settled in Marion County, Kansas. Heinrich, who was 19 years old at the time, had already distinguished himself as a bright student. He immediately took advantage of the new educational environment to further his education, first

David in the mid-1880s as a
student in the teacher preparation course at the Halstead Seminary.

attending public schools in Marion, then Normal School at Emporia,
Kansas, then the Des Moines Institute in Iowa, and finally the Theological Seminary of the Evangelical Synod in Marthasville, Missouri. When,
at the end of this study period, Ewert was offered a position at the newly
established *Fortbildungsschule* in Emmatal, he accepted. He served as
teacher there, then as teacher and principal at Halstead, from 1883 to
1891, after which he assumed leadership of the Mennonite Educational
Institute (now Mennonite Collegiate Institute) at Gretna, Manitoba.
Halstead Seminary had a brief ten-year existence, closing its doors in
1893. Its successor was Bethel College in North Newton, Kansas, which
opened in the fall of that year.

David Toews was one of the 515 students of Halstead Seminary in its
decade of existence. Initially he enrolled in the three-year teacher
preparation course. There was a sense among those who knew him that
he would do well at teaching. One of his fellow students observed some
years later that David "had the ability to bring understanding to youth,
with patience."[14] While at Halstead, David thrived under the influence of
Heinrich H. Ewert who was not only a teacher but also a churchman. He
was involved in the Kansas Mennonite Conference as superintendent of
Sunday schools and was a frequent speaker at Mennonite conferences
and in the churches.[15] This commitment will have impressed itself on the

Halstead Seminary graduates in 1893, including David Toews (seated, front left). Photo: MHC Archives

mind and soul of young David. Ewert was convinced that education was crucial for Christian nurture and conversion. Christian education should be the primary means whereby children and youth were drawn to God and became incorporated into the image of Christ. He believed that Christian discipleship included responsibility and service to both the church and the state. In his view, it was the Mennonite school, especially the school that served youth in their post-elementary years, that played a crucial role in the practical expression of his philosophy of education.[16] David Toews' years under the influence of Ewert were crucial for the formation of his viewpoint for the years to come. The relationship between the two men extended over many decades. At Halstead, Toews not only sat in Ewert's classes but also earned some of his tuition and board by taking care of Principal Ewert's livestock, something he had learned to do well and to love while on the Asian journey and on the Regier farm east of Newton.

First Teaching Assignment

In the spring of 1888, having completed the teacher training program, David left Halstead Seminary to try his hand at teaching. He taught at three different locations in Kansas—two years at Whitewater and then at Elbing and Newton. These were all places where Mennonites had settled. It is conceivable that he would have contributed to the German courses at these schools. One can imagine that he took particular satisfaction in such courses as literature and history. In those earliest years Toews was already making his mark as a community leader. It is said of Teacher Toews that "he was patient with the children and manifested a great sense of responsibility which won him the respect of the community."[17]

During the time that David Toews was teaching in Kansas, the school system among Mennonites was in a stage of initial development.[18] The first Mennonite schools had been organized in 1874, shortly after the arrival of Mennonites from Russia to central Kansas. A variety of schools emerged. Some were begun as private initiatives and were conducted in homes. Some were organized as parochial schools of the church. Soon private home schooling gave way entirely to parochial schools. Between 1877 and 1898, Mennonite parochial schools increased from a dozen to 42 and were integrated with the public school system. In an intermediary stage, they offered supplemental instruction in German and religion to augment the "secular" courses taught in the public schools. During his years of teaching in Kansas, Toews became familiar with this developmental stage in the growth of educational institutions.

About the time that David completed his three-year program at Halstead, he took care of a matter that belonged to his faith development: he decided to be baptized in the Mennonite way upon confession of his faith. The ritual took place on May 20, 1888, at First Mennonite Church. His father had the honour of officiating. One can only imagine the kinds of inner reflections this event evoked in the mind and heart of Jacob and Anna. A biographer says of David at this time that "he found recognition among his superiors, in the churches, and with parents of the children."[19] The stage was being set for greater service.

Return to Halstead

In the fall of 1891 David returned to Halstead to continue his education. By then his friend and teacher, Principal Ewert, had left Halstead and moved to Gretna, Manitoba, to direct a teacher education program similar to that at Halstead. C.H. Wedel had taken Ewert's place as principal of the Halstead Seminary. This time David concentrated on college preparation courses. Principal Wedel had a significant impact on David's life and thought. He instilled in the young student a love for church history, for literature, and for the Bible.[20] By the summer of 1893, David had completed the two-year course and joined the graduating class. With that he would move on again.

4

Manitoba
1893–1898

In the spring of 1893, when David Toews heard that a new Mennonite College was opening its doors just north of Newton, Kansas, he
planned to enroll. But then his life took a different course. That summer
his former teacher, Heinrich H. Ewert, visited Kansas on a recruitment
trip. The Mennonite Collegiate Institute in Gretna, Manitoba, of which
he was now the principal, had recently reconstituted its educational
program as a Normal School (Teacher Training Institute). The aim was
to prepare teachers for the public district schools that were emerging
among the Mennonite villages of southern Manitoba. Ewert had also
been hired by the Manitoba government, through Clifford Sifton, its
Education Minister, as inspector for district schools among Mennonites.[1]
Ewert's reason for coming to Kansas was to recruit teachers for the
public district schools under his supervision. On this particular trip he
was looking for two teachers, one for the school in Winkler and the other
for the elementary school in Gretna. Ewert approached David Toews and
offered him the latter job.

The young Toews, who by now already had some teaching experience, saw this as an opportunity and an adventure. It meant that he would
be working under Ewert's tutelage, something he looked forward to. It
also meant he could indulge his *Wanderlust*, but this time with a personal
purpose. David sought the counsel of his former farm employer,
Bernhard Regier, who advised him to accept Ewert's offer. David's
parents, Jacob and Anna, also gave their support and blessing, seeing the
hand of God in this direction. This was sufficient encouragement for the
23-year-old David to accept the position. His original intention was to go
to Canada for two years and then return to Kansas for further education.[2]

North to Canada

In the late summer of 1893, David Toews packed his bags, took leave
of his parents, and boarded the train for Manitoba. His trip took him
through Chicago where he stopped for a few days to visit the World's
Fair and other places of interest. While in Chicago he also attended a
church service where he heard Dwight L. Moody, the famous American

Heinrich H. Ewert (1855–1934) was a mentor to David Toews at Halstead Seminary in Kansas, Mennonite Collegiate Institute in Gretna, and in his subsequent work as educator, churchman, and immigration administrator.
Photo: MHC Archives

preacher of the day. Toews found the trip enjoyable and satisfying, a sign that he was beginning to feel at home on the North American continent.[3] With all his experience, he knew how to find his way around. He certainly was not afraid of travelling.

David Toews arrived in Gretna, Manitoba, in late summer of 1893. He was greeted by Heinrich H. and Elizabeth (Baer) Ewert, who had extended hospitality to him once before when he was attending Halstead Seminary.[4] In Gretna, Toews boarded at the Ewert home. This contact with his former Halstead teacher and part-time employer of the past gave the young teacher a sense of well-being in this new community.

Educator in Gretna

What was Heinrich H. Ewert doing in Gretna, Manitoba? And why had he invited David Toews to join him? Beginning in 1874, Mennonite immigrants from southern Russia, later Ukraine, had settled in Manitoba. They had come with the understanding that they would be free to conduct their own schools and promulgate their own faith and culture. But times were changing, and very soon the provincial authorities began to exert influence over the Mennonite schools. Their stated intent was to improve the quality of education among Mennonites many of whom resisted what they saw as an intrusion. In their view, this was a recurrence of the threat they had sought to escape by migrating from southern Russia to Canada. They feared the loss of the German language and of their cherished principle of non-resistance. In their view, the school should serve as an extension of the life of the church, not as a servant of the state.

Not everyone was threatened by the prospect of public education. Some progressively minded leaders regarded these developments not as a threat but as an opportunity. Here was a chance to improve the level of education. They would concentrate their efforts in teacher preparation for the public system. They would send qualified and dedicated teachers to the Mennonite village schools. Rather than resist the public educational authorities, they would work in cooperation with them, even supplying inspectors from their own circle. Ewert had been invited to Gretna in 1891 to "sell" this program to the Mennonites and to head up the institution that was to serve this purpose.[5]

To accomplish his goals, Ewert needed young teachers who would provide models of how to teach at the elementary level and who could help with teacher development. David Toews was his "pick." Ewert recognized in him a person who would know how to walk the line between church and public school in the educational world. Toews' assignment was to teach in the Gretna Public School, working with children up to 12 years of age. Meanwhile, he also contributed to the teacher development program organized by Ewert through his teacher training institution. He served on the committee that planned semi-annual conferences for elementary school teachers from throughout the Mennonite school district.[6] Ewert gave Toews various assignments at these conferences, such as making presentations on teaching principles and methods as well as leading discussions that followed the typical demonstration lessons. Toews was also part of a group that evaluated and recommended appropriate curriculum for the elementary schools.

At Gretna, David's first year of teaching went very well but he did not enjoy the second year as much. Besides, he still entertained the dream of furthering his education beyond the Halstead diploma. Although this might have led him back to Bethel College, that was not the route he chose. Perhaps he listened more seriously to the encouragement of Ewert who surely would have advised him to achieve Manitoba teacher certification so that he could re-enter the educational enterprise in southern Manitoba.

Student in Winnipeg

Thus, after two years in Gretna, David Toews decided to enter the Collegiate and Normal School programs at Wesley College in Winnipeg, a precursor to United College which eventually became the University of Winnipeg. What we know of this period in his life is that in the course of two years, from the fall of 1895 to the spring of 1897, he completed the necessary courses for teacher certification. There has been some uncer-

A group of teachers meeting at Mennonite Collegiate Institute in Gretna, Manitoba, ca. 1893–1895 during the time the young David Toews was teaching in the Gretna Public School. Toews is standing (second row, centre); H.H. Ewert is seated (front row, centre). Photo: Mennonitische Lehranstalt: 25. Jubiläum 1889–1965.

tainty as to whether Toews stayed in Gretna for three years or only two and whether he studied in Winnipeg for only one year or for two. He himself settles the matter for us when, in a 1937 letter to Edmund G. Kaufman, president of Bethel College, he writes: "After two years in that school [Gretna Public School] I attended the Collegiate and the Normal School at Winnipeg for two years."[7] These two years of studies in Winnipeg brought his formal education to an end.

Apparently this was still an unsettled time for David Toews. One biographer wrote that for him attending school in Winnipeg "was no easy task, and he was wont to become discouraged, but people encouraged him and he accomplished his program."[8] Another friend reported that "during his year [sic] in Winnipeg there was a recurring dream of taking up farming again."[9] But farming was not an option if Heinrich H. Ewert would have his way.

Teacher in Burwalde

In the fall of 1897 Toews took up teaching again under the inspectorship of Ewert. This time Ewert assigned him to the elementary school at Burwalde just north of Winkler. There Toews was acclaimed by the community as a sincere and successful teacher. In his evaluation at the end of that year, Ewert gave him a high recommendation. Yet Toews was not satisfied. He had difficulty with self-acceptance and with affirmation of his own gifts. It may be that, like a typical idealist, he was overly critical of himself. Ewert counselled him on this problem, and finally told Toews that if he could not bring himself to self-affirmation, he should at least accept others' recommendations about his abilities and gifts. By the end of his year of teaching at Burwalde, Toews had decided to seek new opportunities west of Manitoba in what was then the North West Territory, an area that encompassed present-day Saskatchewan and Alberta.

Go West, Young Man

How did it come about that David Toews left the familiar environs of Manitoba to go west? Perhaps it was *Wanderlust* again. Perhaps he was lured by homesteading possibilities on the western frontier. Perhaps it was the attraction of linking up with people of more recent Prussian emigration whom he had met when they stopped off at Gretna in 1893–1894 on their way westward.[10] About the same time that Toews had come to Gretna from Kansas, Peter and Anna Regier, together with several other families, arrived in Gretna as immigrants from the village of Rückenau in West Prussia.[11] Peter Regier had decided to leave Prussia for religious as well as economic reasons. The small contingent was received warmly by Heinrich H. and Elizabeth Ewert who offered them temporary lodging in newly refurbished quarters of the schoolhouse. The Regiers' plan was to spend the winter in Gretna, with the Regier children attending the school of which Ewert was the director and the adults hoping to find work.

Once the Regier family was settled in Gretna, Peter Regier proceeded westward in search of a place to settle. A land agent by the name of Klaas Peters assisted him in this search. They took the train as far as present-day Alberta where, between Calgary and Edmonton, the Canadian Pacific Railway had tracts of land for sale. Regier also stopped off at Rosthern where some Mennonites had already settled. This area interested him very much, not least of all because Mennonites there were in need of a spiritual leader, and Peter Regier had the status of *Ältester* in the West Prussian Mennonite church. A tour of the region some 16 miles (25 kilometres) or more northwest of Rosthern took him to an area known as Diehl's Creek where two half-sections of land were available for purchase. Regier returned to Gretna, with this potential plot of land in mind. After the harvest in October, he and Anna travelled back to Rosthern by train and then on to the Diehl's Creek area. With Anna's approval, they purchased the two half-sections together with buildings. Before returning to Manitoba for the winter, the couple spent a few days on their newly purchased property. There they ploughed the garden, planted some trees, and dug a fireguard around the buildings. Then they returned to Rosthern and from there took the train back to Gretna. In the spring of 1894 the Regier family proceeded to the Tiefengrund area and settled in there.[12]

David Toews probably observed this coming and going with keen interest. The convergence of his arrival in Gretna with that of the Regiers gave him opportunity to get to know the Regier family. No doubt the Toews-Regier family connection went back further than Gretna. Peter Regier would have known David's father and grandfather from their time in West Prussia. There would have been a sense of kinship between the Regiers and David Toews because of their common recent West Prussian roots. It may have been this connection that provided the incentive for Toews to move westward to Tiefengrund.

There is even the possibility that, during his second year of teaching in Gretna, Toews may have visited the Eigenheim and Tiefengrund areas. In his history of the Eigenheim Mennonite Church, Walter Klaassen tells of a Toews from Kansas who was present in the congregation on November 4, 1894. This brother Toews preached in the Eigenheim and Waldheim churches at that time. According to someone's local diary, Toews had delivered the sermon with power and conviction. One source refers to this person as D. Toews; another speaks of J. Toews. Klaassen says it seems likely that this was indeed David Toews who had moved from Kansas to Manitoba in 1893.[13] He may have been visiting the Prussian families there with whom his parents and grandparents had previous connections in the old country. In particular, he may have come to visit the Regier family with whom he had become acquainted during their stay in Gretna the previous winter. But we cannot know for certain whether or not David Toews made an exploratory trip to Tiefengrund during the fall of his stay in Manitoba. How would it have been possible for a school teacher to leave his classroom for a trip to the North West Territory in November?

While David Toews was pursuing his education in Winnipeg, beginning in 1895 the elementary school in Tiefengrund, where he would eventually teach, was just getting organized. Once the Regiers and other large Mennonite families arrived in Tiefengrund, schooling became a necessity. Arrangements were made and classes began in the fall of 1895.[14] For the winter sessions of 1895 and 1896, Käthe Anna Regier, oldest daughter of Peter and Anna, was the school teacher. She had received a good preparatory education in Prussia. Classes were conducted in the Regier home. After two years, the school moved to the home of Peter's brother, Cornelius, who became the teacher for the 1897–1898 school year. He had a large house, which also accommodated the local post office. But it was obvious that a separate school building was needed where there would be space to accommodate the growing population of children. It was also obvious to Peter Regier and others in the community that they would need help from the outside if they were to upgrade their school so that it could offer good instruction in English along with the current German program.

And so it happened that, after two years in Gretna, another two years in Winnipeg, and a year of teaching at Burwalde, Toews packed his bags once more and took the train west to Saskatoon and then northward to Rosthern. Another hour or two across country by horse and wagon brought him to Tiefengrund. There he found a welcome reception, the chance to acquire some farmland, the opportunity to continue his teaching career, and much much more. Twenty-eight-year-old Toews arrived in Tiefengrund in the summer of 1898.

5

Tiefengrund
1898–1903

Given the pioneering spirit of David Toews, he moved west at an opportune time. Farmlands were being distributed for homesteading and towns were developing. While Rosthern had not yet come into its own as a major centre, it was an up-and-coming place. Apparently the summer before Toews arrived, in July of 1897, an event took place in Rosthern that placed it on the map of the Canadian west. In that year the little town got in on the Canada-wide jubilee celebrations in honour of Queen Victoria. Townspeople bedecked the streets with garlands and lanterns. An organ was brought into town for a musical event, and the town hall was the scene of dramatic productions. People came from near and far to enjoy the celebrations. A train, making its run from Regina to Prince Albert, stopped an extra hour so that the crew and passengers could get a taste of the celebration. News of the festival spread throughout the region by way of newspaper articles. One observer of the day said that this extravaganza served to attract a good number of businesses to the town.[1] Rosthern, along with the surrounding area, was in a mode of growth and development.

Northwestward
No doubt Toews travelled from Winnipeg to Rosthern by rail. He would have taken the Canadian Pacific Railway (CPR) from Winnipeg to Regina, then northward as far as Rosthern on the Qu'Appelle, Long Lake, and Saskatchewan Railroad which ran from Regina to Prince Albert—the CPR was leasing this line at the time. In Saskatoon he would have boarded the north-bound train on the spur line between Saskatoon and Prince Albert. Pioneers of the day depended on this line to get them into what was then only hinterland. About an hour up the line at Rosthern, where he disembarked, a horse and wagon would have been waiting to take him the 25 kilometres across country northwestward to the district of Tiefengrund where the Peter Regier family had settled four years earlier. Regier's description of the soil as having a substantial depth of topsoil (*einen tiefen Grund*) suggested the name *Tiefengrund,* which became the name of the area.[2] It may very well have been Peter Regier

who was at the Rosthern station to greet David and bring him to Tiefengrund. On the way home they would have talked about the new settlement of Mennonites, and Regier may have pointed out the lands that
were still available for homesteaders. The wagon trail led right alongside
a portion of potential farmland south of Tiefengrund that would soon
become David's homestead property.

At the time David Toews arrived in Tiefengrund, the district had
already attracted a number of settler families.[3] Abraham and Margarete
(Regier) Friesen had arrived from the Danzig region of Prussia in 1894,
the same year the Peter Regiers came. John Fieguth, who later married
Maria Harder, took a homestead in Tiefengrund in 1896. John J. and
Anna (Redekopp) Dyck, who came to Manitoba from Russia in 1891,
settled there in 1897. Isaac and Maria (Wieler) Klaassen arrived from
West Prussia by way of the United States in 1897, Cornelius and Anna
Regier via Kansas in 1894. Gerhard Dyck of Russia took up a homestead
in Tiefengrund in 1898, and married Anna Hamm a few years later.
Joseph and Elizabeth (Knopf) Samletzki came from Danzig by way of
Nebraska and arrived in Tiefengrund in 1897.

These were the pioneers who, together with their sometimes large
families, had already settled in the Tiefengrund district when Toews
came on the scene. Practically all of them had come because of the
opportunity to acquire land there. Some had related skills and interests.
Peter Regier was a minister, as was Abraham Friesen. Johann Fieguth
was a blacksmith and a machinery repairman. Isaac Klaassen was a long-
time school trustee. Abraham Funk and Gerhard Dyck contributed to
various social service organizations. Gerhard Dyck owned a Case steam
engine, used in the neighbourhood to turn the first sod of the bush and
the prairie. For each of the men named in this list of contributors to
community life and economy, there were at least as many pioneer women
who made their indispensable contribution in the home, in the church,
and in the community.

By the time the Mennonites arrived, the aboriginal peoples, who had
occupied the land centuries before the appearance of the white race, had
endured considerable unsettledness of their way of life and their
territory.[4] Signs of Indian culture were still apparent, but the impact of
European civilization had all but destroyed the way of life of these
nomadic people, who had in times past followed the herds of bison in
their quest for a livelihood. The first white man to penetrate into what is
today Saskatchewan was Henry Kelsey, who travelled there in 1690 from
York Factory on Hudson Bay. It appears that he explored the areas
around Warman and Hague. This exploratory trip predated the coming
of the Mennonites by 200 years. Within that time, the native inhabitants

had become well supplied with guns and alcohol, with European diseases and remedies, and with Christian teachings. Unfortunately, the Mennonite pioneers who came to the area in the late nineteenth century took little account of the earlier history of the west. The Mennonites had come because of their consuming passion for productive farming and the quest for a safe haven where they could practise their culture and faith. For this, they also needed teachers and ministers to serve their noble aspirations.

Teaching

David Toews came to Tiefengrund with six years of teaching experience—three in Kansas and three in Manitoba. The Tiefengrund community understood that he had come to be their teacher, and so they set him to work. As mentioned, some effort had been made over the previous three years, since the Regiers and other Mennonites first arrived in the area, to get a school started. But until now they were dependent on their own resources, both in supplying a teacher and in arranging accommodations in homes. When David assumed teaching responsibilities in 1898 after the fall harvest, he took over from Cornelius Regier, the brother of Peter. Cornelius' home was located on the quarter on which the Tiefengrund Church was later built in 1910.

That same year the district residents decided they needed a school building. The "home-schooling" facility was at best temporary. Since the Regiers had come to the Tiefengrund area in 1893, others had followed, and the population of children had grown to the extent that the living room of even the largest family home in the area offered only cramped quarters. And now, with a new teacher having come from afar, it was time to take a step forward. In February of 1899 the Board of Trustees held a meeting at the Peter Regier home to initiate plans for a suitable school building.[5] Debentures were sold, and by May of that same year the necessary $450 had been raised. Construction began with dispatch, so that teacher Toews was able to move into the schoolhouse in the fall of 1899, one year after his arrival. About the same time the boundaries of the school district were negotiated with the Department of Public Instruction in Regina. This resulted in a considerable enlargement of the area served by the Tiefengrund School.

Teacher Toews quickly gained the trust and respect of the community. He had free reign as far as the daily operations and the program of instruction were concerned. His salary amounted to $500 annually. There appeared to be no complaints about what he taught or how he taught. He was highly regarded by all parents.[6]

Homesteading
Even while the Tiefengrund community may have been rejoicing that they had acquired a fine teacher for their local school, David Toews was less sure about this vocational direction. He still dreamed of settling down on his own plot of land. There was homesteading land to be had in the area, and he was eager to stake out his claim. Within the first half year of arrival in Tiefengrund, early in 1899, he submitted an application for a homestead patent. In March of 1899 he obtained entry to a property. The plot of land assigned to him bore the number NW32-43-4-W3, a quarter-section that lies southeast of the intersection a mile south of where the Tiefengrund Mennonite Church stands today. The patent was granted later, on April 11, 1904,[7] but already in March of 1899 the name of David Toews appeared on the property assessment roll as a new ratepayer on NW32-43-4.[8]

It was sometimes said that David Toews became a serious farmer at this time, but that was apparently not the case. He never resided on his homestead property, and he developed very little of it. The record shows that in the summer of 1899 he "broke" 20 acres of bush and sod but did not plant a crop. The following three years he did not break any additional acreage, but only planted a crop on the 20 acres he had cleared earlier. In 1903, after four years of access to the property, Toews broke an additional 16 acres but still cropped only 20 acres. In that year his livestock consisted of two horses, five cattle, and five pigs. Clearly, David Toews did not see his future in farming.

It is not that the conditions were adverse to the possibility. The challenge of an undeveloped countryside inspired a work ethic and an entrepreneurial spirit. The new immigrants had travelled a great distance to make a new start. Now they needed to establish themselves. Large families contributed to the work force. New methods of clearing homestead land, such as the iron plough, were being introduced. Growing conditions were good. Mechanized harvest machinery was becoming more and more common. These were relatively prosperous times, and the pioneering spirit was in the air.

Marrying
But David Toews had other things than farming on his mind. On December 15, 1898, even before applying for his homestead, he purchased a quarter-section of land from the railway company. The land was located immediately north of where the Tiefengrund Church was later built in 1910, and diagonally across from the place where the new schoolhouse would be constructed the following summer. Evidently he did not plan to develop a residence and farmyard on homestead property.

His idea was to build a house on this newly acquired land, near to what was becoming the centre of the developing community. For the moment, the house-building project could wait, since the bachelor teacher could live in the teacherage of the new school. Having his own house would be premature and presumptuous, since he did not as yet have a bride to carry over its threshold. But he was thinking ahead nonetheless. Meanwhile, on December 20, 1898, he became a naturalized citizen of Canada.[9] David Toews had settled on his country of residence and of citizenship.

What happened next helped to distract David from his wandering ways and to provide an air of settledness to his life. He fell in love with blue-eyed Margarete Friesen, the eighth child of a family of 12 siblings of whom three were the children of Abraham Friesen's first marriage and nine were the children of Abraham and his second wife, Margarete (Regier) Friesen. The Friesens had migrated to Canada in 1894, coming from the same area as the Peter Regier family—Margarete (Regier) Friesen was a sister to Elder Peter Regier. Abraham Friesen was an important leader in the new community. He served on the team of church ministers. Also, he was a charter member of the Tiefengrund School District and was "responsible for successfully guiding the school's progress through the initial five years of its existence."[10] Daughter Margarete was born July 24, 1881.

Abraham (1849–1901) and Margarete (Regier) (1859–1912) Friesen, parents of Margarete, the wife of David Toews. Photo: *Saskatchewan Mennonite Historian*

It is said that David, being a non-resistant Mennonite, could not resist her winsome character.[11] Although Margarete was only 19 years old when she married 30-year-old David, she was mature for her age. She had learned to take responsibilities in the context of a large family. From 1894 until she married in 1900, Margarete was one of the two older daughters in the home. When her older sister Marie married in 1897, it fell to Margarete to take major responsibilities for domestic work. In this context she learned the meaning of doing her duty as life demanded it. Remarkably, although she did not have the benefit of a happy and carefree youth, she was gifted with a warm and vibrant personality which prevailed and matured in the crucible of the Friesen family setting. Margarete was baptized upon the confession of her faith on June 5, 1898, about a month before David arrived from Manitoba.

The marriage of David and Margarete took place on September 20, 1900, but the record as to the order of service and even the location has been lost. Most likely the ceremony took place in the Friesen home. In any case, we can imagine a dignified service with Elder Peter Regier, the uncle of Margarete, officiating at the ceremony, and Margarete's minister father offering an official word of counsel based on Scripture. We can also imagine the beautiful setting at that time of the year, with the leaves displaying their golden splendour and colourful fall flowers adorning the place of the ceremony.

Those who knew David's spouse spoke highly of her. One unpublished biographer who knew David and Margarete personally in later life, put it this way: "Nicht Geld und Gut brachte sie ihm in die Ehe mit; aber ein Herz wie Gold trug sie ihm als Mitgift zu, ein sonniges Herz, dass von warmer Liebe durchglüht war. Das musz schön gewesen sein!"[12] (She did not bring money and material goods to the marriage, but the dowry she offered him was a heart of gold, a heart of sunshine, glowing with the warmth of love. That must have been wonderful!) David was a fortunate young man to have Margarete as his helpmate! As we shall see, she stood by him faithfully in good times and in bad.

Building a Home
David and Margarete set up their family household in the teacherage of the Tiefengrund school. A year later, by the summer of 1901, they moved out of those cramped quarters and settled, at least for a short time, into their new house across from the school. Built at a cost of $600, the house was two-storied, 24 feet long and 16 feet wide. There was also a stable for the horses, additional livestock, wagons, sleighs, and buggies. The stable measured 20 feet by 18 feet and was valued at $200. A local carpenter, Johann J. Dyck, built the house for David and Margarete

The wedding of Margarete & David Toews on September 20, 1900

where they lived for three years. Two children, Marie (1901) and Benno (1903), were born there.

Educational Issues

In the fall of 1901 David Toews began his third year as teacher at the Tiefengrund school. Besides classroom teaching, he was a proponent of Mennonite educational values generally. In Kansas as well as Manitoba he had rubbed shoulders with leaders who upheld the principle that the school should serve the interests of the church. According to the historic conviction of Mennonites and their Anabaptist forebears, the church and the family bore ultimate responsibility for the nurturing process. Any consideration of public education needed to guard against deferral to the state and its values. State education appeared to imply devotion to the affairs of the state and compliance with its authority. This would inevitably lead to a breakdown of the pacifist stance. David's early life had been shaped by the particular response of his religious community

The first family home built by Margarete and David Toews in Tiefengrund shortly after their marriage. The house was later moved to Laird, Saskatchewan, where it stands to this day.

to this issue. Even though the "great trek" had not achieved its goal, the principle which drove his parents to take that route remained with them, a principle with which Toews agreed.

All the while, the government was pressing the Mennonites to comply with prescriptions laid out by its Department of Education. The public education promoters wanted a curriculum that would fit every school. This left two options for those with Mennonite religious convictions: to petition the government for modifications that would accommodate the values of the Mennonite churches; or to establish their own private schools where they could enjoy greater freedom. The first option required negotiation with governmental departments, the second a greater vision and much money.

Gradually Toews was drawn in as official spokesperson and advocate for Mennonite educational concerns. He had a gift for stating issues with clarity and for thinking on his feet. In his view, Mennonites should seek permission to teach the German language as part of the curriculum in schools where their children attended. David spoke about this with anyone who would listen. And in the year 1900 he and others drew up a petition requesting authorization to teach German in "our public schools" for two hours each week. The church believed it to be essential that the children learn German. How else could they communicate with the older generation? How else could they participate in worship services which included German preaching and singing? How else could they be instructed in the faith, which the older generation could express only in German and for which the curriculum materials were written in German? As Toews and many others saw it, the German language and religious instruction were also the fabric that would keep a Mennonite identity strong, even as a barrier that would keep other ideas at bay in this strange new world to which the Mennonites had immigrated. There was majority support for the petition back home, but there was also opposition. What if everyone wanted his or her own language taught in the public schools? Think of the cost! David Toews was no stranger to such opposition.

In the spring of 1901, he received permission from the Tiefengrund trustees to present a petition to government officials in Regina.[13] This would be his first assignment of the kind where he would negotiate with public authorities on behalf of the larger Mennonite church. It would not have been easy for him to travel to the big city, then boasting a population of about 2500, and to make his way alone to the offices where the Department of Public Instruction (now the Department of Education) was housed. While he presented his request clearly, there was little response from the Department. Since no reply came, in the interim the Mennonites continued to do as they wished. At least until the outbreak of the Second World War they were not hindered in their teaching of German.[14] Meanwhile the alternative idea of a private school was also in the air.[15]

Rosenort Mennonite Church

When Elder Peter Regier left West Prussia and came to Canada in 1893, and then to Tiefengrund in 1894, he came not only for the purpose of farming and preserving his convictions on nonresistance, but also with a willingness to serve the immigrant church that would surely develop with the coming of Mennonites from Russia and Prussia. At first, as immigrants moved into the area, meetings were arranged here and there in local homes. Regier took upon himself the responsibility of serving these groups with sermons and with the ordinances of baptism and the Lord's Supper. Slowly, beginning in 1896, church buildings were constructed where immigrants had settled—first in Eigenheim (1896), then in Rosthern (1903), in Aberdeen, Laird, and Tiefengrund (1910), and in Hague (1911). Local groups in other locations continued to meet in homes or in schoolhouses.

The first organizational meeting of this group of churches dates back to July 2, 1894, the first summer following the coming of the Peter Regier family to the area. The assumption was that the local groups would form one *Gemeinde*. That is, the smaller units would be part of one congregation, one church, with one *Ältester* and as many assistant *Prediger* (preachers, ministers) as necessary. This had been the system in the Rosenort congregation in West Prussia where Regier was ordained as *Prediger* in 1879 and as *Ältester* in 1887.[16] Not only was the West Prussian (and Russian) Mennonite ministerial system carried over, the name was brought from Europe as well. The church or *Gemeinde* in West Prussia, of which Peter Regier had been elder, was the "Rosenort Mennonite Church." At a church meeting on May 27, 1897, the decision was made to give the newly organized immigrant church in central Canada the same name, the "Rosenorter Gemeinde."

Minister Toews

By this time David Toews was recognized as a potential leader in the church. On numerous occasions he had been called upon to speak, to lead meetings, and to lead the singing, even though he was not yet ordained. That would change soon. The occasion for ordination arose when, on June 21, 1901, David's father-in-law, Abraham Friesen, passed away. This was a great loss not only to his large family, but also to the church in which he had served faithfully as a member of the ministerial circle. The death occurred just at the time when an increasing number of Mennonite families was coming to the area, and Mennonite centres were developing quickly in the wider region. With the death of Rev. Friesen, it was important that one or more new ministers be chosen, both to take his place and to serve the growing church, a church which at the time met mainly at local gatherings in homes and in schoolhouses.

In the Mennonite tradition to which the Rosenorter Mennonite Church belonged, ministers were chosen by a democratic process. First, members of the congregation decided whether or not they wanted to engage in a selection of ministerial leaders, and how many candidates they wished to ordain. In this case, the congregation was in favour of moving ahead with the selection of two persons. Next, the congregation was invited to submit nominees for the position. These were received by the church council, which gave the list some scrutiny to ensure that the persons nominated were in good standing with the congregation and would be deemed capable of serving. The submitted names were then placed before the membership for a vote. The two persons with the largest number of votes were invited to submit to ordination.

On August 18, 1901, David Toews was ordained as one of the ministers of the Rosenorter Mennonite congregation. In German, he would be referred to as "*Prediger* David Toews." In the custom of English-speaking churches, he was now also "Reverend David Toews." At a meeting shortly thereafter, it was decided that for the next while Sunday services at Eigenheim and Rosthern would be conducted on a weekly basis, while at Tiefengrund, Waldheim, Hague, Bergthal, Osler, and Aberdeen services would be held every third Sunday.[17] Toews joined the circle of ministers that served these local gatherings as itinerant preachers. Elder Regier took care of all official functions such as baptisms, the Lord's Supper, and ordinations. He also presided over the regular ministerial meetings at which worship schedules were planned, pastoral visits were coordinated, and church issues were discussed and resolved.

With his ordination to church ministry, David Toews entered a new phase in his life. Until then he had been involved primarily with matters of education and with teaching. While this did not diminish, his responsibilities were increased and widened to include the congregation and the wider church constituency. He was enlisted for regular duties at any one of the locations. This included not only the itinerant Sunday morning preaching, but also pastoral counselling, ministerial meetings, follow-up on disciplinary decisions, leadership in music ministry, Sunday school teaching, work with youth, and more. Toews enjoyed relating to people and he saw it as his obligation. He was young, energetic, and understanding.

Clearly he could not have carried on with these added duties if his faithful Margarete had not supported him wholeheartedly. Toews knew this, and he appreciated her support. Years later, when he found it necessary to write her obituary, he noted that when he was inducted into the ministry in 1901, and again when he was ordained as *Ältester* of the Rosenorter Mennonite Church in 1913, this always meant added burdens (*Lasten*) for his spouse. She bore her responsibilities faithfully and without complaint.[18]

The ministry of David Toews in the church went beyond the role of preacher. Given his keen interest in education, it was inevitable that he would get involved in the congregation's teaching ministry. When it became apparent that religious instruction through the public school might not be permitted in the long run, one of the options was to organize Sunday schools. Toews led the congregation in thinking innovatively about the possibilities of biblical instruction in the church context. At first, the idea did not go over well with some, since it seemed that such "work" was not appropriate on the Sabbath. There was also the problem of coordinating Sunday school with the traditional worship service and possibly extending the amount of church activity on a typical Sunday morning. And where in the church would such classes be conducted? Gradually, however, the program of Sunday morning classes for children, and then for youth and even for adults, set in. At the beginning, a Sunday school was conducted for children of all ages in the Eigenheim School near the church. The local elementary school teacher, Gerhard Epp, taught the class. At this time David and Margarete lived in Tiefengrund next door to Ältester Regier.

However, the centre of gravity for the church was elsewhere, namely in Eigenheim. Not only did that area have a greater population of Mennonites, it was a central location for the church, while Tiefengrund was somewhat north of centre. This required much additional travelling for the new *Prediger.* The trip from Tiefengrund south and somewhat west to Eigenheim was ten miles one way. Picture, if you will, Toews and Regier, setting out from Tiefengrund on a late afternoon in January to attend an evening ministerial meeting in Eigenheim. After bidding farewell to spouse and children, they bundle up in heavy fur coats and thick blankets, take their places in the two-seater sleigh, and get the horses moving. After the meeting the faithful horses carry their two conversing passengers home in the light of a full moon and under the vista of a star-studded sky. The only sounds are the animated conversation of the two passengers and the crunching of crisp snow under the horses' feet. They arrive home about midnight, with a prayer of thanksgiving and a long day well spent.

Conference Beginnings

While David and Margarete were living in Tiefengrund, an event of some significance took place within walking distance of their place on the farmyard of Ältester Peter Regier just to the north. On July 18, 1902, nine men met in the Regiers' garden to discuss the possibility of forming a relationship between Mennonite Bergthaler congregations of Manitoba and the Rosenorter Mennonite church of the North West Territory. This meeting led to the subsequent founding of the *Konferenz der Mennoniten im mittleren Kanada* (Conference of Mennonites in Central Canada).[19] The exact place of the meeting on the Regier yard is known to this day: two outdoor benches, arranged in a v-formation, mark the historic spot.

The immediate reason for the gathering was to agree on an arrangement for the orderly transfer of church memberships from the Bergthaler Mennonite Church of Manitoba to the Rosenorter Mennonite Church. Mennonite families related to the Manitoba group were moving to the Rosthern area and Bergthaler leaders wanted to ensure that its members would find a church home on the frontier. The meeting at the Regier home included two representatives of the Bergthaler Mennonite Church in Manitoba, Benjamin Ewert and Johann M. Friesen. The General Conference Mennonite Church of North America had sent J.E. Sprunger from its head offices, located in Berne, Indiana, at the time. David Toews along with five others—Peter Regier, David Epp, Johann Dueck, Heinrich Warkentin, and Gerhard Epp—represented the Rosenorter

Rosenorter (Saskatchewan) and Bergthaler (Manitoba) church leaders meeting in 1902 at the Peter Regier home. They agreed to meet again a year later at what became the first delegate session of the Conference of Mennonites in Central Canada. From left, front row: *Benjamin Ewert, Gretna; Peter Regier, Tiefengrund; Johann M. Friesen, Altona; J.E. Sprunger, Berne, Indiana;* back row: *David Epp, Laird; Johann Dueck, Eigenheim; Heinrich Warkentin, Laird; David Toews, Tiefengrund; Gerhard Epp, Eigenheim.* Photo: MHC Archives

Church. The average age of this group is estimated at about 38 years. David Toews, at age 32, was among the youngest. There was a premonition in the air that this meeting would be of some significance.

While the meeting resulted in an agreement to accept migrating Bergthaler members into the Rosenorter Church, the gathering made a more far-reaching decision: to meet again in one year for a call to convene a delegate conference of the member churches of the Bergthaler and Rosenorter groups. The session would be held in Manitoba at a place to be determined by the Bergthaler Church ministers. And so it was that the first of what became annual sessions of the Conference of Mennonites in Central Canada was held July 20–21, 1903 in the congregational meeting house at Hochstadt in southern Manitoba.[20] Assistant Elder Jacob Hoeppner of the Winkler Bergthaler Church presided over the sessions in Hochstadt. Benjamin Ewert of Gretna, a Bergthaler minister and printer, served as secretary.

David Toews was scheduled to be at the historic first delegate session in 1903. He had been assigned a presentation to answer the question: "How should the scattered members of our church community (*Gemeinschaft*) best be served?" His paper was to follow a talk by his mentor and friend, Heinrich H. Ewert of Gretna, on "The goal, the purpose, and the worth of our Conference." But David Toews was not at the meeting. He had three weighty family matters to take care of. First, there was the imminent birth of the second child, Benno. Then there was the matter of Margarete's health. Several years earlier she had contracted trachoma, a common yet dreaded eye disease, and David was making every effort to facilitate the healing process. Furthermore, this was the summer when Toews completed five years of teaching at Tiefengrund and moved on to a new appointment in the Eigenheim public school. With so much happening in his personal life, David Toews was absent from this first annual delegate session of the Conference.

From the beginning, Conference leaders appreciated the presence of David Toews as a co-worker in their midst. Half a century after the origin of the Conference of Mennonites in Central Canada, Rev. J.G. Rempel wrote: "We regret to this day that the presenter [David Toews], who always had energy to spare for life and work, could not be present."[21] It would have been good for both H.H. Ewert and David Toews to be there, he continued, as this "would have contributed a good breadth of ideas, even if it did not always seem possible, in the working relationship for these two strong personalities, to offer mutually enhancing presentations." It was fortunate, continued Rempel, that "the Lord found a field for each." Then Rempel compared the two to "parents who sometimes negotiate between their children, and give each their toys and their place to play." In a similar way, "our loving God showed his two children (and certainly the two were God's children) their place; and each was able to offer great service to our people." The result of this separateness was positive, as "they did not need to expend their energies in doing battle with one another, even though at times there were severe clashes between them, as between the Apostles Paul and Peter."

Despite his absence, David Toews was drawn into Conference work. Together with Heinrich H. Ewert and another Bergthaler member, Johann M. Friesen, he was appointed to a committee that was charged with studying the feasibility of publishing a church paper (*Gemeinde-blatt)*. This was the first of many Conference committees for Toews. At the close of the first sessions, Rev. Gerhard Epp invited the delegates to meet at Eigenheim in 1904. By then it was a foregone conclusion that there would be continuous annual Conference sessions.

A Widening Conference Circle

With the formation of the Conference of Mennonites in Central Canada, two identifiable groups had pledged to work cooperatively—the Rosenorter *Gemeinde* of Saskatchewan and the Bergthaler *Gemeinde* of

Manitoba. But there are at least three additional parts to the Conference story. First, in Saskatchewan, the Rosenorter Church had already received into its membership some Mennonites who had been excommunicated from their Old Colony Mennonite Church in Manitoba.[22] A group consisting of 11 families moved to the Rosthern area in 1891, even before Peter Regier arrived there. These Mennonites, who came from Reinland, Manitoba, by way of Gleichen, Alberta, joined the Rosenorter Church in 1895. At the turn of the century, more Mennonites of Old Colony background from the Reinland area moved to farmland in the Rosthern area and joined the Rosenorter group.

Second, beginning in 1885, a considerable population of Reinländer Mennonites, who were known as "Old Colony" Mennonites and of a more conservative bent than the afore-mentioned Bergthaler Church of Manitoba, moved from Manitoba onto the Hague-Osler Reserve, a region of four townships between Saskatoon and Rosthern, set aside for Mennonites by the Dominion government.[23] These Reinländer Mennonites were tightly organized and strictly regulated. As a consequence, a considerable number of individuals left this conservative church over various issues, and joined the Rosenorter Church and other congregations of the Conference of Mennonites in Central Canada. For example, if families of this Reinländer church would send their children to public schools, or if members would find it necessary to purchase public fire insurance, they would be banned from the church, and the remaining church members would be restricted from social visits or business dealings with the excommunicated members.

Third, between the years 1898 and 1914 a small but steady stream of General Conference Mennonites from the United States migrated to Canada. In Saskatchewan, they settled in such places as Herbert, Drake, Langham, Aberdeen, and Waldheim.[24] They did not hesitate to link with congregations of the Conference of Mennonites in Canada, as they knew themselves to be of one family with the Rosenorter Church. When church leaders from the United States visited the Canadian churches, they would always find a warm welcome among these former Americans.

For David Toews and his colleagues in the church and eventually in the German-English Academy, this spectrum of persons and congregations presented a challenge. There were constant issues of ethics, of unity, and of doctrine to discuss and sometimes to resolve. One early result of this diversity was that the Conference fostered a spirit of inclusivity and of broadmindedness. This suited the style and the perspective of David Toews, whose concern it was to hold to the essential core of Christian faith and life while allowing a variety of opinions on nonessentials.

Moving Again

In 1903 David and Margarete made the decision to leave Tiefengrund and move to Eigenheim. We can only speculate as to the reason for this move. Perhaps teaching for five years in one rather small community was long enough. They may have felt too, since David was ordained to ministry, it was more practical to locate closer to the centre of the congregations of the Rosenorter Church. The distance to the various congregations was a great deal farther from Tiefengrund than from Eigenheim. Perhaps Margarete felt that by then she could afford to distance herself somewhat from her paternal home. Her siblings were able to manage for themselves. She needed to concentrate on tending her own family which had grown to four members—the parents David and Margarete, two-year-old Marie and infant Benno. Perhaps with the prospect of a German-English Academy on the horizon, and its possible location in Rosthern, Toews wanted to place himself in geographical proximity to the centre of activity.

Whatever the reason or reasons, in the summer of 1903 the family vacated their Tiefengrund home and settled for a time into the teacherage at the Eigenheim school. Their house in Tiefengrund was rented to Abraham and Johanna (Kliewer) Funk, immigrants who recently had arrived from Germany.[25] Toews eventually sold the house and the quarter of land on which it stood to Peter Regier. The house is still in existence, although it no longer stands next to the Tiefengrund Mennonite Church. It was purchased by Bruno and Elsie Neufeldt, who moved it to the village of Laird in the early 1950s. There it stands to this day, somewhat altered over time by renovations.[26]

The new teacher who succeeded David Toews at the Tiefengrund school was William Thomas Diefenbaker of Toronto.[27] Mr. Diefenbaker made the move from the east to the prairies on the advice of his doctor who had diagnosed him as a likely prospect for tuberculosis, or "gallopping consumption," as it was called in those days. He had found the Tiefengrund position through an agency that listed school vacancies across Canada. William was able to speak German so he was somewhat suited for the teaching assignment at Tiefengrund. Together with his wife, Mary, and two young sons, Elmer and John, William Diefenbaker moved into the teacherage in August of 1903. Today this is a family of some historical distinction since William and Mary's younger son, John, grew up to become the Prime Minister of Canada.

John Diefenbaker's later description of the move to Tiefengrund tells us something about life on the prairies at the time when David Toews and family made their move from Tiefengrund to Eigenheim.[28] On its way from Regina to Saskatoon, the train had stopped three or four times to allow the railway workers to go duck hunting at the side of the tracks. According to John, there were millions of ducks in the fields. When the train arrived at Rosthern, about 300 people were milling about at the station. They were not there to welcome the Diefenbakers. Rather, they were immigrants from continental Europe who had just arrived. John wrote that, after a few days' stay in Rosthern, they "started out for Fort Carlton and the area where Father had accepted a school, 17 miles across prairie on a wagon—no roads, you just simply drove in a general direction northwest." Their taxi driver for the trip from Rosthern to Tiefengrund was Mr. John J. Dyck, who came for them in his double-box farm wagon and team of horses. In Tiefengrund, the Diefenbakers found the school quite modest, "equipped with plank seats and the desks themselves were made of rough hewn planks." They found themselves among people of two European racial origins, Russian-German and French-Canadian, with many Metis and Indians also inhabiting that part of the Territories.

Life on the prairies at that time is reflected in John Diefenbaker's comments on his father's salary which was $350 annually. With this he not only had to sustain his family. He and Mary were expected to extend hospitality *gratis* to all who stopped by, which included government inspectors, land agents, implement dealers, door-to-door salesmen, and an assortment of travellers. John Diefenbaker wrote: "This was the spirit of the prairies."

6

Eigenheim
1903–1906

Eigenheim, which means "our very own home," was the name given by Mennonite immigrants to a farm settlement ten kilometres west of Rosthern. The name reflected the passionate motivation that brought Mennonite immigrants to this region in western Canada—they were driven by the desire for their own land. Many were of the poor and landless people in the Mennonite colonies in Russia who hoped they would find exemption from military service and even from compulsory alternative service in lieu of military conscription.[1] The motivation was in some respects no different from the goal that Jacob and Anna Toews had pursued when they took their son David and his siblings on the trek to central Asia a decade earlier, except that the Toews were not economically depressed when they left Lysanderhöhe.

The first Mennonite family to settle in the Eigenheim area arrived in the early months of 1892. The typical pattern of migration in those earliest years was to come as far as Manitoba. The men would leave their families there while they proceeded westward to investigate possibilities for settlement and make arrangements for the possession of homesteads. The stopover in Manitoba also served the purpose of buying farm equipment and livestock, which the immigrants then took to their new home.

When Gerhard Andres of Russia arrived in Manitoba in December of 1891, he immediately made his way to Rosthern to explore homesteading possibilities. After finding a plot of land west of town, he went back to Manitoba to organize the last leg of the journey. Other families soon followed the Andres family to Eigenheim. If the earliest settlers brought good reports back to Manitoba, and even to Russia and western Prussia, others would soon follow in their tracks. In this way the community known today as Eigenheim developed into a Mennonite settlement. It was not a village as such, but a region where farm was linked to farm over a wide area. The name Eigenheim came into informal use by 1894, and in 1899 was given to school district no. 502.

Church Beginnings

At the centre of the Eigenheim settlement was the church, lying to the north of the road that ran east and west. It was organized by Elder Peter Regier in July of 1894, the same year that he settled with his family in Tiefengrund.[2] At first, worship was conducted in homes. Because of distance and winter weather, it was not possible to have services every Sunday, but it did not take long for vigorous church life to develop. In 1895 a 20-acre plot of land was donated by the railway company as a church site.[3] In July, the local group elected Gerhard Epp as minister and Johann Dueck as deacon. During the winter of 1895–1896 logs were cut on an island in the North Saskatchewan River and hauled by sleigh to the site of the future church building. In spring, after the thaw, the men gathered to construct the church which was completed by early June.

The dedication service for the log meeting house took place on June 14, 1896. On that occasion 24 persons were baptized, a sign of the expansive population of the Eigenheim area and of the congregation. The church was filled to overflowing for the celebrative event, a sign that the new building would soon be too small for the growing congregation of immigrant Mennonites. By January of 1902, a new building was on the drawing board. Funds were soon collected, and in the spring construction

The first Rosenort church built in Eigenheim. Dedication for the log meeting house took place on June 14, 1896. Photo: H.T. Klaassen, *Birth and Growth of Eigenheim Mennonite Church*

proceeded.[4] The church was dedicated on November 2, 1902. This second building had a seating capacity of 300, which was adequate for the needs of the community, but was still somewhat cramped for special events. David Toews was a participant in the dedication services that day. In the morning service he led the church choir in the singing of two songs: "Komm doch zur Quelle des Lebens" (Come to the fountain of life) and "O wunderbar suess ist die Botschaft" (O how wonderfully sweet is the message). In the afternoon service, Toews was one of the two preachers. This time the choir sang the popular, "Gott mit euch bis wir uns wiedersehn" (God be with you till we meet again).

According to Walter Klaassen, singing practices had begun in the Eigenheim church in 1901 by a Johann Gloeckler, immigrant from Minnesota. David took over from him, and introduced four-part singing, something he had learned while in Kansas.[5] With the dedication of the Rosthern Mennonite Church building in August of 1903, the area had two permanent locations for worship.

At the time this was still the only local group of the Rosenorter family of congregations with its own church building. Records show that in the summer of 1903 some 175 church members were present at the celebration of the Lord's Supper in the Rosenort-Eigenheim church. Eigenheim was considered unofficially as the mother congregation of the "Rosenorter Gemeinde von Saskatchewan" (Rosenorter Congregation of Saskatchewan). The latter name had been decided upon at a meeting of all local groups in May of 1897.[6]

Teaching
When David Toews became the teacher at Eigenheim in 1903, he and Margarete moved into the living quarters next to the school. It was located three-quarters of a mile west and one mile south of the church. David knew the people very well, since the Mennonite churches in Tiefengrund and Eigenheim were part of one congregation. As one of the ministers of the Rosenorter congregation of churches, he was not only the teacher at the Eigenheim school, but also one of the ministers at the local place of worship.

He was not the school's first teacher. Day-school instruction had begun at that location in October 1894.[7] For the first two years, when attendance averaged about ten pupils, the children had gathered at the home of Johann Andres with Gerhard Epp as teacher. Then the community built a log schoolhouse consisting of a classroom and a teacherage. After three years, Epp was succeeded for one year by Hermann Lenzmann. Then in 1899 David Epp, brother of Gerhard, took over the teaching duties. At that time teachers were paid by the month according to an agreement made with the local school trustee group. Remuneration came both in cash and in household necessities. The first teachers received $2.00 per month plus five bushels of wheat per child. By the time David Epp assumed responsibilities, salaries had risen to $10 a month plus fuel.

When David Toews took over from David Epp in 1903, the log schoolhouse had been dismantled and replaced by a new building. This was now a district school within the public school system.[8] With public control came inspection, the licensing of teachers, the selection of textbooks, and curriculum outlines. At the beginning the emphasis on religious instruction depended to a great extent on local expectations. Bible stories, hymn singing, and German instruction were part of the curriculum. With the inclusion of non-Mennonite families within the school districts, religious instruction became more and more the direct responsibility of the church through its Sunday school.

To understand the role of Toews in this situation, one needs to recognize that the west was pioneer country. The provinces of Saskatchewan and Alberta had not yet come to birth. Schools as well as the roads that led to them were in primitive condition. This made travel difficult, especially in wintertime, and school attendance was somewhat irregular. Besides, planting crops in spring and harvesting operations in fall were judged by most parents to take priority over school attendance. Every capable hand was needed for the farming operation. Nevertheless, the people were in a mood of progressiveness.

Fortunately, Teacher Toews had the will and the wisdom to adapt to the aspirations and operations of the community. One unpublished biographer describes his attitude as follows:

> He soon felt quite at home in the community, and school work was for him a joy, not a burden. Conducting school was no drudgery, no spiritless work, simply carried out against his own will. He had a sense of duty and responsibility. He was not quarrelsome, but rather harmonized with the people. He did not ask for much for himself. He had an open heart for the needs in the surrounding community. To give is more blessed than to receive.[9]

Toews did not appear to be in the teaching profession for his own ego-satisfaction or for personal financial gain. He was in step with the people he served. He desired to build community together.

Higher Education

Sooner or later the Mennonite community would need to consider the question of higher education. Advanced education was part of their European past. In western Prussia and in Russia, the school system had developed well beyond the elementary level to include high schools and teacher training institutes as well as schools of commerce and of agriculture. Furthermore, given the development of educational institutions on the wider Canadian public scene, the Mennonite community would need to consider how they wished to enter the arena of higher education. It was not a question of whether, but of how. It was predictable that Mennonites would seek an avenue of involvement, given the social and cultural interests of these progressively-minded Rosenorter people.

David Toews was at the centre of discussion concerning the school question. It was his conviction, along with others, that a Mennonite identity was worth nurturing and preserving. This meant the Mennonite community would need to take its own educational aspirations and needs in hand. Toews believed that the preservation and development of Mennonite community depended largely on its religious and cultural fabric, and that education played a crucial role in weaving and strengthening this fabric. He saw the pursuit of biblical knowledge, a Mennonite understanding of the faith, and the use of the German language, as essential elements in this intergenerational task. Toews viewed a Mennonite-directed educational system as the necessary vehicle for this goal.

Meanwhile, the situation was becoming complicated for the Mennonites. Many of their neighbours, with whom they were to conduct schools in common, had different religious convictions, or none at all. Also, various cultures were represented in their school district. It was possible to build a religious and cultural identity in the church but not in the public school. The territorial government could not afford to give each group its own kind of school, nor could it allow one particular religious group to have a dominating voice. With communities being pluralistic in ethnic make-up, it was impossible to accommodate each community according to its local religious and cultural wishes. Toews understood both the Mennonite ideal and the practical situation. Together with others, he was intent on finding a solution.

Planning Committee

On January 24, 1903, while the Toews were still living in Tiefengrund, an "extra special meeting" was held in the home of Peter Regier to deliberate on the school situation.[10] David Toews, one of five persons at the meeting, was named as chairman of the program committee. The sense of the meeting was that a German-English school was needed, a school owned and operated by Mennonites. This was conceived as an alternative plan in case the government was not willing to make allowance for the teaching of German in the public system.

David Toews felt the need to inform the Department of Public Instruction in Regina of the Mennonites' initiative. In a letter dated February 24, 1903, he requested that the government should consider a two-track school where both English and German would be taught. There could be two departments and two teaching staffs. The English teachers would be paid by the district and the German teachers would be paid by an association of those who desired German instruction. Would the government consent to such a plan and be willing to support the English part of the school? The answer that came eventually, on June 10, 1903, was negative. The letter stated adamantly that regular departmental grants for the teaching of children would be available only where children were instructed in the English language.

David Toews and his program committee had already suspected that the idea of offering German through the public system would not be acceptable to the Department in Regina. Without waiting for a reply, the Mennonites called a meeting for March 7, 1903. This first official public meeting to be held in the new church building at Eigenheim was well attended. Toews presented one of the three papers, entitled, "The need for our own teacher education institute." The participants were interested and enthusiastic.[11] A noteworthy comment made at the meeting was: "Was unsere Schule ist, wird später unsere Gemeinde sein." (What our school is now, our congregation will eventually become.) By the end of the meeting, a decision had been made to proceed with a German-English Academy. An administration committee was elected. Of the 15 persons nominated, the top five were appointed with Toews receiving the most votes. He was chosen to chair the committee.

Further public meetings were held on May 9 and May 20. The result was that the first school board was chosen with David Toews among the original nine members. The meetings also considered and accepted a constitution. The name of the school would be *Deutsche-Englische Fortbildungsschule* (literally, German-English School for Continuing Education). Apparently not everything had proceeded calmly at this first meeting. At a further organizational meeting on June 10, 1903, Toews read from Philippians 2:4: "Let each of you look not to your own interests, but to the interests of others." He followed this reading with an appeal for "a calm and quiet discussion."[12] A point of some debate was the location of the new school. Should it be in the country? Near a town? Or in town? By the end of the meeting it had been decided that the best location would be near a town, and that Rosthern be named as the desired site. By that time it had 600 inhabitants.

Once he was settled into his teaching assignment in Eigenheim, David Toews would have his hands full with tending to his teaching and to his family, along with fulfilling his obligations in the church. But as the recently appointed chairman of the administration committee (the "Board") for the prospective high school, he had another agenda to attend to. It was left largely to Toews to promote the idea of the school and to collect funds for its start-up operation.[13] His means of travel at the time was mainly by horse and buggy, and he had no modern telephone at his disposal. It took much personal dedication and time to keep in touch with the widespread constituency of the Rosenorter churches.

School Site

On the basis of the decision made at the spring meeting, the Board authorized the purchase of a three-acre plot northwest of Rosthern at a price of $150. When the note came due at the end of the year (1903), sufficient money had not yet been collected. By mid-1904 there was still very little money in the treasury. This did not deter Toews. He purchased the plot on behalf of the school with the expectation that there would eventually be enough money to pay for it.[14] He reported his purchase to the Board several months later, in June, but the matter was not a high priority since the financial situation did not permit purchase of land, much less construction of school facilities. His explanation was that he wanted to secure the land in case the school would be built in Rosthern. This was possibly something of an understatement of his motives. Toews felt strongly that the school should be located in Rosthern, while some supporters spoke for a distinctly rural location.

The task of fundraising tended to fall to David Toews. Even while he was in Eigenheim, he was offered remuneration comparable to a teacher's salary if he would work administratively for the school as fundraiser. But Toews realized that with no money in the treasury a salary would not be forthcoming. So he continued as teacher at Eigenheim and, with the help of others, did fundraising on the side. By the beginning of 1905 donations were coming in quite well, so the Board began to plan for school opening on November 1 of that year.

Some had expected that David Toews would become the school's first teacher. He was offered the position, but he declined. No one seems to know why. Perhaps he wanted to be certain that the new school project was a sure thing before he would commit himself to moving again. Keeping some distance would give him time to promote and do more fundraising for the school. Frank H. Epp, in his history of the school, surmised that Toews may have "taken a year off to take a refresher course (or to teach) at the Mennonite Collegiate Institute in Gretna, Manitoba."[15] But evidence from the Eigenheim school records shows that he continued to teach at Eigenheim during the 1905–1906 school year.[16]

Excerpt from the Eigenheim School District #502 Attendance Record book indicating that David Toews taught there until June 1906. Courtesy: Rosthern High School Records

On October 21, ten days before the announced opening, the Board found a teacher by the name of Hermann Fast, a 45-year-old recent immigrant from Russia. Fast had taught for several years among the Doukhobors in the village of Petrovka. His duties would include instruction, administration, and the care of students in the dormitory. His salary was set at $70 per month. Student fees were $2.00 a month.

Somewhat later than the announced date, on November 14, 1905, the German-English Academy opened its doors to students. The Board had rented an abandoned hotel building on Seventh Street in Rosthern. The hotel, known as Saskatchewan House, was renamed Unruh Hall after its owner, the widow of Peter Unruh. With minimal renovations, the former hotel was able to accommodate classrooms, a student residence for men,

and a teacherage. The building, located two blocks from downtown Rosthern, was envisioned as the school's temporary location until facilities
could be built. As it turned out, Unruh Hall provided a home for the
German-English Academy for its first four years from 1905 to 1909.

Trachoma

Early in life, Margarete Toews had contracted trachoma, an infectious
eye disease. The malady was quite bothersome and practically blinded
her at times.[17] In the summer of 1903, David took Margarete to Winnipeg
for treatment. Since the procedure there was only partially successful, it
meant that he had to exert extra effort to "doctor her" at home. Eventually she was healed, but her vision was always somewhat affected. The
matter of attending to Margarete, together with the work of moving from
Tiefengrund to Eigenheim that summer, may explain why Toews missed
the historic first delegate session of the Conference of Mennonites in
Central Canada in July of 1903. No doubt he would have liked to return
to the Gretna he had left five years earlier.

CMC Sessions

The second CMC delegate sessions, held the next year on July 11–12,
1904, took place in Eigenheim, right on David Toews' doorstep. So
Toews was very much there. No doubt he took part in the local planning
and the hosting. He was appointed recording secretary for the sessions.
He took the place of Benjamin Ewert who had held this position the
previous year but could not be at the Eigenheim sessions. This appointment gave Toews a place on the Conference executive group. He was
appointed as secretary again from 1906 to 1911. The original minutes
reveal his gifts: a clear and beautiful handwriting as well as an accurate
record of proceedings.

At the 1904 sessions, Toews presented a paper on one of his favourite
topics: "What is the worth and usefulness of the school for our
churches?"[18] Toews had in mind both the Sunday school and schools
such as the already existent Mennonite Collegiate Institute and the
envisioned German-English Academy. In the paper he made the
following points: 1) church schools inspire persons to Bible study; 2) the
schools awaken participation in Christian activity; 3) they breed
familiarity with the church; and 4) they contribute to a sense of Sabbath
holiness. "We have waited too long to establish Sunday schools, but now
it's time to move ahead," he urged. In the discussion that followed, the
delegates raised two additional concerns that illustrate current issues of
the day. One person suggested that not only children, but also adults,
should be offered Sunday school classes. Another delegate objected to

the curriculum study guide (*Lexionsheft*), and advocated the straightforward telling of Bible stories to children instead. David Toews was given an additional assignment at the conference: to do the public reading of a paper prepared by his former teacher and mentor, Heinrich H. Ewert, who was unable to attend the sessions. The paper was entitled, "How do we educate and retain our youth for our churches?"[19]

A constitution, which in large measure served to set the tone for the Canadian Conference of that day, was accepted at the Eigenheim sessions. One of the significant statements in the constitution was the statement of purpose: "The purpose of the Conference shall be to promote the fellowship of the Spirit among the various Mennonite congregations and to encourage and strengthen one another in the work of the Kingdom of God."[20] Another important statement addressed the matter of the relationship of the Conference to the congregations:

> The Conference may not interfere in the internal life of a congregation unless the congregation seeks help. It shall not lay down the law, but shall be an advisory body. The unity which it seeks shall not consist so much in sameness of outward forms and practices as in the unity of love, faith, and hope and in the common work in the Kingdom of God.[21]

The polity leaned toward congregational authority. This may well have been necessary, given the distance between the major two entities that constituted the first grouping. Despite these safeguards, one senses a healthy spirit of openness and mutual trust in these samples from the first constitution which, no doubt, was in keeping with the mind and the spirit of David Toews, the secretary of the day.

Two more annual Conference sessions took place while David Toews lived in Eigenheim, in 1905 at Winkler, in 1906 at Eigenheim. Toews was not present at the Winkler sessions. As a matter of fact, these conferences were sparsely attended by persons from out-of-province. Funds were not readily available for travel. But Toews had another reason: he was needed at home to attend to Margarete who continued to be plagued by her eye disease.[22] He had been assigned a paper under the title, "What assignment should the Conference take on in home missions?" In the paper, which was read publicly by someone else in Toews' absence, he made the point that the church should strive to serve all members in outlying districts with personal contact; and he contended that there were too few ministers for the amount of work that needed to be done. He felt that younger people should be drawn into the work of ministry. A decision was made to publish the Toews presentation in *Der Mitarbeiter*, the recently established Conference newspaper. When it came to forming a Program Committee for the next annual Conference session, David Toews was appointed along with Gerhard Epp and Heinrich H. Ewert. It seems that, even in his absence, the other ministers always had David in mind and were beginning to rely on him for leadership.

A year later, the Conference returned to Eigenheim for the fourth annual sessions. Heinrich Ewert was elected to preside as chairman and David Toews was again chosen as secretary. Fraternal visitors from other Mennonite groups and some from the United States were in attendance. All were invited to participate fully in the discussion and, for that matter, in decision-making. David Toews was again one of three persons elected to the Program Committee for the following year.

Invitation to Rosthern

As the summer of 1906 drew near, Toews was again invited to come to Rosthern to become the principal of the German-English Academy. It was clear that the school needed a teacher who could handle not only German but also English. He consented, and made the move from Eigenheim to Rosthern at that time. No doubt he did so with some confidence and with a sense of obligation. The school was close to his heart, and the people trusted his discerning leadership. The move clinched the close-knit relationship between David Toews and the Academy. Historian Frank H. Epp wrote:

> And from that time until his death four decades later, Toews was so closely involved with the affairs of the school as teacher, principal, secretary-treasurer and board chairman, that the very existence of the school seemed to depend primarily on his continuing involvement.[23]

7
Rosthern
1906–1912

The move from Eigenheim to Rosthern in the summer of 1906 was, for David and Margarete Toews, a move from rural life to an urban centre. Relatively speaking, Rosthern as compared to Eigenheim brought the Toews family into a hub of activity. While the population of the incorporated town was less than 1,000 inhabitants, the contrast between the sparsely populated prairie setting of Eigenheim and the bustling life of Rosthern was significant. In 1906, the latter was a centre of activity with no fewer than eight grain elevators. At this time in its development, it was one of the largest grain shipping hubs in the newly formed provinces of Alberta and Saskatchewan with Mennonites being the primary producers of the grain that passed through Rosthern.[1]

The move for David and Margarete was not as formidable an undertaking as some of the others had been. Socially, they were going to familiar surroundings. Congregationally, they would still be in the centre of Rosenorter activity. However, this move was significant: it would be their last and final relocation. The family would establish a permanent home in Rosthern which was, for them, the end of a long sojourn. Geographically speaking, David had conquered great distances in his 36 years—from Lysanderhöhe to Turkestan to Kansas to Gretna to Winnipeg to Burwalde to Tiefengrund to Eigenheim, and now finally to Rosthern. His longest stay had been in Lysanderhöhe, his shortest in Burwalde, but in each place he had gathered significant experiences and perspectives. No doubt the journey from Lysanderhöhe to Rosthern had brought home to him that life is a pilgrimage that moves one ever forward toward a changing horizon. In each of the places where he had settled for a time, he had found a "place of refuge" amidst people who encouraged him and accepted him.

Given the transportation systems and communication networks of the day, all of these moves entailed the conquering of considerable distances. One can surmise that at this point in his life he would have looked forward to settling down for a longer stay. This would certainly have been preferred by Margarete. She too had traversed considerable distances in her 25 years of life. First there had been the long trek from

David & Margarete Toews with Benno, Marie & Margaret in 1907.

western Prussia to Tiefengrund in Canada. Rosthern was to become the fourth home in six short years of marriage. With an increasing number of children "in tow," it was time to stay a while. Rosthern became home to Margarete for the rest of her life. There she would raise her family and attend to the comings and going of her husband. As for David, Rosthern would become the "launching pad" for his widening ministry. At the same time, it also afforded him a sense of place and a degree of permanency. It was the hub of his school and church communities, two important centres for his own identity and for his life's work. For the next 40 years, Rosthern provided home base for the Toews family.

Unruh Hall

The 1906 school year began on October 1 and concluded at the end of June 1907. The late fall starting date was designed to accommodate farm work. Even at that, only 15 of the 30 students who had registered for the year made their appearance. The others were needed at home for a few more weeks.[2] The male students occupied the improvised dormitory at Unruh Hall; the women boarded in local homes. It was expected that the principal would move into Unruh Hall which David dutifully did together with Margarete and the children of whom there were now three. Marie and Benno had recently welcomed sister Margarete (sometimes called Gretchen, to distinguish her from mother Margarete) into the family. The teacherage facilities and the rest of the building were somewhat decrepit, but in the early years everyone was expected to make the best of what was available. For better or for worse, the buildings would serve as a symbolic reminder of the tentativeness of the whole idea of the school. Some constituents were not at all convinced that the project would survive. Historian Frank H. Epp quotes one Abram Richert as saying: "It's a miracle the way the school weathered those early years, for it was at the point of closing many times."[3]

With the coming of David Toews to Rosthern and to the leadership of the school, there was a new sense of optimism. He had a good reputation as a young leader, and he could handle English equally as well as German. Hermann Fast, teacher at the Academy in its first year of operation, had been proficient in German only. Besides, Toews had a passion for the school. A paragraph in the December 1906 edition of *Der Mitarbeiter* illustrates how Toews teased his constituency into futuristic thinking:

> As a temporary facility, the current school building will do, but for the long term it leaves much to be desired. We must pursue the thought, how we might be able to build our own facilities. Also we need to come to grips with the thought of hiring a second teacher. We have the capacity to resolve these two problems if we apply our will and our abilities. The possibility is there, provided we are willing to act sacrificially.[4]

Richert, quoted above, said: "The school was the thing most dear to David Toews' heart."[5] John H. Epp, another old-timer from the early days, said: "The school was Toews. If he would have stepped back the thing would have folded up."[6] Toews' move to Rosthern was in a sense a declaration that he would give his heart to the Academy.

For the Love of the School

David Toews was the life-line of the school in another area of work. In the spring of 1908 he offered his services as a collector of funds for the coming summer and fall. As he said, he would do this "for the love of the school."[7] Apparently he was quite successful in this work. Old debts were paid off prompting renewed talk of building a new school. Possibly it was this gesture of good will, or perhaps of desperation, that caused people to assume Toews would continue indefinitely as collector for the school. In any case, that's what happened. To be sure, others helped, but Toews was considered the driving force in keeping the school on its financial feet. When at one time it was in financial difficulty, with a mounting deficit already at $17,000, Toews mused aloud at a Rosenort Mennonite Church congregational meeting as to whether this was the time to close down the school and continue with the Bible school department only. That brought a ministerial colleague, David Epp, to his feet. He addressed this uncharacteristic attitude with the words: "You must not be so pessimistic. It's you we depend on to encourage us all!"[8]

Fortunately, Toews was able to make the best of this thankless task. He had creative ideas for how to go about the work of exacting contributions from potential donors. People knew that he was collecting not for himself but for the school. It is said that he was always concerned that the salaries of the other teachers would be paid first, with his own stipend coming last. In the early years he travelled by horse and buggy, drawn by his "pony." During the winter the men from the church would sometimes drive him from place to place with their horse and sleigh. Horse conveyance meant that he was often away from home for days on end. He travelled far and wide, believing that everyone in the constituency and even beyond should contribute to the cause. In later years he drove a car. His first automobile was a Model-T Ford while later he owned a Chevrolet.

David Toews' poetic style, his direct approach, and his sometimes humorous twists won him a reputation for good results.[9] The story is told of an occasion when he and his church colleague, John G. Rempel, were visiting constituents together. The meal was placed on the table and when they were seated, Toews began to chuckle, and said: "My dear friend, I find myself in the same situation as Eliezer when he was invited to a meal with Laban. I too do not wish to begin eating until I have brought before you the reason for which I have come." With that comment the subject of a donation for the school was introduced. On another occasion the wife was bringing the food to the table. The husband, knowing the purpose of the visit, proceeded to explain: "I have debts, and I must pay those first. If I give something for the school, then I give away another person's money." Just then the wife placed a delicious piece of pie before Toews. He set it aside and said: "Thank you, but I do not feel it is right for me to eat this piece of pie. If it had been paid for with your own money, I would eat it. But as your situation now stands, it really comes from someone else." The visit ended with Toews eating the pie and also receiving a donation.

David Toews liked to tell the story of his visit to Heinrich Bartel, *Ältester* of the congregation in Drake, Saskatchewan. When Toews arrived, Bartel was busy with the milking. Toews was patient and waited at a distance behind the cows with receipt book in hand. "Shall I write the receipt for the $100 you promised?" asked Toews. "Make it $200," said Bartel. Toews was about to begin writing before he would change his mind, when Bartel spoke up from among the cows: "You may as well make it $300." Once finished with the milking, Bartel opened his wallet and handed Toews the $300, a substantial sum of money in those days. Then looking into his wallet, he produced an additional $10 bill and said: "This is for you. You probably receive scoldings in many places. Here, take this $10 bill in compensation for letting yourself be scolded."[10]

Toews went to great lengths to gather funds for the school.[11] He wrote to the Rockefeller Foundation for a grant. The request fell on deaf ears. He did manage to elicit a one-time donation from the Honourable William Lyon Mackenzie King, Prime Minister of Canada. This seemed legitimate since David Toews was one of his constituents. Mackenzie King was Member of Parliament for the constituency of Prince Albert which, until 1933, included most of the Mennonite settlements in and around Rosthern. But these big plans yielded very little in the long run. Toews realized that the school would need to depend on the good will of its Mennonite constituents. They had an understanding for its mission and they would benefit directly from its efforts.

Not Everyone on Side
The key to Toews' work on behalf of the school lay in his visionary thinking. Even while he was dealing with the "nuts and bolts" of the school's everyday existence, he was always able to hold the larger vision before the people. John G. Rempel recounted a story from the mid-1940s when the school was beginning to flourish.[12] He and Toews were walking from the school to the Toews home. As they passed some new construction on campus, Rempel remarked: "That will be a wonderful dormitory." To this Toews replied: "It is not enough that one constructs a school outwardly. More importantly, the school must fulfil its obligations toward our churches." Toews was always thinking in broader terms of the purpose and goals of the school even as he struggled with daily operations and programs. When the opportunity presented itself at Rosenort congregational meetings, he would often say: "Try to imagine our churches without our school!" On one occasion he elaborated: "About 200 graduates of our school are currently teaching in Mennonite school districts, or at least did so for a period of time. They utilize the half hour for teaching religion in our mother tongue still allowed by our laws. In addition they teach our children another half hour of German language."[13] In this way Toews upheld the significance of the school for the long term.

Sometimes this was an uphill battle but he could be philosophical about the realities he needed to face. His approach is typified by the introductory paragraph to the published minutes of the important annual meeting held in January of 1909, where he began as follows:

> Every good endeavour has its opponents. It belongs to the strategy of the human adversary to find any reason at all to find some source of evil in something good, in order to hinder the progress of the good. It is no surprise to us that committed Christian education will not be supported by the enemy of light. We are not surprised by the fact that our school project in Saskatchewan is not recognized by all in our community.[14]

Then he proceeded to outline the careful way in which the decision to begin the school was processed in the constituency, and the integrity with which the school had been developed in accordance with the wishes of the church.

At the 1909 annual meeting, with plans for a new school already in the works, a building committee was charged with finding a site on the outskirts of town. They settled on "Block 49" to the northwest of Rosthern, only to find out that back in 1904, five years earlier, Toews had already purchased that plot for a potential school location. Although his original cost had been $150, he eventually sold the plot to the Academy in 1914 for $100.[15] A building was erected on the land in 1909–1910, and this became the permanent site for the German-English

Dedication on April 28, 1910 of the red brick building which was the home of the German-English Academy (later Rosthern Junior College) for over 50 years. The building is now a local museum and archives. Photo: Frank H. Epp, *Education with a Plus*

Academy for the next 50 years. The property of today's much-expanded Rosthern Junior College includes the original 20 acres secured by Toews. The first building erected on the plot was dedicated on April 28, 1910.[16] Today the building serves as a local museum and archives.

Given his vision and drive, David Toews tended at times to get ahead of the constituency and even of the Academy board. While he invited the school board to give counsel on issues, he would sometimes make decisions on his own, as for example, the hiring and firing of teachers. In such cases he would have to convince the board members of the rightness of his actions after the fact.

Be Chiselled

In character, Teacher Toews possessed an interesting combination of characteristics. He was a strict taskmaster but also a gentle leader. He stuck by the principle that a considerable number of the courses should be taught in German. He discouraged social interaction in Low German, as he maintained that the its use did more harm than the English language to the learning of German. But when students floundered because they simply did not have the necessary background in German, he closed one eye to their dilemma, but stuck to his principles publicly.[17] There would always be students who assumed that rules were there to be broken. Toews had a patient attitude toward such students, even while he let them know where he stood.

His philosophy was well expressed in a little rhyme which he repeated often: "Willst du dass man dich hinein in das Haus baue, Lass es dir gefallen, Stein, Dass man dich behaue."[18] (If you would want to give yourself as a building stone for the house, then permit yourself to be chiselled into a suitable shape.) Toews did not like to expel students, although this would happen on occasion. He felt that failure on the part of a student reflected the failure of the teacher.

Increased Church Involvement

By 1906, church life and work had seen considerable development. Each local district provided its own ministerial leadership as much as possible, except that Peter Regier occupied the overall office of elder. Besides the sacramental functions of baptizing, ordaining, and distributing the Lord's Supper, this included chairing the ministerial meetings and the congregational meetings of the wider Rosenorter Mennonite Church. Local ministers planned the details of the Sunday morning worship services, prepared the young people for baptism through catechetical instruction, provided for pastoral care in the immediate community, and attended to stewardship and local statistics. The districts also planned and carried out their local building projects. When ministerial candidates were needed in the local setting, the local group would nominate potential persons. These would be endorsed by the entire Rosenorter Church at its annual meeting. In districts where resources in personnel and material needs were not adequate, the entire church assisted. While this institutional arrangement entailed a heavy schedule for Peter Regier, it also meant that the ministers had much to do and to think about. All were involved in both the local and overall ministry of the church.

Since its beginning before the turn of the century, the Rosenorter Church had experienced considerable growth. With new migrants continuing to settle in the larger centres as well as the outlying areas, many with large families, the Mennonite population kept rising. This placed a heavy demand on the Rosenorter ministerial group which was attempting to serve its expanding congregation from a central base. In time this became an impossible task, especially for Elder Peter Regier. In the year 1909, the Rosenorter Church made a major organizational change which was designed to help the situation.[19] The *Gemeinde* was divided into six districts, each of which was given certain local administrative and pastoral tasks. The districts were: 1) Rosthern, together with Bergthal to the east and surroundings; 2) Hague and Osler and surroundings; 3) Aberdeen and its surroundings; 4) the school districts of Eigenheim, Danzig, Silberfeld, Friedensfeld, and Ebenfeld; 5) Laird and its surroundings, including Carmen, Waldheim, Springfield, and Snowbird; 6) Tiefengrund, along with Johannestal and Hamburg. Local responsibilities included pastoral initiatives, preparing candidates for baptism, maintaining the local church building, and keeping local records. The elder of the Rosenorter Church baptized and served communion in each local district.

Since David Toews now resided in Rosthern, he served as part of the local ministerial circle of the Rosthern Mennonite Church where his family attended regularly. Additionally, he would be present at the monthly district meetings of the ministerial council where he represented the English-German Academy and entered into discussions of wider church concerns. Besides these obligations, there was the regular itinerant preaching schedule, the constant round of celebrations such as weddings, 25th anniversaries, and more.

Along with his contributions to pastoral work, David Toews continued to make a special contribution to the Sunday school movement in the Rosenorter churches. With his background in teaching, this was not surprising. For example, the report of a church-wide Sunday school convention on October 22, 1911 in Laird indicates that Toews chaired the convention, gave the opening sermon, and made one of the major pre-

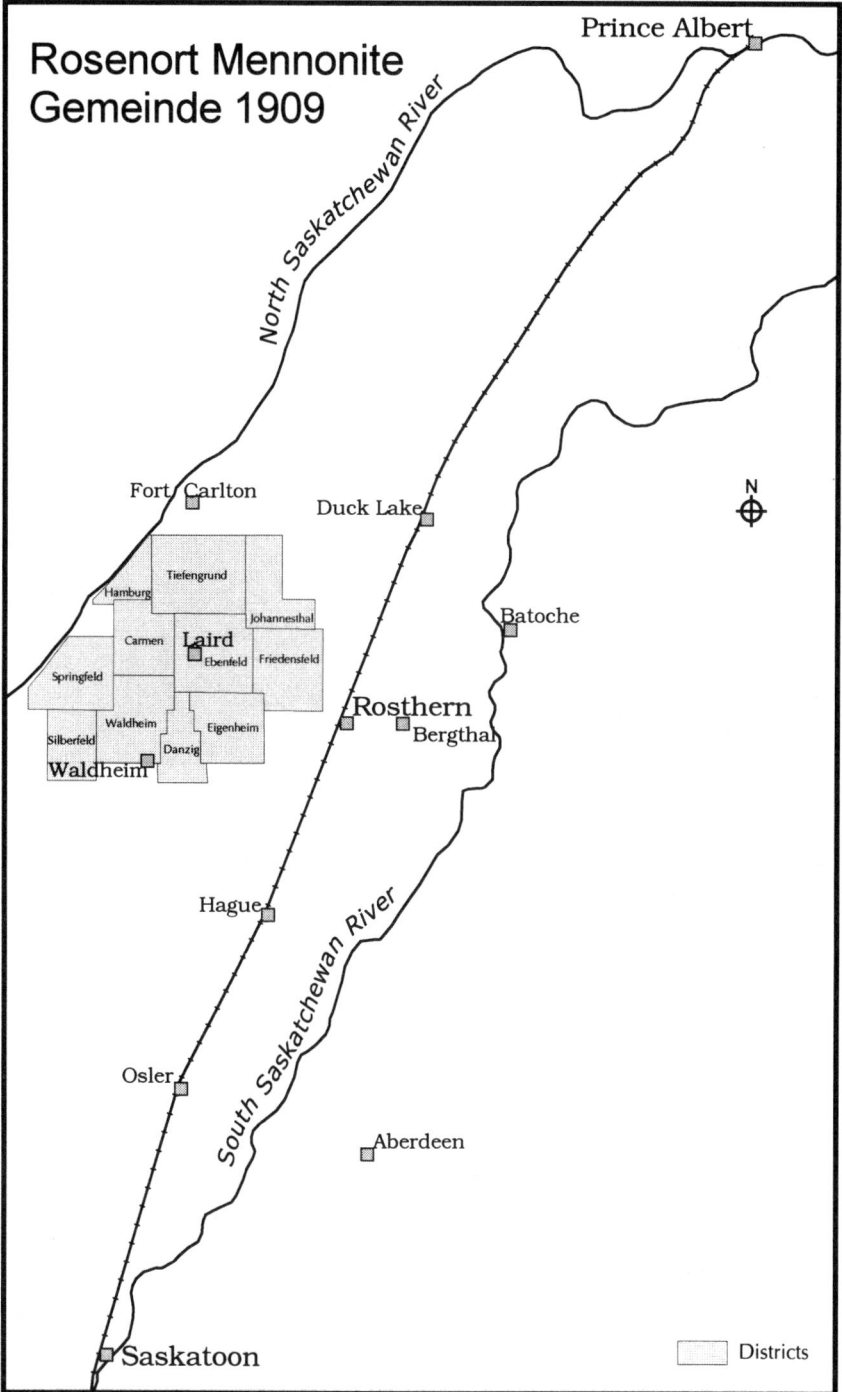

Rosenort Mennonite Gemeinde 1909

Prince Albert

North Saskatchewan River

Fort Carlton

Duck Lake

Batoche

Tiefengrund

Hamburg

Johannesthal

Carmen

Laird

Ebenfeld

Friedensfeld

Springfeld

Waldheim

Eigenheim

Rosthern

Bergthal

Silberfeld

Danzig

Waldheim

N

Hague

South Saskatchewan River

Osler

Aberdeen

Saskatoon

Districts

Map: Christopher Werner

sentations on the topic: "How can we address the shortage of Sunday school teachers?"[20]

In some ways, David Toews did not "tow the line" of the conservative element of the church. Walter Klaassen reports on a time of testing for the Eigenheim church when Herman Roth, whose background was Moravian Brethren, wished to marry Elizabeth Wieler. This pushed the acceptable edges of the Mennonite tradition. Could the marriage of a non-Mennonite with a Mennonite be conducted in a Mennonite church by a Mennonite minister? When the matter was put to a vote at a church meeting, there was considerable opposition, even while the membership voted 16 to 12 to allow it. Not wanting to alienate the opposition, the leading minister, Gerhard Epp, declined to officiate at the wedding. The marriage, which took place on March 13, 1913, was solemnized by David Toews. Two years later, when another person was planning to marry an "outsider," Gerhard Epp again declined so as not to cause offence. Toews again officiated.[21] Since the community was divided on matters such as this, it was left to the ministers to decide how to find their way through to a resolution. In this case, it came down to the question of who was willing to risk status and reputation in the eyes of constituents among whom there was a wide range of opinion.

David Toews had been called upon from time to time to speak to government officials on behalf of the Mennonite people. One such occasion occurred in December of 1908 when the Saskatchewan Ministry of Education sent a Commission of Enquiry to Warman. Its assignment was to try to understand the Old Colony's educational system and its attitudes. The government had encountered some roadblocks in its attempt to implement a province-wide public educational system. Toews found himself before the Commission, explaining the difference between Old Colony Mennonite educational ideals and those of the progressives he represented.[22]

Conference Work

In 1906, during the summer in which the Toews family moved to Rosthern, the fourth annual sessions of the Canadian Conference were held in Eigenheim. This being the home congregation of David Toews, he was involved in local arrangements. Also, he helped set up the program for the sessions. Heinrich H. Ewert was elected to chair the sessions, and David Toews was chosen as secretary. A unique feature of the Eigenheim conference was the variety of guests present.[23] According to the record, these included Hermann Epp from Asia, Jacob Quiring from Russia, Johann Gerbrandt of Quill Lake (Drake), Brother Bowman representing the "Old Mennonites" of Ontario (this person could well

have been Bishop Amos Bauman of the Alberta-Saskatchewan Mennonite Conference which originated in the west in 1903), Peter Schulz of
the Bruderthaler congregation in Langham, Jacob Dyck, elder of the
Bethesda congregation at Langham, Gerhard Siemens representing the
Mennonite Brethren, and Jacob J. Balzer of Mountain Lake, Minnesota.
Balzer delivered the conference sermon. This wide range of visitors was
indicative of the early attitude of openness in conference circles. Not only
were all guests welcomed, but they were invited to participate both in the
discussions and in the voting. An open invitation was extended to any
congregation that wished to join the conference.

One significant decision of these sessions led to the launching of a
Conference paper: a monthly publication named *Der Mitarbeiter*. The
great distances between congregations of the constituency required such
a means of inter-church communication. A group of three persons would
see to its publication: Heinrich H. Ewert as editor, David Toews as
assistant editor, and Benjamin Ewert as manager. It was indicated that an
annual budget of $150 would suffice. The first edition appeared in Octo-
ber of 1906. The publication served the Conference membership for
nearly 20 years until its closing in 1925. Over the course of its brief
lifespan, the paper had a rough time financially. Again, Toews did
substantial collecting of funds to keep the project afloat.[24]

In the summer of 1907, rather than return to Manitoba, the conference
moved to Herbert, Saskatchewan. H. H. Ewert was again selected to chair
the conference with Toews once more appointed as secretary. The Publications Committee, which included Ewert and Franz Sawatsky, reported
on the fledgling paper. According to John G. Rempel, conference
historian, H.H. Ewert and Toews "have been able to work together with
good mutual understanding."[25] Toews was elected to a further term on
both the Program Committee and the Publications Committee.

The sixth annual sessions of the Conference took place in mid-July of
1908 in Drake, Saskatchewan. This was the third conference in succession to be held in Saskatchewan. One wonders whether this was a wise
decision as there were no Manitoba Bergthaler Church representatives
present. In Ewert's absence, Johann Gerbrandt, *Ältester* of the Drake
congregation, was appointed chair, a position he held for the next three
years. David Toews again served as secretary. Gerbrandt had emigrated
from Kansas in 1906, and the following year he organized the North Star
Mennonite Church at Drake with 20 members. Thus the Conference was
meeting in a place only recently settled by Mennonites.

David Toews delivered the keynote conference sermon in the absence
of Ewert, to whom this duty would naturally have fallen. It is interesting
to note the thoughts which Toews expressed on such an occasion. His

The 1910 annual sessions of the Conference of Mennonites in Canada in Eigenheim during the time when Toews was secretary, on the Program Committee, and on the Publications Committee. Above are participants at the missions conference held prior to the Conference sessions. Photo: J.G. Rempel, *Fünfzig Jahre Konferenzbestrebungen*

chosen text was John 15:8: "My Father is glorified by this, that you bear much fruit, and become my disciples." John G. Rempel summarized his address as follows:

> Brother Toews points out that it is our duty to give glory to God, since everything that is created praises God. This includes the flowers which praise God through their beauty and fragrance; the birds which praise God through their songs, etc. The people of Israel drew near to God in holy awe; we people of the New Testament have even more reason to praise God, since he sent his Redeemer for our sake. How do we praise God? By bearing fruit through discipleship. We have much opportunity to do so, given the lack of true knowledge, the lack of genuine spiritual life, the lack of unity among our people. We have been given a vast field within which to work in the hope that fruitfulness will result.[26]

The address was typical of the recurring emphasis we find in Toews' preaching. He was sensitive to the world of nature and often began from that point of view. The person and work of Jesus Christ were central in his theology. Discipleship was one of his recurring themes. His concern was to build up the church and promote inner-church development. He made a point of speaking words of encouragement to church leaders.

During the next five annual Conference sessions (1909–1913), Toews continued to serve in a supportive role. He was elected as secretary from

1909 to 1911 after which Benjamin Ewert took over that responsibility. He served on the Program Committee from 1909 to 1912 and continued on the Publications Committee until 1913. By then the format of the sessions was well established. The main feature was the *Referat* (presentation or lecture). Any one conference meeting would have seven or eight such presentations on the program. A topic of current importance was chosen, a minister was assigned to address the topic, and a discussion followed. Topics included themes such as home missions, educational institutions, church development, pastoral concerns, and the overall purpose of the Conference. One might have thought that of the 50 or more themes assigned during these five years, David Toews would have made a presentation or two, but in the period 1909 to 1913 he never did. Perhaps, as a member of the Program Committee, he was in a position to refuse and to ensure that others were selected. His motive for declining may have been his busy schedule with the church and also with the Academy, which closed each year on the last day of June, shortly before the regular Conference sessions were scheduled to begin.

The records show that, from time to time, Toews offered a question or a comment in the discussion. Following H.H. Ewert's presentation on "speculation," Toews asked whether it was "speculation" when farmers withheld their grain in hope of a better price or when they bought up land in order to sell it later at a higher price.[27] On another topic, the use of courts to settle disputes, he made the comment that the use of such legal means was a sign of the "stagnation of a people."[28] Toews liked to probe into motives behind people's actions, and he was adept at interpreting motives within broader contexts.

Trip to Kansas
Margarete Toews lived near her family, but David had left his parental home behind. His parents lived in the Newton, Kansas area, while his siblings had scattered to Oklahoma, Idaho, and Nebraska. David had not seen his parents for a decade when he made a trip to Kansas before beginning his year of teaching in Burwalde. His family had not met Margarete or the children. It was time to go home for a visit. So after the Conference sessions in Herbert in early July of 1907, the family packed its bags and boarded the train for Kansas.[29] Some had hoped that Toews would be able to collect funds for the school in the United States, but this did not materialize. Instead, this became a family vacation.

The train ride took them to Winnipeg and then southward to Newton via St. Paul, Minnesota, and Topeka, Kansas. After four days of travel, they arrived at their destination. The reunion with family members, especially parents, and with friends, required some emotional adjustment. The parents had grown noticeably older, as had David's siblings. David was no longer the young bachelor they had last seen. Old acquaintances needed to be revisited, and new relationships forged between the relatives and his family.

The visit, which lasted five weeks, was marked by Sunday preaching assignments in six congregations—Newton, Gnadenberg, Emmaus, Brudertal, Hillsboro, and Herold. Toews complained somewhat about the practice of inviting visiting preachers to deliver Sunday morning sermons during their vacations—that defeated the purpose of the vacation. On the other hand, he cherished the contact with churches in the south. He also made a point of telling *Der Mitarbeiter* readers of the way Sunday schools had developed in Kansas. Not only the children, but also the adults attended. He prodded Canadian readers to learn a lesson about adult education from the Americans.

Apparently almost everything went very well during the visit, except for one near catastrophe. During an evening outing the horses pulling the buggy were frightened by an automobile and bolted full-speed down the road. The buggy capsized, ejecting its occupants. Father Jacob Toews was knocked unconscious, and mother Anna Toews sustained a broken rib and other injuries. The David Toews family had only minor bruises. It took two weeks for the parents to recover. The trip back to Rosthern was uneventful, and the family was happy to be back home again.

Another Trip South

Three years later, in August of 1910, Toews again travelled south, this time by himself, to visit his family. He stopped off in Beatrice, Nebraska, where his brother lived, but did not find him home. He then proceeded on to the Newton area where he stayed for several weeks. After a side trip to Oklahoma to visit his sister, he headed for Idaho where two of his brothers lived. From there it was still a four-day trip back to Winnipeg. Everywhere he stopped, he gathered impressions on farm conditions, on church life, and on the development of Mennonite institutions such as schools and hospitals. He was particularly concerned about whether there was harmony or discord in the congregations. He thought the Canadian Mennonite churches had much to learn from their more advanced American brothers and sisters. This included such areas as church budgets, religious education, development of institutions, interest in mission work, and mutual service organizations in the church. Among Mennonites in Kansas, Toews found several practices worthy of note. One was the enviable option of allowing private school teachers the freedom to pursue their professional development in the summer break rather than obligating them to collect money for their schools. He also noted, although without evaluation, that there was a trend toward the one-pastor system in the churches. While he thought Canadian Mennonites could learn much from their American neighbours, without question he preferred life in Canada. But he did not say why.[30]

Within a period of five years, between 1908 and 1912, three more children were born to David and Margarete: Else (Elsie) in 1908, Dorothy (Dora) in 1909, and Louise in 1912. Louise was the first of the Toews children to be born in a hospital. In fact, she and a second infant were the first babies born in the recently opened Rosthern Hospital.

By the summer of 1912 it was becoming evident that the task of principal of the Academy was becoming overload for David Toews. His church duties and his family obligations detracted significantly from the attention he could give to the school's daily program and to its residence life. He was too often absent on church assignments and collecting duties to give adequate attention to matters such as discipline. Besides, Peter Regier was gradually withdrawing from serving the church, which meant that more of the pastoral work fell to Toews. On the basis of a faculty review, Hermann Fast, who had provided leadership for the school in its first year of operation, was brought back as principal for the 1912–1913 year. Toews still remained deeply involved in the school, but in this way he could distance himself somewhat from daily operations.

8
Elder Toews
1913–1918

On a Sunday afternoon at the end of June in 1913, members of the Rosenorter Mennonite Church and guests from other congregations gathered in the Eigenheim church to celebrate the 25th anniversary of the ministry of Peter Regier as *Ältester*. Elder Johann Gerbrandt of Drake gave the main address, and David Toews was one of the speakers on that occasion.[1] Regier took the occasion to inform the church that he wished to withdraw from active ministerial duty. Given his waning health and the increasing demands of a growing church, he could no longer do justice to his many obligations. He requested that the church should proceed to choose his replacement. Who would succeed Peter Regier as *Ältester* of the Rosenorter Mennonite Church?

The procedure that followed was democratic and straightforward. All church members were given the opportunity to submit the name of a

Elder Peter Regier (1851–1925). David Toews succeeded him as Ält- ester of Rosenorter Mennonite Church in 1913. Photo: J.G. Rempel, *50 Jahre Konferenzbestreb- ungen*

candidate they would prefer to see on the slate. Only already ordained ministers could be nominated. These names were submitted by the local districts to a central committee. The eight persons named by the membership were made public, and elections were conducted in each local district on a one-vote-per-member basis. In the end, David Toews received the most votes, and Johannes Regier the second-highest number.[2] Thus the matter was settled. David Toews would succeed Peter Regier, his friend and mentor, as *Ältester* of the Rosenorter Mennonite Church.

A Sacred Occasion

The ordination service was announced for Sunday, September 14, in the Rosthern Mennonite Church. People came from near and far, with some from Herbert, Drake, Aberdeen, and Tiefengrund already arriving on Saturday. Unfortunately Jacob and Anna Toews, David's aging parents, were not able to make the trip from Newton, Kansas. This was a keen disappointment for David. Jacob himself was currently elder of First Mennonite Church in Newton. His presence would have given familial and spiritual support to David on this important occasion.

The ordination ceremony took place in the morning, and the festivities lasted all day.[3] The morning began with congregational and choir singing. John C. Peters of Waldheim introduced the service with a text that expressed God's promise to faithful servants: "I will not fail you nor forsake you. . . . Only be strong and courageous, being careful to act in accordance with the law that my servant Moses commanded you; . . . for then you shall make your way prosperous, and then you shall be successful" (Joshua 5:1–9). Outgoing Ältester Regier gave the main address based on Genesis 24:31: "Come in, O blessed of the Lord." Just as Eliezer, the servant, was bent on finding a bride for Isaak, Toews should be zealous in seeking a bride, the church, for his Lord.

Then Regier called David Toews forward for the ordination ceremony. Regier reminded him of his solemn duties as *Ältester*, and asked whether he agreed to assume these obligations. Duties would include inducting leaders into their offices, baptizing, serving the Lord's Supper, and exercising discipline when church members were not obedient in their Christian walk. Toews answered with a firm: "Yes, as God gives me grace." He then knelt, and all five *Ältesten* who were present laid their hands on his head while Elder Regier spoke "a highly earnest prayer." The circle of confirmation included the leading ministers from outlying congregations such as Langham, Herbert, and Drake. At the conclusion of the prayer, Toews rose, and each of the elders and assistant ministers extended their hand of welcome together with a personal word of encouragement and comfort.

After a song of welcome and blessing by the choir, the newly ordained Ältester Toews delivered his response. His chosen text was John 21:15–17, with the theme: "Simon, son of John, do you love me?" Toews applied the thrice-repeated question of the risen Lord to himself. Twenty-five years earlier, at his baptism, the first question, "Do you love me more than these?" (21:15) together with the answer, "Feed my lambs," led him to the teaching ministry in schools and in Sunday schools. After 12 years he was ordained as a minister. At that time the question, "Simon, son of John, do you love me?"(21:16) had to be answered again, and having responded positively, Toews heard the directive: "Tend my sheep." Now he was hearing the question a third time in the call to become the leading minister. And he again heard the command, "Feed my sheep"(21:17). Toews concluded: "With the help of the Lord, supported by a church that will pray for me, I will do my best to be found a faithful steward."[4] To conclude the morning service, Elder N.F. Toews of Langham offered some thoughts. Two of his points, worthy of note, were that when God calls a worker he also calls his wife whose special task is intercessory prayer, and that a minister's children are often spoiled and contrary because the minister has to neglect his family in order to serve the church.

During the noon hour, the women of the church served a hot meal to the 500 persons present. Most certainly there was vigorous social interaction during the break. And what a great amount of work such a dinner would entail for the women. The lunch break was cut short by the second service which began at 2:00 p.m. It was opened by Ältester Jacob Dyck of Langham. Ältester John C. Peters of Waldheim preached on 1 Chronicles 28:10: "Take heed now, for the Lord has chosen you to build a house as the sanctuary; be strong, and act." The thrust of his message was that it is the will of the Lord, and not of humans, that Brother Toews be called to this ministry, and that to fulfil his calling would require a battle (*einen Kampf*) which would call forth all of Toews' talents and energies in service to the Lord. The session was framed and punctuated with more singing by the congregation and by choirs from Laird, Hague, and Rosthern. At the close of the service everyone was again invited to *Faspa*, a late afternoon light meal.

The evening service began early, at 6:00 p.m., so that those who had come from a distance would still be able to return home in reasonable time. It featured two speakers, Rev. Gerhard Buhler of Herbert and Ältester Johann Gerbrandt of Drake. Biblical passages referred to included Isaiah 6:1–7, Psalm 27:1, 1 Timothy 5:17–18, and John 21:17. At the end of the day, David Toews had the last word. After listing the many personal blessings of the day, he remarked that this occasion had been for him the most satisfying day in his memory, despite the weight of the many things he would need to ponder and the abundance of advice he would need to take seriously. With that the day of David Toews' ordination as "bishop" of the Rosenorter Mennonite Church came to an end, and his new duties began.

The Elder Office

What was required of an *Ältester*? While congregations in Anabaptist and early Mennonite history desired to function in a democratic way, as compared to an Episcopal system which tended to operate from the top down, they still allowed a role for delegated leadership to defend the faith.[5] This had been necessary in an earlier day when the church community was being tested severely by persecution from society. This practical necessity, coupled with biblical teaching in such texts as Acts 14:23 and 1 Timothy 5:17, suggested the congregation should choose and ordain servant leaders of three kinds: elders (*Ältesten*, bishops), ministers (*Prediger, Diener am Wort*, preachers), and deacons (*Armendiener*, servants to the poor). Beginning in early Anabaptist times, there was the understanding that elders had special functions reserved for them: the administration of baptism and of the Lord's Supper, the ordination of ministers and deacons, the exercise of discipline, and the chairmanship of the ministerial circle and congregational meeting. It was common for elders to have responsibility for more than one local congregation.

In some Mennonite congregations, the distinction between elder and minister disappeared by the latter part of the seventeenth century; in other settings the distinctions remained even into the twenty-first century. In the early decades of the Conference of Mennonites in Canada, which included the Rosenorter Mennonite Congregation, the elder system, within the scheme of the three-fold ordained ministry, was the acceptable practice. This system had been brought to Canada from western Prussia and from Russia. In some Mennonite groups of Swiss or South German origin, the term "bishop" was sometimes substituted for the designation "elder" or "*Ältester*," but here too the organizational structure was similar. While elders of western Prussian and Russian background, now in Canada, might have been referred to as "bishops" at times, this was not a title prescribed in the ministerial handbooks of churches of this background. If and when the term was used, it was done informally.

Ten Meeting Places

The congregation for which David Toews assumed oversight was wide-ranging geographically as well as spiritually. In early spring of the year following his ordination, Toews wrote a sketch of what was happening in the various locations.[6] The church encompassed ten places of worship, ranging from large congregations to small groups. The largest was at Eigenheim, the district shepherded by Gerhard Epp, Johann Dueck, and C.C. Ens. In his report on a visit to the Eigenheim church in the following winter, Toews noted there were 40 Sunday school children in four classes. The Eigenheim ministers served the local group at Danzig where sister Justina Wiebe conducted the Sunday school faithfully. West of Eigenheim were two places of worship, Laird and Carmen. They were led locally by Jacob Janzen, David Epp, H. Warkentin, and C.F. Sawatsky. Both places had vigorous Sunday schools and *Jugend-vereine*—Sunday evening youth and young adult programs attended by young and old. Laird led the way among Rosenorter churches in fostering music through a well-organized choir. Next came Tiefengrund where Peter Regier and his son, Johannes, lived and served. This congregation distinguished itself in its harmonious working relationship, its joyful attitude of service, and its willingness to cooperate with church-wide projects.

Immediately south of Rosthern was Hague where C.C. Ens, an elderly minister, preached sermons that were enriched by his depth of experience. The Sunday school was doing well there, but choir and youth programs were not thriving. In Aberdeen there had been problems earlier, but these had been alleviated, and A.R. Dyck was providing good leadership. A church group had just begun gathering in Osler where brothers from Rosthern and Hague served on Sundays. There was some hope of assigning a local school teacher who could also serve the church. In Great Deer, the most distant location, it was finally possible to build a church. But soon thereafter a dance hall was erected next to the church, creating an unwelcome problem. In the Rosthern church, where the Toews family was at home, the membership was growing. Because this was Toews' place of residence, he was expected to provide the leadership there, with the assistance of the brethren Galle, Isaak, Rempel, and Gloeckner.

In total this added up to ten places of worship, with a composite membership of 800 and a Sunday school of 400. With the help of the aging Peter Regier, David Toews was responsible for serving this constituency with baptisms, communion services, ordinations, and generally establishing good working relationships within the ministerial group which met on a monthly basis. It was clear that he would have much to attend to in the next years. Besides the official duties were the constant rounds of home visitations which he had done earlier, but now they took on greater importance. At a congregational meeting on June 5, 1918, Toews reported that he had visited 200 families in their homes in a two-month period during that winter. It is reported that during the winter of 1917–1918 many deaths resulted from an influenza epidemic in the wider community. This kept Toews busy with pastoral care and funerals. He also contracted the flu and was confined to his home for a time.[7]

In his report of Toews' pastoral accomplishment, church historian J.G. Rempel writes: "When one takes into account that these families were scattered far and wide, that the distances needed to be conquered mainly with horse-power, then one gets a picture of the amount of energy such congregational ministry required. One should also consider the biting cold that comes with winters in the west in January and February."[8] We would like to know more about Rosenorter church life during these years. Unfortunately, much of the activity of the church and of its ministerial leaders at this time is lost since in 1917 fire destroyed earlier records.[9]

Confronting Sin

From the accounts we do have, there is some evidence that David Toews often found himself in the middle of the fray when it came to the call to holy living. Writing in *Der Mitarbeiter*, he cited a lengthy list of shortcomings. He complained that people did not attend church services regularly.[10] Benches were empty in churches with a large membership. Some appeared only on festive occasions; other came to the services but appeared sleepy and listless. "What's the problem?" he asked. His own answer to his question was multi-faceted. While some wanted to blame the pulpit, and others the benches, the problem lay in both directions. Ministers were sometimes caught up in their own importance. Some did not take their ministry seriously enough to prepare their sermons well. Perhaps because there was little or no remuneration, some had become too casual about their ministry. Toews wondered how much preparation time was spent in prayer. Turning to "the bench," Toews named materialism and worldly allurements as a major source of distraction. The quest for this world's goods hardened the heart and wearied the body so there was little energy left to concentrate on God's word on a Sunday morning. Then there were the "pleasures" of life such as drinking, dancing, horse racing, theatre attendance, sports, and the saloon. How could one indulge in these things during the week and then enter wholeheartedly into singing the songs of Zion on Sunday morning? And what of the willingness to help people in need? Where were the good Samaritans among them? And just look at the power of false teachings. Almost anything anyone said in the name of religion, however false, gained some following. This came about when people were not well grounded in their faith. "The only solution to these problems is for both ministers and lay people to humble themselves, to repent, to seek salvation in Christ, and to serve God and one another with a holy seriousness and an inner love."[11]

An additional issue immediately after the close of the First World War was the illegal production of home brew for money-making purposes. These were prohibition days, an extension of the policy during the war. The ministers did battle against these evils in the congregation. A specific incident, reported by Walter Klaassen, illustrates the problem.[12] In March of 1918, David Toews was involved in a matter in the Eigenheim church during Bible Week services. According to the journal of Rev. Gerhard Epp it came to light that someone had secretly stashed away some brandy in the church barn. During the evening service Toews was called out to hear a young man confess that he had done it and that it was his liquor. Toews then invited the young man to give his life over to Jesus who would help him to overcome such temptations. The prevalence of liquor was a problem to the extent that it prompted Toews to warn church members publicly not to accept any invitations to social events where liquor would likely be used.

Great Possibilities

The concerns of David Toews went beyond his beloved home church. He had a heart for home missions as well, by which was meant the development of Mennonite churches in outlying areas. Many Mennonite families lived on the outskirts of their church community. Given the limitations of transportation, the harsh climate, and the vast distances between households and communities, it was a major challenge to provide spiritual sustenance to the people. The challenge needed to be addressed through the work of inner missions (*innere Mission)* or home missions. In mind and heart, Toews had a deep concern for the extension of the church into the far corners of frontier settlements.

In an article in *Der Mitarbeiter,* Toews revealed some of his vision for home missions.[13] He believed there was a great need as well as opportunity for mission in local districts. Think of what could be accomplished with good counselling, he prodded. People needed encouragement to attend church services. The church needed workers who would visit the members in outlying districts on a regular basis. In the article Toews mentioned his concern over the troubled conditions and relationships within some families. He was concerned about those areas in Saskatchewan and Alberta where people did not have a church nearby and where Mennonite families rarely received ministerial visits. He wondered: Why can't we do more on the home frontier? The problem was not money, but workers, or rather, the assignment of workers. Since it was the General

Conference and not the district conferences that assigned workers, the needs of the districts were often overlooked. But there would be a solution if we had the vision for it, Toews urged. Why not appeal to local ministers and potential ministers to broaden their ministry in their district? Why is it that mission work is not mission work unless one comes from a great distance or one is sent to a distant place? Why not use the travel money to encourage residents in their local districts to reach out to the borders of their constituency? he suggested. What such persons might lack in knowledge and gifts would be gained in their understanding of local conditions and their acquaintance with the people among whom they lived. Toews had a heart for visitation ministry. He did not want to negate the good work of the General Conference in mission overseas; he only wanted to make the point that mission begins at home. In his view, to neglect the mission field at one's doorstep only weakened mission abroad.

In another article, David Toews pointed to the ministry of hospitality.[14] He noted how, in worldly and business matters, salespersons put forth great effort to present their wares in appealing ways. But in the church things were supposed to happen by themselves. The church had failed to make the gospel appealing to the general public, he complained. He noted that while in the "English" churches in the cities visitors were made to feel welcome, in Mennonite churches the people were not greeted in a welcoming way. Visitors often felt like strangers. It was not surprising if they did not return. The problem lay in the fact that the ministers were overburdened, and that lay people appeared to have little time for the work of God's kingdom. Toews ended the article with a call to renewal: "Our people needs an awakening to the great possibilities of our ministry as churches in the world."[15] David Toews was reflecting an engaging theology of mission.

Chairman of the Conference

In 1914 the Conference sessions were held in David Toews' home town of Rosthern. While the first conference in 1903 in Hochstadt, Manitoba, had between 16 and 19 participants in attendance, the Rosthern event, 12 years later, brought together 55 delegates and an additional 400 or more attendees for the two-day program. Of the guests who had come from a distance, about 40 travelled by rail and another 40 came by automobile.

David Toews was chosen as the chairman of the Conference for the first time at its meeting in 1914 in Rosthern. This was a temporary appointment to replace H.H. Ewert who was unable to come. However, it had permanent consequences, since thereafter Toews continued in this position for decades. Besides chairing the annual sessions, he served on the Publications Committee and on the Program Committee. He was also the presenter of one of the themes: "How can we better serve the needs of our people through our 'higher schools?'" His concrete suggestions were that schools should appoint church-minded teachers, that a spirit of harmony be fostered among the staff, that the German language be promoted, that the schools aim to prepare ministers and Sunday school teachers, and that a common and cooperative instruction plan be developed for all Mennonite high schools.

While the Conference sessions took place on Monday and Tuesday, events were also planned for the days before and after. Missions Conferences were held in three locations—Laird, Eigenheim, and Rosthern—on the preceding weekend. The annual Ministers' Conference met for an entire day on Wednesday after the close of the regular sessions.[16] At the Missions Conferences, the emphasis was on home missions, which David Toews summed up as follows: "The circle of mission influence is widening; we are facing new challenges such as the need for more workers, more interest, more support, and more prayer for the work."[17] Toews expressed great appreciation for the simple and unassuming presentations of Missionary Linscheid of Montana who reported on "the work and the sacrifices among the poor heathen." Toews chaired not only the Conference sessions, but also the more intimate Ministers Conference the following day. Its program focused on pastoral and doctrinal concerns. At the end of the conference, the 44-year-old Toews was recognized publicly "for his visionary leadership."

The present-day historian will be mindful of the fact that the year 1914 brought with it the beginning of the First World War. Was the cloud that hung over Europe at the time reflected at all in Conference discussions? In the reports, little attention was given to world events. At the Ministers Conference Rev. Gerhard Epp of Rosthern addressed his colleagues on the topic, "Recent world events seen from the Christian standpoint—Matthew 24:33,"[18] but there is no record of the content of his presentation or of discussion on the issue. During the war itself, these events would have their impact on the Mennonite people of Canada and on the agenda of David Toews.

The 1915 conference, held in early July in Herbert, Saskatchewan, followed the same format as in 1914. The Missions Conference, held on the weekend preceding the two days of deliberations, drew an unprecedented crowd of 600 to 700 attendees. Special speakers were Michael Horsch and William Gottschall, General Conference ministers from the United States. The sessions on Monday and Tuesday had an audience of between 400 and 500. About 50 persons came from a considerable distance. David Toews was again elected to chair the sessions. At his request, a vice-chairman was appointed in the person of Ältester Johann Gerbrandt. Of the many topics presented and discussed, the great majority concerned themselves with inner-churchly issues. One of them touched on the world situation. Horsch dealt with the question of what could be done practically to further the biblical peace teaching in their day. At this conference session Toews declined further appointment to the Publications Committee, but continued on the Program Committee.

Along with the invitation to the 1916 sessions held in Altona, Manitoba, Chairman Toews and Secretary Benjamin Ewert published a statement of the purpose of this annual gathering: "The primary purpose of the Conference is so that our Mennonite churches might experience unity, so that we might cultivate fellowship, and so that we might confer together on what we can do to further the kingdom of God."[19] These two conference leaders were masters at stating things in a succinct yet comprehensive style.

The conference days were again preceded by a missions festival. A large tent with a seating capacity of 700 had been erected, and every seat was taken. There were three addresses in the morning, three more in the afternoon, including one by David Toews, and two in the evening. The sessions, which began Monday morning, featured the conference sermon by David Toews. He began by pointing to the problems that faced the church. Solutions are found when we are obedient to God, he said. Building the kingdom of God comes through inner renewal of the believer and of the church. Renewal begins with earnest prayer. If we are obedient and prayerful, blessings will flow.

Apparently Toews had struck a cord with the delegates. There was lively and creative discussion, especially following the report of the Home Missions Committee. One person made the point that more could be accomplished through house visitation than through preaching. Another suggested that travelling ministers should be hired by the Conference to explore and serve outlying areas. Another urged that a large budget was needed to accomplish mission work. On the second day attention turned to the war and to nonresistance. Michael Horsch spoke on the topic: how to foster the peace teaching in those difficult times. Menno Galle addressed the question: what could the church learn from the current wartime situation?

A committee was named to formulate and send a letter of thanks to the Canadian government for the fact that they had not yet drawn the Mennonites into military service. The letter was drafted and sent to Prime Minister Robert L. Borden. In his reply the Prime Minister assured the Mennonites that they were highly respected as citizens and residents of the Dominion of Canada. The reply was particularly significant in light of occasional difficulties endured by Mennonites in some places due to their pacifist position and their promotion of the German language.[20] Again, there was a day-long Ministers Conference following the two-day regular sessions. There seemed to be a new awareness of the difficult political and social times in which the church was finding itself.

The next two annual sessions were held in Langham (1917) and in Drake (1918). Toews was again elected as chairman for these meetings. His opening sermons set the stage for the mood and the deliberations. At Langham he based his remarks on Nehemiah 2:18: "They replied, 'Let us start rebuilding.' So they began this good work." Like the people of Nehemiah's time, he said, we live in a period when we face many foes. If we as leaders approach our work with courage, the people will follow. But we need to have a heart of love for our people in the church and a heart of love for our ministry. Toews was addressing the situation of the day which presented the challenge for building the church in new settings. There was much virgin soil, spiritually speaking. The situation required new and creative initiatives.[21] At Drake, Toews began with Romans 11:22: "Consider therefore the kindness and sternness of God." In his reflections he emphasized the present day as a time of testing which they should not resist. That is, they should allow themselves to be tested in those difficult times. The war years should evoke repentance, love, strength of faith, and a willingness to suffer. In the face of the disunity that threatened them, God's word would lead them forward.[22]

While the reports of Conference sessions throughout the years gave an account of the presentations and deliberations, at times the keen reporter would also observe and relate things that took place on the periphery. One eyewitness at the conference in 1918 in Drake noted that, among the Model T Ford cars parked on the church yard during the sessions, one could spot quite a few of the larger and more expensive automobiles such as the Maxwells and McLaughlins.[23] Was this a sign of economic blessing or an indication of materialistic allurement?

Eternal Optimist

During the first seven years of its existence, the German-English Academy had its ups and downs. The school always seemed to be teetering between survival and demise. What kept it going was the drive of David Toews and the dedication of committed groups and individuals within the Rosenorter Church. Through their untiring efforts a significant foundation had been laid with the completion of the new school building in 1910. At the beginning of the eighth year of instruction in 1913 Toews appeared optimistic. His vision had not flagged. In the September issue of *Der Mitarbeiter* he could write: "It is certainly an occasion for joy that here in Canada interest in the school is on the increase, and due to this fact we can surely promise ourselves much for the future of our churches."[24] Of particular significance was the privilege that the government allowed the Academy to teach German and Religion, "since we consider it to be essential for those who will instruct our children in the future and who will become leaders in our churches."[25] In the same article he addressed the often-asked question, "What do our schools offer?" by pointing to results. He noted there were about ten public schools in which graduates of the Academy were teaching, and there were two students at the university. In a mood of optimism he assured the constituency that the school would grow. The teaching staff had increased to three qualified teachers, not including himself.

The German language was very close to David Toews' heart. So when the question arose at the 1913 Conference sessions as to whether it was even permissible in principle to teach and learn German in Saskatchewan, Toews promised to clarify the matter with the government. On the basis of a discussion with the Solicitor-General of the Province, Toews established that, while English was the language of instruction and French might also be offered, a local board had the right to offer instruction in whatever language it pleased. This should be understood as half an hour a day of German instruction, while more instruction time could be offered if time and interest allowed. Toews was pleased with this arrangement, and encouraged teachers in local communities to take full advantage of this allowance.[26] Meanwhile, he concluded that, after much anticipation and numerous requests for assistance, no funds would be coming from the government for the support of private education. This called for sacrificial effort on the part of the Mennonite people together with continuing reliance on the grace and goodness of God.

Again and again, David Toews was called upon to offer a case for the existence of Mennonite private schools. In a paper delivered at the Canadian Conference held in Rosthern, July 6–7, 1914, he again addressed this issue.[27] He began by making a case for the teaching of German. He saw the Mennonites' possession of the German language as a privileged gift that should not be rejected. It would help in commerce, in acquisition of knowledge, and in their relations as citizens in the world. More than that, a language was essential for the formation of peoplehood. If they wanted to remain a Mennonite people in the midst of a predominantly English society, they would need to keep the language, he maintained.

The second purpose of the Mennonite "higher school" was to teach religion, he went on to say. Quite simply, the people's appreciation for and commitment to biblical faith would be lost if the word of God was not taught. Also, ethics and proper social conduct would inevitably deteriorate. The teaching of religion afforded the teacher opportunity to get next to the student and speak to the heart.

Thirdly, a good church education would provide training for work in the kingdom of God, Toews claimed. The original purpose of the private schools was to prepare workers for their schools and their churches. Toews was thinking not only of teachers and ministers, but also of faithful discipleship in daily life. Unfortunately our people were lured into thinking of possessions and the enjoyment of life. Where was the dedication to selfless suffering service? The schools needed to mould young people willing to follow Christ's way of love. He felt that this should be the primary aim of the church's educational efforts. Here we see the passionate ideals of David Toews.

During those years, he was always willing to do what had to be done for the school. Because it was usually in a precarious situation, he adjusted his work for the sake of the institution. It was not that he made these adjustments without complaint. When in 1912 it became evident that someone was needed to promote the school in the constituency, he stepped aside as principal to devote his available time to the task of soliciting funds. For two years teacher Menno Galle took on the role of principal to relieve Toews. But then it was time for him to return to the helm, which he did in the summer of 1914. Galle became Toews' assistant. When the funds were depleted, the Board prevailed upon Toews to go to work in the constituency. When there was no money in the treasury, Toews as staff member, as board member, as secretary-treasurer, and as principal felt the problem most—especially when teachers' salaries could not be paid on time, as was the case on several occasions. Almost annually he would complain and ask to be released, but then the decision would be made that Toews should do it again. Frank Epp says appropriately that "if the school would not have continued to exist in the mind and heart of Toews, it would not have existed at all."

In 1917 he tried to put his foot down. Being a fundraiser, he said, was "incompatible with the work of a minister."[28] It was probably incompatible with being a teacher, too. So Toews was released from his teaching duties at the school, but on the condition that he would give about one- third of his time to the school. This should include consulting with the faculty about the school's direction and program and collecting money for the school. Since by that time the Rosenorter Church was complaining that he was not giving enough time to the churches, the church board took some comfort in the thought that Toews would now be able to devote major time to the care of the flock over which he was

Ältester.[29] It was expected that the church would provide him with a salary. Meanwhile, he continued to provide leadership on the school board and remained the principle spokesperson for the school.

While problems of existence continued to plague the Academy, it is significant that in the next year it reached a peak enrolment of 82 students. This included 37 from the Conference of Mennonites in Canada, 21 Mennonite Brethren, four Krimmer Mennonite Brethren, and three Evangelical Mennonite Brethren.[30] By then the school was also attracting some Catholics, Lutherans, Presbyterians, and others from beyond Mennonite circles. This was fine with Toews. He was confident that the Mennonites would continue to conduct the school in accordance with their ideals.

Parasites We Are Not

The First World War began in August of 1914 and ended officially on November 11, 1918. It was a tumultuous time for Mennonite immigrants to Canada. Just when the Canadian population was beginning to recognize them as loyal citizens, due to their hard work and farming skills, the sentiment turned against them. Their German language and culture made them suspect and open to the charge of being collaborators with the enemy. Their pacifist convictions added fuel to this suspicion.

Students of the German-English Academy in 1918 when the school reached a peak enrolment of 82 students. Photo: Frank H. Epp, *Education with a Plus*

While earlier, Prime Minister Borden had referred to Canada's German citizens as "the very best" in the country, soon after the outbreak of the war there were "repeated calls for disenfranchisement, compulsory work at low wages, internment, and censorship of foreign language publications"[31] directed at the German populace, which included Mennonites, particularly in western Canada.

Who would speak for the Mennonites in this cross-fire? In Ontario an official "secretariat" had been appointed in the person of S.F. Coffman to represent the Mennonite cause and convictions in Ottawa. The west was not organized in this way. But the lot fell mainly to Benjamin Ewert of Winnipeg and David Toews to take up the task, "not because they were appointed, but because they were the most knowledgeable and, consequently, most able and willing."[32]

In December of 1916 David Toews found himself on his way to Ottawa with three other Mennonite delegates from the west. In addition to Toews, the group included Klaas Peters, also of Saskatchewan, and two Manitobans, Abraham Doerksen and Benjamin Ewert. The purpose of the trip was to meet with government officials to gain clarity on the status of Mennonites on the issue of exemption from military service. The meeting gave the delegates opportunity to remind government officials of the 1873 Order-in-Council which had assured the Mennonites they need not engage in battle on Canada's behalf. They also took the opportunity to recall the speech of Lord Dufferin to the Manitoba Mennonite pioneers on August 21, 1877, in which he said: "The battle to which we invite you is the battle against the wilderness. . . . You will not be required to shed human blood."[33] The delegation left Ottawa with a feeling of success and with the assurance that the historic arrangement would stand. Back home, they invited their constituencies to make a financial contribution for relief work, aimed at financial support for victims, invalids, widows, and orphans.[34]

With the confusion about conscription requirements and the added aggressiveness of the Saskatchewan military department, David Toews found himself called to represent Mennonite youth before the Canadian government. This required repeated trips to Regina and countless counselling situations with young people and their parents. On June 5, 1918, Toews reported to a church meeting at Eigenheim that he had recently journeyed to Regina twice within a three-week period concerning military participation of young people. The problems had to do both with young men being drawn into the military inadvertently due to their lack of knowledge about the process and with complaints from officials about the indecisiveness of young people regarding their status as Mennonites. Added to the problem was the questionable ethical and

moral conduct of some young men. It appeared to their English neighbours, who had "sacrificed" their sons to the cause of war, that these
young people were hiding under the shelter of the Mennonite name and
the Mennonite community, but that they were otherwise not convinced
pacifists. Toews frequently appealed to the young people to present
themselves in public in such a way that they would not give the occasion
for criticism from non-Mennonites in the community. Toews knew what
he was talking about. As spiritual leader of the largest Mennonite church
in the region, every Mennonite parent and youth, whether Rosenorter or
not, came knocking at his door when in trouble with the authorities and
asked him to intercede on their behalf. Toews was conversant in English;
he was a good negotiator; and he knew how to speak with judges and
military officials. He also cared about upholding Mennonite convictions.

Some of these wartime concerns hit very close to home. Apparently
one evening, when David was not at home, there was a knock at the door.
Margarete Toews answered and found a group of young veteran soldiers
recently returned to the community. They demanded to see "Bishop
Toews." Louise, who was eight years old at the time, recalls how the
children anxiously stood behind their mother in fright. Margarete had
informed the young men that Rev. Toews was not at home. Indeed, he
was on a trip to Alberta and British Columbia. Upon hearing this, the
agitators proceeded to the Rosthern Mennonite Church, where, according
to a later report by Toews, they "uttered profanities, romped around,
flung the Bible between the pews, and even wanted to drag a cow along
the aisle, suggesting that surely the cow too is a Christian; and in the end
they hung a black shield on the front doors."[35] The end result was that the
agitators were severely reprimanded by the local law enforcement officer.

Through it all, David Toews remained a staunch pacifist and a firm
promoter of the peace position as an immovable object of faith for the
Mennonite people. Nonresistance was not an individual choice; it was the
way of life for a people. It was preferable that the community should
speak for the individual rather than that the individual be left to decide
whether or not to be pacifist. He may well have learned this lesson as a
youthful participant in the great trek to Turkestan. Was it not for the sake
of their children and their church that Jacob and Anna Toews had
undertaken that dangerous journey? One saw this same parental
conviction in David. His stance was keenly reflected in a statement
prepared at a conference of Mennonites in Saskatchewan in mid-1918
that dealt with the issue of conscription. At the core of a petition to the
Governor General, asking that the public harassment of Mennonites be
stopped, we find these words, sometimes attributed to David Toews:

Parasites we are not. We are earning our bread by honest labour, and if we mistake not, our labour has assisted materially in advancing the material wealth of our country. We do not depend for our living on the sustenance or efforts of others excepting as we give and take. We do not require any one to shed his blood for us. We would rather die ourselves or languish in prison or leave our home and again settle in some wilderness, the same as our forefathers have done, than to require a sacrifice of any kind by any one on our behalf.[36]

Toews would have more opportunity at some future date to speak for the peace principles of his people. It is readily admitted by Mennonite historians that the peace churches in both Canada and the United States were ill-prepared to defend their stance at the time of World War I. They did somewhat better in the next round which faced them in the late 1930s.[37]

Love at Home

While David Toews was teacher and minister, collector and conference chairman, peace advocate and political negotiator, he was also husband and father. Since the birth of Louise in 1912, Toews' sixth child, two more daughters, Elma (1915) and Anna (1918), were added to the family. In 1921 one more daughter, Irene, would be born to them. This completed the family of eight daughters and one son.

David Toews' parents, Jacob and Anna, celebrated their diamond wedding anniversary in 1917 with extended family, including David and Margarete (standing, middle row, left of centre). Photo: Mennonite Library & Archives

What was family life like in these years? Today, the aging children recall a happy home, with mother Margarete always at the centre of domestic activity. Father's comings and goings were taken for granted; it was part of the milieu. His times at home were always special, since he was a friend to children, particularly his own. In his tribute to Margarete Toews, Rosenorter minister and historian John G. Rempel put it this way:

If one may speak of an ideal family life, then one could speak of Ält. David Toews' family life in that way. Whoever has visited in the home throughout the years when the children were growing up or when they were already grown and came home, one would gain the impression: Love dwells here, along with well-being and satisfaction! Surely one does not do an injustice to the name of Ält. David Toews if one ascribes this spirit in the home and this attitude of all members of the family, in the first place to Mrs. Toews, the heart of the home. She herself came from a home where it was no small thing to banish Mrs. Worry on a daily basis. Had Margarete not been the second oldest [sic] of the seventeen siblings of Rev. Abraham Friesen's second marriage? And while not all of these survived life, a full dozen were always around. And we are speaking here of the home of a pioneer preacher. It is hardly necessary to elaborate on the situation. The calm loving Mrs. Toews, who received many a guest with a quiet laugh, who gave all she had, not only in the home but also in her church and social circle beyond the home, exercised a noble influence and left a marked impression despite her modest nature.[38]

No doubt the fact that David Toews was able to face the heavy demands of his daily work was attributable in large measure to the encouraging and quiet support of his beloved Margarete and the peaceful and orderly atmosphere in the Toews home.

9
Advocate for His People
1919–1922

Before World War I, the Canadian government was known for its open door policy on immigration.[1] Pioneer farmers were needed for Canada's wide, open spaces. The railways had been built to provide a means of transporting people to the west who would populate and develop some of the 25,000,000 acres of land owned by the railway companies. Eventually the railway cars would return to the east with the produce of the land. This would prosper the economy of Canada. The west was organized into provinces which facilitated a more systematic development of the unpopulated regions. Mennonites played a prominent part in this early immigration initiative. They were desirable citizens, particularly due to their farming skills and their reputation as hard workers.

However, the attitude of the Canadian government was about to change. The depression of 1914 caused the immigration department to have second thoughts about a wide-open immigration policy. Too many immigrants would increase the already high unemployment. This fear was accentuated at the conclusion of the war when returning veterans needed some assurance that there would be jobs waiting for them. Public sentiment focused in particular on those ethnic groups, notably Mennonites, Hutterites, and Doukhobors who, besides speaking German, had displayed little national support for the war effort. In addition, Mennonites and their historic "cousins" had gained a reputation as isolationists who resisted public education and Anglicization in general.[2] The Canadian public had entertained some hope that the war years would serve to nationalize all Canadians, but in this they were disappointed. The public was coming to realize that for most Mennonites opposition to war was born of a religious passion, and that the Mennonites were not easily nationalized.

As a response to public sentiment, the Canadian government passed an Order-in-Council on May 1, 1919, which closed the doors of immigration to Mennonites, Doukhobors, and Hutterites. The immediate occasion for the Order was the influx, during the war, of Hutterites who sought to evade conscription in the United States,[3] although in the minds of many

Canadians, Mennonites had shown themselves to be unwelcome citizens during the recent war. Understandably, the railway companies were not very pleased with this restriction since they needed good agriculturalists for their large tracts of land. Even so, some 100,000 immigrants a year entered Canada after 1918, but the industrious Mennonites were not among the newcomers.

Defending the Mennonite Reputation

Even before the passing of the Order-in-Council, David Toews saw the need to defend the reputation of Mennonites. Apparently in the public press, Mennonites were accused of committing fraud by falsifying documents claiming exemption for individual young men. In a letter to the Honourable J.A. Calder, Minister of Citizenship and Immigration, dated October 16, 1918, Toews defended the Mennonites against this accusation. He wrote to Calder that Mennonites had done all they could to comply with directives given by the authorities in Ottawa. Toews had been in Ottawa twice to get information and directions. "If it is found that I have made false statements," he said, "put me in jail."[4]

This is how the matter stood when, a year or two later, Canadian Mennonites in the west began to consider a major migration of their people from the Soviet Union to Canada. Closer to home, David Toews also found himself doing "damage control." The unruly behaviour of some young people eligible for the draft had caused a major headache for the church and its leaders. Sectors of the non-Mennonite population had turned against the Mennonites for their stance of nonparticipation in war. In the public press they were being depicted as "undesirable citizens" and were even referred to as the "Mennonite menace."[5]

David Toews often bore the brunt of this public anger. He had gained a reputation as defender of any and every Mennonite as nonresistant, regardless of his deportment. When the young men got themselves into trouble by submitting to conscription, but then changed their minds—or had their minds changed by their parents—it was Toews who was called upon to convince the military administration that the youth was "one of ours" and should be released from military duty. The public press in Saskatoon had maligned Toews more than once for his attempts at advocacy. On one occasion, the papers reported on a case against a young Mr. Hamm who was in court for some misdemeanour. The news article added the comment: "If Mr. Toews had been present, he would swear upon it that Hamm was a good Mennonite."[6] Such was his unconditional faith in his people.

Internal Issues

While Toews found it troubling that Mennonites were being criticized in the public arena, he found it even more distressing to be misunderstood by his own people. At one point he was confronted by a fellow church member with the criticism, "In your view every good-for-nothing is a Mennonite."[7] In his view, the position of nonresistance was not a matter for each member of the Mennonite church and of Mennonite families to decide on their own. The peace principle was to be upheld by the church on behalf of everyone in the church, members and adherents. Historically, the Mennonite people as a whole had held to this position and currently the church as such confessed it. For Toews, this was sufficient reason to claim the peace stance on behalf of all who belonged to a Mennonite family, whether they themselves held the position firmly or not.[8]

Understandably, Toews was caught in a dilemma. On the one hand, he wanted to uphold the historic principles of the Mennonite people. On the other hand, there were young men of Mennonite families who did not want for themselves what Toews wanted for them. Besides, the behaviour of some youth heaped disgrace on the church, especially when young men would get in trouble with the law while at the same time claiming to be free of conscription because they were Mennonites. At one congregational meeting, Elder Toews was heard to complain, "As for me, my head is sometimes in a spin over it all."[9] These troubles, which continued until well after the end of the war, generated considerable internal agenda for the Rosenorter Church's ministerial meetings.

At the 1919 sessions of the Conference of Mennonites in Canada in Gretna, Manitoba, the focus of concern was still on internal matters. In his conference address, David Toews spoke of how the New Testament church did battle against the principalities and power.[10] Then he pointed to the Anabaptists of the sixteenth century who confronted the wrongs of their day with conviction and courage. That brought him to the current situation. He lamented the fact that the Mennonite people had not fought their recent spiritual battles with sufficient vigour. During the recent time of war, they had been ill-prepared to give a reason for their peace stance with the result that their witness had become marred. What would it take for people of faith to withstand the onslaughts of evil? Toews had the answer: Mennonite youth needed to be grounded in the faith of their forebears, and this grounding would come by way of solid higher education in the religious values of their tradition. According to the minutes of the sessions, the delegates affirmed the concerns and the perspectives Toews had raised. The church needed to give careful attention to its internal life, particularly as this applied to the youth in its midst.

Relinquishing School Duties

In 1917 the church had requested Ältester Toews to relinquish his school duties and devote himself fully to the work of the church. The request placed Toews in somewhat of a dilemma. On the one hand, he had obligated himself to the eldership of the church which was considered a holy and life-long calling. The church was growing and his responsibilities were increasing. On the other hand, the school had come to depend heavily on his leadership. Would it survive if he withdrew his services there? Toews was not only on the teaching staff, but he was also the chief administrator and fundraiser. He had his fingers in all those aspects of the school that were crucial to its very existence. This situation put undue pressure on him, especially in the financial department. Not only was Toews responsible for seeing to it that there were enough funds to keep the school afloat; he also had to make decisions about the dispersal of funds. Often it was a matter of deciding at the end of the month which bills absolutely needed attention and which could be left for later when hopefully there would be sufficient funds. This dilemma impinged on his own financial situation. As Toews said: "With the available money I had to satisfy the other teachers, and in the end I got what was left over."[11] Two questions faced him as he considered resigning from the school and devoting full-time service to the church. Would the school survive? And, would he survive financially, as he would now need to depend on a church that was not used to supporting their ministers? These were risks to be considered.

Consequently, Toews did decide to resign from teaching duties and give more attention to the church. At the same time, he continued as chairman of the board and as fundraiser for the school. Toews was willing to give this arrangement a try. He quietly hoped, and perhaps assumed, that the church would provide him with a stipend, but it became evident after some time that there was little support forthcoming. Although deeply disappointed, he was not ready to give up, even though he wrote of this as a time of "much worry, grief, and brokenheartedness."[12] Rosenorter congregational historian, J.G. Rempel, added his own explanation of the situation.[13] He saw two reasons for the failure of the church to provide for their Ältester's monthly support. First, the churches of that day were not used to paying their ministers a salary. Second, it never was clear who was responsible for collecting the money needed for this budgetary item. Apparently not even those who had urged Toews to make himself available on a full-time basis saw it as their responsibility to provide the financial means to make that possible.

As Toews' financial woes increased, he tried his own hand at alleviating the problem. At one time he invested in some real estate, hoping to purchase land cheaply on borrowed money and then sell at a profit. But this did not work out well. By his own admission, he did not have the wisdom to choose good land and so became an easy target for prospective land developers. As a result, his debts only increased, and he had little hope of paying back the money he had borrowed. Eventually a fellow church member, Isaac P. Friesen, lent Toews the money to retire the bank note. But this meant that Toews was indebted to Friesen, which generated another set of problems. In time, hard feelings developed between the two. Friesen had not expected this to be a long-term loan, and he pressed Toews for his money. From his winter vacations in California, Friesen wrote to suggest that Toews did not want to pay and wondered if he should take legal action. Toews wanted nothing more than to retire the debt but insisted that he simply did not have the funds to clear up the loan. The conclusion to this matter will be told in another chapter.

Return to Teaching
    As the year 1921 wore on, David Toews realized he would need to find his own personal source of income since the church was not forthcoming with a stipend and fundraising for the school did not yield enough to pay the fundraiser. Debts were pressing. A maturing family and the recent birth of their ninth child, Irene, increased the need for financial resources in his family. And then there was always the keen sense of obligation to the church. At one point in the spring of 1921, when Toews was sensing the demands upon him, he inserted the following defence in an article in *Der Mitarbeiter*: "The writer of this article has been gone from home constantly throughout the past winter due to church work. Whoever might think that is easy is welcome to accompany me for a week."[14] What should he do? To teach at the Academy during the 1921–1922 school year was out of the question since the positions there had all been assigned. So he applied for a teaching position at the elementary school in Heidelberg, five miles west of Hague. He began his teaching duties there in January of 1922. It appears that the church found out about this only after the fact. Toews simply took matters into his own hands.
    Think of the situation! It was the middle of winter. At the end of a busy weekend of church responsibilities, which no doubt left many pastoral duties "up in the air," Toews had to make his way ten miles south and five miles west to his outpost. Each Sunday evening, with food provisions in hand for the week, he took the train from Rosthern to Hague, then either borrowed the horse and sleigh of his brother-in-law, Jacob Friesen of Hague, for the lonely five-mile trek to Heidelberg, or

had his brother-in-law take him Sunday night and bring him back to Hague again on Friday afternoon. After the week of teaching, he returned to Rosthern late Friday afternoon to fulfil his obligations to family and church as best he could during the weekend. Then it was back to Heidelberg again on Sunday evening. All the while he continued as secretary-treasurer and acting principal of the Academy and, of course, as elder of the large Rosenorter Church.[15]

Toews accepted the Heidelberg assignment with a heavy heart and found the arrangement very difficult. It meant that he was removed for the entire week from his family and from the life of the church. While he loved children and enjoyed teaching, and while the Heidelberg community showed love and kindness toward him, the months there proved to be very lonely. His situation dipped to a low ebb when he received news from Aberdeen, Idaho, that his aged father had passed away. To attend the funeral service was completely out of the question, so he bore his grief alone in the dead of a Saskatchewan winter away from family and friends. As the months wore on, he knew that he would not continue at Heidelberg, even though the community found many ways to express love and appreciation for their teacher and the local school board offered him a sizeable salary increase for the next year. The continuing request of the church for more and more of his services added to the pressure. At this time David Toews was 51 years of age.

Turmoil in Russia

While these events were taking place in Saskatchewan, another drama was unfolding in far-away Russia, a country that had been in turmoil for some decades. With the organization in 1898 of the Russian Social Democratic Labour party led by Lenin, a revolutionary movement against the tsar, Nicholas II, was taking shape. Wars, depression, and populist strikes plagued the government of the day. World War I accentuated the crisis when the effects of a costly war produced drastic repercussions among the common people, with shortages of food, fuel, and housing and a general depletion of social services. With the famous Revolution of October 1917, the Bolsheviks, led by Lenin, formed a new Russian government under the "Russian Communist Party." The Revolution evoked more chaos which turned the area of the Mennonite colonies, among other places, into a battleground between the Bolshevik Red Army and the anti-Communist White Army. The peasants generally supported the Reds, believing they would lose their land if the Whites won. The Reds were stronger and better organized and won out in the end. The Mennonites, being successful land owners, had their own interests and hopes but in the main resisted the temptation to get involved.

The territory of the Mennonite colonies was one of the battle grounds for these factions. The main forces in the conflict there were the White Tsarist Army and the Red Communist Army. As the armies moved back and forth in a see-saw battle, they demanded horses, food, and shelter from Mennonite colonists. To make matters worse, a third destructive force entered the fray. An anarchist group, led by Nestor Makhno, directed its vengeance against them. Makhno claimed to have a score to settle with the Mennonite people, charging that he and his Russian compatriots had been badly treated as servile workers for Mennonite landlords. The band plundered and destroyed villages and violated the people in unimaginable ways.

In the wake of this upheaval, it was feared that the Mennonite community faced the destruction of its entire way of life—indeed, of life itself. The spread of typhoid fever, brought on mainly by contact with the revolutionaries, resulted in more deaths than the war and anarchy put together. The scarcity of seed grain combined with severe drought added to the crisis. It seemed that a time of dying had begun for Mennonites.

When David Toews later took up his pen to write his memoirs, he began his 55 pages of recollections in this way: "It was probably in the year 1918, perhaps already at the beginning of 1919, that the first reports of gruesome events in Russia reached our ears. The war had brought much suffering, but the Russian Revolution brought even more."[16] News of the gruesome murders, with entire families being slaughtered, estate owners either murdered or sent fleeing, and reports of a catastrophic shortage of food made such a deep impression on Toews that for him and others in Canada and in the United States the question of what they could do to help became ever more pressing. These persecuted people were the relatives and friends of Mennonites in North America.

In his memoirs Toews recounted how, in the spring of 1920, Gerhard Ens of Rosthern had approached him one day with letters in hand that he had recently received from Russia.[17] Ens was a former Mennonite and a local politician. He had an interest in helping, partly as a service to his Mennonite constituents and partly by virtue of his Mennonite background. Perhaps he also saw this as an opportunity to invite additional industrious Mennonite farmers to Saskatchewan. Toews and Ens discussed the question of what should be done to help the troubled Mennonites in Russia. It was decided that Toews would call a church meeting at Eigenheim to lay the matter before the Rosenorter Church.

Changing Agenda

The Rosenorter Church meeting in late June of 1920 proved to be a turning point in its congregational agenda.[18] Internal issues were overshadowed by concern for the suffering brothers and sisters in Russia. Following Toews' report that evening on the grim picture of the plight of their people in Russia, the thought of a mass immigration came to public expression for the first time. At the meeting, Toews was quoted to have said: "We must bear in mind that these our brothers and sisters, stripped of all resources, will want to immigrate, and we should begin to gather resources in order to expedite their rescue from this slavery."[19] It was decided "that we should do whatever is feasible within the realm of possibilities."[20] The evening concluded with the passing of a resolution that expressed the desire that Russian Mennonites be helped to come to Canada in the near future. Toews admitted later that he could not see how this could be accomplished; he had hoped conditions would improve so that a bold initiative would not be necessary.

Similarly, on the level of the Conference, there was a marked difference between the agenda of the 1919 meeting at Gretna and the Laird conference in 1920. While the Gretna conference had been preoccupied with internal church agenda,[21] the Laird meeting wrestled with the question of how to understand the suffering of people in Russia and how to facilitate their emigration to Canada.[22]

First Initiatives

How should the Mennonite constituency in the west respond to the need? This was a question that David Toews took seriously as spiritual leader of the Rosenorter Church and as chairman of the Conference of Mennonites in Western Canada. It seemed clear that contributions of money would help, but this only meant another fundraising project for David Toews. He travelled to congregations far and wide to present the need and to organize collections. It was decided to channel assistance through the newly formed Mennonite Central Committee (MCC). By the fall of 1920 an initial sum of $3,500 was forwarded to the MCC office in Scottdale, Pennsylvania.

The Mennonite Central Committee originated on July 17, 1920, with the joining of five distinct Mennonite bodies: the Mennonite Church, the General Conference Mennonite Church, the Mennonite Brethren, the Lancaster Conference, and the Krimmer Mennonite Brethren.[23] Soon there was cooperation between MCC and two relief organizations in Canada, one in the east and the other in the west. In the east, the Ontario constituency was served by the Nonresistant Relief Organization of Ontario, founded in 1917 from among various Mennonite groups and the Brethren in Christ.[24] In the west, representatives from Manitoba, Saskatchewan, and Alberta met in Regina on October 18, 1920, to form the Canadian Mennonite Central Committee.[25] These Canadian Mennonite organizations, along with others that emerged during World War II, joined forces with MCC in the 1940s. On March 15, 1940, at a meeting in Winnipeg, the western Canadian sector of MCC was organized under the name, Mennonite Central Relief Committee (MCRC).[26] Within Canada, the Ontario relief efforts continued to be centred in the east, while there was close cooperation between the eastern and the western organizations. Beginning in 1924, and for some years following, the work of the Canadian MCC in the west was taken over by the Canadian Mennonite Board of Colonization

Beyond financial contributions it seemed obvious that persons should be sent from America to Russia to help in the distribution of material aid. A first attempt was made to enter Russia by way of Constantinople, but this turned out to be unsuccessful. Upon hearing this, Toews sent a letter to Scottdale, suggesting they try to access Ukraine with relief contributions by way of the Latvian city of Riga. This venture was a success. By this time, three MCC representatives, Orie Miller, Arthur Slegel, and Clayton Kratz, had arrived in the Mennonite colonies where they hoped to facilitate the movement of supplies from America to the stricken areas and to help Mennonite leaders in Russia organize their relief efforts. Because of blockage tactics by the Communists, it took until the spring of 1922 for American relief efforts to reach Ukraine. On the Russian side, it was Benjamin B. Janz who, with great commitment and much personal risk, headed up negotiations with government officials.[27] Toews and Janz would have many occasions to work side by side on immigration and relief projects.

Clearing the Way

Realizing their desperate situation, the Russian colonists took concrete action to facilitate immigration. Their focus was on North America as such. In December 1919, a *Studienkommission* (Study Commission) comprised of Abram A. Friesen, Benjamin H. Unruh, C.H. Warkentin, and J.J. Esau, was sent across the Atlantic to report on the situation of Russian Mennonites and to explore immigration and settlement prospects.[28] All members of the delegation were educated and well qualified to speak on behalf of their people. Meanwhile, in Russia Mennonites established offices in Kharkov and Moscow from which to direct their affairs and provide a point of reference to negotiate with the government. They also established organizations for the purpose of engaging in economic development and reconstruction. Many in Russia had the view that immigration was not the only option, that conditions might still improve.

It was A.A. Friesen who suggested, at a meeting in Herbert, Saskatchewan, in June of 1921, that every effort should be made to persuade the

Canadian government to rescind the Order-in-Council of 1919 that disallowed Mennonites to immigrate to Canada. That summer, the idea of a delegation to Ottawa was approved by the Mennonite Brethren Conference and by the Conference of Mennonites in Western Canada. At the latter sessions of 1921, there was a call for the formation of an inter-Mennonite relief organization to assist the suffering kinfolk in Russia.[29] A delegation of five persons was appointed: Heinrich H. Ewert, A.A. Friesen, H. A Neufeld, and two (Old) Mennonites from Ontario, S.F. Coffman and D.M. Reesor. In Ottawa, their discussion with the acting prime minister, Sir George Foster, was not very encouraging, even though the delegates did their best to impress on the Conservative politician that their co-religionists in Russia were progressive in their views of culture and education. The delegates also had a meeting with Liberal opposition leader, William Lyon Mackenzie King.[30] This interview held more promise as Mackenzie King assured the group that, if he were successful in the forthcoming election, he would see that the Order-in-Council was removed. King, who was from Waterloo County in Ontario, knew the Mennonites well and thought highly of them.

The Liberals won the election in the fall of 1921, and the Mennonites wasted no time in moving forward. David Toews took the initiative in organizing a second visit to Ottawa.[31] He himself could not go as he was teaching school in Heidelberg at the time. The delegation included H.H. Ewert, Gerhard Ens, A.A. Friesen, S.F. Coffman, and Sam Goudie. In Ottawa they met with three government leaders, Prime Minister Mackenzie King, Charles Stewart, the Minister of Immigration, and W.R. Motherwell, Minister of Agriculture. As in the previous visit, the Mennonite delegates sought to clear up some prejudicial attitudes of the Canadian public against them. Among other things, they noted that in recent years over $100,000 had been donated by non-resistant Menno-nites for relief work. The five Mennonites were received very positively and were given the assurance that their request would be granted. On June 2, 1922, that Order-in-Council, which had blocked immigration of Mennonites to Canada, was repealed.[32] The way was now open for a "Mennonite exodus" to Canada.

Forming an Organization

Even before the Order-in-Council was repealed, Mennonite leaders swung into action to organize for the envisioned immigration. David Toews invited the various conferences in the west to send representatives to a meeting in Altona on April 11, 1922. At that meeting it was decided to form an immigration commission.[33] David Toews and Heinrich Ewert were the two members chosen to represent the Conference of Mennonites in western Canada on the new organization. Other representatives were to come from the Church of God in Christ Mennonite, the Kleine Gemeinde, the Bruderthaler, the Mennonite Brethren, and the Brethren in Christ churches. The Sommerfeld Church decided not to participate.

May 17, 1922 was the date of the organizational meeting held at the home of Heinrich H. Ewert in Gretna.[34] David Toews could not be present as he was occupied with teaching duties back in Saskatchewan. In any case, he had given indication that he could not serve on the new commission as he was fully engaged with his responsibilities of teaching, carrying on with church work, and chairing the board of the German-English Academy. His personal financial limitations also played into his decision.[35] Besides Ewert, the meeting included Rev. H.A. Neufeld (Mennonite Brethren) of Herbert, Saskatchewan, A.A. Friesen, P.H. Wiebe (Church of God in Christ Mennonite) of Steinbach, Manitoba, and Gerhard Ens, whom David Toews had sent as his substitute. The group decided that the official name of the new organization should be "Canadian Mennonite Board of Colonization."[36] The executive committee consisted of David Toews as chairman, C.J. Andres as secretary, and H.A. Neufeld as a third member. A.A. Friesen was appointed as corresponding secretary with a monthly salary of $100.[37] The group selected H.H. Ewert, David Toews, and Cornelius J. Andres as permanent members of the Board.

One might have thought that Ewert would play a major role in the new organization but he appears to have deferred to David Toews. It was sometimes said that Ewert and Toews did not get along too well, that they had strong and differing views on various matters, yet Ewert appears to have had confidence in the younger man. With the election of David Toews, it was not at all sure that he would accept the position. But the meeting went even a step further. Gerhard Ens and A.A. Friesen were assigned to approach Toews back in Saskatchewan and prevail upon him not only to chair the Board but to become its chief executive officer.[38]

Following the Gretna meeting, Toews received a visit in Heidelberg from Friesen and Ens. They carried with them an invitation from the Board asking Toews to assume the directorship of the entire immigration project. A.A. Friesen had been offered the job of secretary and treasurer. While Toews had some reservations about his ability to do the job, he was immediately attracted to it for several reasons: it would expand his horizons beyond the somewhat restrictive Heidelberg experience and he would be able to do the major part of the task in his home town of Rosthern. At a subsequent meeting of the Board on June 24 in Rosthern, David Toews formally accepted the assignment. He was offered an annual salary of $1,400, comparable to what the Heidelberg school board had offered. But he told the Board he would be satisfied with $1,200, so that was the amount agreed upon.

Meanwhile, at its semi-annual meeting in June of the same year, the Rosenorter ministers voted 46 to one in favour of urging Toews to serve the church full time. They were feeling keenly the need for his services.[39] They admitted to defaulting on his salary and intended to do better. But with the matter of remuneration left to the discretion of each church district to do what it could, it seemed inevitable that the financial issue would not be resolved. The Rosenorter Church took a proactive step to provide for its leadership when, on July 8, 1923 at a service in Eigenheim, five persons were ordained to the ministry. They were H.T. Klaassen, Rudolf Gaeddert, Isaac P. Friesen, Gerhard G. Epp, and Isaac I. Friesen.[40]

Given the new arrangement, David Toews would be working in the same office with A.A. Friesen. Abramovich A. Friesen, born in 1885, was a bright young man who had made his mark in Russia where he had taught at the school of commerce in Halbstadt, Ukraine.[41] Since coming to America in January of 1920, Friesen had actively pursued the possibility of remaining in Canada. In time he received permission to stay but he left behind his fiancée, Maria Goossen. After a separation of almost three years, including a two-year period where they did not hear from each other, Maria left Russia on her own and undertook a six-month journey to Canada. David Toews officiated at the wedding of Abram and Maria on August 31, 1922. They made their home in Rosthern and later moved to Rabbit Lake, Saskatchewan.

Finding a Way

At the May 17, 1922 meeting, the question of how to finance the immigration had been discussed. H.H. Ewert had the idea that individual families in Canada should be asked to sponsor and host immigrant families, but because this plan was not favoured by the others he did not press his idea. A decision was made to form a corporation, the "Mennonite Colonization Association of North America," through which the transportation and settlement of immigrants would be undertaken.[42] With this step the organization for carrying out the immigration project was in place. But how would the transportation and settlement be financed and carried out?

Even before the June 2 decision, on March 31 a Mennonite delegation, comprised of Heinrich Ewert, A.A. Friesen, and Gerhard Ens, had visited the Montreal offices of the Canadian Pacific Railway to explore the possibility of arranging transportation facilities and financial credit for a large-scale movement of Mennonites from Russia to Canada. The

A.A. Friesen (1885–1948), a colleague of David Toews in the office of the Canadian Mennonite Board of Colonization from 1922 to 1926.
Photo: *Mennonitisches Jahrbuch*

initial talks with officials of the CPR went well, thanks mainly to Colonel John Stoughton Dennis, Chief Commissioner of Colonization and Development for the CPR. Col. Dennis thought highly of the Mennonites from earlier days when he worked on *The International*, the boat that ferried Mennonite immigrants down the Red River in 1874. The delegation left Montreal with a promise in hand that CPR officials would draft a transportation contract. The railway had colonization on its mind ever since the First World War when it had expressed interest in Mennonite farmers from Russia.[43] Quite simply, Col. Dennis assured the delegation that the CPR would advance credit to the Mennonites if they would promise to pay back the debt.

The Infamous Contract

The first order of business for the Canadian Mennonite Board of Colonization was to find a way of financing the immigration project. It was out of the question to expect that Canadian Mennonites would have money to put up front. In the first place, their own financial resources were limited; secondly, the project would have required an unusual financial commitment. So the Board turned to a source that had helped them in the past. In the mid 1890s, when the newly arrived immigrants in Tiefengrund, Eigenheim, and surrounding areas had to rely on Manitoba Mennonites for food and for seed grain, the CPR had transported the goods free of charge.[44] The point was not missed on the CPR that there would be something in it for them as well. New settlers with a reputation for honesty and hard work made them a safe risk to farm the railway company's land. Thus Col. Dennis was able to persuade his colleagues at the Montreal office that the transportation costs would be a worthwhile and safe investment.

David Toews' first duty as director was to fulfil the Board's request that he send a telegram to Col. Dennis in Montreal asking him to send a draft of a transportation contract to Rosthern.[45] This he did in June of 1922. The crucial aspects of the contract were the line of credit with the CPR and the price of the trip per person by ship and rail from Russia to Canada. There was some reservation within the CPR about the arrangement. The Vice-President of Finances called it "one of Col. Dennis' crazy ideas!"[46] Even Toews admitted that "in view of our poverty and the huge responsibility toward the Company and toward our congregations the entire matter was for me a frightening prospect."[47] On June 20, Col. Dennis informed Toews that he was prepared to go ahead with a contract. The CPR was willing to grant transportation credit for 3000 immigrants.[48] The cost would amount to $400,000. Terms of the payment stipulated that 25 per cent of the total cost was due ten days after the invoice was issued. Another 25 per cent should be paid within three months, the remainder after six months. Interest was calculated at 6 per cent. The contract was between "The Mennonite Church of Canada and the CPR Co." Interestingly, no such entity as "The Mennonite Church of Canada" existed. As for the government, it gave full support to the venture, provided the Mennonites would carry out three requirements: 1) Mennonites in Canada would supply shelter and support for the incoming immigrants; 2) the immigrants would become farmers; and 3) no immigrant would become a public charge.[49]

Toews' first challenge was to convince the Mennonites in Canada that this was a good and workable plan. The first test in the constituency came in July at the annual sessions of the Conference of Mennonites in Canada in Winkler. Two plans were presented to the delegates, one by H.H. Ewert and the other by David Toews.[50] The two men were of differing opinions on how the immigration project should be financed. Ewert's idea was that groups of five sponsors should be found who would take responsibility for each immigrant family. Toews judged this to be impossible, given the amount of work this would take and the number of sponsors this would require. By then reports surfaced that about 3000 immigrants, or about 750 families, had arrived in Odessa with the expectation that ships would be there to transport them to North America. Toews saw it as an impossible task to find five or six sponsors per family in Canada who would be willing to vouch for these relative strangers. His idea, with which most of the Board agreed, was to form a corporation and to arrange for a line of credit. Toews describes the proceedings at Winkler this way: "When it came to the immigration issue, Brother Ewert explained his plan. I then explained ours, the corporation plan as worked out with our lawyer, Mr. March. I succeeded in presenting the plan in a calm and straightforward manner, whereas Brother Ewert became quite agitated. He emphasized: 'I have nothing against Brother Toews, but the other members of the Board do not want to get the opinion of the constituency, and I cannot work with them.'"[51] The Toews proposal was accepted with an overwhelming majority. Toews surmised that it passed not because people liked it but because it seemed to be a more realistic possibility.

Permission to Sign?

Then came a somewhat dramatic moment in the course of the Winkler Conference and in the story of Mennonite immigration. While in Winkler, Toews had received a telegram from Col. Dennis in Montreal, informing him that a contract had been forwarded to his Saskatchewan address and that it would require a signature from the Mennonites. This should be done with dispatch since much time had already been lost. But who would sign it? And under what authority? Toews tells the story this way:

> I put the question before the assembled delegates, whether I had permission to sign the awaited contract. Everything was quiet. I asked my question a second time. Still no response. I repeated my question a third time. No answer. A brother Hildebrand from Winkler wanted to know what Ewert had to say. At that point I became anxious, thinking that Ewert would reply in the negative. But he remained silent. Then I did something for which I later incurred heavy criticism. Likely I was in error. I said: "For the time being the Rosenorter Church will take responsibility until such a time as the other churches join in."[52]

On the last day of the conference a resolution was presented and accepted, which affirmed the work of the Board of Colonization, voiced the expectation that further undertakings of the Board would be done in a practical, healthy and business-like matter, and gave the Board permission to arrange a loan for the necessary funds.[53] Thus a rather lengthy and involved process was concluded.

According to Toews, the two other delegates from Rosthern lost no time in stirring up negative sentiments in their area. Toews' remark about the Rosenorter Church taking responsibility was enough to sow seeds of fear and mistrust which eventually turned to hostility. In Rosthern and surrounding area a petition was circulated designed to prevent Toews from signing the contract. While this did not stop the process, the fallout in ill will and bad relationships was hopelessly irreparable. Just when the storm in Rosthern was subsiding, a meeting of the congregation at Hepburn on July 27 resulted in a telegram to Col. Dennis in Montreal, indicating they did not support what Toews was doing. Letters expressing opposition were also sent by individuals in Rosthern. Similar sentiments were expressed to A.A. Friesen and Toews by a delegation from Dalmeny.[54]

Thus things did not get off to a good start, although the Board took the Winkler discussion and resolution as their green light to proceed. In the view of Toews, the detractors lacked clear information which always results in unclear thinking. Driven by his compassion for the desperate situation in Russia, Toews saw no other option than to move ahead resolutely. He wrote: "Inwardly I was convinced that we would have to bite into this sour apple if we wished to help our people."[55]

While Friesen stayed back at the office, now situated in the National Hotel in Rosthern, Toews engaged in getting the project off the ground and seeking to answer the critics as best he could. He and Gerhard Ens left for Saskatoon on July 24 for preliminary discussion with CPR representatives there who had the contract in hand. Instructions from Col. Dennis were that it should be signed in Saskatoon or they need not bother coming to Montreal. Toews had great hesitation about signing:

> After all, we were on our way to Montreal for the purpose of negotiating a better deal. That's why Gerhard Ens was sent along. I hesitated to sign for that reason. Ens had no such reservations—after all he did not carry the mantle of responsibility as I did. He recommended signing. Taking into consideration the advice of Brother H.A. Neufeld in Hepburn and of Gerhard Ens, and in view of the fact that I would eventually sign even if no better deal could be achieved, I signed my name to the fateful document and we continued on our way to Montreal. . . . According to the minutes of the Board of July 14, 1922, I had actually received authority to sign the contract even if we were not able to obtain better conditions.[56]

The signing, which probably took place on July 24, gave Toews the reputation among some Mennonites of being "the million dollar man." He had signed a contract that had the potential of obligating the Canadian Mennonite Board of Colonization, and thus also the Mennonite people of Canada to whom the Board was responsible, to an initial loan that could easily amount to one million dollars.

"Bishop" Toews

In Montreal David Toews met Col. Dennis for the first time. When the latter addressed him as "Bishop" Toews, Toews objected, but to no avail. Henceforth he was regarded, at least by the CPR officials, as having the hierarchical authority to speak (and sign) for all Mennonites in Canada, indeed in North America, as their "Bishop." Due to the sentiment and influence of Col. Dennis, chief negotiator for the railway company, the contract signified a "gentlemen's agreement" made in trust. Toews believed that the project was seen by Col. Dennis and a significant number of his associates not only as a good business venture but also as a humanitarian cause. It was a win-win situation. People caught in misery and suffering would be rescued from their situation, while the Canadian west would gain a new population of good farmers who would develop land—including CPR land—that had the potential for productivity. This is how Toews understood it as well.[57]

From Montreal, Toews proceeded to Bluffton, Ohio, for a meeting of the historic peace churches—Mennonites, Quakers, and Tunkers—on the theme of nonresistance and peace. He went to Bluffton with the hope of presenting the immigration cause and the plan of action. While he was somewhat disappointed in the amount of time he was given to make his presentation and in the sparse attendance, he did gain the assurance of support for the cause he represented.

Some Resistance

Back home it was quite another matter! Soon after Toews arrived in Rosthern, two persons from Dalmeny and one from Hepburn were at the church door wanting a copy of the contract. A large congregational meeting was planned in the Hepburn area at which they wanted to read details of the contract to the gathering. Toews refused to give them a copy but suggested he or someone from the Board would come with contract in hand, read the document in public, or have it read, and be ready to offer explanations and answer questions. This did not suit the visitors, so they left Toews' office only to "confer with Isaak P. Friesen until late into the night."[58] Subsequently there was a large protest meeting in Hepburn after which a telegram and a letter were sent to Col. Dennis in Montreal to report that "a public meeting was called for the purpose of reading the contract, but that they were refused a copy."[59] The letter named nine congregations opposed to the immigration and made it clear that these congregations would take no responsibility in the relief effort. Col. Dennis also received a letter from the Chortitzer Mennonite Church in Manitoba, stating they wanted nothing to do with the immigration project. In time the Mennonite press became involved in the issue. One particularly hurtful statement appeared in the Mennonite Brethren *Zionsbote* at the beginning of 1923: "It has come to light that those who are working with the immigration project have their own interests in mind." The note was signed by a J.F. Strauss of Hepburn.[60] To this note Toews responded quickly with a request for evidence to support this statement, but none was offered.

In these difficult months, Toews found comfort in biblical texts such as 1 Peter 2:20: "But how is it to your credit if you receive a beating for doing wrong and endure it? But if you suffer for doing good and you endure it, this is commendable before God."[61] He recalled a stirring sermon preached by Jacob Kroeker, visitor from Russia, in August of 1922. The text from 2 Kings, 6:8–18 was a comfort for Toews, particularly verse 16: "Do not be afraid, for there are more with us than there are with them." When someone suggested that the Mennonites in Russia were unconverted and had brought their suffering on themselves because of their sinfulness, Toews replied: "It is not a question of judging their beliefs. They have fallen among thieves, and that is how they are there for me." In a letter to a member of the Board of Colonization, dated January 19, 1923, Toews wrote graciously regarding a proposed reconciliation among those who had hurt one another in the exchange illustrated above:

> As for a reconciliation with our opposition, you know that we did not ask for a fight. We were openly slandered by the press without basis or reason. Despite that, we are prepared even now to offer the hand of reconciliation to everyone who in sincerity wishes to work together with us for the rescue and well-being of our suffering brothers abroad. We do not have a specific plan to propose as to how this could happen but would be willing to consider whatever sincere suggestions well-intended brothers in this regard would propose.[62]

David Toews carried in his heart a deep conviction that he was representing a just cause. It was not a matter of changing his mind but of convincing the opposition to come on side. He took solace in the faith of Elisha, that there were more on his side than on the side of the opposition.

In time there were those who recognized the faith of Toews. The American Mennonite historian, Cornelius Krahn, is quoted as follows: "One is deeply moved when one reads the account of how one man with a strong faith and commanding personality dared to assume tremendous responsibility in the face of great obstacles which made others desert him or even turn against him."[63] At the beginning the Board had the notion that as many as 100,000 immigrants could be coming. A Corporation Charter establishing "The Mennonite Colonization Association of North America, Limited," approved by the Canadian Department of State on July 26, 1922, set the limits of the Canadian Mennonite Board of

Colonization at $10,000,000.[64] That is, the Board could issue stocks for that amount. The conceived arrangement was that the Board would extend up to that amount of credit to immigrants who would eventually pay off their obligation. Then it was a matter of selling shares. The Board envisioned this as possible both in Canada and in the United States among Mennonites and others as well.

Looking South

In early February of 1923 David Toews left for Kansas with the idea of selling the immigration project as well as shares in the company to the Mennonites there and in Oklahoma. After all, American Mennonites appeared to be more prosperous than their Canadian brothers and sisters. Even though this would also give him a chance to visit family members and earlier acquaintances from his years in Kansas, Toews admitted that he did not look forward to the venture southward. He wished he could have persuaded H.H. Ewert to go, who would have understood much better how to approach the situation and who surely would have had greater success there. But of course Ewert had withdrawn from the work because of his "falling out" with the Board, so that was out of the question. As chief executive officer for the work, Toews would have to go. When he arrived by train at the station in Elbing, Kansas, on a Sunday evening, no one was there to meet him, so he took suitcase in hand and began to walk toward Newton. Soon someone picked him up and took him to his former farm employer, Bernhard Regier, where he arrived unexpectedly. The Regiers were happy to see him and invited him to stay with them during his time there. The next day Regier took him to Newton and to Hesston to meet with various Mennonite leaders, including D.H. Bender, chairman of the newly-organized Immigration Committee.

Responses to Toews' presentation of the immigration cause were mixed. One farmer with considerable means greeted him with the words: "What are you trying to do up there in Canada? You are chasing a dream. What you are attempting is completely impossible." Another said: "We should be sending missionaries to Russia. It's their own fault that they are having a hard time of it. In Molotschna modernism has taken over." Toews had hoped he would be able to agree on a plan of action and would be able to begin selling bonds. But nothing came of it. By this time he was seeing clouds before his eyes when he thought of the task that faced him.[65]

A group of land speculators in Newton wanted Toews to come with them to Washington State where they had a large plot of land in mind for settlement. Although Toews did not see much point in the trip, given the fact that the United States was not even open to immigrants at this time, he went along with the suggestion. However, the trip confirmed for him that he was looking in the wrong places for help. On the way back to Newton he stopped at Aberdeen, Idaho, to visit his aged and widowed mother and his siblings. Back in Kansas Toews faced more challenges to the Canadian plan. One man brought news that the Lancaster bishops were not supportive of the Canadian idea. Another made the comment at a public meeting that he could not see how Toews could sleep at night after having signed the contract. To this Toews replied that he would not have been able to sleep at night if he had *not* signed. Someone surmised that the Canadians would not be able to come up with more than about ten dollars to support the immigration effort. Another person made a statement implying that the Colonization Board would be getting 15 dollars from the Canadian government for every immigrant they would bring over.[66] In the midst of this negativity there were also some encouraging sentiments. It is not surprising that Toews returned home quite discouraged and somewhat more realistic about the prospects of putting the plan together.

To top it off, back in Rosthern A.A. Friesen had received a letter from D.H. Bender, chairman of the American Immigration Committee, in which he spoke of organizing a Colonization Board which would see to the settlement of immigrants from Russia. In part, the intent was to steer the prospective settlers to Mexico, a location some Americans favoured over Canada. In the letter he invited A.A. Friesen, H.H. Ewert, and several other men onto this new board, and indicated that he wanted to assign Friesen to be the middleman for those arriving by way of Quebec and Orie Miller for those coming by way of New York. To this, Toews commented later: "It appeared as though Bender believed that, with one letter, he could set aside our organization. I have to wonder at his audacity but also at his limited understanding of the matter."[67] The American initiative did not get off the ground as nothing more was heard of it.

Back in Canada, Toews continued to promote the plan and the contract. When some in the Board wanted to "throw in the towel," he led the way, insisting that, although they might fail, they must be unflinching in the pursuit of their goal. The hope had been that a shipload of immigrants would come by the fall of 1922. At least in Russia plans were moving in that direction and some prospective immigrants were becoming impatient. But that plan needed to be cancelled. News came that Russian ports had been quarantined because of an outbreak of cholera. As well, international hostilities between Greece and Turkey involved some waters through which the immigrant ships were scheduled to pass.[68] Furthermore, matters such as medical clearance had not been finally arranged between the Canadian travel agency and the Russian government. In short, plans to begin immigration in 1922 were cancelled. The anxious pilgrims in Russia would need to wait until spring.

Many times it seemed as though the entire project would come to nothing. Given the logistical complexities, the opposition in Canada, and the hindrances in Russia, the average individual would have given up. Frank H. Epp gives David Toews the credit for the success of the venture: "Luckily for the Mennonites waiting in Russia, Toews was one of those rare individuals who stood his ground during the worst adversity and whose character thrived on courageous action."[69] Just when it seemed that the project might falter and fail, news came in June of 1923 that a group of 750 immigrants were on the *Empress of France*, scheduled to dock at Quebec City on July 19. Toews received the telegram in early July, while at the Conference sessions in Langham. The announcement generated great excitement among Conference attendees.[70]

David Toews Was Here!

It is reported by John G. Rempel that on that occasion, Christian Krehbiel of the United States, editor of the *Christlicher Bundesbote,* advised Toews: "It would be best to leave it with this one group that is now on the way and let it go at that."[71] To this, Rempel adds that Krehbiel did not really know David Toews who would never do only half a job. Rempel depicts David Toews as a man who was present to life with his entire being. In his words:

> Concerning assistance and relief, Ältester Toews spoke in season and out of season. In holistic fashion (*als ganzer Mensch*) he embarked on his own course of action whereupon we, his coworkers, could only shake our heads in disbelief. If then he would get into a situation where he needed to give account, he would gladly quote the verse from Karl Gerok's poem, "Es reut mich nicht" (I have no regrets).[72]

It was this quality of character that made Toews the leader he was, particularly in the face of opposition and adversity. He was truly "the man for the task."[73]

But Toews Didn't Do It All by Himself

A biography of David Toews will inevitably focus on his particular contribution to the Mennonite "exodus" of the 1920s. Obviously he did not accomplish the work single-handedly. On the Canadian side, for example, persons other than Toews did the initial negotiating with the Canadian government and with the CPR. In his book, *Lost Fatherland*, John B. Toews gives an account of activity on the Russian side.[74] In particular he names B.B. Janz as the chief overseas mover.[75] He also names two organizations that were crucial to the initiative: "The Union of Citizens of Dutch Lineage" and "The All-Russian Mennonite Agricultural Union." Their frequent contact with Russian government officials made them apprehensive about the future of Mennonites in Russia. Hence, they saw the practical necessity and the urgency of immigration.[76] While this biography concentrates on the story of David Toews, there were also other major contributors.

10
A Mennonite Moses
1923–1925

It was almost five years since Mennonites in both North America and in Russia had talked of immigration. Preparations by way of negotiations with governments, community meetings, and the formation of planning committees and boards had been in place for over a year. At one time it was anticipated that an initial contingent of immigrants would arrive in Canada in the fall of 1922, but this was not to be. One can only imagine how difficult it was for those who had staked everything on the antici- pated exodus to live between anticipation and frustration, between hope and disappointment. The wait will have seemed endless. But then things began to happen.

They're Coming!
Early in July of 1923, about 750 immigrants boarded the train at Chortitza in Ukraine and set their faces and their hearts in the direction of Canada.[1] With great interest and mounting intensity, David Toews and the other members of the Canadian Mennonite Colonization Board followed the sojourn of this first group of immigrants. Excitement soon turned to discouragement when, at the border between the Soviet Union and Latvia, Canadian officials subjected the would-be Canadians to severe medical scrutiny. About 10 percent of the group was diagnosed as carriers of trachoma, a contagious eye disease. The obvious cases as well as those even slightly suspected of carrying the disease were transferred to Lechfeld, a detainment centre made possible through the good graces of the German government. There they would stay until healed.[2] The rest boarded the *Empress of France* and embarked on their journey across the Atlantic Ocean.

The immigrant ship with its precious cargo docked in Quebec City on July 17, 1923. Gerhard Ens and P.P. Epp had been sent by Toews to welcome the group and conduct them to their destination. Meanwhile, Toews and his staff made preparations for their reception in Rosthern. While there would have been other possibilities, such as Kitchener or Winnipeg or Saskatoon, it made good sense to bring the travellers to Rosthern—the town which housed the offices of the Colonization Board and its executive staff—and to Saskatchewan—which lay on the edge of the frontier that the new immigrants intended to conquer.

Would they be welcome there? The problems of the past year and a half might cast doubts on the prospects. While David Toews had not given up, he certainly *had* absorbed a great deal of animosity from his own people. However, along the way there were positive indicators. When the train made a stop at Schreiber in northern Ontario, the group received permission to disembark for a brief worship service on the station platform. Soon they attracted a local audience. One spectator, impressed by the piety and decency of the immigrant group, was heard to say: "Is that the kind of immigrants you are bringing here? Why, then bring in lots of them!"[3]

An Emotional Moment

At five o'clock in the afternoon of July 21, the immigrant train, comprised of ten passenger cars and three baggage cars, pulled into the Rosthern station. All day, Mennonites from near and far had been gathering. They came in cars, in buggies, in wagons, and in hayracks, prepared to take their assigned families back to their homes. Frank H. Epp describes the event in this way:

> The immigrants disembarked north of the station and east of the tracks. The scene that followed defies description. There was crying and there was hearty rejoicing. When the first wave of emotion had passed, the immigrants gathered in one large body. Gerhard Ens mounted a small platform and introduced David Toews, who addressed the newcomers briefly, assured them of his sympathy and understanding for their sorrows and privations, and welcomed them on behalf of the Canadian Mennonites. After he had spoken the immigrants sang a song of greeting, "Gott grüsse dich" (We greet you in the name of God). The second line of the hymn expressed the sentiment that "no other greeting than this is more appropriate at this time." This was followed by a hymn of thanksgiving, "Nun danket alle Gott" (Now thank we all our God). With that, Abram Hamm, leader of the travellers, arose and expressed appreciation for the warm welcome. He assured the Canadians "that the ambition of the immigrant Mennonites was to adjust themselves to Canadian conditions, to adopt Canadian customs, and to become, not an alien race with Canadian privileges, but fully Canadians worthy of the name."[4]

No doubt this welcoming event stirred the heart of David Toews deeply. Now the visions and dreams he had held close to his heart were turned to reality before his very eyes. In remembering the sentiments of that day, Toews wrote simply: "We all rejoiced because of this first step of success

On July 21, 1923, Mennonite immigrants from Russia are welcomed by Canadian hosts at the train station in Rosthern. Photo: Centre for Mennonite Brethren Studies

to our work; the day brought its deeply satisfying reward after all the strife and trials we had endured."[5]

Before the sun had set, every immigrant family was on its way to the Canadian family to which it had been assigned. In the weeks preceding this day, an organizing committee had given each church district a quota of homes that would be willing to receive immigrant families, to offer hospitality to them until the following spring, and to help them find work. This arrangement worked very well.

Teacher Re-Training

Not all immigrants had been farmers in Russia or wanted to be farmers in Canada. A considerable number had been teachers. The excitement had barely subsided in Rosthern when, at the beginning of August, Toews was on his way to Manitoba. There he met with H.H. Ewert to discuss a plan for teacher re-training so that immigrants, who were teachers by profession or who had planned to pursue a teaching career but could not because of the Revolution, could continue on their chosen path in the new country. As we know, both Toews and Ewert had teachers and education on their mind at all times. The plan was simple: to allow immigrants to pursue their education at Gretna or at Rosthern on credit. The financial offer would apply to their training at the Normal School (Teachers' College) as well. Once they had a teaching position, they would begin to pay back their debt to the school. This was a good plan and it proved helpful for many. The only drawback, in Toews' view, was that those attending at Gretna were counselled to give higher priority to repayment of their school debt than to their *Reiseschuld*. He was typically anxious about the transportation debt.

The Contract?
     On that same trip to Manitoba, Toews continued south to Freeman, South Dakota, where the triennial sessions of the General Conference Mennonite Church were to be held from August 29 to September 6, 1923. The General Conference dated back to 1860 when, in the interest of renewal in worship and mission, a group of congregations broke from the (Old) Mennonite Church, and formed their own church organization. Initially, the group centred in the United States. The majority of Mennonite immigrants who arrived in the United States from Russia in the 1870s joined the General Conference through their local congregations. Over the first half of the twentieth century, a considerable number of Mennonite congregations of Russian background in Canada also joined the General Conference. This was in part because of common historical ties in Russia and also because of the mutual interest in both international and home missions.
     The General Conference Missions Committee, of which David Toews was the Canadian representative, met in Freeman at that time. It came as no great surprise to Toews that the skepticism he had encountered earlier in Kansas over the immigration project was still in the air at Freeman. In anticipation that there would be floor discussion on the immigration issue, a committee was named to meet with Toews to get clarity on where things stood. The main issue was still the fear that the contract which Toews had signed with the CPR would implicate the American Mennonites. Mennonite church papers in the United States had spread this impression in no uncertain terms. When Toews appeared before the Committee, it felt to him like an interrogation. He recounted the conversation as follows:[6]

     C.E. Krehbiel: "Did you sign the contract?"
     David Toews: "Yes."
     Krehbiel: "Upon whose recommendation and on whose authority?"
     Toews: "Upon the direction of our Board."
     Krehbiel: "Who is named in the contract?"

Toews: "The Mennonite Church of Canada."
Krehbiel: "In that case I am reassured that our churches in the United
    States are not named. Did you bring the contract with you?"
Toews: "No."
Krehbiel: "Why not?"
Toews: "I knew of no reason for bringing it along. I had no assignment
    on the program in this regard."
Krehbiel: "Would you be willing to send for the contract yet?"
Toews: "No."
Krehbiel: "Why not?"
Toews: "It wouldn't arrive here on time and, aside from that, there is no
    reason the contract should be presented here."
Krehbiel: "Did you bring your financial statement with you?"
Toews: "No."
Krehbiel: "Why not?"
Toews: "Our Board was not founded by this Conference and I received
    no request to make a presentation on the program. . . . I am rather
    weary of all this. If we don't get help among our own people, we will
    look elsewhere."
Krehbiel: "Do you have other prospects?"
Toews: "No, but I will find help if it comes to that."
Krehbiel: "Did you not promise me that you would close down the
    project now that 750 have come?"
Toews: "No, how could I do that? Once the first group had arrived, a
    second group was preparing itself to leave. The initial contract allows
    for 3000."

While criticism about what the Canadians had done continued to be
voiced, it seems that this conversation satisfied the General Conference
leadership in that they saw that what Toews and the Board had done did
not place financial obligation on the Americans.

During the remaining time at Freeman, C.E. Krehbiel was seen
gathering signatures from persons willing to make a contribution to the
transportation debt. In his memoirs, Toews expressed appreciation for
Krehbiel and regarded him as the most competent leader among the
Mennonite people. His caution must be regarded as a virtue, said Toews.[7]
After the sessions, lawyer M.H. Kratz travelled to Montreal to find out
for himself and for the Conference Executive just what the facts were
about the contract. Back home he reported that Col. Dennis had satisfied
him that the Americans had no reason to fear Toews might have made
them accountable for the *Reiseschuld.*

At the meeting of the Board of Home Missions in Freeman, Toews
requested that a monthly sum be budgeted as stipends for immigrant
ministers who could serve their people in Canada. When a counter-
suggestion was made to the effect that the current ministers of the

Canadian Conference could take care of such duties, Toews expressed his opinion rather strongly that the needs and the inner spirit of the immigrants was best understood by those ministers who had lived through their time of turmoil and suffering. Toews' request was brought to the Conference floor by the Mission Board and was accepted.[8] He returned to Rosthern from Freeman with the somewhat surprising comment: "I am convinced the Americans will not abandon us with our problems."[9] A month later, in a letter to D.H. Bender, chairman of the American Immigration Committee, Toews gave a progress report on how the new immigrants were doing, and he reiterated his hope that there would be good cooperation with Mennonites in the United States:

> Our brethren who have come from Russia are generally making a good impression. They are at work in the harvest fields and at the threshing machines. . . . We are keeping them in our homes and providing for them. This is not to cost the settlers anything. We are sure that many a cow and many a horse and many a bushel of grain will be given them free of charge. You see that we are not shirking our responsibilities toward these people. We have their welfare in view and hope that, by proper cooperation with our brethren in the United States, we shall be able to do something to start these people on new lands and put them on the way to prosperity.[10]

In the same letter Toews admitted to some major problems with entry of immigrants into Canada because of the severe restriction regarding communicable diseases. But he warded off the persistent proposal from the American committee that negotiations be made for resettlement in Mexico. It appeared to Toews that the American Mennonites were too quick to discount the possibility of a viable future in Canada.[11]

For David Toews, living with the immigration project was something of a roller-coaster ride. On the up-side was the satisfaction of seeing the immigrant groups arrive. On the down-side was the disappointment of the detention of a considerable number in Europe, both in Lechfeld and in Atlantic Park in England. Again, on the positive side was the good harvest of 1923 which meant that immigrants had work opportunities and there should be "money in the bank" for payment on the contract. On the negative side was the formidable debt that grew ever larger with every new group that came. While many made it their priority to pay off the *Reiseschuld* as quickly as possible, others chose to concentrate first on getting themselves established. This was bad news for retirement of the travel debt.

Then there was the task of finding suitable land for farming. Canada was a vast country but had some harsh conditions to contend with. Yet in the face of these odds, Toews did not back down. He was tough, he was optimistic, and he had a passion for the cause. He was bound to see the project through to a successful conclusion.

Toews would never have been able to do the work single-handedly and, indeed, he did not intend to. While he had strong feelings about some issues and directions, he believed in community ownership and mutual accountability. Of particular help was the formation of the Central Mennonite Immigration Committee (ZMIK).[12] About 130 recent immigrants gathered on September 9, 1923 in the Eigenheim Church to organize this Committee and spell out its mandate. A major task of Committee members was to search for suitable land for settlement. Besides this, their assignment included advising the Board on immigration matters, receiving new immigrants, distributing clothing and supplies, regulating money transactions, distributing monies, lending money, keeping a list of persons to be brought out from Russia, nurturing religion and the German language among the immigrants, ensuring that there was ample good literature for schooling, finding financial support for the education of prospective teachers, founding a benevolence fund for the sick, promoting the retirement of the *Reiseschuld*, and generally encouraging a sense of solidarity and peoplehood. Dietrich H. Epp, editor of *Der mennonitische Immigranten-Bote,* chaired the Committee.

Another Church Paper

One notable decision made by the ZMIK was to initiate a church paper that would serve the expanded Mennonite population. The first issue of *Der mennonitische Immigranten-Bote* (The Mennonite-Immigrant Messenger) appeared on January 14, 1924. In an introductory article David Toews, in a picturesque way, likened the appearance of this new paper to the birth of a child:

> As when a child is born into a family the older brothers and sisters approach the cradle with curiosity to view the little brother and to show him love, so it will likely be in the publication family. For quite a while already it was whispered that a new paper would be making its appearance. Now it has arrived. In a family, mother and father instruct the older siblings: Handle your younger brother with respect and be friendly to him. In our larger publication family that will not be necessary. The older brothers do not begrudge the little fellow a place in the sun, and so it should be.[13]

The *Immigranten-Bote* soon changed its name to *Der Bote*, a German church paper in circulation to this day.

Bring Money!

While in the office A.A. Friesen served as the main staff person for the ZMIK, David Toews concerned himself with the *Reiseschuld* and with other matters related to overall planning and negotiation with government, with the transportation company, and with the wider constituency. By the end of September 1923, the debt to the CPR stood at $68,000 and was growing. At that time there was still optimism that this amount and the ensuing bills could be paid off in short order. But this became more and more difficult as the debt mounted and immigrant families struggled to meet their daily financial needs. Toews applied all his wisdom to the challenge of finding funds. He contacted the Mennonite Board of Missions and Charities of eastern Pennsylvania and asked for an immediate loan of $30,000. When the Board said they were. sending Orie Miller and two others to Canada to gain more information, Toews said: "Bring money with you." They didn't follow his request, but the visit resulted in an agreement that the Board would send $5000 monthly for 11 months, a loan totalling $55,000.

Another mildly successful plan was to apply for money at local banks on the strength of credit-worthy immigrants. The Rosthern office did send a $30,000 cheque to Montreal, although some weeks after the deadline. Toews felt badly about this since, to maintain a good reputation, he wanted the first payment to be prompt. With high anxiety he waited for a reply acknowledging the payment and perhaps anticipating a reprimand. Instead, Col. Dennis sent a letter thanking profusely for the payment and noting that it had been received well within the previously arranged 30-day period of grace for each invoice. Toews had forgotten about that arrangement. He was greatly relieved![14]

By the end of 1923 the immigration count stood at about 3000 persons. The bills received for transportation costs amounted to $360,000. Although the CPR office was prompt in reminding the Board of its indebtedness and its payment schedule, it had not yet issued any harsh demands. The creditor seemed to be reasonably satisfied. Now it was time to move on with plans and arrangements for the year 1924.

Fräulein **Hooge**

One staff person without whom the work could never have been accomplished was Kaethe Hooge, long-time office secretary to David Toews and the Board. Miss Hooge was among the immigrants who came to Canada in the summer of 1923.[15] She had acquired secretarial education in Russia, including typing and some knowledge of English. Toews always called her *Fräulein* Hooge. She began employment in the office of the Board of Colonization on October 16, 1923, and retired from her position in 1962, after almost 40 years of faithful service. For 23 of those years she was Toews' secretary; for the remaining 16 years she was secretary for J.J. Thiessen, successor to Toews.[16]

Miss Hooge was an indispensable help to David Toews especially since he was out of the office for considerable stretches of time. One of her enjoyable tasks was to administer the books for the home mission work of the Canadian sector of the General Conference. She was not only secretary in the office, but also a close friend of the Toews family. Kaethe was a regular invitee to family birthday parties over the years. Her brother, Abram Hooge, married Elsie Toews (1908–2000), the third oldest daughter of David and Margarete. Fräulein Kaethe Hooge deserved most of the credit for keeping the office staff on schedule and the office books in order. Locally, in the Rosthern Mennonite Church, she was a faithful and enthusiastic teacher in the children's Sunday school department.

A New Year—1924

At a meeting of the Rosenorter Church during the first week of the new year, David Toews was able to give a positive report of immigration proceedings. Nearly 3000 persons had been welcomed in Canada to date, and the hospitality extended by Rosenorter church members had been commendable. But Toews had second thoughts about his work load. At the meeting he laid before the congregation the question whether he should withdraw from his involvement in the school and in immigration work so that he could give full attention to pastoral and administrative work in the church. It is noteworthy that, even at this stage, Toews seemed to have recognized the primacy of his role as *Ältester*. The congregation discussed the matter and passed the following resolution:

> We would wish that our *Ältester* would do more *Gemeindearbeit* (church work). Yet we recognize and appreciate the other work he is engaged in, from which our church gains blessing directly as well as indirectly. Thus we leave it to him to do as he sees best for the good of all, and we promise to support him as best we can through prayer and in practical ways.[17]

While this decision was an indication of support for the continuing leadership of Toews, it did not resolve the question of his availability. Immigration work was sure to increase rather than decrease. It would take several years before something concrete was done. In June of 1929, Johannes Regier was ordained as assistant-elder to David Toews.[18] By that time there was also a movement afoot to appoint a leading minister in each of the larger congregational centres. The issue of financial compensation for Toews' services was also never regulated. In June of 1924 the church's Finance Committee proposed that each district should compensate Toews for his work and submit the monies to the central treasury. But with that the matter was dropped. Meanwhile Toews received his regular support through his Board's financial arrangements with the CPR.

In February of 1924, the Board met to assess progress to date and to lay plans for the future. A sense of success for what happened in 1923 and a sense of urgency on the part of Mennonites in the Soviet Union motivated the Board to enter into negotiations with the CPR for a second wave of immigration in 1924. The railway company indicated its willingness to work out a deal. The Board had learned from its mistakes in the first round so this time they authorized two additional persons besides David Toews to place their signature on the contract. This was done for the sake of constituency relations, not because it was demanded by the CPR. Thus the interim president of the Board, Eli S. Hallman,[19] together with Jacob Gerbrandt, Board secretary and treasurer, placed their names on the contract along with David Toews. In March, Hallman, Toews, and A.A. Friesen travelled to Montreal to negotiate the terms. The trip to Montreal was successful. The contract specified the transport of 5000 credit passengers and 2000 passengers who would pay their own way. It is significant that Hallman of the "Swiss Mennonite" group was willing to approve the contract when in western Canada there were so many opposing voices among those who had much closer ties to the "Russian Mennonites."[20]

Toews had written to S.F. Coffman of Vineland, Ontario, whom he had never met, to join the group in Montreal. He had in mind that in 1924 some of the immigrants should stop off in Ontario to consider settlement possibilities there. For that he would need the help of Ontario (Old) Mennonites. This proved to be a good move as Coffman made a commitment to arrange hospitality for at least 1000 immigrants in the coming months. Toews spoke very appreciatively of Coffman, stating that "he certainly deserves the respect that people show him."[21] Indeed, Toews developed a high regard for the (Old) Mennonites. He wrote: "I have found these people to be open and faithful. All things are tested openly, without embellishment, and without thinking highly of themselves when they accomplish something."[22] Seated on the train while homeward bound from Montreal, Toews wrote to Coffman in a brotherly way: "We were glad to have you with us. We were much encouraged by your sympathetic attitude and I assure you that it will always be a source of great pleasure for me to recollect our meetings in Montreal."[23]

Look to the Heavens!

The twenty-second sessions of the Conference of Mennonites in Canada held in July 1924 in Drake, Saskatchewan, were special because this was the first conference where the Russian Mennonites were in attendance. Everyone was aware of the special significance of this moment. Even the women of Drake had sought to do their part by agreeing to dress simply so that the immigrant women would not feel inferior. J.G. Rempel reported that "this worked out very well."[24] And of course, David Toews was there! In his summary of the event some years later, Rempel noted that, while he had heard David Toews speak many times, "this conference sermon made the greatest impression on me of any presentations Toews made."[25] Drawing on Revelation 3:7–13, the letter to Philadelphia, he noted how a small force can accomplish great things for God. His illustrations ranged from biblical times to historical occasions to current events. He admonished church leaders to be faithful in small things in the school, in the church, and in the family. And he pointed to the great opportunity to help suffering kinfolk in Russia who found themselves in a dangerous situation.

Rempel also remembered how persons came to Ältester Toews with downcast demeanour during the conference to complain about the lack of rain. Spring had been unusually dry and the crops were languishing. Toews' memorable comment was: "Why do you stare at the ground? Look to the heavens. That's where the rain comes from!" And, added Rempel, the rains really came already during the Conference sessions.

On the subject of immigration, Toews could report with some satisfaction that, of the $360,000 bill received from the CPR in 1923, about $141,000 had been paid off. Of this amount the immigrants had contributed about $60,000. A new contract had been arranged with the CPR extending credit for 5000 more to come in 1924. The constituency was considerably more at ease now that their leader and the Board had shown their credibility. And the Board was pleased to commend the constituency for the welcome afforded their brothers and sisters in need.

Signs of Tiring

During all this time David Toews was deeply involved with the German-English Academy. He still served as secretary-treasurer of the school board. This was no simple matter since the financial problems persisted and stories of discipline problems circulated in the constituency. Toews was the constant advocate for the school even at such times. Yet, even while he tried to encourage others, he himself was showing signs of weakening. The immigration issues involved him in heavy agenda, given the burden of facing mistrust and suspicion. Then there was his continuing obligation to the Rosenorter Gemeinde with its preaching assignments and the task of baptizing and serving communion at the many local meeting places. Add to this his leadership role in the Canadian Conference and it was understandable that Toews would be tiring. Given his condition, it is not surprising that Toews overreacted when, at a delegate meeting of the school on August 1, 1924, some said that the treasurer's report was unclear and one delegate registered lack of confidence in the present secretary-treasurer. Toews took this as an insult and resigned from that position. A week later he accepted the position as chairman of the school board, which meant that he became responsible for the main oversight of the school. Typical of Toews, he took up this greater task with vigour and vision, curbed only by limitations of the time he could give to this role. He remained chair of the Board of the German-English Academy for the next 20 years until 1944.[26]

Our Beloved Canada

By then the immigrants were coming in greater numbers. Of particular significance was the hospitality provided by the Ontario Mennonites. S.F. Coffman had committed his people to welcoming over 1000 of the new arrivals, and this worked out well. David Toews was buoyed by the spirit of cooperation that prevailed and wondered why this had not been possible from the beginning. Delegates from the United States came north to check out the immigration movement and returned with good reports. The situation inspired Toews to place a statement in *Der Bote*, welcoming and encouraging the newcomers. It read, in part:

> You have come to a land that offers every peaceful citizen protection of life and possessions, and where each of you can worship as he chooses and can nurture his children in the fear of the Lord. In this respect we believe that there is no country that offers the advantages as does our beloved Canada. . . . May you, beloved brothers and sisters, find a real home here! May you live here successfully, and may your succeeding generations one day bless the day on which their forebears set foot on Canadian soil. May a bond of love and brotherhood surround us all! This feeling will allow us to discover the true word and teach us to do good deeds—so that both those who give and those who receive can rejoice.[27]

During the course of the year 1924, a total of 5048 new immigrants had arrived. As they kept coming, so did the bills from the CPR, from the detaining centres in Europe, and from hospitals in Canada. The Board of Colonization had promised Canadian officials that the Mennonite newcomers would not be a burden to the government. This meant that, when the need arose, the Board had to cover medical expenses for persons who needed hospital care, whether physical or mental. For David Toews, the financial undergirding for the project was a constant worry. And there was always the concern that immigrants were not paying as they could and should. In October of 1924 he wrote a passionate and compassionate article in *Der Bote*, requesting that immigrants, relatives, friends, and congregations do everything possible to contribute to the travel debt. He pointed out that, while the CPR had graciously trusted our people and the Board of Colonization had done the same, it was now time for churches and individuals on the local level to trust the immigrants as well by making contributions and offering loans so that the Board could liquidate the debt and the transportation company could receive its monies.[28]

To America Again

While Mennonite leaders in Canada had initiated the immigration project and had settled the first immigrants in Canada, there was always the feeling that this project was too large for them alone and the hope that Americans would want to offer substantial help. David Toews' first attempts in South Dakota, Kansas, Oklahoma, and Washington had been deeply disappointing, but he was certainly not ready to give up. In December 1924, the Board decided that he should go south to procure loans of money from Mennonites with means. Something needed to be done soon so that payments could be made to the CPR. Borrowing money from Mennonite constituents was one way to cover the fast-mounting bills. In 1924 the Board paid the railway company $146,000 of which $60,000 was borrowed money. This was still only a partial payment for the 5048 immigrants who had come during 1924.

Shortly after Christmas, Toews set out, travelling first to Kitchener and Vineland. In Kitchener he made contact with A.R. Kaufman, owner of a shoe factory, who provided a loan of $25,000 on this visit with the promise of another $25,000 at a later date. In Bluffton, Pandora, and Archibold in Ohio, as well as in Berne, Indiana, Toews found many individuals who were sympathetic to the immigration cause, and he was able to gather some funds. He was considerably more encouraged by this trip than by previous attempts.

After a short stop back home, he set out for the United States again, this time on a seven-week trip to Minnesota, South Dakota, and Kansas. For this excursion he was joined by a recent immigrant, Jacob H. Janzen. Toews and Janzen had quickly developed a mutual appreciation and respect for each other. Toews felt that it would add to the integrity of his visit to take along someone who could speak first-hand out of the Russian experience of turmoil and suffering.

Toews' report on this latter visit was mostly positive, as people expressed their sympathy for the immigrants and shared of their means. Evening presentations in the churches were followed the next day by numerous contacts of all kinds. We are told of an elderly mother who brought $150 from her savings box, of an aged man who provided a loan of $400, and of another person who added another $1000 to the loan of $700 he had made previously. Then there was the person who paid the *Reiseschuld* for an entire family and extended an additional loan of $1000 to assist others.[29] Toews also reported that the General Conference executive, with whom he conferred while in Kansas, had declared willingness to support the Canadian effort through solicitation of funds and through the home mission program.

A Matter of Trust

It became evident from Toews' writings in *Der Bote* during the first six months of 1925 that the transportation debt weighed heavily on his mind and on his conscience. In a message to the immigrants of 1923 and 1924, published in mid-March of 1925, he outlined the various ways in which the Board was carrying and seeking to alleviate the weight of its obligations. Then he followed with an urgent appeal to the new immigrants and to each of the churches to take their obligation to the CPR with utter seriousness. While no one should be expected to contribute beyond what they were able, the *Reiseschuld* should be a matter of top priority. Those who had benefitted to date by leaving Russia should remember that many more were waiting to come. But their coming would depend in large part on whether the current debt could be retired. The article served to announce the appointment of H.B. Janz as the person authorized by the Board to visit all regions where immigrants were to be found, there to discuss their obligations and make arrangements for collections.[30] In a follow-up article in early July 1925, Toews spoke passionately and persistently to the same issue:

> If there would be a united response to the situation among those who are able to help, it would be possible to carry forward with the work this year. This is what we expect. We believe God will open doors for us. Would we be able to justify ourselves if, because of mistrust, misdirected convenience, or misdirected initiative, we would default on our obligation? The matter is large, serious, and pressing. It is not appropriate to do petty calculations or to defer because of business-minded distractions. The time has come to act. If it were your brother, your sister, your father, your mother, or your child who was among those for whom everything was at risk, who were waiting over there for the possibility of immigrating, then I surmise that much would be possible.

In the word of God we are admonished to exercise love for the wider community in addition to our families. The question the apostle Paul once asked our Lord on the way from Jerusalem to Damascus is in order for each of us: "Lord, what would you have me to do?"[31]

Toews followed up on this emphasis in his Conference address at the 23rd annual sessions of the Canadian delegate body in July of 1925 in Eigenheim. Basing his remarks on 1 Thessalonians 1:1–2, he centred on faith as the key to good works. Faith evokes works which find expression in our offer of assistance toward all suffering people. In his immigration report, Toews noted that to date 7601 immigrants had arrived in Canada. The total debt to the CPR for the years 1923–1924 was $812,718, of which $308,000 has been paid off. In addition there had been the debt accumulating as immigrants continued to come in 1925. The CPR was willing to offer further services, provided they received a payment of $100,000 by August 31. And the money was found! In an article dated August 31, Toews began: "Bless the Lord, O my soul, and all that is within me, bless his holy name; bless the Lord, and forget not all the good he has done to you." Then he added: "With these thoughts August 31 will long be remembered by us." The $100,000 was in hand and was sent to the railway offices in Montreal. He closed with a note of thanks to all who contributed and with an appeal for material aid for the needy both in Canada and in Russia.[32]

An Inner Bond

September 20, 1925 was a special day in the life of the Toews family. On that date, 25 years earlier, David and Margarete had joined hands and hearts in marriage. As was the custom among Mennonites, this anniversary date called for celebration to which everyone was welcome. As David Toews said, "We had not sent special invitations to people, but we believed that all who would find it possible to come and who loved us would make a point of being there."[33] The editor of *Der Bote*, D.H. Epp, had announced the "silver wedding" across Canada and had invited greetings. A large tent was erected on the Toews' yard, food was prepared, and on the appointed day everything was in readiness. As expected, people came from near and far, and soon the tent was filled to capacity. Relatives from Aberdeen, Idaho, also took the occasion to pay a visit to Rosthern at that time.

The program featured at least seven speakers—Johannes Regier, brother-in-law Jacob Klassen, Johann J. Klassen, Daniel Loewen, D.H. Rempel, Johann Gerbrandt, and David Epp. Three women from the church offered poetry recitations. The choir, led by Dietrich H. Epp, sang

The David Toews family in 1925, the year of Margarete and David's 25th wedding anniversary. Front row, from left: *Elsie, Anna, Mother Margarete, Irene, Father David, Elma, Dorothy;* back row: *Herman Riesen, Marie (Toews) Riesen, Louise, Margaret, Catherine (Friesen) Toews, Benno.* Photo: *Saskatchewan Mennonite Historian*

several songs. The Toews children made various contributions. Greetings and good wishes were conveyed from persons throughout the Canadian constituency. Many well-wishers brought gifts, but according to the parents,

> the best part of the day was to think that our children—Marie, Benno, Margarete, Else, Dora, Louise, Elma, Anna, and Irene—have all been kept in good health and that an inner bond of love encircles our family. We saw in our children the most precious thing we have. Their poems were of special significance. We have come victorious through many a battle; we have weathered many a storm; we have carried many worries and endured many troubles. There we stood in the circle of our loved ones, in reasonably good health, after twenty-five years of pilgrimage.

Toews always gave special recognition to Margarete, his faithful spouse. The sentiments he felt on the occasion of this anniversary are best conveyed in his own words, written some years later:

> My beloved wife has had to carry a heavy load because of our children for whom she was constantly a devoted mother. Because of me and my

formidable responsibilities in the school, in the church, and in society, she had extra burdens. Besides, because of my many obligations, I found it difficult to take care of my personal financial situation, a matter which often made me glum and depressed.[34]

The mention of Toews' financial situation motivated him to reflect on the difficulty of the minister in this regard. He continued in his "Memoirs:"

Our people are strange in that they expect the minister, and in particular the *Ältester*, to be ready at all times to do sacrificial service without help or remuneration. But when something goes awry, then the criticisms come, sometimes very severe and unjustified. In such matters I am too sensitive, awaiting a thank-you and some recognition after I have really worked sacrificially and put myself on the line, while others only think of themselves and then demonstrate how they can manage quite well without any help. But enough of that! On festive occasions such as this, and also when I got into deep trouble, loyal friends stood by me. At such times I saw love in operation and there was a willingness to help.[35]

These reflections revealed the inner heart and soul of David Toews.

The October 14 issue of *Der Bote* carried a note signed by David and Margarete Toews. They expressed warm thanks for all the letters and gifts that came their way. They spoke of September 20 as an abiding point of reference that would give them encouragement. If dark days should come again, they would "retreat for a brief period to bask in the sunshine of the love represented" by the festival. The note closed: "We couldn't have imagined a better day."[36]

David Toews Was Here!

At an end-of-the-year meeting of Russian Mennonite immigrants on December 10 and 11, 1925 in Rosthern, David Toews gave his report on the progress of immigration and the state of the debt.[37] During 1925, 5000 new immigrants arrived, bringing the total over three years to 12,000. In 1925, the debt was decreased by another $240,000, of which $100,000 was money borrowed by the Board. In total, $449,000 had been paid to the CPR, of which the immigrants had collected and paid $252,000. The $449,000 included $185,000 of loan money of which $45,000 came from the Eastern Mennonite Board of Missions and Charities in Pennsylvania, $27,000 from Mennonites in Ontario, and another $50,000 from a non-Mennonite friend of the cause. The rest of the loan money came from contributors in western Canada.

Toews felt both thankful and challenged by what had been accomplished. In his written report for the December meeting he stated:

Many of our immigrants would like to shake the hands of those who have given gifts, and say, "May God reward you." Yet—is there anything, O man, that you have not received? To give is more blessed than to receive. . . . It is certainly not to our personal credit that we have come away luckier than most in these difficult times. One thing is clear to me: We who have been spared the difficulties will be put to the test on the basis of our Christian attitude toward the misfortunes of our brothers and sisters. It would be good if in these times we would not forget the words from the Epistle of James: "Faith without works is dead."[38]

Toward the conclusion of the meeting the immigrants decided to forward an expression of thanks to David Toews. The citation read as follows:

Dear Brother Toews! The delegate conference of the Russian Mennonite immigrants has today gained a clear picture of the activity of the Board, in general, and of your personal work in the great task of immigration, in particular. The delegate gathering recognizes the great role you have played and the highly significant impact you have made in this historic work on behalf of our people, which was dependent finally on your personal advocacy with a heart full of love and compassion for our need. It was you who brought the influence of your person and of your entire existence to effect the rescue of those hard-pressed brethren in the faith in Russia who were yearning for rescue and who are now afforded the opportunity to find a new home land. The gathering recognizes that even the continuing work is thankfully dependent upon your tireless efforts, and therefore it is the desire of the delegate gathering to express its deeply felt gratitude and recognition of your service. Your selfless work cannot be repaid in any material way; it will have a firm place in the history of our people, and we can only extend to you a hearty, "Vergelt's Gott" (May God reward you). The God of all grace, who sees what happens in secret, will not leave unrewarded your advocacy on behalf of our faith community, and we thank Him that in you he has sent us a helper.[39]

Words of encouragement and assurance, spoken to a sometimes maligned David Toews, helped him stand his ground and move forward in the sometimes overwhelming task that had become his lot.

11
Travel and Trouble
1926

With the great "Mennonite exodus" on track, and many pilgrims already settled in the "promised land," David Toews turned more and more to matters of business that arose as a result of the immigration as such. This entailed trips to Ottawa and Montreal as well as an extensive trip overseas to visit those travellers who were held up, so to speak, by the wayside. The year 1926 brought not only those kinds of expected obligations but also some surprises, mostly of the troublesome kind. During the course of the year, David Toews' faith was severely tested more often than he might have expected.

Ordination of Jacob H. Janzen
It was February 11, 1926. David Toews bade farewell to his family and embarked on an extended trip that would take him across the ocean to Europe. Before boarding ship, Toews needed to attend to assignments along the way. The church in Waterloo had invited him to officiate at the ordination of his good friend, Jacob H. Janzen, as elder of the congregation.[1] The service took place on Sunday, February 14 at First Mennonite Church on King Street which was packed for the occasion. Sermons were delivered by local ministers, Jacob Reimer and C.F. Derstine. David Toews gave the main address and conducted the ordination service.[2]

To Ottawa and Montreal
Next morning David Toews and Jacob H. Janzen made their way to Ottawa by train. There a number of government officials awaited them, including the Prime Minister, William Lyon Mackenzie King. King had been instrumental in reversing the earlier Order-in-Council that had placed a prohibition on Mennonite immigration to Canada. Toews always found King to be friendly toward him and a true friend of Mennonites.

From Ottawa, Janzen and Toews travelled to Montreal where they met CPR officials in the railway's Office of the Department of Colonization, Agriculture and Development. The date of this meeting was probably February 16 and 17. Its purpose was to negotiate further credit for immigrant passage to Canada. Again the signing of documents was part of this visit, but this time Toews was confident that he was signing on behalf of the Board and by now it was clear that, at least formally and legally, his signature was not encumbering all Mennonite organizations in North America. Yet in a way the reputation of all Mennonite people was on the line. Upon his return home, Janzen wrote an article for *Der Bote* on the encounter between Toews and Col. Dennis in the CPR building. Dated February 19, it depicted Col. Dennis as a stately and dignified man with kind eyes. Then Janzen wrote of David Toews:

> Opposite [Col. Dennis] sits Brother David Toews, a humble man of our people. I have often observed him as he speaks on behalf of them. The worries, which this work brings with it, have engraved deep furrows in his brow. Much weighs on his shoulders. He is the man who took it upon himself to give his personal signature on behalf of our people, even while many thought this was too risky a step and withdrew from the immigration project. He is the man whose endorsement was accepted and recognized as valid by the clever and business-like Canadian Pacific Railway Company, for in him the CPR recognized a person who stands by his word. Despite wrongful judgment which he experienced from many sides, he is one who carries through with a task, and not for his own gain. Even while many calculate how much he gains from the whole enterprise, they miscalculate. Despite the massive operation which Brother Toews leads, he is today by no means a rich man, and I fear that he never will be. And why? I respect him as too good-hearted and too honest for that! With that I am not saying that all rich people are mean-spirited and dishonest. . . . What I meant to say is that, because of his sincerity, Brother Toews would never be able to acquire great wealth from the immigration project. On the 24th of February [more likely the 17th of February] two men faced each other in the Office of the Department of Colonization and, on the basis of the simple and honest word of Brother Toews, a far-reaching agreement was reached. It was agreed that many more who do not feel safe in Russia should yet be helped, and I am of the firm conviction that they will be. In those times of serious decision-making and in private conversations with immigrants I have always admired the confidence and the faith in God shown by our Brother Toews.[3]

After the meeting with CPR officials, Janzen returned to Waterloo and Toews took the train to St. John, New Brunswick, where, on February 19, he boarded the CPR ocean liner *Montclaire* for the seven-day journey to Liverpool, England. The trip had to be taken on a CPR ship since that company was providing the ticket as well as accommodations in Europe.

To Europe

The idea of a trip to Europe was suggested in the fall of 1925 by Col. Dennis of the Canadian Pacific Railway who was present at a meeting of the Board of Colonization. Such a visit would afford the Board a chance to view the immigration enterprise from the other side of the ocean. When it came to choosing who should go, there was no question who that would be. The numbers of would-be immigrants detained on the other side of the Atlantic Ocean because of communicable diseases remained substantial. Families who had left loved ones behind were anxious about them. So it was that David Toews found himself on the high seas headed for Europe. His dear Margarete had been hesitant about this undertaking as he would be away from home for a long time, but she knew David must go. He, too, had his reservations, but he went, trusting in God, the One who prepares the way and who provides resources in times of need. Before setting sail, Toews sent a message to his constituency:

> I have no idea what I will accomplish in England and in Germany. The law does not permit persons who carry communicable diseases to enter

Centre front is Irene, youngest of the Toews girls, with sisters Anna and Elma (right) and two friends, ca. 1926. Even though Toews felt duty-bound to make his many trips, he missed his wife and growing family a great deal.

the country. There's nothing I can do to change the law. I sincerely want to do whatever I can to help. Remember me in your prayers and commit this matter to the Lord. As I close, the train is pulling into the station at St. John. May God watch over you. Till we meet again![4]

In any case, his heart was considerably lightened by successful arrangements completed in Montreal. The CPR had extended further credit to the project that lay so close to his heart. Then again, Toews' positive spirit was considerably dampened by seasickness during the entire seven-day voyage. While on the high seas he resolved that this would certainly be his last ocean trip. However, upon arrival in Liverpool, the discomfort left as quickly as it had come. A four-hour train ride brought him to historic London where CPR officials were awaiting his arrival.

Office Fire

Perhaps Toews' anxiety would have increased considerably if he had known, as he found out by way of a telegram delivered upon his arrival in London that, on February 21 while he was on the high seas, the office of the Board of Colonization in Rosthern had burned down. A fire, which had begun in the building adjacent to the bank in which the Board offices were housed on the second floor, had also engulfed the bank building. Fortunately the files were rescued before the fire reached them. Damage to Board property amounted to $210. In the telegram, office manager A.A. Friesen suggested it would probably be a good idea to take this occasion to move the office to Saskatoon so that administration could be done from an urban centre. While Toews saw some advantages to this, not the least being that the Board administrators would be better shielded from constituency scrutiny, he did not support the move because of the higher costs this would entail. By the time Toews returned from his travels, the Board office had been moved to rented quarters in Rosthern. To his chagrin, Toews found that, in carrying out remodelling in the new facilities, Friesen had relegated Toews to a small office in the back corner. Toews considered this to be a "somewhat odd and quite 'step-motherly'" treatment. "The arrangement had the appearance that as manager, Friesen wanted to control me as well," wrote Toews in his "Memoirs."[5] In time, Toews rearranged the space to suit himself.

London

In London Toews engaged in high-level discussions with officials of the CPR, with immigration officials, and with medical doctors. Toews was hosted by Mr. Baird of the CPR who showed him the sights of the historic city of London and introduced him to important officials. Of particular importance were meetings with the official doctors who had the responsibility to scrutinize Mennonite immigrants. There was Dr. Jeffs, a rather reserved man entrusted with applying Canadian restrictions, which he did with great exactness. Then there was Dr. Hummel, the CPR's medical doctor, who also upheld rigid principles with respect to communicable diseases. These men gave Toews the impression that there would be little he could do for the immigrants who were held back.[6] Mr. Baird took Toews to Atlantic Park, the detention centre in Southampton where 39 Mennonite immigrants were housed. Toews found the conditions of their care to be good and their treatment adequate. In the local hospital he visited three seriously ill immigrants, all of them suffering from tuberculosis. Of the three, one eventually returned to Russia; another suffered a mental breakdown because of the stress of his situation; and a third was able to come to Canada, thanks to Toews' negotiations on his behalf.

Germany

From England, Toews proceeded to Hamburg, Germany, by way of Holland. There he was met by Benjamin H. Unruh of Karlsruhe and Christian Neff.[7] While a teacher at Halbstadt in Russia, Unruh had been centrally involved in representing the Mennonites immediately following the Russian Revolution of 1917. He had chaired the All-Russian Mennonite Congress, called in the summer of 1917, that sought to deal with crucial issues of that day.[8] He had also been part of the four-person Study Commission that came to North America in 1920 to report on conditions in Russia and to explore immigration possibilities.[9] At this time, Unruh lived in Karlsruhe, Germany, where he was teaching and from where he was offering assistance to the immigration cause. Unruh had a theology degree in church history. Christian Neff, long-time pastor of the Weierhof Mennonite Church in the Palatinate in Germany, was a prominent scholar and leader in German Mennonite circles. Unruh and Neff had worked in Germany to provide a bridge for immigrants on their way from Russia to Canada. Toews was impressed with these two men with whom he had often corresponded but was now meeting for the first time.

At the immigration centre in Hamburg, Toews visited with the 18 people, most of whom had been there for about three years. In the recent past as many as 700 had been detained at one time. Toews spoke positively of the way the German Mennonites were offering a helping hand to these people in need. Then he went on to Lechfeld where many more were awaiting their release. Some were eventually able to continue on to Canada; others chose to stay with their detained family members. The trip had the effect of reminding officials that they should do everything possible to provide good care for the immigrants and, if at all possible, to send them on their way to their intended destination. The trip touched the heart of David Toews so much that these folks were continually on his mind. He knew from earliest childhood what it was like to be underway and to yearn for a place of refuge. He resolved anew to do all he could to urge the resolution of this problematic aspect of the Mennonite exodus. His travel report in *Der Bote* included the following reflection:

> How many times have I sung the song to myself: "Befiel du deine Wege, und was dein Herze kränkt . . ."(Commit your way to the Lord, and whatever your heart finds troublesome . . .), but I came to cherish this hymn in a whole new way when I heard it sung out of the depths of the heart by our detained immigrants at Atlantic Park and in Hamburg. We learn many of the truths and lessons of Scripture only in the crucible of life's experiences.[10]

Toews' compassion for detained immigrants revealed his pastoral heart.

Following his visits to Atlantic Park, Hamburg, and Lechfeld, he travelled with Unruh to the Weierhof, a village of historic Mennonite importance in central Germany. There he attended a Bible Conference which brought together Mennonite leaders from Germany and Switzerland. Unruh was one of the conference speakers. At the Weierhof, Toews became reacquainted with Jacob Kroeker of Wernigerode who had visited churches in western Canada in 1922 at the height of the time when the Board was under severe criticism. Kroeker had provided encouragement to Toews at that time and did so again now. At the close of the conference, after Toews had addressed the group on a biblical text and reported on the immigration project, Kroeker invoked a blessing upon Toews with the following words:

> Blessed, yes blessed indeed, is he whose help is the God of Jacob;
>   he who lets nothing separate him from God;
>   who trusts with confidence in Jesus Christ;
>   whose support comes from the Lord.
> Such a person always receives the best counsel for his onward way.
> Hallelujah.[11]

David Toews was greatly encouraged by this expression of support for his difficult ministry, coming as it did from European Mennonite leaders.

Prussia

Leaving the Weierhof, Toews travelled by way of Berlin to Marienburg, the area from which his parents had migrated to Russia in 1869. Many of Margarete's relatives as well as some of David's distant relatives still lived there. He found a hearty welcome among these Mennonite people and was asked to preach on several occasions. Everyone was interested in the situation in Russia and the circumstances of the new immigrants to Canada. Of special significance was a meeting in Danzig of Mennonite leaders from all over Europe to confer on international relief efforts. There Toews sometimes took centre stage since the major agenda of the discussion dealt with the suffering Mennonites in Russia. In reflecting on this mini-conference in Danzig, Toews wrote:

> The coming together in Danzig will remain in my memory for a long time. Especially in these difficult times it becomes important that we have connections with various groups of our brotherhood all over the world so that we can give mutual help and support to one another. We do not all have the same gifts nor the same means with which to help others, but if the relationships are there, we will always find opportunity for one person to help another, and to lift weary hands. Perhaps in our day we spend too much energy in strife, and we sin by speaking too harshly and unjustly against those brothers in the faith who are geographically distanced from us. Such things accomplish nothing.[12]

Holland

Soon it was time to turn westward. In Holland Toews met with Mennonite leaders to discuss questions of migration and transportation. The Dutch Mennonites tended to promote the use of the Holland American Steamship Line. As well, they were inclined to help immigrants settle in Mexico. Toews was able to provide a satisfactory rationale for the continued use of the CPR. As well, he cautioned against Mexico and spoke in favour of resettlement in Canada. Toews found the Dutch Mennonites to be reasonable and understanding in their outlook and he quite enjoyed his relationships with them. He said of them:

> I have learned to appreciate the Dutch folk the more I have come to know them. In their religious views they may be somewhat liberal (*frei*); yet there are many positive Christians and persons of Mennonite conviction who stand firmly upon the foundation of our fathers. I am very pleased that I could get to know some Dutch leaders and that I was able to work with them in various ways. A number of our immigrants were hosted by them and received good care so they could be healed of their illnesses.[13]

Back in Southampton Toews again met with officials. His purpose was to urge that those detained should be given every possible benefit of the doubt. A.A. Friesen had wanted Toews to request that the CPR should bear the cost of their upkeep along the way. But Toews felt he could not request this, so their "room and board" was added to the ever-increasing *Reiseschuld.* Meanwhile, his urging did produce some results. Most of the detainees at Atlantic Park in Southampton, whom Toews had met on his way westward, were already on their way or scheduled to leave for Canada shortly.

Home via Scotland

In London, Toews was informed that Col. Dennis was on the high seas, heading for Liverpool, and that he would be arriving shortly after the Easter weekend. It was hoped that Toews could wait to meet with him and the England-based officials. Rather than stay in London, Toews expressed the wish to take a weekend side-trip to Scotland. A ticket was readily provided by the CPR and an official was contacted in Glasgow who would look after him there and take him to Edinburgh as well. Thus it was that he experienced Easter in Scotland. Back in Liverpool after the weekend, Toews and an entourage of officials—Moore, Baird, Edwards, Hampson, and Drury—met Col. Dennis as he stepped off the ship and accompanied him to a hotel for a meeting. There it was agreed that in 1926 another 1800 immigrants could come on credit and 3000 on up-front cash. It was also emphasized that only persons of good character and persons free of certain diseases should be allowed to come. There was agreement that some flexibility would be considered in cases where only one member of a family was found to have a communicable disease. While the problems were minimal compared to the number of immigrants that were being transported and resettled successfully, the difficult cases had created a great deal of work and worry.

After the meeting, the group accompanied Toews to the train which took him to Glasgow where he boarded the *Metagama* bound for Canada. He was given first-class accommodations and was assigned a place at the captain's table. The captain befriended Toews, invited him repeatedly to sit on the bridge, and gave him a personal tour of the inner workings of the entire ship. On the way home, Toews was seasick for only four of the seven days. After a stop-over in Montreal where he reported to the CPR officials on his trip, he had an uneventful train ride back to Saskatoon and then to Rosthern. Back in the family home, he found that things had gone their normal course.[14]

Toews arrived home on April 23 after two months of travel. At the Rosthern train station he was met by a welcome group of friends and relatives. In the evening a choir of young people, under the leadership of teacher Franz Thiessen, gathered outside at the front of the house and sang a song of welcome:

Gott grüsse dich!
Kein andrer Gruss gleicht dem an Innigkeit;
Kein andrer Gruss passt so zu aller Zeit.
Wenn dieser Gruss so recht von Herzen geht
Gilt bei dem lieben Gott ein Grusz so viel wie ein Gebet.
Gott grüsse dich!

Greetings to you in the name of God!
No other greeting equals this one in sincerity;
No other greeting is as suitable for all occasions as this one.
When this greeting truly comes from the heart
It counts before God as much as would a prayer.
Greetings to you in the name of God.

Toews ended his written account of the Europe trip with warm sentiment about his work in Canada:

> Surely the nicest part about travelling is coming home. So it was now again. It is interesting to travel in a strange country, yet such a country can never be called home. My earthly home has become Canada and that is probably how it will remain. In future it is here that I want to dedicate myself to work in the church, to the school, and to the newly arrived immigrants. May my life increasingly become a life of service and may it please the Lord to make me a blessing to others.[15]

As is true for every trip that David Toews made, he had become fully engaged with the people and the situations he encountered. While he had left his mark on those he met, his heart was in turn touched by those he encountered along the way. Of his sojourn to England, Germany, Prussia, and Holland, it can be said once again, "David Toews was here!"

A.A. Friesen Resignation

It would have been good if everything back in Rosthern had been running calmly and smoothly in Toews' absence, but that was not the case. Only a few weeks after Toews returned, office manager A.A. Friesen submitted his letter of resignation. On the one hand Toews regretted this decision. Friesen was an astute business manager who had kept the massive amount of administrative work under good management. On the other hand, there had been tensions between Toews and Friesen. Early on, Toews had reluctantly given Friesen permission to smoke in his office, but this was becoming an irritant, in part because he and the other co-workers had to breathe the office air, in part because visitors from the constituency who regarded the work of the Board as church work found the atmosphere inappropriate. One might expect this in a secular corporation office but not in the office of the Mennonite Board of Colonization.

There were other tensions as well. The arrangement was that both Friesen and Toews were required to sign cheques that were sent out from the office. On at least one occasion, Friesen objected to a certain payment and refused to sign a cheque that Toews had requisitioned and signed. In his opinion, the payment was not justified. In one case, Toews had promised that the sanatorium bills would be paid for Margaret Wiebe, a tuberculosis patient. Friesen questioned whether Toews had the right to make such a decision and disagreed with Toews' policy on this matter.[16] Such incidents influenced the relationship of these two leading persons in the immigration story. The final straw apparently came when, upon Toews' return from his trip, Friesen asked whether he had approached the CPR on his behalf to ask for an increase in his monthly stipend. Toews had not done so because, as he said, it had slipped his mind and also that such a request would have fallen on deaf ears in Montreal.[17] Furthermore, there had been the "renovations incident" reported earlier. In any case, Friesen addressed his resignation to the Board which met on May 6. It was a brief letter stating that the basis for his resignation, effective as soon as possible, was "the necessity of providing better for my family."[18]

At a subsequent Board meeting on May 27 at which Friesen was present, he was asked whether he still held to his decision—in its reply the Board had expressed the wish that he should continue on as long as possible. When no clear word was forthcoming, the Board voted to accept his resignation. Regarding the resignation, Toews commented:

> Friesen and I did not always agree but I believed, nonetheless, that we could work well together. There were some things about him that I did not appreciate, and from time to time we had minor disagreements. I did not appreciate how he sometimes handled people . . . very much from a position of superiority.[19]

As for Friesen, he was a keen administrator who had distinct ideas about how things should operate. He sometimes found it frustrating to work alongside and under Toews who, of his own admission, did not have administrative skills but took a more pastoral approach to matters. Friesen and his family eventually moved to Rabbit Lake, Saskatchewan, where he developed a lumber and hardware business. People in that community who remember him to this day, speak well of his contribution to community life there. Daniel P. Enns was appointed as secretary-treasurer in Friesen's place and served in this position for many years.

The Braun-Friesen Fiasco

Of the immigrants who arrived in Canada, a few made life difficult for David Toews and for the Mennonite constituency. The reputation of the immigration project depended not only on a contract and on successful debt retirement but also on the good character of these new would-be citizens of Canada. Among the immigrants was one Isaak Braun of Halbstadt, Ukraine, who, together with his wife and two children, arrived in Rosthern in July of 1924. Like most of the others, Braun made plans to buy a plot of land. He had his eyes on a piece of property in Renata, British Columbia. While in Rosthern, Braun became acquainted with Heinrich P. Friesen, a business man and farmer involved in some land deals with Old Colony Mennonites who were selling their properties and moving to Mexico. Friesen was the brother of Isaak P. Friesen from whom David Toews had borrowed money earlier, which he still owed at the time. Before leaving for Renata, Braun borrowed $5000 from H.P. Friesen, at 6 percent interest. With that he was on his way to the mountains.

In the next months, H.P. Friesen received letters from Braun who implied the reverse of what had actually happened; that is, Braun asked Friesen to return the $5000 he had (supposedly) lent Friesen since he had found a piece of land and needed to pay for it. When Friesen objected, Braun claimed he had a note to "prove" it. He came to Rosthern in December of 1924 and, with the help of friends in the area, he took Friesen to court over the matter. Meanwhile, Braun was able to rouse considerable public sentiment in the community against Friesen.

What did this have to do with David Toews? Early in December of 1924, Heinrich P. Friesen visited Toews at his Board of Colonization office, showed him five letters received from Isaak Braun, and told him his side of the story. According to brother George P. Friesen—who later wrote an account of the whole affair in a booklet entitled, *Fangs of Bolshevism*—Toews had little to say to Heinrich P. Friesen on that occasion.[20] Perhaps he was taken aback by the whole affair; perhaps he was reluctant to take sides, not knowing the facts of the situation. This hesitation on the part of Toews brought him under suspicion, particularly by Heinrich Friesen. He felt Toews should immediately have come to his aid.

A somewhat bizarre incident, which involved David Toews, occurred in Rosthern the evening of February 20, 1925, a few days before the Braun-Friesen court case was to open in Saskatoon. On that day Heinrich P. Friesen paid a visit to the home of a Mr. Berg whom he wanted to question about Braun. Friesen had heard that Berg might be able to help him get perspective on his plight. Berg told Friesen to come back in an hour and that, for a bribe, he would give him important information. Friesen returned and was just getting settled when Isaak Braun and Isaak Ediger rushed in and held Friesen down. Then one of them left and came back with David Toews. As Toews surveyed the scene, they told him they caught Friesen trying to bribe Berg to testify against Braun. According to George P. Friesen's account of this event, "Bishop Toews did not say a word,"[21] which could imply that he favoured Braun and his supporters rather than his own parishioner.

What did David Toews know about the facts of the situation? Was he siding with Braun? Or did he just want to wash his hands of this fiasco? These were some of the questions circulating in the rumour mill of the constituency. It seems that A.A. Friesen of the Board office had some connection with Braun and went with Braun to the office of the Rosthern lawyer, Mr. March, who assisted him in preparing his case. March had often provided legal counsel for the Colonization Board. Be that as it may, Heinrich P. Friesen had expected that Toews, as his pastor, would believe his story and would discipline Braun. The fact that, for whatever reason, the bishop of the church and director of the Board did not commit himself one way or another left him open to criticism and rumours that the Board might have been supporting Braun's claim that he had been wronged.

The hearings commenced on February 24, 1925. Braun told the court that when he came from Ukraine he had brought along $5000 dollars, which he had stored in the bottom of his trunk. He also produced an "I owe you" note with what looked like the falsified signature of Heinrich P. Friesen on it. What is more, in court he called forth two youths from the Rosthern area, Jacob Friesen and Frank Hildebrand, as witnesses. They claimed they had seen an envelope pass from Braun's hands to Friesen's in the foyer of a hotel in Saskatoon on August 29, 1924. This hearing, which was only the first chapter in what became a notorious case, ended with Braun winning. Historian Frank H. Epp drew this conclusion: "[W]ith the help of forged documents, false witnesses, and through unusual trickery and cunning, Braun won his case at a non-jury sitting of the Court of King's Bench in Saskatoon, Feb. 25, 1925."[22] A troubled Friesen had to pay out $5000 plus interest plus court costs, although that was by no means the end of the matter. The fact that the court ruled against Friesen and in favour of Braun would have given David Toews some reason to support Braun.

Seven months later, in October of 1925, the case was reopened. This time Heinrich P. Friesen had registered a judgment against Braun for the recovery of his money. Since by now both young men, Friesen and Hildebrand, had confessed they had lied about seeing Isaak Braun hand

Heinrich Friesen money in a Saskatoon hotel lobby, the case against Braun seemed to be mounting. The two young would-be witnesses were charged with perjury, and each served time in jail, nine months and eight months respectively, in Prince Albert.[23] The arduous court case of Friesen against Braun, presided over by Justice McKenzie, lasted several months. In the end, Friesen won his case and Braun was ordered to return the original $5000 to Friesen. The judge suggested that Braun be deported back to the Soviet Union and that the Mennonite society take responsibility for his return. Meanwhile, Braun was committed to prison in Prince Albert. He appealed the McKenzie decision but on May 3, 1926, five judges upheld the verdict against him.[24] Then Braun brought forward a charge of perjury against Friesen, supported by some falsified letters. After a four-month lull during which time Braun was still in the Prince Albert prison, the Appeals Court was ready to hear Braun's defense. With the help of his friends, he had gathered monetary and moral support for yet another court process that began in September of 1926. By mid-October the court had decided in favour of Friesen. Braun appealed the conviction and was released on bail. Proceedings on the appeal began in May of 1927, continued in November of that year, and finally concluded on October 17, 1928. On that date Braun was conclusively charged with fabrication of evidence. On October 28, 1928 he was sentenced to five years in the penitentiary to be followed by deportation back to Russia.[25]

What was David Toews' stand during this time? Apparently he still chose to reserve judgment on the case. In an open articles in *Der Bote* he wrote as follows:

> The actual case is this, that Braun says he lent Friesen $5000, and Friesen denies this. Only God and these two men know what the actual situation is. As a consequence of the process, Braun is now in prison for five years. How, after all this, a human being can still take satisfaction in throwing stones at this poor man and his family after all their misfortune is a mystery to me. . . . The evidence could be clearer. . . . However, I do not want to sort out the case here, since I am not in a position to do so. I do want to address the matter of people finding fault with our Board.[26]

Toews then went on to say he was absolutely certain that the Board as such had nothing to do with the case, although some Board members were drawn into the matter as individuals. In that regard he mentioned A.A. Friesen, but assured his readers that Friesen was an honourable person. Toews then noted that he himself was named in the letter with the implication that he was a collaborator with Braun. Toews clarified his involvement:

First, when Braun was in prison and unable to work on his citizenship papers, I assisted him in this matter. Secondly, when Braun did not have money to bring his situation to court, I accompanied some brothers to seek financial help for him. These two things I did from the standpoint that I regard every person as sincere until such a time as I am convinced to the contrary. And every person should have the chance to prove his possible innocence.[27]

It seems that Toews was not easily persuaded of Braun's guilt. In any case, he felt that Braun was entitled to a trial that would clarify the matter once and for all. In principle, Toews wanted to think well of his immigrants but in this case he probably strained his principles unduly. By the time he wrote his "Memoirs" in 1934, he had developed a clear opinion and said that "[Braun] was a villain of the highest order."[28]

Criticisms

Meanwhile, there was considerable "foot dragging" by recently-arrived families when it came to travel-debt retirement. In a letter dated June 9, 1926, Toews once again encouraged immigrants to "pay up." "Consider this," he wrote, "that when we undertook this project, we were not establishing it as a business venture. The whole enterprise was based on trusting relationships. We trusted our brothers, whom we as yet did not know, and the CPR trusted us."[29]

After reporting on the number of persons who had already come, the amount of debt incurred, and the amount of debt retired, Toews admonished constituents not to think that the CPR would wait forever: "Rather, we have obligated ourselves, and we need to honour our commitments. Those who are tempted to think they can put things off should say: 'Get thee behind me, Satan.' And those who are totally negligent should feel appropriate judgment upon themselves."[30] His final appeal was on behalf of those who still wanted to escape their lot in Russia: "We can only help our brothers overseas if we pull together in meeting our obligations at home."

But the criticisms kept coming anyway. In the spring of 1926 a letter from someone in Dalmeny, Saskatchewan, appeared in *Der Bote*. The anonymous writer charged the directorship of the Board of Colonization, specifically David Toews and A.A. Friesen, with enriching themselves personally by charging a tax of seven dollars per immigrant above the actual cost of the travel ticket. Toews was assigned by the Board to answer the charge. After expressing his disbelief that an anonymous letter of this kind would be published and his mystification over the unfounded charges, he apologized for even answering the letter. He would not do so except for the prospect that people read and believe such letters, which would hurt the good and noble rescue operation Canadian Mennonites were engaged in. To help with clarifying the issue, members of the Central Committee of Mennonite Immigrants in Canada (ZMIK) issued a statement in which they reiterated once more:

> that no member of the Canadian Mennonite Board of Colonization has made himself rich at the expense of the immigrants; that all financial matters are recorded accurately and conscientiously in the books of the Board Office; and that the books are controlled regularly by a state-appointed auditor.[31]

Toews had explained many times that the seven dollar charge per immigrant covered operating expenses of the Board and extra costs necessary for running the non-profit corporation. As for Toews and Friesen, their modest stipend came from the offices of the CPR.

Even the Conference of Mennonites in Canada, at its sessions in Altona in July of 1926, addressed the problem of criticism. After some discussion, a resolution was passed by the delegates:

> The Conference receives as regrettable the knowledge that through various organs the Mennonite press puts hindrances in the way of immigration work, throwing suspicions and even dirt at the Board. The Conference considers this kind of activity as unjust, not springing from a spirit of Christian love. Hence the Conference registers its full confidence in the Board and prays that it will not tire in its work. As for the Conference, it expresses the firm resolve to work cooperatively and with encouragement in accordance with earlier Conference resolutions.[32]

On the first day of the 1926 sessions, moderator David Toews had delivered his Conference address based on Exodus 33:10: "When all the people saw the pillar of cloud standing at the entrance of the tent, all the people would rise and bow down, all of them, at the entrance of their tent." His message was straightforward: Today secular people build their own horizons and live by them. The children of Israel, on the other hand, were led by a cloud. We Christians have Jesus as the horizon to which we look and by which we are oriented. If we would allow God to lead us, the evil one would be sent to flight, and misunderstandings in the churches and in the family would be overcome.[33]

Later in the year, Toews was again defending the Board in church papers. To his credit, he always drew attention to the larger picture and the greater vision. A letter appearing on December 1, 1926, ends this way:

That we are engaged in a great work becomes clear to us again and again. I doubt that in the Mennonite world of today there is anywhere as much suffering as is expressed in the various letters and comments submitted to our office in Rosthern. We receive letters from China, from Africa, France, Rumania, Bulgaria, Poland, Atlantic Park in England, from Hamburg, Rotterdam, and Mexico; practically everyone always with the same request: Help! We think of those among us who are ill in sanitariums in Canada, in three mental institutions in which we have patients, in hospitals from which requests come to us. We think of the many widows and orphans among our immigrants, of those who come to us with little to wear. Every day we face problems for which we do not have solutions and to which we can only respond with help from our benefactors. And in the context of this mass of human suffering, a piercing and callous word, "band of swindlers," is flung into the midst of our sincere efforts.[34]

It is remarkable how, in the face of constant criticism, Toews maintained a positive spirit. In the midst of much misunderstanding and ill will, he could still write, as he did in early December:

Until now we have received about 14,000 of our people. Ontario, Manitoba, Saskatchewan, and Alberta participated in the reception and received their allotment according to how many they were able to care for. In some places the hosts tired of their responsibility for a time; then other doors opened. Just as soon as they had their own dwelling, those who were the first to come were willing to receive others who came later. It was touching to see how frugally some lived only to be able to receive new immigrants. . . . With this I am not claiming that much more could not have been done. Some hearts remained cold, some doors remained locked, many a loveless word was spoken, many hindrances were placed in our way, but the Lord found the faithful in the land and they did what they could.[35]

He must have seen himself, along with others who encouraged him, as the bearer of the burdens of his people. This included not only the hardships of those suffering in revolutionary Russia but also of those in Canada and the United States who were burdened and bound by a critical spirit.

A positive disposition and firm sense of direction influences others. Mrs. Mary Harder, now of Vineland, Ontario, has a childhood memory of David Toews' visit to her home church in Leamington, Ontario, in the mid-1920s.[36] She can still see "Onkel Toews" in her mind's eye and hear his voice. The church was packed to hear his report. The children and young people sat on the floor at the front of the sanctuary. She remembers to this day that Rev. Toews cited the following lines, which she took to heart:

Üb' immer Treu und Redlichkeit
Bis an dein kühles Grab;
Und weiche keinen Fingerbreit
Von Gottes Wegen ab.

Do your best to be faithful and upright
Even to your very last breath;
And do not veer from God's pathway
Not so much as an inch.

Aunt Mary says that on that Sunday evening long ago she perceived David Toews to be "ein Mensch," a significant human being.

A Disastrous Night

It was a cold and stormy weekend in Rosthern with night temperatures dipping to bitterly cold minus 30 degrees Fahrenheit. On Saturday, December 11, several immigrant families had arrived in Rosthern by train. While standing on the platform and awaiting their arrival, Toews recalls that he had expressed the fear that this kind of weather often caused one of those all-too-common chimney fires resulting from ovens stoked with extra wood and stovepipes overheating.[37] On Sunday morning, Franz F. Enns of Manitoba, one of the travelling ministers assigned to itinerate among the immigrant settlers, was the preacher. His text was Romans 8:28: "We know that all things work together for good for those who love God, who are called according to his purpose." At the evening church service, where Enns told of their flight from Russia, it had been almost impossible to produce heat in the church. Back at the Toews home, where it was also chilly, Dora and Louise vacated their room for F.F. Enns, while they bedded down on the floor of their father's study. The extra room upstairs was occupied by Herman Riesen, a son of David Toews' cousin and a student at the German-English Academy.

In the early morning of December 13, at about 4:30, Louise awoke to the smell of smoke and the sound of crackling wood. She saw fire snaking its way up the stair carpet and immediately ran upstairs to awaken the others. Dora grabbed Rev. Enns's fur coat and ran to the street where she laid it down and stood on it to protect her bare feet from the ice and snow. Louise soon joined her. Meanwhile, mother Margarete had awakened and rushed into the adjacent bedroom to awaken Marie and Elma. By then it was impossible for those upstairs to descend on the burning steps. When Marie saw the flames shooting up the stairs, she ran into the room occupied by Rev. Enns who had just shattered the pane in his bedroom window. Marie crawled out the window and, after slipping part way down the eave pipe, dropped the rest of the way into the snow. She ran around the house and tried to mount the veranda roof to help her mother. But, barefoot and in her night dress, the cold was overcoming her, so she ran to neighbour Abrahams' house. No one there answered her cries for help, so she continued on to the home of Pastor Mahlstedt, but there too everyone was sound asleep. She continued on to the Penner house where she collapsed and would surely have frozen to death if the Penners had not already been awake, preparing their horses for a trip to the bush to bring home a supply of firewood. They helped Dora into their house, then ran to assist the others. By then the Abrahams were also awake.

Meanwhile, Rev. Enns had jumped from his upstairs window which resulted in a break in his pelvic bone. Unable to walk, he crawled on hands and knees to the neighbour's house. David Toews, with 11-year-old Elma in his arms, was able to negotiate the burning stairway, although with great difficulty. Mother Margarete broke the window above the roof of the porch, pushed Anna through it onto the porch roof, and went back for Irene. She made several attempts to bring her out onto the veranda roof but to no avail. Thereupon Herman, who had also escaped by running through the flames of the burning staircase, climbed

The first Toews home in Rosthern which was destroyed by fire in 1926. Several family members and guests escaped from the burning house through the upstairs window over the porch roof.

onto the porch roof from the outside, entered the burning house through the window, and succeeded in getting the unconscious Irene out onto the roof. Toews stood on the ground and helped them to safety. Eventually everyone was out of the house and sheltered in safety at the neighbours. When the three town doctors arrived, the old Abrahams couple was doing its best to attend to the distraught and injured group.

At about 5:00 a.m. the townsfolk of Rosthern were awakened by the sound of the fire siren. By the time the fire engines arrived, there was nothing left to save. The Toews house was going up in flames—with furniture, clothing, family records and photos, silver wedding gifts, books, and all! Everyone was injured in some way by frost, by fire, and by the daring escape. But at least for now, everyone was alive. As for the house, five-year-old Irene was heard to exclaim: "Our house is totally burned down, but we will build a new one."

All three medical doctors of the town of Rosthern arrived at the Abrahams house to attend to the injured. They were wrapped in blankets, put on stretchers, and transported singly or in pairs to rooms in the National Hotel where medical care continued. Later that morning, F.F. Enns and Herman Riesen were transported to St. Paul's Hospital in Saskatoon for special attention. The three children who had not been at home that night arrived from their places of study and work—Elsie from Normal School in Saskatoon, Benno from the University, and Margaret from Hague where she was teaching school. Friends and local relatives dropped by to express concern and offer support.

But the worst was yet to come. At 2:00 a.m. on Tuesday morning, December 14, 22 hours after the fire, little Irene died. The burns she sustained to her body had been too severe. This was a terrible blow to the family, especially to the parents. To this day the children remember how their mother cried out in anguish when she heard the news. It is said that Irene took her last breath while in the comforting arms of Kaethe Hooge.[38] Some years later David wrote: "I cannot picture for you what we experienced when we heard the news. The Lord only knows. Never in my life have I experienced such anguish of soul as when I heard that our little Irene had died."[39]

The funeral was held the afternoon of the very next day, December 15. The doctors had determined that this would be best, given the physical and emotional condition of the family. Before the coffin was taken to the church, it was brought into David Toews' hospital room. Those injured in the fire were also brought into the room. After some words of comfort spoken by local ministers, the family bade their sad farewell to their youngest daughter and sister. Because of injuries and trauma, the Toews parents were not able to attend the funeral service in

Irene!

Sie winkt aus lichten Himmelshöhen,
Euch Eltern heute freundlich zu.
Sie ruft, könnt ihr es nicht verstehen,
Ach gönne mir die süsse Ruh.

Today she greets her parents dear
From heavenly realms above,
She calls—can you not understand?—
Do not begrudge me this sweet peace.

Er trug mich heim auf seinen Armen
Ins Land der Freuden, Wonn', und Lust,
Wo sanft ruht sich's an seiner warmen
Und süszen, sanften Jesusbrust.

In his arms he carried me home
To a land of joy, of rapture, of bliss,
Where I have found eternal rest
In the warm and soothing arms of Jesus.

Ihr Lieben dürft nur nicht verzagen
In neuem Jammer, Weh und Schmerz.
Dürft weinend Jesus alles sagen,
Und fliehen an sein liebend Herz.

Dear loved ones, you must not despair
In your grief, your woe, and pain,
Tearfully you can tell all to Jesus,
And take refuge in his loving care.

Mit Jesus könnt ihr es ertragen,
Dasz ich so frühe muszte geh'n.
Durch Jesum winkt nach kurzen Tagen,
Uns ein frühes Wiederseh'n.

In Jesus you can bear the tragedy
That I was taken from you so early,
Jesus has promised that we will meet
After a few short days of separation.

Ich wart auf euch am Perlentore,
Denkt nur ihr Lieben, wo ich bin,
Voll Himmelslust, beim Engelchore,
Wo Blümlein unverwelklich blüh'n.

I'll wait for you at the pearly gates,
Just bear in mind, where I am,
As part of heaven's joyful angel choir
Where flowers bloom and never wither.

O könntet ihr es einmal sehen,
Des Himmelsglanz, voll Licht u. Pracht,
Die immergrünen Salemshöhen,
Wo keine Tränen, keine Nacht.

O, if you could only see/The glory
of heaven, full of splendour and light,
The heights of Salem eternally green,
Here there are no tears, and no night.

Kein Unglück mehr, das uns aufwecket,
Kein Ach und Weh, und keine Not,
Kein Trost, kein Feuer, uns erschrecket,
Und niemals mehr trennt uns der Tod.

Here no tragedy disturbs our sleep,
No remorse or pain, and no more want,
No accident, no fire to frighten us;
No death to part us from one another.

Darum, ihr Lieben, wandelt stille,
Getrost mit Gott, durchs Tal der Zeit
Bis uns einst, wenn es Gottes Wille,
Ein sel'ges Wiederseh'n erfreut.

Therefore dear loved ones, tread softly,
Trust in God, through the valley of time,
Until one day, if it is God's will,
We will enjoy a blessed family reunion.

This German poem, penned by Rev. Isaak P. Friesen of Rosthern, was reflective of the words of comfort offered to the bereaved at the tragic death of Irene, David and Margarete's youngest daughter. Literal translation: Helmut Harder the church. From the hospital, the coffin was taken to the Rosthern Mennonite Church where it was carried into the sanctuary by four girls. In the church, Johannes Regier, J.J. Klassen, as well as Rev. Cudderford of the United Church, spoke. In his memoirs, Toews wrote: "If only it had not all happened so suddenly. But it did, and we had to be careful not to succumb too much to our pain and anguish."[40] Today, a visitor to the cemetery in Rosthern will find the grave plot and memorial stone of little Irene beside the graves of her parents.

The cause of the fire was never determined for certain. Rumours spread quickly that this was a case of arson, that the fire had been set by adversaries of David Toews. But Toews himself discounted this option. The possibility of the fire starting because of furnace problems seemed dubious as well. When Mrs. Toews had checked the furnace at 11:00 p.m., everything appeared in order. Besides, by early morning the furnace would already have cooled down somewhat, making a furnace-generated fire unlikely at that time. Also, Dora and Louise, who were sleeping directly above the furnace pipes, would have noticed the fire earlier than they did if it had originated there. The most plausible theory is that a short-circuited electrical wire in the north wall had caused the surrounding wood to smoulder and eventually to ignite into flames.

Thus the eventful year of 1926 ended in trouble and tragedy for David Toews and his family. Later in life, Toews would speak of the latter half of December as the most difficult time of his life and of the life of Margarete. And yet, there was life after December 13, 1926, as the community responded and as, by the grace of God, physical and emotional healing did its slow work.

12
Immigration Ends
1927–1929

News of the December fire spread quickly across Canada and throughout the Mennonite world. Major newspapers in Canada carried the story. The Mennonite grapevine, fostered by word of mouth and personal correspondence, by way of church papers and through telegraph lines, saw to it that the constituency heard of the tragedy. The community was quick to respond with sympathy and help.

Mutual Aid

With embers from the fire still smouldering, an article in the December 15 issue of *Der Bote*, entitled, "Rosthern Immigrant Children," announced a "Christmas Fund" designated for gifts for the Toews children. The article stated simply that David Toews was a man who had contributed so much during the great tragedy which befell the Mennonites in Russia and now, that disaster had struck the Toews family, it was up to those who had benefitted from his kindness to offer something in return. Since the father of the Toews children was now so poor that he could not offer his children any Christmas gifts, the community was invited to contribute money so that some Christmas joy might come to his children too.[1] Letters expressing sympathy and encouragement, along with monetary contributions, poured in from Canada and the United States and even from Europe, including Russia. Sunday school classes gathered clothing and bedding; women's auxiliaries sent letters of condolence and money to Mrs. Toews.

Within one day of the fire, Col. Dennis of the CPR sent a letter to "Bishop Toews." Having just heard "by telegraph of the calamity which you have met with in the destruction of your home by fire, and the injury to yourself and some members of your family," he asked his representative, Mr. Herzer, "to proceed to Rosthern and to do what he could to give a helping hand."[2] The helping hand came not only in the form of a hospital visit but also a cheque of $1000 from the CPR treasury to help in the replacement of the house. Official letters also came from the Canadian National Railway office, from immigration officials, and even from Prime Minister Mackenzie King.[3]

Most letters of sympathy included money. One group, the detained immigrants at Atlantic Park in England, sent a moving note of sympathy with apologies for not including a monetary contribution since they had nothing to give in that respect. The note contained about 100 signatures. Someone in Rosthern offered the Toews family a house they could occupy as long as they needed it. This was mutual aid at its best.

Recovery
Emotionally, the loss had a devastating effect on the parents. Even today the surviving children recall their mother's cries of agony in the first days brought on by her excruciating remorse over the tragic death of Irene. Fourteen years later, the person who penned Margarete Toews' obituary made this comment:

> The night from December 12 to 13, 1926 was the most difficult time in our life. Mother Toews was able to recover from this blow and she continued the various aspects of her work with joy and in peace. Every summer she gave special and willing attention to the flowers in her garden which she tended with much work and great care.[4]

David was constantly overwhelmed by feelings of hopelessness, but he managed to dictate numerous thank-you letters which his faithful secretary, Miss Hooge, sent on their way. She was a staunch support to the Toews family during this time. In the end, Toews could write: "We went through a period of hopelessness, expecting nothing from the future. But we have been overwhelmed by what has come our way."[5] Clearly it was the support of friends far and near that helped them recover from the trauma.

Physically, the healing process took more time than at first anticipated. On December 30, Toews wrote to Col. Dennis that he was confined to bed, unable to use his feet or his right hand, but expected to be back at work in two or three weeks. The rest of the Toews family was mobile by then and getting along fairly well. On January 12, 1927, Toews wrote to Johann Bueckert of Gretna: "Our recovery is coming along satisfactorily. We hope to be on our feet soon."[6] Mother Margaret and the children were "on their feet" by mid-January with Margarete attending to the household and the children back at school. But it took David somewhat longer. By the end of February he was seeing some improvement in his condition and beginning to believe that things would eventually return to normal. In Toews' view, the good recovery was because "we were treated in the hospital like millionaires."[7] Three months after the fire, Toews wrote to a sympathizer in Norristown, Pennsylvania: "We are all up again and about our work; and outside the loss of our child, who cannot be replaced, our losses have for the most part been covered, thanks to the kindness of so many dear friends."[8] By this time the physical wounds were pretty well healed.

Herman Riesen and Rev. Enns spent a month and a half in hospital before they were released. By the end of January, Herman had resumed his studies at the high school. Shortly after Christmas, Rev. F. Enns wrote to David Toews to report on his condition.[9] His right hand was completely healed. He could already move the thumb and finger of his left hand and hoped it also would be restored to health in a week's time. The pain in his broken pelvic bone had left him, which was an indication that the break was healing properly. It had been difficult to lie constantly on his back, but he was in good spirits and was able to manage. He thanked David Toews for the $25 Christmas present, and assured Toews that he should not feel responsible or guilty for what happened to him. Enns was released from St. Paul's Hospital on February 4 and was escorted back to his home in Winkler. Being in the employ of Home Mission work as an itinerant minister, his hospital expenses of $400 were paid by the Board of Colonization fund designated for immigrant social care.

Now it was time to think of permanent housing. The decision to build a new house came somewhat readily once all the donations were tallied. Earlier Toews did not know what to do since, as he said, "the fire had taken everything from us but our debts."[10] In early March, he wrote to C.F. Claassen in Newton, Kansas: "We have received more in (financial) gifts than I had hoped to borrow to build a new house."[11] The house, built on the same lot as the former one, was constructed during the summer of 1927. The relatively spacious structure, which can still be seen in Rosthern today, was financed by the $7000 contributed by friends and organizations. Interestingly, in his "Memoirs" Toews expressed some regret that he built so large a house. He mused:

> The decision shows that I do not have the practical sense that I would like to have. When I assess things today [1934], then I tell myself that I allowed the house to be built too large and at too much expense, and later I came to regret that I put so much money into the building.[12]

What was the lesson in this tragedy and its aftermath? Five weeks after the fire, Toews wrote to John F. Dick in Scudder, Ontario: "It is clear to me that through this fateful event the Lord wants to tell us something. What the message is, is not clear to me as yet, but we believe that no hair on our head falls except by God's will. It is clear to me that our Father in heaven has allowed this to happen and we need to listen attentively to what the Lord wants to tell us."[13] The dictum, "God makes no mistakes," appears to have been a driving force for Toews' faith and life. A little later he began to hint at some insight into the question of the meaning of the tragedy. In early February he wrote to an acquaintance in Germany: "I believe that through our tragic experience we may have come to a greater understanding of our suffering brothers in Russia and that, when we seek to help others, we find consolation for ourselves, especially for the loss of our child."[14] Along the same lines, he wrote in late April to a friend in Kansas: "Whoever has been in misery can better understand the misery of others; and when we seek to help others in their pain, we are the recipients of consolation in ours."[15] In being mindful of the many Mennonite people who had been strong in the face of their suffering in Russia, Toews found the same courage in his own tragedy. The experience appeared to inspire him to renewal, perhaps to a new level of dedication to the causes he represented. His above-mentioned letter to Heinrich Ediger included the lyrics of a hymn:

> As long as God ordains,
> I will continue to carry my cross,
> And do faithful battle in this world;
> Yet penitently and secretly I sigh:
> Please take me home.[16]

It was typical of Toews to speak of himself in two ways—as a sinner, not worthy of all the grace and goodness he had received, and as a humble servant, ready and willing to live responsibly in this world. The tragic event of December 13 and its aftermath seemed to deepen David Toews' sense of the vulnerability of life. At the same time, the event strengthened his resolve to continue with the tasks at hand.

Appeal for Help

1926 was the last year for large numbers of immigrants to arrive on Canada's shores.[17] It was becoming apparent that the years of opportunity were passing. By mid-1927 about 18,000 Mennonite immigrants had arrived in Canada from Russia and another 446 had been directed to Mexico. If it had been up to the Canadian Mennonite Board of Colonization and its visionary leader, the immigrants would have kept coming to Canada. The CPR was willing to continue its cooperation, even though it already had advanced $1,500,000 in travel credit, of which $500,000 had been paid back. But the obstacles to further immigration were becoming formidable. In the Soviet Union the situation was becoming increasingly urgent as the economic and social situation worsened. The government had increased the cost of exit permits substantially, while at the same time it had reduced the number of permits issued. The chief medical inspector for the CPR, Dr. Drury, who had travelled the length and breadth of the colonies to check out prospective immigrants, was being restricted in his travels in the Soviet Union.[18] Immigrants had to come to his office in Moscow, which made things very difficult, and the sentiment of the Soviet government and the Russian people was turning against the exit of Mennonites and against the Mennonite people as such. In Canada, the citizenry increasingly was raising its voice against the immigration policies of the Liberal government. With unemployment rising and with more immigrants choosing the city rather than the rural context, the prejudice of the general populace against new immigrants increased substantially toward the end of the 1920s.[19] This situation gave David Toews new concern for the immigration project. Meanwhile, his own health and well-being were always on his mind.

On the Road Again
   The spring of 1927 found Toews on the road again to Ottawa, Montreal, and New York on behalf of the immigrant project. Two letters, written to his family while he was on this trip, reveal his sentiments and his condition at this stage of life.[20] The first, dated April 2, 1927, was posted in Montreal. Father Toews began by assuring his wife and children that he and his travelling companion, Gerhard Ens, were in good health, although his feet were sore from the walking he had to do on his stopover in Winnipeg and again in Ottawa. In Montreal, he took a hotel near the train station, which meant less walking, but he had a restless night with much dreaming and much waking from sleep. After a day in Montreal he complained of being particularly tired. There a telegram awaited him, asking him to proceed to New York City for a day of meetings. He and Ens would leave in 45 minutes and return again Monday morning. From there the journey took them back to Ottawa for two or three days of meetings. On the way home they had one-day stopovers in Waterloo and in Winnipeg. He hoped to be home by Tuesday or Wednesday before the Easter weekend. The letter ended: "I have you constantly on my mind. May the Lord protect you. Hearty greetings to you all. Your, David Toews." One senses that he was growing physically weary by this time.
   A second letter was written a few days later, dated April 5, 1927, and again sent from Montreal. By then Toews had returned from New York where he had conferred with Brother Kratz of the Mennonite Relief Commission about the ongoing immigration project and payment of the transportation debt. It was most interesting, he said, to spend some time in America's largest city. The theme of weariness recurred again. By then

Margarete and her daughters in 1927 after the death of Irene, youngest member of the Toews family.

his feet were tired and painful. He had retired to his hotel room as soon as possible after the evening meal and had exchanged his leather shoes for slippers. He ended the letter: "I am glad this trip is coming to an end and that I can soon return home. Hopefully I will find you all in good health. The Lord keep you in his care. Please convey hearty greetings to all our dear friends. I greet you heartily. Your, David Toews." Father Toews would rather have been at home with the family than on the road, but duty called and he did what he had to do.

Endless Needs

David Toews' address at the opening of the 25th annual sessions of the Conference of Mennonites in Canada in Herbert, Saskatchewan, in July 1927, reflected some anxiety, although with his typical dose of optimism and vision, about the immigration project and about conditions among Mennonites in Canada.[21] Basing his remarks on 1 Corinthians 3:11–15, he noted that, while the churches were engaged in the great work of building up the kingdom of God, the evil one was busily destroying much good in the world and in the church. He called for a forthrightness born of conviction and awareness of what people of faith were up against. He identified two kinds of Christians: those found wanting and those who were victorious. The latter kind followed the Apostle Paul in building on a good foundation. Our schools, our families, our congregational work, our mission work, and all our endeavours would stand the onslaughts of the evil one if the church stood firmly on the good foundation. "For no other foundation can anyone lay than that which is laid, which is Jesus Christ"(3:11).

On the last day of the Conference sessions, chairman Toews put forward a resolution to the effect that the congregations should be reminded to increase their efforts to help the needy. He focused in particular on the need to gather funds to help those who were still being detained in Europe and to collect clothing for the destitute among the immigrants in Canada.[22]

Shortly after the conference in Herbert, Toews sharpened his appeal for help.[23] The entire project was begun without money and now, after four years, the budget was tight and all incoming funds were spoken for. Meanwhile there were specific demands. The first was the travel debt which was always before them, Toews asserted. There the Board depended on the sense of obligation of the people to fulfil their promises.

Second were the immigrants who had been detained and were receiving medical help. At one time 700 persons had been held back at Lechfeld and 300 at Southampton. By now there were only six in Hamburg and 30 in Southampton. Still, this was a continuing concern both pastorally and financially. Toews recognized the graciousness of the Mennonite people in Europe, especially through Benjamin H. Unruh, the generosity of the German government, and the personal interest of President Hindenburg in helping the detainees.[24]

Third, some immigrants in Canada were not able to pay their medical expenses or needed social assistance because of joblessness. At that time, this item alone required between $700 and $800 monthly. The Board had promised the Canadian government that no immigrant would be a burden to Canada, at least for the first five years. Fourth, there was the need for pastoral visits to the emerging churches in Canada. This too required financial assistance, for which the General Conference Mission Board was providing substantial assistance.

And finally, there was the project of establishing hospitality homes in the big cities—Winnipeg, Saskatoon, and Vancouver—for working Mennonite women. By mid-1927 the Winnipeg home was already up and running and the Saskatoon home was on the drawing board. Having named these five areas of financial need, Toews, in typical fashion, stepped out on a limb and drew attention to another area:

> In respect to the above-mentioned crying needs I can hardly dare to mention yet another matter. Yet there may be special friends among you for whom this point would be of special interest. We have been able to bring a number of good teachers to Canada. What they miss is the language facility to be able to serve our people in the schools.[25]

Toews was inviting constituents to contribute to a bursary fund in support of continuing education for prospective teachers among the immigrants.

At the end of this overwhelming recital of needs, Toews reiterated that the first obligation was the *Reiseschuld*: "I emphasize again and again that clearing the travel debt is a matter of honour for our people. Just as 50 years ago through the faithful clearing away of their debts the pioneers in the Red River Valley gained a reputation on the basis of which our current project was made possible, so also through faithful payment of our responsibilities today, blessings will abound for later generations." He ended the article with the statement: "We will not consider our work complete until we have paid the last penny to the CPR and until the very last of those who have been detained will have arrived here."

During the fall months of 1927, David Toews appealed often to Mennonite brothers and sisters in the United States for financial and material help.[26] The letters were directed mainly to Alvin J. Miller of Belleville, Pennsylvania, director of Mennonite Central Committee. On September 9, he appealed for contributions to an investment fund that was set up to help the 4000 landless immigrants who as yet were not placed on farms. He assured Miller that "from our knowledge . . . of the character of these brethren we are confident that they will prove a safe investment . . . and we believe that they will make good." Another letter, dated December 4, outlined the need for financial support for hospital expenses, for material aid, and for assistance to those who had had crop failure. In the following months and years the appeals for help turned increasingly to needs in the Soviet Union. An excerpt from a letter of August 3, 1929, stated: "We are particularly interested in the needy in Canada and the people in Russia, and we will be very thankful for anything you can do to help us relieve suffering along these lines."

In an article written in December 1927, Toews assessed the situation of the previous year. He reflected on the summer when fields in western Canada looked promising at first but then were damaged severely by frost, rust, and hail. This raised fear in the hearts of those who had hoped for a good crop so that the *Reiseschuld* could be paid off. Then winter arrived early, and there was added concern that recent immigrants would not have sufficient warm clothing. Against this backdrop, Toews paid tribute to God for the outpouring of aid in clothing and money, especially through the Mennonite Relief Commission in the United States. The article included comments from recipients of aid, particularly some widows, who expressed their thanks. Toews was greatly encouraged by this help and quoted the text: "Cast all your cares upon the Lord, for he cares for you."[27]

Always, Toews took the lead in expressing heartfelt thanks to those who contributed aid financially and materially. In an article entitled

"Herzlichen Dank" (Heartfelt thanks), he reported on the number of bundles of clothing that had been received at the Rosthern office and the number of packages that subsequently had been sent to individuals, to families, and for distribution through local churches. "Many times," he wrote, "the words have come to mind: 'I was naked, and you clothed me. . . . What you have done to the least of these my brethren you have done unto me.'"[28] Toews was relieved that the Lord had heard and answered the cry of needy people.

He himself lived by example in this regard. The story is told of a poor immigrant who came to the Rosthern office for advice.[29] It was a bitterly cold winter day and Toews saw that the man's shoes were worn thin. He called home and asked the children to bring his recently purchased felt boots to the office. These he gave to the poor man, following the precept of Jesus about sharing of our abundance with those who have nothing.

It was not always easy to distribute the available aid justly. Sometimes rather arbitrary decisions needed to be made. The story is told of a shipment of seed potatoes sent by the Rosthern office to families that had settled at Truax, Saskatchewan.[30] A local Mennonite leader, Johann Pankratz, was to see to the distribution. Some time later a local farmer wrote to Toews to complain that he had been "discriminated against" and had not received any of the potatoes. When Toews checked things out, Mr. Pankratz explained that anyone who owned a radio was not considered eligible to receive potatoes. Such persons obviously had the means to take care of themselves. Toews wrote to the complainant that he supported the principle that governed the distribution with the added comment that he himself did not as yet own a radio either.

Enduring Hardships

On the last Sunday of November in 1927, David Toews was in Didsbury, Alberta, officiating at the marriage of Cornelius D. Harder and Sara Paetkau. Cornelius' pilgrimage is a moving story of hardship and faithful service.[31] He (1866–1946) was born in the village of Blumstein in Ukraine but moved with his family to Orloff, Siberia, where he grew up, married, and served the church. He was close to the age of David Toews and had been ordained as *Ältester* of the Orloff church in Siberia in 1912, about the time that Toews was ordained as elder of the Rosen-orter Church in Saskatchewan. In May of 1926, at 60 years of age, Harder, together with his wife and two unmarried children, attempted to leave Russia for Canada. They travelled to Moscow in the hope of making the necessary arrangements. It happened that mother and children were granted exit permits but he was not. After a few agonizing days of decision-making, it was decided that his wife and children should continue on to Canada while he would return to Siberia. Toews received Mrs. Harder and children in Rosthern and, together with others, saw to her needs. Then she turned ill, died, and was buried in Rosthern in January of 1927. When Harder finally did arrive in Canada six months later, he was reunited with his children, but he could only visit his wife's gravesite and grieve his loss.

About that time the newly founded church at Didsbury, Alberta, needed an *Ältester.* Toews assigned Harder to the role where he entered into a second marriage with Sara Paetkau. Three years later, in 1930, the Harders moved to Rosemary, Alberta, to organize the Mennonite church. Rev. Harder was also instrumental in founding the Alberta Conference of Mennonites and did much itinerating work in the newly emerging Alberta churches.

Islands of Encouragement

If church work and immigration concerns became difficult, there were always the wonderful summer conferences to look forward to. For David Toews these were islands of encouragement in the midst of difficult work. In his invitation to the 26th annual sessions, to be held July 2–4, 1928 in Rosthern, he quoted from a hymn: "Come, let us gather to build Zion, with faith and confidence, Zion, the city of God. Zion must become enlarged, so large that no person upon the earth is outside of its walls" (literal translation). Toews ended his invitation with the comment: "Our Mennonite people have great responsibilities. Let us approach our task with courage, with joy and with love, and let us seek to fulfil our obligations in a way that pleases the Lord."[32] If the one-day mission conference, which typically preceded the conference sessions, was an indication of growth, then Toews should have been encouraged. It was reported that some 2000 persons attended the Sunday mission conference which featured the work of both home and international missions.

At the sessions, the Board report given by David Toews was mostly upbeat. By July 1928, the total number of immigrants had reached 18,427. During the fiscal year, July 1927 to July 1928, another $97,000 had been paid down on the CPR loan. In addition large amounts of clothing had been gathered to assist immigrants and funds had been donated to pay hospital and sanatorium costs for the ill. Those retained in Europe were receiving pastoral care, particularly from B.H. Unruh, for whose travels the CPR bore the cost. A good spirit of support was evident, but there were also some discouragements. The Mennonites in Russia, where there was increased turmoil and suffering, were encountering great difficulty in obtaining exit visas. Toews then lauded the CPR for its support. In his Conference report, he wrote:

People can criticize us if they want. Yet if there is left in our Mennonite people at least a trace of self-respect, then let us not multiply the difficulties of our honourable friend, Col. Dennis, whose attitude toward our Mennonite people means so very much to us. He has persistently done everything possible for our immigrants. Anyone who is prepared to respond with ingratitude and distrust toward such goodness of heart and trust should blush with shame. . . . We are convinced that the Lord is with us. And if this is the case, then with prayerful support we want to work further with our churches and not be discouraged.[33]

In the closing resolution of the 1928 sessions, the Resolution Committee noted a good spirit of support for the work of immigration and for the work of the Conference as such. This was certainly a change from the sentiment just a few years earlier.[34]

First Family Wedding

The first of seven weddings in the Toews household occurred a month before the Conference. On June 7, 1928 Benno Toews, only son of David and Margarete Toews, was married to Catherine Friesen, daughter of Isaak P. and Katherine Friesen of Rosthern. At the time, both were elementary school teachers in Saskatchewan, Benno at Sheo and Catherine in Laird. The newlyweds began their life together in Sheo, after which Benno served as teacher, pastor, and missionary in a variety of places both in Canada and the United States. He took positions at the

The wedding of Benno and Catherine (Friesen) Toews on June 7, 1928.

German-English Academy in Rosthern; with the General Conference Home Mission Board as missionary to the Cheyenne and Arapaho in Oklahoma and as teacher at the Hopi Mission School in Bacabi, Arizona; as Bible School teacher in Rosthern; as teacher at Freeman Junior College (1946–1948) and at Bluffton College; as teacher and president at Canadian Mennonite Bible College in Winnipeg (1949–1954); as pastor of Three Oaks Mennonite Church in Paso Robles, California, and of Calvary Mennonite Church in Liberal, Kansas. Catherine Toews, who earned a music degree from the Royal Conservatory of Music in Toronto, taught private piano lessons and served as church pianist in the many churches that they attended and in which they worked.

Endless Criticism

Family celebrations were important to David Toews, and he managed to find time for them in his busy schedule. They were also a source of encouragement for him. Yet it seems that it was his lot in life to walk the line between encouragement and discouragement. While good things were happening, reasons to worry were always present. In the fall of 1928, about the time the Friesen-Braun case was coming to a close, there was still public nervousness about the whole affair and the role of the Board of Colonization. On September 20, 1928, Toews answered a letter from H. J. Brown of Freeman, South Dakota, who accused the Board of using funds to support Braun in his court battle.[35] Brown charged that, since many in Canada were accusing Toews of having his hand in the affair, there must be something to it. Brown's letter placed Toews on the defensive again: "Please, Mr. Brown," he wrote, "come and examine our books. It should be obvious there since we are not so far advanced that we would be able to camouflage our dealings." Toews appealed to his own good standing in the congregation and the Conference, and pointed out that the matter had been taken up time and time again in his church. Toews continued: "I very much regret this whole affair, but on one point I challenge you. You do not have the right on moral or Christian grounds to drag my name into the affair. . . . You have made one big mistake in that, when people have come to you to complain about me, you did not come to me directly." Then Toews added this telling testimony:

> I can assure you that, especially since the beginning of our immigration work, I have often had to do my work with deep sighs. At times it seems so odd to me that our nonresistant peaceful people will so readily listen when someone speaks evil of his neighbour. Admittedly it may have been good for me that in recent years I often served as the object of assaults and slanders. Despite everything, I want to continue to strive, before God, to present myself with a clean conscience.

The 58-year-old David Toews at his desk in Rosthern in 1928.

It pained David Toews deeply to find among the Mennonite people those whose custom it was to condemn a person before giving the accused person a hearing.

With respect to Isaak Braun, the most one can say that, in his own heart and mind, he was undecided about the matter. In the end, Toews admitted his error. To the accusation against Toews, that he may have contributed to Braun's court costs in the last round of hearings, we will need to take Toews' word that he did not do so.[36] At the same time, we can conjecture that he knew of persons, "friends of Braun," who will have made contributions on behalf of Braun. What we do know is that in 1931 there was an open and public church meeting of reconciliation between Toews and the Friesens. However, the events and sentiments of the past were not easily dispelled.

Sure Leadership

Drake, Saskatchewan was the scene of the 27th annual Canadian Conference sessions held in July 1929. Fifty-nine-year-old David Toews was again chairman of the proceedings. By then 25 congregations, extending from Manitoba to British Columbia, comprised the membership. The theme of the Conference sessions read: "Our Obligation as Churches." Toews based his opening address on John 11:51–52: "Jesus was about to die for the nation, and not for the nation only, but to gather into one the dispersed people of God." He emphasized the obligation of member congregations to tend to their children, their youth, their schools, the sick among them, the poor, the aged, and to support the work of mission. The Board reported that about 19,000 immigrants had arrived, and that the debt stood at about $1,000,000. About 400 persons were still in holding centres in Europe, hoping to arrive in Canada once they were healed of their diseases. Toews expressed the hope and confidence that the debt would be paid and that all detainees would eventually complete their journey. At the end of the conference, a special resolution was passed:

> The Conference states its deeply felt thanks to the director of the Board, Ält. David Toews, and all his coworkers. The full confidence of the Conference, that herewith is affirmed for David Toews and his coworkers, should also encourage them in the future to miss no opportunity to help the poor.[37]

In his reflections on the sessions, J.G. Rempel observed that all matters were conducted in a spirit of love and peace and he made the following observation about Chairman Toews:

> The sense of belonging together has probably never been experienced as strongly as at this conference. To some extent this spirit was brought by each of the delegates, but the calm and sure leadership of Ält. David Toews was a major contributing factor.[38]

The 25th session of the General Conference of the Mennonites of North America was held August 20 to 28, 1929, in Hutchinson, Kansas.[39] Even though a disastrous flood had hit the area three weeks before the sessions, leaving three feet of water in the new Convention Hall in which the conference was to take place, everything was in readiness for the week. On the first full day of the program, David Toews presented an address on "Mennonite Immigration to Canada in the Future." In his report, he emphasized the precarious situation of the Mennonite people in Russia. Churches were being transformed into club houses and theatres. Ministers who dared to baptize young people under the age of 18 were sometimes sent into exile in the far north. Generally, ministers had been stripped of any rights. Sunday was a work day. Young people who refused military service were jailed and sometimes shot. The aim of the government was to force everyone into the Communist system. The organizations in the Mennonite colonies that assisted those who wanted to immigrate had been dissolved. These and other obstacles were making it almost impossible to bring more immigrants to Canada. Then Toews added what could be seen as a note of regret for the way in which some

Mennonites in North America, particularly in the United States, had responded to the immigration project in recent years: "How many more could have been brought out, if our people in the United States and in Canada would have stood united in our support, I cannot estimate."[40] Toews offered a prophetic note on possibilities for the future: "I will venture the prophecy that our immigration work in the future will greatly depend on our disposition towards our indebtedness at the present time."[41] Again, as so many times in the past, he concluded his report with a free translation of some lines he had earlier received in a letter from an elder in Russia:

> God knows the hands, although I may not know them, that have helped the poor. Before God nothing is unknown. May they be unknown to me until I pass to the great beyond. God will have their names in his book. Let us thank God who blesses those who give. May the Lord show them that he loves them tenderly. Take those, O Lord, who helped into that city that has the finest gold in its eternal walls.[42]

One of the issues discussed at this conference was modernism, a burning issue in some circles. Toews observed that this was a concern in the United States more than in Canada. He made two comments about modernism. First, he proposed that our fortification against modernistic thinking lay in giving careful attention to what our traditional forebears in the faith had taught us. Second, he analyzed that much of the problem stemmed from mistrust toward our neighbours, a problem which would largely be resolved if we would take the time and effort to understand one another better. In his report on these sessions, Toews expressed great appreciation for the readiness of the General Conference constituency to engage in mission work and especially also to assist in the relief effort. Evidently by then the tide of sentiment in the United States had changed from skepticism to acceptance of the Canadian immigration project. After the sessions, Toews went on a fundraising tour in the United States to solicit donations for relief work. His reflection on this experience was positive. He wrote: "If the work of gathering funds is an undesirable task, nevertheless people have made it easy for me, so today I am a more firm believer than ever in the good attributes of our people and also of our youth."[43]

Church Division
Until then the Rosenorter Church was still one church (*Gemeinde*) with David Toews as *Ältester* and with numerous local places of meeting, but it was becoming apparent that something needed to be done. The Church was growing ever larger and the demands on Toews were on the

increase not only in the local church but also in the school, the Conference and, above all, the work of immigration. Despite his good health and his untiring energy, at times the heavy agenda was becoming too much for him. In addition, some had raised the question whether it was time to form the Rosenorter Church into local independent church groups. Already in June of 1923, before the arrival of the first immigrants, the idea of dividing into separate congregations, each with its own *Ältester*, had been voiced. Although at that time the congregation made the decision to explore this direction, the matter was dropped.[44] It may be that the coming of immigrants from Russia overshadowed such internal concerns, or perhaps the idea of separation had only mild support when it was raised the first time.

At a church meeting on January 26, 1927, a proposal was brought to the floor that addressed both the largeness of the Church and the need to alleviate the work load of Rev. Toews. The matter was presented by Rev. Jacob Klaassen of Eigenheim. The proposal was to separate the Rosenorter congregation into six districts: Tiefengrund, Laird, Eigenheim, Rosthern, Hague, and Aberdeen, with the smaller centres of Silberfeld and Danzig to be attached to the district of their choice. Each congregation could consider Toews as their *Ältester* but there would be no need for an *Ältester* over the whole group, as the large unit would be dissolved. Nor would there be a central treasury. Each congregation would compensate Toews for the amount of time they asked of him. Beginning with Hague, congregations would in time appoint their own ministers and senior elders.[45] In the discussion, some feared that separation would cause splintering. Klaassen then drew attention to the churches in Kansas which still worked together even though they were separate local units. It was decided there would be discussion in each church centre, led by Toews, to be followed by a future meeting of the Church.

At a congregational meeting a year later, on January 11, 1928, the matter was reintroduced. Ministers were invited to identify advantages and disadvantages. Rev. Isaak P. Friesen feared that the forces of evil would overwhelm the church if it divided its strength. He suggested that an assistant *Ältester* be elected. David Toews expressed the view that, with smaller local units in place, more intensive and concentrated work could be done. Yet he saw disadvantages for the smaller districts where it would be difficult to build up the church because of limited resources. Then the local groups reported on the results of their separate discussions of the issue. Laird and Tiefengrund were against separation. In Eigenheim the result was mixed. Thereupon a vote was taken which showed 56 against, 24 in favour of the proposal to separate. It was decided to return to the issue at a future meeting.[46]

A year later, on January 16, 1929, the matter was again put on the agenda of the church meeting. Toews stated at the outset of the discussion that he simply was not able to keep up with all the obligations, especially the schedule of baptisms and communion services at the various locations. He made the suggestion, which he had already proposed earlier at a meeting of the ministers only, that Laird and Tiefengrund should consider electing one *Ältester* for their two congregations and Eigenheim should elect its own *Ältester*. Already before January 16, the Eigenheim leaders had shared this suggestion with the people of the Eigenheim district. The local group favoured such a move and, encouraged by Toews' suggestion, decided to make their preference known to the wider church. Meanwhile, at the January 16 meeting, a proposal was brought forward to carry through with the election of an assistant *Ältester* to help Toews with his many duties. This motion passed, although the delegates from Eigenheim abstained from voting since they already had other ideas. Thus it happened that the elections to choose an assistant for Toews were held in the course of the following two weeks. Toews travelled to each local district to conduct the elections, with the exception of the Eigenheim district. It chose not to participate in this process since it was there that the desire to separate from the Rosenorter Church had taken root.[47]

At a Rosenorter meeting the following June, Toews announced that Johannes Regier of Tiefengrund had been elected as assistant *Ältester,* and that the Rosenorter ministers group had voted to grant the wish of the Eigenheim district to form its own separate congregation, which included electing their own *Ältester*. He also stated that, in his view, the Eigenheim group had acted too hastily and independently. When he had expressed the wish that Eigenheim, as well as Laird and Tiefengrund, should share one *Ältester,* he had intended this to be discussed and decided at a meeting of the entire Rosenorter Church.[48] By then some hard feelings had developed between Toews and some leaders of the Eigenheim church. Toews had not wanted the Eigenheim group to move as resolutely and as hastily toward separation from the Rosenorter circle of congregations. To some it appeared that he was holding out on the decision altogether.[49] Nonetheless, on May 5 Toews was in Eigenheim to conduct their elections of an *Ältester*. The lot fell to Rev. Gerhard G. Epp. On that occasion Toews read the text from Acts 4:32–35, which reads in part, "Now the whole company of those who believed were of one heart and soul." On June 16, 1929, Toews officiated and preached the sermon at a double ordination service in the Eigenheim church for Johannes Regier and Gerhard Epp. This was the last of the Rosenorter Church meetings where Eigenheim was part of the larger church.

Toews and Thiessen

Jacob J. and Tina Thiessen and their daughters Hedie and Katie were among the immigrants who arrived in Canada in the late fall of 1926.[50] Leaving his family in Waterloo, Ontario, Thiessen continued on to Rosthern where he was to attend a December meeting of immigrant representatives and report on the situation in Ukraine. Thiessen had looked forward to a personal meeting with David Toews. The two men met briefly during the immigrants meeting and at the Sunday morning worship service, and had arranged for a longer conversation on Monday morning. But plans became skewed when, during the night before their anticipated discussion, Thiessen and his hosts, Daniel P. and Katharina Enns, were awakened by the ringing of bells at the town fire hall. It was that fateful night of December 12 to 13 when the Toews' house burned to the ground. Thiessen and Enns had rushed to the Toews home along with others, but they could only stand and watch as the flames demolished the building. The Monday meeting amounted to a brief hospital visit to the bedside of David Toews after which Thiessen returned to Waterloo.[51] These were the circumstances under which the two men first met.

But this was certainly not the last that Toews and Thiessen saw of each other. Over the next 20 years they became colleagues and friends. Their close relationship began when, upon invitation from the Board of Colonization, Thiessen moved to Rosthern to assist H.B. Janz with collecting the *Reiseschuld*.[52] He did not find this assignment satisfying so, in the fall of 1927, he returned to high school in the hope of continuing in the teaching profession, this time in a new country and with a new language in hand. That fall he also took a job as staff person for the newly established "Zentral mennonitisches Immigranten Komitee" (Central Mennonite Immigrant Committee) or ZMIK. Thus it was that J.J. Thiessen, now in his early thirties, went back to high school and got involved with immigration work at the same time. Soon he and Tina joined the Rosenorter Church at Rosthern and became involved in youth work, Sunday school teaching, and in the preaching ministry.[53] These were not easy years for the Thiessens. It was particularly their friendship with David and Margarete that sustained them in this time of new beginnings.

Thiessen graduated from the German-English Academy in June of 1930, thinking he would return to teaching. It is likely that during the course of his student years, Toews, who was always on the lookout for potential church workers among the immigrants, had spoken often to him about church ministry. But would there be a place for him? Toews was attracted to Thiessen who had already distinguished himself as a teacher and preacher in southern Russia. They shared their joys and sorrows intimately, as is indicated in one of the earliest pieces of correspondence on record between the two. A letter, dated September 2, 1929, from Thiessen in Rosthern was sent to Toews who was then in Newton, Kansas, on one of his many trips. The letter is significant in that it brought to expression something of the relationship between these two colleagues and their spouses. Thiessen wrote in part:

> Yesterday we missed you greatly. We were gathered as a circle of friends, celebrating my birthday. Your better half, and the darling of your household, was also there. Your loving wife gave me the impression that she was pining for you. She spoke strikingly little, which affirmed my impression. Later my dear wife and I expressed our empathy and our highest respects to her, and our prayer is: Dear God, repay these folks even for this pain of separation.[54]

Thiessen then expressed the wish that Toews would have been available for counsel in the previous few days. In Toews' absence he had had to make a decision whether to accept an invitation to teach at the Rosthern school. But, he said, he had already made his decision. The salary of $400 annually was appealing—and he worried at times about how he would get through the winter. Nonetheless, he could not bring himself to accept the offer, given his current work load.

During the decade of the 1930s and into the 1940s, Toews and Thiessen carried on a vigorous correspondence between Rosthern and Saskatoon. In a day when telephones were still somewhat rare and costly, the mail served their interests well. Thiessen would often post his letter in the evening. The next morning the train, on its daily run from Saskatoon to Prince Albert, would drop the letter off in Rosthern. Toews would write a reply in time for mid-afternoon pick-up as the train stopped at Rosthern on its way back to Saskatoon. The friendship they had established in the latter 1920s continued through the years.

Dinner with the Prime Minister

By 1929 the work of immigration was running into more and more obstacles. In Russia, the officials were doing everything possible to hem in the Mennonites who wished to make their exodus. In Canada, government officials shied away from welcoming immigrants. Financial hardships and some second thoughts about the number of immigrants that could be accommodated influenced the government's attitude. The federal government was being pressured by some provincial officials to scale down the flow of immigrants. Toews worked tirelessly to influence Ottawa as much as he could. Then, when immigration matters were deferred to the provinces, he visited each western government office in turn, hoping to engender a policy of openness. In Saskatchewan the Conservative government under Premier Anderson was negative toward continuing immigration. In Alberta there was some openness. Manitoba was willing to receive a quota of 800 families. However, mounting difficulties in both economic and political areas weakened these commitments.

On one of his many trips to Ottawa, David Toews had an unusual experience that he related on Palm Sunday evening to a youth-sponsored church gathering at Rosthern.[55] In March of 1929, Toews had been invited to Ottawa, along with other denominational leaders, for a consultation on immigration. At one of the sessions, attended by church leaders, several government ministers, and Prime Minister William Lyon Mckenzie King, the latter had to leave the meeting for another appointment. As he was leaving, he turned to the Minister of Immigration, Mr. Forke, and said: "Grant to the Mennonites everything allowable on the basis of our laws. Mennonites are the best citizens we have in Canada." At the Rosthern gathering, Toews commented that such praise was highly honourable, but did we, the Mennonites, really deserve such trust?

After the meeting, he and some of the other visitors were invited to the Prime Minister's residence for dinner. There Toews had the honour of sitting to the right of their host. He was particularly impressed when, before the meal, the Prime Minister folded his hands and offered a spoken prayer of blessing. Following the sumptuous meal, the guests were taken into the drawing room where they noticed a white marble figure of a woman. King explained that this was a sculpture of his mother. Nearby, in a glass cabinet, he showed them a lock of hair and a wedding ring that belonged to his mother. Toews was impressed again with what he considered to be King's respect for the fifth commandment: "Honour your father and your mother." Next they moved to the residence library that housed shelves of historical books and memorable items. The Prime Minister showed Toews a set of religious books, including various Bible commentaries. In times of leisure, said the Prime Minister, these books afforded him much pleasure and sustenance.

In his Palm Sunday evening address to a full church of younger and older people in Rosthern, Toews pointed out that the people of Canada were fortunate to have a person at the helm of government who honoured his parents and was not afraid to profess his faith openly. If a person like this could appreciate Mennonites, then we should not be ashamed of our faith. And we should do our utmost not to give the Prime Minister cause for thinking negatively of the Mennonite people. Toews concluded his talk with the comment: "When I think of Russia, then I cry out with deep thanksgiving: Thanks be to God that we live in Canada!"

A letter, written by David Toews to Margarete and the children while on this trip to Ottawa and Montreal, did not mention his meeting with the Prime Minister. However, the letter did reveal some of Toews' inner thoughts at that time in his life.[56] It was Sunday, and he had just returned to Montreal from Ottawa where the meetings had gone very well in that there was sympathy and good understanding for the Mennonite people and their needs. However, he complained that by then he was finding time spent in these large cities somewhat boring: "If it were not a matter of necessity, I would rather not do so much travelling." He assured the family that he often thought of them and wondered how each one was doing. He was glad that spring was coming and looked forward to planting a nice garden of flowers and vegetables. He expressed the hope that he would be home more in spring than he had been of late. Addressing Margarete, he wrote: "I often think of you, mother, because of the heavy load you carry, especially when I am away. Don't make it too hard for yourself. Be sure to get some help." The next day Toews attended to some business at the CPR offices. Then it was back to Ottawa to meet with some important businessmen. After that he was homeward bound.

Immigration Halted
   In late fall of 1929 reports were coming from Moscow that a large group of Mennonites had fled there from the colonies in the hope of emigrating to Canada. With the implementation of Joseph Stalin's Five-Year Plan the situation in Russia had become intolerable. Upon hearing the news, Toews immediately sought to make the Mennonite constituency aware of the situation and to stir up public sentiment on behalf of these desperate folk. "We have received information," he wrote, "that in Moscow there are 5000 Mennonite refugees, mostly from Siberia, but also from the Crimea, Orenburg, Kuban, and other regions of Russia." Describing their situation as "utterly hopeless," he appealed to Canadian Mennonites to "remember the poor, the widows, the orphans, who have been deprived of everything; let us sacrifice time, money, and clothes for those who have been stripped of all their belongings."[57]
   Moscow was quick to excuse itself. No visas would be issued unless the Canadian government would assure the immigrants of a welcome entrance into Canada. Meanwhile, the Canadian government demanded that only those would be accepted who had at least $250 in hand per person. This created an impossible situation. Unfortunately, the doors to immigration were slowly but surely closing. Many eventually got to Brazil and Paraguay, while a few came to America, including Canada. But the majority were driven back to their homes or deported to the far reaches of the Soviet empire.[58]

13
Relief Work Begins
1930–1931

By 1930 hope for the movement of large numbers of Mennonites from Russia to Canada, in the manner it had been done in the 1920s, was all but abandoned. In Russia, the Communist government had tightened its grip on German colonists. The new regime saw a challenge in making a show of Mennonite *kulaks*, the land owners, by forcing collectivization and by exiling many to Siberia. Mennonite community life, with its traditional fabric of cultural and religious life, was being dismantled —but to permit dissatisfied citizens to leave in droves would send a negative message to the international community. In Canada, the government had lost much of its zeal for inviting new immigrants to its shores. Along with the rest of the world, Canada was facing recession and eventual depression. There were enough jobless and homeless people in the country without adding to the population of displaced citizens. With this, the Canadian Mennonite Board of Colonization turned its attention away from immigration to relief work, internationally and at home.

I Have a Plan
At the beginning of March 1930 David Toews sent a public note to all Mennonite congregations in Canada.[1] In it he implored the churches to send money to the Board of Colonization office which would be forwarded to specific persons in Russia. Even 10 to 15 dollars per family from time to time would help. There was good evidence, he said, that these designated amounts arrived safely at their destination. He wrote that "alleviating suffering in this way at this time is now the only way we can help our brethren; this is the only mission work we are able to do for them." He added the ominous note: "We must work while it is day; night is coming when no one can work."

Despite the emphasis on relief work, Toews did not abandon the possibility of schemes that might continue the flow of immigrants, at least to some extent. He even wrote to Thomas B. Appleget, an executive of the rich and famous Rockefeller Foundation of New York, asking for help for the Mennonites—and it wasn't the first time he had done so. The letter is worth quoting at length, since it tells us something about Toews' relentless quest for assistance along with his forthright approach to people of power and wealth:

> I hope you will pardon me for again approaching you regarding a very unusual circumstance. You may have read in the papers that many of those in Russia, who at one time had any possessions, have been deported into the northernmost regions where it is intended by the Russian Government to have them perish. Simply shooting these people would be an act of mercy in comparison with what is being done now. But shooting hundreds of thousands would stir the world, whereas the entire world remains quiet when they are being starved to death. We cannot afford to lie down quietly knowing that so many of our people in Russia are perishing. You know that not only Mennonites, but also Catholics, Lutherans, Baptists, and all the so-called *kulaks*, with women and children, have been taken to the far north to perish. I think I have a plan that might work and would like to discuss this, if you would possibly grant me an interview with you and, if possible, also with Mr. Rockefeller. . . . If you would kindly send me a favourable reply as soon as possible, I would appreciate this very much.[2]

In a prompt reply from the Rockefeller office, Toews was told there was little chance of a positive response.

We do not know what plan Toews may have had in mind, but it is entirely conceivable that he could have presented Rockefeller with a grand scheme. After all, he had once approached a large railway company, the CPR, with success. Why not the Rockefeller Foundation? At the same time, Toews had not given up on the Mennonite community, both in Canada and internationally.

Second Voyage to Europe

At the July 1930 sessions of the Conference of Mennonites in Canada in Winkler, the delegates moved a hearty vote of thanks to the Board of Colonization for its work of the past. The resolution read in part: "The Conference fully recognizes the service rendered by the Board and expresses its deeply felt gratitude to brother Toews and all his coworkers." The delegates then promised "full confidence in the future work of the Board" and encouraged the Board to do all it could to "help our poor severely tested brothers in Russia in their dire circumstances" as well as those still detained in England and in Germany.[3] This expression of urgent concern, along with similar proddings received earlier, prompted the Board to ask David Toews to plan an extended trip to Europe.

Meanwhile, through the initiative of the European Mennonites, notably Christian Neff of the Weierhof congregation in Germany, a second international gathering of Mennonite leaders had been announced for the city of Danzig in Prussia/Poland. The dates were August 31 to September 3, 1930. Appropriately, the Conference theme was "Mennonite World Relief Work—Mennonites in the USSR." Given the theme, it seemed imperative that David Toews should be there. The CPR again graciously extended free passage to Toews as well as to C.F. Klassen of Winnipeg. In the end, these two Canadians together with Harold S. Bender of the United States were the only North Americans at the Danzig gathering. Toews and Klassen travelled together.

David Toews was anxious when he left home in early August bound for Europe. In a later report, he reflected his initial hesitation to embark on the trip: "Inwardly I resisted the thought, but when the insistence came from various sources and when my presence was requested via an urgent telegram, I finally gave in. My thought was constantly this, that we should spare nothing if there was any opportunity at all for help."[4] As he stepped on board the *Empress of Scotland* in Quebec City, his recorded thoughts reflected his deep faith and sense of mission:

> We are pilgrims and strangers on the journey. In faith and trust, in the midst of much confusion and many complaints, we can trust our God as we come to him with our questions and our needs. Also concerning the great needs in Russia, He will bring everything to a good conclusion, if we can believe the words: "You guide me with your counsel, and afterward you will receive me with honour."[5]

Before departing for Europe, Toews had a full schedule of activities in Canada. In Winnipeg he met with C.F. Klassen and others. He also arranged some financial support for his family while he was away. In a letter to his beloved Margarete he wrote:

> From Winnipeg you will receive $100 every two weeks, except the last week of September. Please, as much as possible, use this to pay off debts, but be sure that you yourselves lack nothing. Gretchen must not worry so much about obtaining a (teaching) position. We will probably be able to help her somewhat.[6]

One wonders how so much could be accomplished with such meagre funds. Evidently by then the family had learned some lessons about stretching a dollar.

Toews proceeded directly to Montreal to arrange free passage to Europe for C.F. Klassen. In this he was successful, which greatly pleased Toews, because now he would not have to travel alone. Then he went back to Toronto where he had arranged to meet Jacob. H. Janzen. Together they approached some officials on behalf of the immigration cause. From Toronto, Toews continued on to Ottawa for contact with government officials. Then he travelled to Philadelphia via Waterloo for some meetings with Mennonite leaders. From there he headed to Quebec City, again passing through Waterloo and Montreal. The additional stopovers in Waterloo gave him a chance to report on his meetings and to receive counsel from Janzen. On August 19, he boarded the *Empress of Scotland* in Quebec City. While waiting on board for preparations to be completed, he sent a farewell letter to "mother and the children." In these lines we catch a glimpse of Toews' family relationships and his inner thoughts:

My thoughts are constantly with you all. I commit you to the care of our heavenly Father. Benno, may I request that you take the bran to the mill. I know you dear children will do everything possible to help your mother. I had some pictures taken for my passport and am sending the extras to you as a greeting from afar. Brother Janzen thought that on the photos I look sterner than I actually am. I am also sending you the key for our post box. I assume you will bring the mail to the office each day so it can be answered. . . . The ship is about to set sail. The trip will again bring much restlessness and much work. As long as it helps the poor folks over there. How we would rejoice! I am very pleased that I do not need to travel alone. Brother Klassen will be a beloved travel companion. The food is good. The rooms are also comfortable and the service is good. But who knows how we will fare with seasickness this time? Yet these are small details. As long as there will be some success with our major agenda. How that would please us!"[7]

The ocean voyage went quite well with only minor bouts of seasickness. Toews' description of the amenities sounds quite inviting:

We are very comfortable on board. In the morning when we arise, we just press a button and the steward brings warm water for washing. If we desire, he prepares the bathtub with saltwater. I have taken two baths already while en route. Then we dress and go to breakfast, which is served at 8:30 a.m. . . . The food is very good, but it does not taste like home cooking. I fear, nonetheless, that I will not have lost weight by the time I arrive at home.[8]

Toews observed that many of the passengers were in a party mood. But he could not be hilarious; he was on a serious mission.

Always and again my thoughts turn to our poor folk in Russia. Oh, if only a way could be found to help them! I would return home with great joy if we could find a solution. . . . If we could get our people out of

their red paradise, the rest would take care of itself, even if our government would not give permission to immigrate. God the Lord can help
where human plans come to naught.[9]

Then David's thoughts turned to home again:

How are you getting along? I think much and often about you. How
gladly I would like to take delight in the beautiful flowers in your
garden, dear mother. I know that I will see beautiful flowers in England,
in Holland, and in Germany, but they will not attract my attention as
much as ours at home.[10]

The letter was written on the fifth day at sea, two days before the
anticipated docking at Southampton, England.

Once ashore, Toews and Klassen were met by CPR officials who
brought them to their hotel. The next day they were taken to Atlantic
Park where they spoke with the five remaining detained immigrants.
Toews was able to encourage them and assure them that, according to his
information, they would soon be on their way to Canada. The next day
the two travellers were on their way to Hamburg where they arrived in
the evening. They were greeted by several CPR officials and by Dr.
Benjamin H. Unruh who had come from Karlsruhe to meet his colleagues. Toews had been looking forward to meeting Brother Unruh, his
co-worker at-a-distance, for whom he had developed great respect. These
gentlemen took their visitors to the immigrant holding centre at Möln,
where some 450 detained Mennonite refugees were awaiting clearance
to proceed to Canada. In Danzig they would meet a large group as well.

It was already late when the delegation arrived at the holding centre
but the people were expecting them. A choir sang: "Gott grüsse Dich"
(We greet you in the name of God) and "Vertraue auf Gott" (Trust in the
Lord). Brother Unruh addressed the gathering and then Toews was asked
to bring a word of spiritual encouragement. He observed that these
refugees are "beloved brothers and sisters," and that "it is difficult to
understand how Canada can deny entrance to such persons who would
only be an asset to the country."[11] All the while Toews had the rescue of
suffering people in mind. For him, the entire trip to Europe had a single
purpose, namely, to facilitate the exit of his suffering people from Russia
and to ensure that those detained would be able to complete their journey
and join their loved ones in Canada. When he met CPR and government
officials in Canada and in Europe, he persistently raised this matter. He
hoped to place this issue front and centre at the Conference in Danzig as
well. From Hamburg he wrote in a mood of optimism: "Today Brother
Unruh was in my room and he told us about a number of prospects for

our people through various organizations. I am very hopeful."[12] Toews closed this letter with the double wish: "May the Lord protect you, and may the work we are doing for our brothers succeed."

In Danzig

David Toews arrived in Danzig on Saturday, and was met at the train station by relatives and family friends. His parents were known in the Danzig area where his father had farmed and served as minister before migrating to southern Russia in 1869. Margarete had left the Danzig area with her family when she was already a teenager. Both had left relatives and friends behind. David was billeted with family acquaintances, but he would have to leave any serious visiting until after the Conference. Its business occupied him from morning until evening so the nights were already short enough.

The Conference began on Sunday, August 31, with worship and celebrations. About 1500 persons were in attendance. Toews had been asked to preach the morning sermon but had declined, for which he was much relieved when he noted the presence of learned pastors and high officials. His duties, as a representative of the Board of Colonization, included bringing greetings to the assembly on behalf of the majority of Mennonites in Canada. On Sunday afternoon the delegates enjoyed a three-hour boat cruise on the Weichsel (Vistula) River. Business sessions began Monday morning and continued until Wednesday, September 3.

The main theme of the sessions centred on relief work in view of recent turmoil in Russia. Toews was asked to chair the sessions for one of the days. Understandably, he also took his place among the presenters, outlining the work of immigration to Canada over the past decade and expressing concerns about the current state of affairs in the Soviet Union. B.J. Schellenberg, who knew Toews personally and was in a position to assess his impact and attitude at the Conference, wrote:

One has the impression that Toews was a person whom one must take seriously. On this trip, which took him through England, Holland, and Germany, he again had to appear before all kinds of important people of this earth; he, who apparently had not known nor had he nurtured any other ambition than to be a farmer, lived by the watchword, "Let us regard one another as greater than ourselves." In his contact with Mennonites in Europe he was struck by the amount of education many of these people had amassed. Yet in many respects these persons marvelled at this American: a faithful servant of his Lord and Master, warm in love toward his fellow man, distinguished by a high sense of responsibility for the work of rescue in which he was engaged. Thus he could take his place of leadership with dignity and honour.[13]

Writing to his family from Berlin on the day following the Danzig Conference, Toews mused: "In my view people were prone to pay too much attention to me."[14]

At the same time he reported that the Conference had been a success in that there had been significant sharing of information and that a sense of unity resulted among the various Mennonite groups. Toews was impressed with the desire on the part of European Mennonites to help the suffering people in Russia and those detained in camps. The North Americans and Europeans seemed to be of one mind. Toews noted that the entire delegate group "wished there to be no pause in the [relief] work, but that all should be fully engaged wherever there was need."[15] Discussion had focused on how the international organization might be strengthened so that the inter-Mennonite network could respond when opportunity would arise. Toews expressed high regard for Harold S. Bender, especially when Bender proposed a specific Sunday for worldwide collections among Mennonite congregations in all countries to help the immigration project. To his family he wrote: "I am enjoying much love here, but my thoughts are constantly with you, my family."[16]

After the meetings in Danzig, Toews travelled to Berlin where he engaged in high level talks with various relief agencies and governmental officials. Consultation had to do with understanding the situation in Russia and with finding ways to convey relief materials to places of need. While the talks were encouraging in that there was sympathy for the cause, Toews was hoping for concrete results. But the political and social situation made this difficult. With discussions in Berlin concluded, he returned to the Danzig area for several days to visit with relatives and friends who had urged him to spend some time with them. Toews felt at home there, comparing the reception to the times when he would return to Newton, Kansas, or to Beatrice, Nebraska, or to Tiefengrund, Saskatchewan.[17] He was invited to preach in the Heubudener Mennonite Church and visited Weiszhof, the village in which his parents had once lived. He also made a sojourn to Quadendorf where his father had begun his work as minister years earlier.[18] Toews was overwhelmed by the hospitality in these familial surroundings. Back home he reported: "My, how many loving people I was able to meet! The thought that I will likely not see many of them again makes my heart ache."[19]

One other side trip took him to Karlsruhe where he planned to engage in extensive discussion with Benjamin H. Unruh. Unfortunately, Toews became ill with a kidney stone attack and was hospitalized for two days. This incident signalled the beginning of health problems, although for several years already he had complained that he was losing his hearing. Despite this setback, the trip to Europe was an enriching and encouraging experience, and he returned home with renewed spiritual and emotional strength for the tasks ahead.

Cast Your Bread upon the Waters

Back home, David Toews continued his advocacy on behalf of his suffering people in Russia. On October 4, 1930, he wrote a letter of appeal to the Rev. Dr. J. Chisholm, a government representative in Ottawa. Could the Canadian government not allow into Canada at least some of the prospective immigrants who were waiting in Moscow and might be sent to Siberia? Toews' argument knew no bounds, as we see in his pursuit of the following line of argument:

> We do many things on humanitarian grounds even for dogs and horses. Quite properly so. But could not Canada receive about 400 people, some 80 families, and permit Mennonites now here to receive them into their homes and care for them?[20]

Although his letter, with its compelling comparison, fell on deaf ears, this did not deter him. In the spring of 1931 he and Ältester Jacob H. Janzen of Waterloo visited Senator William Borak in Washington, D.C., again on behalf of the Moscow refugees. Apparently Senator Borak was sensitive to human rights issues. In a follow-up letter to their visit, Toews wrote: "We believe that the best solution would be for the Soviet Government to modify its policy in such a way that peaceful and

Wedding of Marie Toews & Herman Riesen on October 11, 1930.

obedient citizens of that country would be allowed to live a peaceable life in the country where, for many years, they have served God according to the dictates of their own conscience." He then informed the senator of the prevailing conditions:

> We have proof from many letters that we have received from people whose word we have not the slightest reason to doubt, that the so-called *kulaks* are being driven from their homes, that ministers are being put in jail on account of their religion, and that many thousands have been deported to the northern forests where they are crowded together in miserable barracks, given scant food, and forced to do slave labour in the woods. We know that many people, especially children, have already perished through lack of the most elementary sanitary conditions. We also know that people have been separated from their families and that famine conditions prevail in many parts of Russia because grain is taken away from the people and they are left to starve.[21]

We do not know that anything came of this appeal.

It was one thing to address persons to whom one can appeal on purely political and humanitarian grounds; it is quite another to challenge people of one's own community. To his people, Toews could speak heart to heart. He could remind them of a common spiritual foundation: Jesus Christ. He could appeal to a common history and culture: the Mennonite people. He could appeal to a common commitment: to follow Jesus. And so in an article in *Der Bote*, dated September 2, 1931, he began by pointing to the compassionate heart of Jesus on the basis of which he identified compassion as the heart of Christianity. From that standpoint he called for people in the churches to have compassion for their own people in Russia. Yes, there are many needs in the world, but our first mission is to rescue our own people from destruction.[22]

In a letter to John P. Andres, Toews revealed the situation of some of his own relatives in Russia:

> My cousins from Alt-Samara have pretty well all been exiled to Archangelsk where they must live out their days in deplorable barracks. The weak young women are compelled to drag trees, shovel sand, and do similar kind of work. They are destined to "go under," and they will if things do not soon change. Many have been banished to prisons even further north, among them Gerhard Riesen, husband of my cousin Katherina Riesen. As much as we know, any trace of him has vanished. Apparently their crime was that they had received letters from abroad.[23]

The letter to Andres was written in response to a request for specific information on conditions in Russia.

At times Toews became defensive and prophetic in his advocacy for the suffering people in Russia. "I realize that many of you are already provoked with me that always and again I come with urgent requests, but I dare not neglect to do so," he wrote. His prophetic note was clothed in a positive spirit:

> I do not believe at all that our people have become so lackadaisical that they would think only of themselves and look out for themselves. Our people help gladly when they see need. How could it be otherwise? Does not the image of a people flash before us—torn from their homes, half-starved, apathetic, without tears, having to take up their assigned hard labour? And we, who are no better than they, live in warm homes and are privileged to sit at sumptuous tables and indulge ourselves. We speak of hard times but what is that compared to the suffering of others beyond our land? May the Lord make us willing to fulfil our duty toward those who live in indescribable misery. If ever there was a time when our people are asked to sacrifice, then it is in this time with respect to those who must exist in their awful barracks devoid of even a ray of love upon their dark way of life.[24]

He ended his appeal with a quotation from Ecclesiastes 11:1: "Let us cast our bread upon the waters, and it will return to us in due time."

Toews stood among his people as a gracious yet persistent prodder of conscience. His appeal, and the appeal of others throughout the Mennonite community in Canada, resulted in a significant outpouring of donations to help the destitute in Russia as well as those whose flight eastward came to a halt in China. Yet the need was overwhelming just at a time when at home in Canada the Depression was making existence difficult as well. When others might have given up in despair, Toews appealed to the "bottom line:" "Wo Menschenhilfe versagt, da bleibt uns der Blick nach oben frei." (When human resources collapse, we still have open recourse to God.)[25]

Hard Times in Canada

While relief work focused mainly on assisting Russian Mennonites, even if in some small way, there were also troubles at home in Canada. Signs of the coming Depression were beginning to show. Severely depressed grain and commodity prices cut into incomes of the agricultural community. Most of the immigrant farmers were already strapped with heavy indebtedness due to the cost of settling and developing their farms. Then drought and the accompanying plagues of grasshoppers and other insects multiplied their problems. In 1930 the southern part of Saskatchewan and large regions of Alberta had total crop failure. At the beginning of December of that year, Toews wrote to Alvah Bowman, vice-chair of the Board of Colonization: "Conditions as they are in Canada at the present time are not known within the memory of the oldest settlers. . . . I hope that brotherly love will again prompt us to do what we can to relieve suffering among our brethren in Canada."[26] In a note in *Der Bote* later that month, Toews made a plea for clothing and money so that hard-pressed farmer immigrants who had had no crop and who faced a hard winter could be offered some relief.[27]

The next summer the drought prevailed. In Saskatchewan, the southern parts were hardest hit. Thus, in the fall of 1931 Toews organized the shipment of three railway carloads of potatoes to the dried-out areas. One went from Laird to Eyebrow, another from Rosthern to Herbert, and a third from Hague to Truax. Toews and the Board designated this relief effort not only for Mennonites but for anyone in need. At the same time, he argued that government aid should be available to Mennonites as well since they paid taxes the same as others. There should be no discrimination either way.[28]

Seizing the Initiative

With the *Reiseschuld* on everyone's mind, immigrant families were on the lookout for work opportunities for their grown children. Jobs were not plentiful in the early 1930s. One opportunity presented itself in the big cities where wealthy Canadians who owned large homes employed good live-in housekeepers. Since Mennonite women had a reputation for their domestic skills, the combination worked out well. In Winnipeg, in Saskatoon, and in Vancouver a considerable number of young women came to the city for work. It did not take long for the churches to organize pastoral care for this workforce. This included providing residences where the women could stay overnight and could participate in worship and Bible study programs. From the beginning, David Toews had regarded the ministry among house-maids and among students to be important. The situation in Saskatoon lay close to his heart, partly because some of his children spent time in Saskatoon attending Normal School and the University of Saskatchewan. Also, he was quite aware of the need for hospital visitation there. In the summer of 1930, the initiative was taken to establish a permanent church ministry in Saskatoon with Rev. J.J. Thiessen as the church worker.[29]

As with other projects, Toews sometimes moved ahead in faith even when material support was not yet in place. Thus it was only after the work was begun that W.S. Gottschalk of the General Conference Home Missions Board received a letter from Toews in which the latter suggested that it would be good to open a home for working women, and that the Mission Board should consider a financial commitment of $100 a month to this ministry. This would be considered a joint venture of the Board of Colonization and the Mission Board.[30]

While Toews' initial suggestion to the Mission Board was low-key, his goal was specific and urgent. Two months later he sent a lengthy letter to remind Gottschalk and the entire Home Mission Board of his earlier suggestion to which he had not yet received a reply. He also suggested that J.J. Thiessen, who was already commuting to Saskatoon from Rosthern, would be an excellent candidate for the project.[31] Another month went by without a reply. At that point Toews informed Gottschalk that he had assigned Thiessen to the work, and that Thiessen had already taken up residence in the city two weeks earlier. He hoped he had not acted hastily before the entire Board had consented. In his words:

> If you think I have been too hasty and should have waited until the consent of the Board came, I apologize, but I am sure that all the Board members will agree with me that it was about time that something should be done and I hope that you will not cenjure [sic] me too severely for taking the step that I did take.[32]

It appears Toews was inviting and expecting a strong word of criticism for his actions, but he had decided it was better to ask for forgiveness later than to be denied permission at the outset. This way of working was reminiscent of the signing of the famous CPR contract. On February 6, 1931, Gottschalk wrote to Toews concerning his request. He was convinced the work in Saskatoon was necessary and personally he supported the move. However, Toews should bear in mind that letters take about six weeks to travel 8000 miles, the accumulated distance between the addresses of Mission Board members, all of whom would need to give their approval. Thus he should expect that the final answer would be some time in coming.[33] Eventually the Mission Board did confirm support for the project.

In Saskatoon there were desperate economic situations as well, as J.J. Thiessen discovered when he made his pastoral rounds. Judging from the correspondence between Toews and Thiessen at this time, it would appear that the two of them bore the burden of poverty-stricken depression casualties on their shoulders.[34] Pastorally, at least, this may well have been the case, given their jurisdictions and sense of responsibility.

School Concerns

Throughout the 1930s, David Toews continued his involvement with the German-English Academy. While in the 1920s the immigrants had brought new life into the school, particularly by raising enrolment, financial problems continued to plague it. Money was tight and this meant that teachers were not getting their full remuneration on time. The problem only got worse as the Depression of the early 1930s set in.[35]

The main burden of carrying the school continued to fall on the shoulders of Toews. He felt responsible for raising funds and capable of doing so. Did it have to be this way? Toews made an effort to single out others to help him. Not long after J.J. Thiessen had settled into church work in Saskatoon, Toews wrote to him with a request:

> I want to write about one other matter. I would very much like you to work on behalf of the school in Saskatoon as well as in Osler and the surrounding region. But I will discuss this matter personally with you in the near future. At this time I must as yet raise a large amount of money for the school so that we can bring the year to a fairly good conclusion.[36]

Later that fall he wrote to Thiessen again: "To keep the school going this coming year we will need to apply all our energies."[37]

Among the teachers, who all too often had to wait an extra month or two for their salaries, was David Toews' son, Benno. In the fall of 1930, he began a four-year teaching stint at the Rosthern school. Then from 1936 to 1938, he taught at both the Academy and at the Rosthern Bible School which had begun operations alongside the high school program. Benno was not able to sustain himself financially on the meagre salary he received there so in time he moved into the public school system and

Benno & Catherine (Friesen) Toews with son Theodore. Benno was teacher at the German-English Academy in Rosthern from 1930–1934, 1936–1938, 1944–1945.
Photo: Frank H. Epp, *Education with a Plus*

into mission service in Oklahoma and Arizona He was back at the Academy for a third time in the mid-1940s.

Some in the Rosenorter Church felt the financial obligation for the German-English Academy did not need to rest on the shoulders of David Toews. At a church meeting in June of 1930 in Hague, H.B. Janz proposed that each of the Rosenorter local congregations should obligate itself to raise its fair share of the financial budget of the school. That way the local group rather than David Toews and his helpers would take responsibility for the collection of funds. The idea was seconded and was agreed upon, although in the discussion David Toews did not commit himself. Apparently he was not warm to the plan. The decision was not implemented at that time and the old system, with Toews taking the primary responsibility, continued. It seems he felt both responsible for, and capable of, seeing projects through, especially if he had initiated them.

A Different Bed Every Night

In the early 1930s, David Toews travelled extensively. Besides the major trip to Europe, he continued to traverse the North American continent on behalf of the Board of Colonization and the church. One wonders how he found the physical and emotional resources to keep up the pace. From time to time, he confided to his family: "I'd rather be home." Writing to Margarete and the children from Ottawa on March 7, 1931, he admitted: "Travelling gives me no pleasure, and I find it particularly difficult when I am left alone to represent important matters, but it has to be that way because we are so short on money. If the CPR officials could accomplish what needed to be done, then I would not have to spend so much time and money on these kinds of trips." He went on to say that "the trip from Rosthern to Ottawa went quite well, although it was understandably quite boring, but [he] shortened the time with reading."[38]

The purpose of this latest trip to Ottawa, which took him away from home for about two weeks, concerned those hundreds of Russian Mennonites detained in Europe. They desperately needed to gain entrance into Canada lest they be sent back to Russia. "I want to do everything possible for them," he wrote to his family, "but what I will be able to accomplish I do not know."[39] His negotiations began in Montreal where he spoke with CPR officials. They advised him to see Mr. Blair of the Immigration Department in Ottawa, so after one day he made his way to Ottawa where he had numerous discussions with government officials. There he had to stay at the old Windsor Hotel, with its small rooms, dust on the furniture, and spider webs on the ceiling. He would much have preferred the Chateau Laurier, but it was "too expensive for us poor people."[40] After a day in Ottawa, he returned to Montreal for further consultation, then on to Waterloo for Sunday where he again gained inspiration and guidance from his good friend, Jacob H. Janzen.[41]

From Waterloo, Toews proceeded to Philadelphia to confer with Maxwell H. Kratz, member of the executive of the original Mennonite Central Committee,[42] and with the Quakers. Depending on that conversation, he would proceed either to New York or Washington to look up someone who might be able to help with the dilemma concerning the refugees in Europe. Then he went back to Philadelphia to confer again with Kratz and others who had gathered for a meeting on matters of relief. On the way home he stopped off in Ontario for a few days of meetings before returning home to Saskatchewan.

How did Toews stand up under this kind of schedule? To his family he wrote from Philadelphia: "This past night we were in the YMCA Hotel. For tonight we have found a different hotel, although I am not really happy with this one either. But it's only for one night, so we will endure. Hopefully we will have better luck after that. Otherwise I am in good health, able to sleep reasonably well if and when we have decent accommodations, but I'm in a different bed every night and have to put up with a great variety."[43] We sense in these comments the signs of a wearying traveller. In February 1931, Toews had turned 61 years of age.

Do Not Tire

Fortunately, by this time those who had been critical of the Mennonite exodus were becoming smaller in number and quieter in their criticism. News of dire circumstances in Russia and the positive presence of new immigrants in Canada contributed to a significant change in sentiment and culture. Along with this changing mood came encouraging expressions of appreciation for the work which David Toews had done and was doing. The Conference of Mennonites in Canada, meeting in July of 1931 in Langham, Saskatchewan, passed the following resolution of thanks:

> We are thankful that Ält. David Toews was willing to help the poor. Even though we have not rewarded his service with money, nonetheless our deepest expression of gratitude stands as a sign of our love for and our trust in him. We request that he continue to be active in untiring service to our brothers. Our prayers shall be his support. In the future we also want to entrust our donations into his hands, and pray that God will make us willing to do good and not to tire. It is our holy obligation to carry our brothers' cry for help to our congregations and to inspire them to actively help and support our poor brothers.[44]

To open the conference, Moderator Toews had preached on Hebrews 12:1–2, on the basis of which he admonished Conference delegates not to neglect their duties of building the family and the church in accordance with God's will. Toews always had his heart and vision set on the wider horizon of future possibilities.

He had little time to complain of or think of his own tiredness. Hardly had he returned home when the endless requirements of his church office faced him. He wrote of his activities to J.J. Thiessen:

> Yesterday morning I was at the mission festival in Laird and in the afternoon at a wedding east of Rosthern. Tomorrow I go to a funeral in Aberdeen where two men were killed by a freight train, one of them a member of our church. Day after tomorrow there is a funeral in Laird where our minister-brother Jacob Janzen will be buried.[45]

Was the weekend of July 20 typical of David Toews' activity?

There appeared to have been no reprieve in his busy schedule. On August 10 he arrived in Waterloo, hoping to meet Jacob H. Janzen, but Janzen had gone to Pelee Island to serve the church there. Writing from Waterloo to his family in Rosthern, he said: "My thoughts are constantly with you, and I wish so much that this whole trip would be behind me."[46]

The daughters of Margarete and David Toews in the early 1930s. From left, front row: *Dora, Marie, Elsie;* back row: *Elma, Louise, Margaret, Anna.*

In the morning he was off to Montreal, then to Toronto, to Ottawa, and on to New York City. In each of these places he made contacts on behalf of the refugees in Europe. Of that situation he wrote in the aforementioned letter that "the news concerning their plight is sad; if only something could be done for the most desperate ones. I am still hopeful."

But Toews' travels were not all business. In early October he took his wife and some of the children on a vacation trip to Vancouver. They had a delightful time together there. The scenery in British Columbia was new to the family, although not to him.[47] Then in November he was "on the road" alone again. First he went eastward to Ontario. His itinerary began with a provincial immigrant delegates' meeting in Vineland, Ontario, after which he itinerated in churches in Waterloo, Leamington, Harrow, Pelee Island, and made further official contacts in Toronto. Several weeks later, in December, he went west to attend ministerial meetings in Didsbury and Coaldale, Alberta. Then he headed home where Margarete was making preparations for Christmas.

Forgive One Another

At the beginning of the 1930s, the longstanding tensions between David Toews and Isaak P. Friesen had not yet been resolved. Hard feelings continued to fester over the debt that Toews had incurred when he borrowed money from Friesen for a real estate purchase. The speculative venture had been a failure, but Toews remained indebted to Friesen for much of the balance of the money. In the March 17, 1931 letter to his family, Toews reminded them to "take some of their bi-weekly household money to pay the debt owed to Friesen and Epp." Toews was trying to pay back what he owed, but it was slow going, especially in those hard times. Friesen tended to be business-like and impatient, and felt that Toews was neglecting his obligations. To make matters worse, Friesen had been critical of Toews' immigration work from the beginning and continued in this mode. An added complicating factor was that Toews and Friesen had children in common: Benno, the son of David and Margaret, was married to Catherine, the Friesens' daughter. The unresolved issue between the two men cast a shadow over those extended family relationships. It was not easy for the children to find happiness in their marriage as long as there was something unresolved between their two fathers.

Eventually several persons from the ministerial council of the church were appointed to bring the matter between Toews and Friesen to resolution.[48] This was not an easy process as it was also complicated by the ongoing troubles between Isaak Braun and Heinrich P. Friesen, the brother of Isaak P. Friesen. In a letter written by J.J. Thiessen to Isaak P.

Friesen on May 11, 1932, Thiessen reported on a meeting of the ministers of the Rosenorter Church concerning the issue. There David Toews told his colleagues that he had accomplished a reconciliation with Heinrich P. Friesen and also with several others with whom he had severe differences of opinion over Isaak Braun. Writing on behalf of Toews, Thiessen urged I.P. Friesen to leave the past behind and to be reconciled with Toews as well.[49] The two men begged forgiveness of each other and the matter was laid to rest.

No Abiding Place

Life was not easy for David Toews. There was the constant struggle with unfinished agenda brought on by the immigration project of the 1920s. The *Reiseschuld* should have been cleaned up by this time but it lingered on. The hundreds of persons detained in western Europe were, for the most part, still awaiting permission to complete their trek. However, some issues were moving toward resolution. There was a groundswell of support for the work of Toews and the Board. This held true for the Mennonites of both Russian origin and Swiss background. Toews felt and was buoyed by this sentiment of appreciation. Some strained personal relationships persisted, although there was also significant movement toward clarity and closure.

Personal health was something of a concern. David was having difficulty with his hearing and he had suffered that kidney stone attack while in Germany. Now at the beginning of 1932, Margarete was ill. In a letter to J.J. Thiessen, Toews wrote that she had not been feeling well for four weeks already and had been in bed for some of that time.[50] Yet in the midst of these challenges, Toews kept a positive and hopeful attitude. Writing to Thiessen the day after his 62nd birthday, he spoke with appreciation of his family relationships:

> Our children have afforded me much joy, particularly on this occasion. The red and white carnations that bedecked the table this morning said something to me. They spoke of love, of a warm bond, and of fulfilment. The best fortune that can befall us is, of course, the fortune of a good home, and the Lord has blest us in this far beyond what we are worthy of or deserve.[51]

In the same letter, Toews bared his soul with respect to the future: "What the new year will bring for me is in God's hands. We have no abiding place here; we seek a future eternal home. May this also apply to my endeavours."

14

Some Laurels But No Rest
1932–1935

In an unpublished manuscript, B.J. Schellenberg wrote from an immigrant's point of view about how things should have been for David Toews by the early 1930s:

> We were now happily settled in Canada where we had much to be thankful for: clothes on our back and bread on the table. Glorious freedom beckoned us; we knew no fear; our children could attend school; the climate was moderate. Furthermore, one should have expected that our cherished "saviour" would rest on his laurels, and we would surround him constantly, singing songs of thanksgiving and praise to him.[1]

Unfortunately, that was not entirely how things turned out. Some laurels did come to Toews. It seems that at sessions of the Conference of Mennonites in Central Canada the delegates felt the urge to reaffirm their confidence in the Board and in David Toews. Thus, again, at the 30th annual sessions, held in 1932 in Laird, Saskatchewan, one of the closing resolutions stated: "We thank our chairman, David Toews, for his selfless service as leader of the Conference and for his sacrificial work on behalf of the brothers in need in far-off Russia."[2] In part, these affirmations may have served to compensate for the harsh criticism that had come to Toews over the months and years since 1923. In any case, for David Toews there was no letting up. Schellenberg continued:

> But as far as rest was concerned, that seemed quite out of reach for the time being. There were 21,000 immigrants, fully new and strange in the land, all of them wanting to be provided for and cared for; 21,000 of whom most would have wanted immediately to acquire a debt-free, comfortably furnished farm which they could call their own.[3]

Of course, Toews had no intentions of letting up. At times he could have left the work to others but instead he chose to place himself at the centre of the action. He was driven by the passion to give his all and his best to the development of the Mennonite church and of Mennonite communities. It is not that he thought only his ideas counted and only his presence would make the difference, although some may have interpreted his efforts that way. Toews was driven by a sense of responsibility for what he had helped to begin, whether it was the school, the church, or the immigration movement. By now he had invested so much in these projects, he wanted to ensure that they remained on course. Worrisome situations created considerable anxiety, but anxiety seemed to energize him.

Concern about the travel debt was a case in point. At a provincial gathering of the Colonization Board in Manitoba in the early summer of 1932, he began with the text: "He who knows to do good, but does not do it, to him it is sin." Then he reminded his listeners of the deteriorating situation. The troublesome *Reiseschuld* was increasing rather than decreasing. The debt to the Canadian Pacific Railway now stood at $1,200,000. In a somewhat disciplining tone, but with a note of thanksgiving, Toews said:

> A common banker would probably laugh at the methods we are using to collect the monies. Even our young people sometimes want to be very wise. But they should rather heed their elderly parents and learn good practices of reducing debt from the older generation.[4]

On the positive side, Toews then reported on the partial success in 1930 when Mennonites of Germany and North America, with the help of the German government and other organizations, were instrumental in resettling about 2500 Mennonite refugees from Russia in South America —900 in Brazil and 1600 in Paraguay. But then again, there were difficulties. Many could not escape what had become indescribable conditions in Russia. Toews concluded that "the reality of persons suffering and dying knocks at our conscience and complains against us if we neglect to do all that we can."[5] The address gives us a picture of how he walked the line between despair and hope, between suffering and rescue. At the conclusion of the gathering, the delegates gave resounding affirmation to the work of Toews and the Board, and expressed assurance that the Manitoba churches were fully behind their initiatives.

Fear of Deportation
Toews feared that if those detained in Germany were not soon allowed to proceed to Canada they would be sent back to Russia. In his view, this was as bad as a ship at sea standing by and only watching while a sister ship nearby was sinking. It was incumbent on Mennonites in North America to do all they could, even at the risk of their own well-being, to rescue those who were going under.

Then there was also the prospect that immigrants, who found themselves under long-term care in hospitals or in institutions for the mentally ill, could be deported to Russia by the Canadian officials if in one way or another they became a burden to the state. The Board of Colonization had obligated itself to undertake the support of all such cases for the first five years of residency in Canada. Now, with a tightening economic situation in the land, Toews feared the worst. At this time, the situation in Russia was becoming unusually grim. The years 1932 and 1933 saw a devastating famine sweep the land with millions of lives lost. All Toews could do was inform the constituency and make another appeal for funds.[6] In a note in *Der Bote*, dated May 25, 1932, Toews thanked his readers for generous donations, and also drew attention to the fact that recently one person had been deported to Russia because his debts could not be paid.

Somewhat later, in the spring of 1933, Toews reported on a certain Johann Grunau who was in a mental institution in Selkirk, Manitoba. Since neither his family nor the Board of Colonization had the funds to pay for his hospital expenses, notice had been given by the immigration officials that he was on the verge of being deported back to Russia. There may well have been additional reasons for the prospect of deportation in this case, although they were not stated. Toews had worked along with others to avert the action, but the matter was not yet resolved. He recommended that a central fund be established to assist in such cases. This kind of situation motivated Toews to urge that Mennonites in Canada establish their own "Bethania" mental institution such as they left behind in Ukraine.[7] By the end of 1933, most of the provincial Mennonite groups had begun to take responsibility for the mentally ill in their region which greatly relieved the anxiety that came with calling on the state for help.[8]

Visiting Relatives in America

In February of 1932, David Toews left on a trip to the western United States. His main purpose was to visit his relatives, mainly in Aberdeen, Idaho. Three of David's siblings had moved there about the turn of the century: his brother Heinrich and wife Anna, brother Johannes and wife Agathe, sister Anna and husband Frank Wenger. David's parents, Jacob and Anna, had moved to Aberdeen after their retirement from ministry at First Mennonite Church, Newton, Kansas. They died in 1922 and 1924, respectively, and were buried in Aberdeen.

The specific occasion of David Toews' visit to Aberdeen at this time was to attend the 50th wedding anniversary of his brother, Heinrich, and his sister-in-law, Anna. Apparently Heinrich was in failing health by this time so David's visit was very important to him. According to David's report to his family, there was much evidence of love and affection

Brother Heinrich and sister-in-law Anna Toews in 1932 at their 50th wedding anniversary in Aberdeen, Idaho.
Photo: F.R. Belk, *The Great Trek*

among the siblings. The presentation of a photo of the David Toews family to Heinrich and Anna brought tears to the eyes of Anna, who, in the words of David, "retreated to the kitchen for a while." The photo was brought to the church and, according to David's report to Margarete, it "had a strategic place on the piano during the service, so that you [my family] were also present, although you were not able to benefit from being there."[9] At the golden wedding celebration service on Sunday afternoon, David Toews gave the main address. During his one-week stay in Aberdeen, he preached in the church on Sunday morning and gave English presentations, including reports on the work of the Colonization Board, on Wednesday and Thursday evening.

While he was in Aberdeen, David Toews' siblings prevailed upon him to take the train to California in the interest of visiting other Toews relatives. There had been a death in the extended Toews family living in Paso Robles, and David was singled out as the person to represent the family and bring comfort. The Toews relatives took David to American Falls, Idaho, from where he travelled by train to Paso Robles by way of San Francisco. In a letter to his family, dated March 1, and written underway from Ogden, Utah, Toews instructed his family to check with his secretary, Kaethe Hooge, whether he might be on the preaching list for Sunday, March 13, and if so, she should ask Isaak P. Friesen to find an alternative to take his place. He also asked Margarete to bring his personal greetings to those who were ill, in particular "Tante Lehn und Frau Dyck." Even from a distance, Rev. Toews was mindful of his pastoral duties. In the letter he mentioned that he would much rather be home in the midst of his parishioners and attending to his work at the office, than travelling about the continent.[10] David arrived home from this extended trip in mid-March.

These kinds of arrangements from a distance occurred from time to time in David Toews' working life. On June 7, 1934, he found himself in Winnipeg, wondering if he had made adequate preparations for weekend events at Rosthern Mennonite Church. In Winnipeg he heard that Isaak P. Friesen, who was scheduled to preach at the Rosthern Church the coming Sunday, was on a speaking tour in southern Manitoba, which meant that both men would be away from the church on the weekend. And his son Isaak I. Friesen was likely not home either to take his father's place. Thus he wrote to Margarete to check with Johann J. Andres whether alternate arrangements had been made for Sunday morning. Meanwhile, she should also ensure that someone was able to officiate at the wedding scheduled for the coming weekend. Actually, David had expected to be home by the weekend but was being urged to stay on in Manitoba for immigration meetings scheduled for Monday and Tuesday in Winkler.[11]

While, on the one hand, we may wonder about the loose and open-ended arrangements of that day, on the other hand, the operative principles reflected a deep-seated dependency on community support. Toews' way of working the "system" had less to do with bad planning and more to do with trust in his supportive network. Unpredictable circumstances, the order of the day, assumed a back-up system dependent upon mutual communal commitment. What would Toews think of today's tightly knit world which is engendered, governed, and fortified by such modern technological facilitators as telephones, fax machines, e-mail, electronic memo pads, and air travel?

We Must Not Despair

David Toews' trip to Aberdeen seemed to have stirred some interest in the plight of the Mennonites in Russia. A number of financial contributions came to the Rosthern office in the next months. In a thank-you note to one of these contributors, Toews reported that the Board office was receiving an average of about 60 letters a day from Mennonites in Russia. All of them described desperate situations and issued a plea for help. Toews was perplexed as to why the international community kept silent about this obvious genocide. Their silence, he surmised, only gave the Russian government cause to drive its satanic cause forward. "Meanwhile, the nations of the world do business and trade with Russia when and where they can, but for the desperate cause of the poor, whose livelihood is being taken from them, one gives no thought whatsoever."[12]

Toews and J.J. Thiessen had much occasion to talk with Canadian government officials and with other church and social agencies about relief aid to Russia. As far as government initiative was concerned, they were gaining the impression that little help was coming their way. In other words, if something was to be done, the Mennonite people themselves would need to take the initiative. The government appeared to be hindering rather than facilitating the possibility of an immigration. As for sending relief aid, there appeared to be little interest.[13]

Toews characteristically believed in the impossible. Perhaps a miracle would happen and the immigration doors to Canada would be flung open. Yet if that were the case, no financial means would be available to bring refugees to Canada since the travel debt from the 1920s was still on record. The message in all this was: Clean up the travel debt so that, if and when a miracle could happen, they would be able to respond. In a moment of regret for having argued in this way, Toews wrote to the readership of *Der Bote*: "I promise I will not again write in this manner."[14]

Toews' mood of optimism in the face of extreme hardships continued into the new year. In his New Year's greeting to the Canadian Mennonite constituency he began with 1 Corinthians 16:13: "Keep alert, stand firm in your faith, be courageous, be strong." Then he listed the challenges facing the church at the turn of the year: 13 immigrants in Canadian mental institutions, 62 immigrants detained in Germany, refugees halted in China, the nagging *Reiseschuld*, shortage of funds for our schools, a host of personal family problems throughout the constituency, and a flood of letters from Russia with the message, "We are going under!" In the face of these seemingly insurmountable obstacles, Toews concluded:

> God has promised that for those whom God has given grace, he will break open iron doors, etc. May we believe this in 1933. We need to pull together. We are our brothers' keeper. Paul says: "Be alert, stand firm in your faith, be courageous, be strong."[15]

While some said it was no use, nothing helped anyway, the situation only spurred Toews on to renewed hope and to do what he could in response to the despair.

Meanwhile, the flood of letters kept coming to his desk. Some came directly, while others were sent by way of Benjamin H. Unruh, his cherished colleague in Germany. Within a period of four months, January to April 1933, the Rosthern office was the recipient of about 7000 letters from persons in Russia begging for help.[16] This desperate situation continued for several years. Toews was particularly touched by a letter received from an individual who begged for help. She wrote that their mother had died, their father had been sent away into exile, the oldest sister had recently died, and the younger children, among whom were two deaf-mute siblings, were alone and forsaken.[17]

At a brotherhood meeting of the Rosenorter Mennonite Church on February 3, 1933, Toews asked the question, in a reportedly emotional tone: "How can we rescue our brothers in Russia from the famine that besets them at this time?" He reported that in the past three weeks he had received over 1000 letters with pleas for help. Toews challenged the meeting: "Brethren, will we be asked some day: 'In the year 1933 I was hungry in Russia and you did not give me food?' We must gather donations and we must help!" From the hymn, "Throw out the lifeline," he then quoted a stanza:

> Soon will the season of rescue be o'er,
> Soon will they drift to eternity's shore,
> Haste then, my brother, no time for delay,
> But throw out the lifeline and save them today.

The point of all this was summed up in Toews' conclusion to his address: "Blessed are we, if we have extended compassion." In his commentary on the compassionate Toews, J.G. Rempel added the following: "This report on how DT made his appeal was typical of the man who always gave himself wholeheartedly for a cause."[18]

It became a rather overwhelming task to coordinate this relief effort which was concentrated on sending individual care packages to individual addresses supplied by donors in Canada and determined in part by letters received from Russia. There were also always detractors to deal with. Toews made short work of their complaints in an article entitled, "Our Problem," when he wrote that our problem is not those who send anonymous letters and in other ways try to deflect our relief efforts in Russia. Rather, our problem is where to find bread for the hungry and how to get it there.[19]

Thankfully, some $40,000 had already been received since the beginning of the new year. Toews was pleased to note that a fair share of the contributions came from the Rosenorter church people. While it was not possible any more to send missionaries or even Bibles to Russia, where atheism was being spread systematically and the break-up of the family system was anticipated, "a contribution of money from afar says something to our people there about practical Christianity."[20] At the same time, compassionate sacrifice needed to continue. In the fall of 1934, Toews reported to the constituency that, according to what he had been told, some five million persons had died of hunger in Russia in the past year and the number might double in the coming year. For this reason, the last Sunday in October was designated as a special day for prayer and for collecting funds for Russia. "Let's remember," Toews appealed, "sooner or later we will be in a situation where it will be our turn to need help."[21]

While it was not possible to continue immigration of Mennonites from Russia in the 1930s, the relief efforts in material aid turned out to be quite remarkable. In 1934 David Toews reported that since 1929 the Mennonites had sent some $160,000 in relief support for their suffering brothers and sisters in Russia. Most of this money had come from Mennonite immigrants of the 1920s. Toews added that this fund-raising campaign for a desperate cause had been much more successful than monies coming from the general populace.[22]

Somehow

David Toews had already gained something of a reputation for a certain style of leadership. When a situation appeared hopeless to his colleagues, he would think of a way through. When others shrank back, he would press forward with new vigour. Some were critical of his style, yet even his critics had to admire his tenacity and stubbornness. One of Toews' detractors wrote a poem about him that walks the fine line between criticism and admiration. It is entitled "Irgend wie" (Somehow):[23]

Mein lieber Bruder "irgend wie"
Verzweifelt wirklich nie;
Er läszt die Dinge ruhig gehen,
Ohn' ihnen in dem Weg zu stehen,
Und glaubt, die allerschwersten Sachen
Werden sich irgendwie schon machen . . .
Und sieh, wir leben Tag für Tag,
Was immer uns auch kommen mag;
Behalten unsern frohen Mut;
Am Ende wird doch alles gut.

My dearest brother "somehow"
To despair will never bow;
He lets things run their chosen course,
Without applying any force;
He thinks the gravest situations
Will get resolved if we have patience . . .

Somehow we live from day to day
Doing our duties, come what may;
Always maintaining a cheerful mood,
Knowing that things will turn out good.

Ordination of J.J. Thiessen
The ordination of J.J. Thiessen as minister took place on Sunday, May 29, 1932, in Saskatoon, with David Toews officiating. In 1931 Thiessen had moved from Rosthern to Saskatoon to serve as pastor of the newly opened congregation which met in Victoria School. The congregation, which served the growing population of Mennonites moving to the city, had become an official member of the Rosenorter Mennonite Church on January 26, 1932.

The ordination of Thiessen as leading minister of the Saskatoon church meant that an urban-oriented pastor was now part of the ministerial leadership of the Rosenorter network. It also meant that David Toews, as continuing elder of the Rosenorter Mennonite Church, would not be required to fulfil all official church functions in Saskatoon. It took some time for Toews to establish the point that the Saskatoon work could function quite well under Thiessen. For example, Thiessen had invited Toews to speak at the Thanksgiving and Mission Services in October of 1932. Toews wrote back to say he was much too busy on that day and would not be able to come. Whereupon Thiessen wrote again in an urgent tone: "That you are declining the invitation to come to our celebration is unfortunate. This gathering and similar ones here are unthinkable without you. It is most important that you come, and so I will risk urging you to reconsider."[24] Eventually Toews conceded, saying he would come; however, he still maintained that his presence had little meaning there.[25]

The newly-ordained Rev. Thiessen had no easy time of it in Saskatoon. There was enough pastoral work, which he enjoyed, but for the first years there was always a shortage of funds. This affected not only the financial situation of the Thiessens but also the extent to which they could and could not help those who came to their door for money, food, and clothing. Thiessen's own stipend was forwarded to the Rosthern office by the Home Mission Board. From there, David Toews dispensed the funds to Thiessen on a monthly basis. This proved difficult when the money was not received on time in Rosthern or when less than the agreed-upon amount was forwarded by the Home Mission Board.

Thus it happened quite frequently that, in desperation, Thiessen would send Toews a note to say he was far behind in payment of his bills and did not have enough funds to pay the rent. Toews would apologize and sometimes forward money out of his own pocket, temporarily. On one particular weekend in the fall of 1933, Thiessen was scheduled to preach in Rosthern on Sunday morning. He did not have enough money to buy a train ticket for the trip to Rosthern, but he had hoped, until the last hour, that somehow the funds would become available. They did not, and Thiessen found himself calling Isaak P. Friesen on Saturday evening to ask Friesen to substitute for him.[26]

On another occasion, Thiessen wrote to Toews that he was in arrears with his bills to the tune of $105.19. He was embarrassed to bring this matter forward again yet he dared to do so, albeit in desperation. In the same letter he apologized for having been absent from the recent ministerial meeting, but that he could not come because he could not leave his wife to manage the household all alone. On that day there was laundry to do; there had been 22 phone calls to answer; and the doorbell rang 12 times. "Don't scold me," Thiessen pleaded. "I dare to be open because it is you to whom I am speaking." He admitted that, even as he wrote, his face was turning red with embarrassment, but he had no other recourse than to ask the Home Mission Board for money again.[27] Toews replied the next day with the comment: "In my view, the funds from the Home Mission Board are coming in all too slowly, and I would think they should make some effort to send the money more quickly."[28] On yet another occasion Toews wrote to Thiessen: "I know the money I am forwarding to you is not adequate for your needs, but before things get too serious for you, write to me and I will do what I can."[29]

Despite these hardships, the Thiessens had much joy in serving the Mennonite student population as well as the young working women who were housemaids in well-to-do homes in Saskatoon. Toews also related well to the young adult Mennonite women and men in the city. On more than one occasion he met with the group that gathered at the Thiessen home and served them with encouraging talks and congenial conversation. Their affection for Toews was warmly expressed in a Christmas greeting forwarded to David Toews with 80 signatures from the *Mädchenheim* (home for young women) which was the responsibility of the Thiessens:

> We can sense how heavy the responsibilities are that you need to carry in your service to our people. Therefore our prayer is: Faithful God, in the coming year, continue to give guidance, protection, and power to our beloved *Ältester* so that under his leadership our people may bring the great work of rescue from Russia to an honourable conclusion.[30]

The *Mädchenheim* in Saskatoon, as in Winnipeg and later in Vancouver, represented frontier mission work in its day. The Winnipeg home was begun in 1926 at a time when about 100 young women of General Conference background were doing housework in the city. Rev. J.H. Enns served as spiritual advisor to the residents of the Winnipeg home. In Vancouver, a residence for working women was begun in 1935. Rev. and Mrs. Jacob H. Janzen moved from Waterloo to Vancouver for a two-year period to begin the work there while also serving seven church groups in British Columbia as elder. Upon his return to Waterloo, Rev. and Mrs. Jacob B. Wiens continued with the work in Vancouver.

Rural churches and immigrant parents on the land often feared that the city would have a negative effect on their young adult children and on the Mennonite church. Toews encouraged the churches, the parents, the women doing housework, and the students studying in the city, to utilize the services offered by the emerging urban Mennonite church and to maintain their Mennonite principles in this new environment. Toews believed that the way to counter negative influences was to provide positive institutional opportunities.[31]

Sixty-three

On February 8, 1933, David Toews turned 63 years of age. His good friend, J.J. Thiessen, recognized the day with a heart-felt tribute that included a lengthy and thoughtful sentence:

> Tomorrow is your birthday; not your special day only, but a special day for the church as well. We rejoice heartily with you and yours, that—under the gracious protection of God, the support of your family, the Rosenorter Church, the large General Conference of our suffering people in Russia, and of the entire Mennonite people, scattered across the face of the earth, who pray and who strive for a humble existence—you have been kept safe to this day. Today many friends and relatives take part, directly and indirectly, in your family festivities, and all of them have but one wish, namely, that you and yours may continue to enjoy happiness and peace in the future.[32]

David replied to his friend the day after his birthday with the words, "One does not expect more from the steward than that he be found faithful. Above all, I want to be faithful in the tasks that have been given to me; may the Lord give strength for this." Then he added that at the end of the week he would be off to British Columbia for provincial gatherings and for Bible presentations in one of the congregational settings. He felt others could do much better than he could with Bible lectures but, with God's help, he would do it.[33] In a follow-up letter, J.J. Thiessen affirmed and encouraged Toews in support of his Bible teaching assignment in British Columbia, and spoke of such contacts as significant contributions for building up our people and our church for the work of the kingdom of God on earth.

The Toews Children

Where were the eight Toews children by this time, the early 1930s? In a letter to his nephew in Paso Robles, California, dated December 5, 1933, David Toews gave a person-by-person account to their American cousin.[34] Benno was teaching school in Rosthern at the German-English Academy. He and his wife Catherine (Tena) had a four-year-old son, Theodore. Marie was married to Herman Riesen and they had a daughter who would soon be one year old. Margaret was a school teacher in the neighbouring village of Hague; she came home by train every Friday and returned Sunday evening. Elsie was a school teacher in Rosthern in the public school. Both Margaret and Elsie were doing well and loved their work. Dora had a teaching certificate as well but had as yet not found a suitable position. Louise, who was 20 years of age, taught private piano. At this time she was working toward her Associate Registered Certificate in Teaching (ARCT) in piano. Elma and Anna were students.

In summary, as of the end of 1933 there were eight children, of whom two were married, and there were two grandchildren. Of the eight children, one was a homemaker, one was a high school teacher, three were elementary school teachers, one was a music teacher, and two were still in school. It appeared that most of the children were following in the footsteps of their father's first career, the teaching profession.

In the fall of 1934 Benno left his teaching position at the German-English Academy to pursue seminary studies in Dallas, Texas. On the way through Saskatoon, the family paid a visit to Rev. and Mrs. Thiessen whom they had come to regard as their friends and pastoral advisors. After they left, Thiessen wrote to David Toews about the visit:

> Benno appeared very serious, inwardly agitated, yet courageous. May the Lord watch over this dear brother who takes his work in God's vineyard so seriously; may he be protected from disappointments and may he be brought safely to his goal. I know that his father's heart is deeply touched. The feeling must be mixed: joy and pain vie with one another for domination. And yet joy must take the upper hand, for the son did not leave home as prodigal son but as redeemed in order to redeem others. That should evoke joy and thankfulness in you. We rejoice with you and we try as well to partake in your sorrow in the parting.[35]

In a day when sons were highly prized, and in a family setting of eight (later seven) daughters and one son, it is understandable that a father

The Toews family in 1932. From left, front row: Anna, David and Margarete, Catherine (Friesen) Toews holding Theodore, Elma; back row: Louise, Marie (Toews) and Herman Riesen, Elsie, Benno, Dora, Margaret.

would have had high expectations of his only son. Thiessen may well have sensed this and did what he could to express empathy and encouragement to Toews.

The School Again

During these years, David Toews was still centrally involved with the German-English Academy. Fundraising was part of his agenda and, since the idea of asking each congregation to be responsible for its share internally was not implemented, he continued the work himself and tapped a few others on the shoulder to help. Thus in June of 1932 he wrote to J.J. Thiessen in Saskatoon and asked him to devote some time to collecting for the school.[36] Thiessen replied that he was quite busy with his church agenda but to Toews that did not mean "no." Thiessen did his best to comply.

While Toews was a persistent and enthusiastic promoter of the Academy, he did want to be realistic about its future. At the 1932 annual meeting, when it again had to be reported that because of hard times the financial picture looked grim and it was difficult to meet obligations to teachers, he encouraged the small gathering of corporation members not to be discouraged. Just as there would be no reason for optimism if many members were present, there was no reason for pessimism if only a few came. The best way to meet optimism or pessimism was with realism. "We want to look the situation straight in the eye and not make the bad worse or the good better than it actually is. Our best progress is made when we face the facts and accept the situation as it is."[37] And with that the corporation members found renewed courage to continue on, somehow assured that their leader would continue to lead the way. Optimism showed itself in that a five-month Bible School program was begun that year. J.J. Nickel of Aberdeen, Saskatchewan, was the sole teacher for the first three years. Then J.G. Rempel of Langham took his place. In 1937 a second teacher was employed, then a third, and then a fourth.

Even at that, the critical situation persisted for some time due to the severe economic depression. David Toews was again in dire straits. In a letter to J.J. Thiessen dated May 2, 1934, he commented that his finances were tight, and that consequently he had not as yet produced even last year's baptismal certificates. He could not finance these himself and did not know where he would get the funds otherwise. He continued to have outstanding medical bills, and the school was hard-pressed for funds. Concerning the latter, he wrote: "The school is causing me great worries at this time. Money is needed and I have no idea where to obtain it."[38]

In time, things appeared to have turned around. A provincial school inspector's report at the end of 1935 gave evidence that the Academy was offering good quality education and that the deportment of the students was laudable. This gave Toews further reason to admonish the constituency to support the school generously.[39] By the beginning of 1936, the mood was again quite positive. According to a report by Toews, student enrolment was up and the financial situation was somewhat easier. There seemed to be a firmer foundation for the school's future. Not unsurprisingly, Toews concluded that this was no reason to relax, but rather to keep building for the future.[40]

Tough Times in Canada
   When the agreements were made in 1922 to arrange for the immigration of Mennonites from Russia, one of the stipulations of the government was that the newcomers would be brought onto the land as farmers and that the Mennonites receiving the immigrants would take care of their health and social welfare. The Canadian Mennonite Board of Colonization sought to take its obligations seriously. One of David Toews' concerns was that those who had started out on the farm should find their prosperity there. This wish became more difficult when the Depression of the 1930s hit the prairies. Many wanted to give up and move to the cities. In an article in *Der Bote,* Toews drew attention to the migration of immigrants to the city since they had not been able to make it on the farm. He warned that life in the city could be difficult as well. Besides, if immigrants would find themselves facing poverty in the city and apply for relief, their names might well be reported to Ottawa and they might be deported. They had been allowed into the country with the assumption they would not become a burden to Canada. People should exercise extreme caution about this kind of eventuality. Toews called upon the Mennonite people to "pull together and stay together so that during this time of depression our people can retain their good name."[41]
   Then there was the travel debt, a never-ending matter of concern. Given the financially hard times of the 1930s, the problem only persisted and worsened. Always there was a sense of urgency in his tone as Toews addressed his people on the debt. His anxiety was heightened somewhat when, in 1934, C.F. Klassen of Winnipeg, the person on whom the Board relied to organize debt collection, became seriously ill.[42] However, Klassen recovered and his work continued. Toews approached the matter with little sympathy for the immigrants. His goal was to conquer the debt which would require self-sacrifice on the part of everyone. Thus he had praise for those who made a sincere attempt to pay and critical words for those who couldn't care less about their obligations and the reputation of the Mennonites. It's a matter of personal integrity, he said. It's an obligation before God. In a December 1935 article on the subject, Toews

reported several instances where immigrant families disallowed themselves a proper bed or a new suit of clothes or butter on the table until the *Reiseschuld* had been paid off. He expressed his profound respect for such disciplined action, and ended his admonition with Isaiah 56:1: "Maintain justice and do what is right, for soon my salvation shall come, and my deliverance be revealed."[43]

Tensions with A.A. Friesen

David Toews' concerns seemed to move back and forth between large issues and personal relationships. The reader will recall Abraham A. Friesen who, as a young man, played an important role as a member of the delegation that first came from Russia in 1919 to investigate immigration possibilities. After returning to Russia to report on what he had found and to help prepare for the eventual immigration, Friesen soon returned to North America. In 1922 he was appointed as manager of the Board of Colonization from 1922 to 1926. The fiancée of A.A. Friesen, Miche Goossen, who had grown up on the Wintergrün estate north of the Molotschna Colony in Ukraine, followed him to Rosthern three years later. Abraham and Miche were married in 1922 with David Toews as the officiating minister. Miche's mother and some of her siblings also came to Canada and settled at Rabbit Lake, Saskatchewan. Following a somewhat abrupt resignation from his position on the Board in the spring of 1926, Friesen had moved to Rabbit Lake, where he acquired and operated a lumber business in the town until his death in 1948. His wife Miche passed away in 1934; the next year Abraham married Helena, the sister of Miche.[44]

There had been tension between David Toews and A.A. Friesen when they worked side by side at the Rosthern office. While it was difficult to pinpoint the problem, one source of tension was Friesen's tendency to criticize Toews for certain of the latter's policy decisions. Friesen was astute in business matters and wanted the immigration project to be operated more as a corporate business than as an arm of the church. Toews was more oriented to the way of the church and to the sentiments of the church constituency.

These issues bred a negative relationship between Friesen and Toews which carried on into the 1930s. In a harshly critical letter written by Friesen to Toews in April of 1935, he told Toews in no uncertain terms that the latter had confused his pastoral office with his assignment as director of the Board of Colonization. He went on to say that he found Toews to be self-serving, egotistical, and power hungry, and he called on Toews to repent of his ways.[45] Toews was taken aback by this attack, although it did not come entirely "out of the blue."

A year earlier, on August 18, 1934, when Toews officiated at the dedication of the new Mayfair Mennonite Church building near Rabbit Lake, he met with Friesen to ask whether it was he who was spreading false rumours in the community about the work of the Board, having to do with the question of their jurisdiction over a large sum of money.[46] It was not a question of false use of funds but whether the funds should be administered by the Board at all. Friesen denied any involvement in the accusatory rumour but the conversation of that day must have annoyed him considerably. To him it felt like a personal accusation. On the basis of further investigation by the Board, it was ascertained that, indeed, the source of the rumour lay elsewhere than with Friesen.

Toews and others tried to rectify the matter, even to the extent of making a public statement at the subsequent annual Board of Colonization meeting in Waldheim, Saskatchewan, in 1935. But that, together with a statement in *Der Bote* in which Toews sought to clear up the matter on the basis of what he had learned from his conversation with Friesen on August 19, 1934, appeared not to have been satisfactory. Toews then proposed to Friesen that an independent study commission be formed to determine the truth about outstanding issues between them and to propose a resolution to their relationship. But Friesen would not agree to this, fearing that such a commission would only take sides against him.[47] In a letter to Friesen, Toews expressed his view that as much clarity as possible had been achieved and that he had a clear conscience about the matter.[48] With that, the issue appeared to have been concluded, although perhaps not resolved.

In a characterization of A.A. Friesen and David Toews, written by Jacob H. Janzen in 1950 following the death of both Toews and Friesen, Janzen compared these two servants of our people.[49] In A.A. Friesen, he saw a person who was exacting and intelligent. Janzen quoted Benjamin H. Unruh, who said of Friesen: "Er war ein Mann saubersten Denkens" (He was an exceptionally clear thinker). He could summarize a situation well and could formulate clear proposals for future action. Friesen was business-like, concerned that the books would balance. He preferred to lend money to the kinds of people who conceivably could pay it back. In David Toews, Janzen saw a strong character who gave priority to human relationships. He took his chances on future outcomes, provided that people in need were served. When Toews did engage in business ventures, he was prepared to "fashion his own cross, which he was then left to drag along with painful steps to the blessed end of his earthly journey." Janzen observed that, when a person who is steeped in exacting business walks and works alongside a person whose mission is to relieve suffering, these do not make compatible travelling companions. If they exercise patience and forgiveness along the way, they can travel together, but the achievement is rare in human experience. Janzen has offered a compelling depiction and comparison of A.A. Friesen and David Toews.

1935 General Conference Sessions

At the beginning of August 1935, David Toews had the privilege of attending the General Conference (GC) sessions in Upland, California.[50] On Sunday afternoon of the sessions, he addressed the assembly on immigration work, including the work of home missions in Canada. In his own words, the report was well received. During the sessions he also supported an initiative on the part of the General Conference to send a protest petition to the international League of Nations concerning the persecution of Christians in the Soviet Union. Regarding this initiative, he said:

> We fear that again this protest will fall on deaf ears, but we dare not neglect to open our mouth on behalf of those who are not permitted to speak for themselves and who have already endured untold suffering for so many years.[51]

The trip to California gave opportunity to spend several days after the GC sessions to visit relatives who lived there. In a letter to his family back home he mentioned the beautiful flowering plants in the area and the

Wedding of Elsie Toews and Abram Hooge on July 11, 1935.

scrumptious feasts of fruit. He also expressed regret that his bad hearing prevented him from understanding everything that was said at the conference.[52]

Health Concerns

The reference to troublesome hearing was an indication that David Toews was experiencing health problems in the mid-thirties. As noted earlier, he was hospitalized for a time when in Germany in 1930. In the summer of 1933, he was under medical care for a time. It took him some time to recuperate to the point where he was able to come to the office again.[53] In February of 1936, two days after his 66th birthday, he wrote to his friend J.J. Thiessen:

> I don't feel as well as I did 10 or 20 years ago, yet my health is bearable. How I long to see the day yet when the problems which press upon us today will move toward resolution. Whether or not we will be given that privilege I do not know.[54]

Now in his mid-sixties, David Toews increasingly felt the weight of two personal struggles, his physical maladies and the burden of unresolved issues brought on by the challenges of immigration and resettlement.

15

Third Trip to Europe
1936–1938

On June 12, 1936, David Toews, together with Margarete, set sail from Montreal for Europe. The main purpose was to attend the Mennonite World Conference sessions in Amsterdam.[1] The Conference was scheduled to coincide with the 400th anniversary of the exit of Menno Simons from the Catholic Church in 1536. Toews and C.F. Klassen, the two Canadian delegates, were selected by the Board of Colonization to represent not only their respective Mennonite denominations but all the Mennonites in Canada.[2] David was delighted that his "dear wife" could travel with him, and that she would be able to visit relatives she had left behind in Prussia some 40 years earlier.

Fortunately, the journey by sea was relatively smooth. No doubt Margarete enjoyed a running recount of all that veteran traveller David had experienced on his two previous ocean journeys. The couple disembarked at Liverpool and went to London by train. On Sunday they attended the service at Metropolitan Tabernacle where Charles Spurgeon had once been the regular preacher. On that particular Sunday the sermon was delivered by Rev. Oswald Smith on the topic, "Victorious Living," based on Romans 8. Toews noted that the congregation was comprised of mostly older people and that the church was not full, as he would have expected. From London, they travelled to Berlin and then to Danzig where David Toews left Margarete to visit relatives. He went on to Amsterdam for the Mennonite World Conference sessions scheduled for June 29 to July 3.

They were held in the Singel Mennonite Church, a building tucked back behind the street that bordered one of Amsterdam's main canals. Toews was impressed with the inconspicuous position of the building and with the church's rich library collection. To commemorate Menno Simons' resignation from the priesthood, there was much recounting of history as well as assessment of contemporary Mennonite faith and life. The opening address by Dr. A.K. Kuiper, a Dutch Mennonite scholar and pastor, was based on 1 Corinthians 3:11: "No other foundation can anyone lay, than that is laid, which is Jesus Christ." Menno Simons often quoted this text on the front page of his writings. Toews knew the text well, but he claimed to have understood very little of the substance of Kuiper's sermon since it was delivered in Dutch. But he did hear the repeated mention of the name of Jesus Christ and concluded that, while the Mennonite people did not agree on every point of doctrine, they did agree that Jesus Christ was central to their faith.[3]

In his report to the Canadian readership, Toews expressed his enthusiasm for the presentations on Mennonite history featured on this anniversary occasion. The address by Pastor N. van der Zijpp was especially impressive. In his outline of Mennonite beginnings in Holland, the pastor focused especially on the humble characteristics of Menno Simons. Humility was one of the themes Toews would often address in his sermons. For him, the significance of the Conference lay in the opportunity it gave Mennonite churches to become conscious and reflective about their particular existence in the world, and to commit themselves to unity in faith and faithfulness.[4] Listening together to addresses on Mennonite history and its significance served this purpose.

Toews spoke twice at the Conference. His first address dealt with "The Story of the Mennonites in Canada."[5] He reported that there were about 15 different Mennonite groups in Canada at the time with a membership of about 81,500. The differences between and among the groups were minor, he felt. More importantly, the Canadian Mennonite churches were united in the central beliefs of the Mennonite faith—mutual aid, nonresistance, baptism upon confession of faith, and non-swearing of oaths. He ended his first address with a heartfelt statement: "May the Conference contribute to the recovery of those values for which our forefathers stood."

Toews' second presentation focused on relief work. He took the opportunity to thank: the Mennonites of Holland, Germany, France, and Poland for their significant support of those detained in Europe because of medical problems; and the American Mennonites for the contribution of clothing received in Canada—which amounted to about 15,000 pounds annually for more than a decade—for their financial contribution to support ministers, and for their monetary aid in the construction of churches and related institutions. Then he listed continuing problems that were placing sacrificial demands on the Mennonite people of Canada: the debt remaining from the immigration of the 1920s; development of vigorous congregational life; the need for good leadership in the churches; and the challenge of nurturing youth. He invited Mennonites worldwide to continue to respond with compassion to the most critical of all needs, the suffering people in the Soviet Union.

Toews then turned to the situation in Russia. He admitted that the day of opportunity for rescue was past. He summarized the problem thus:

The 66-year-old David Toews in 1936, now a player on the Mennonite world stage at the Mennonite World Conference in Amsterdam.

> After the emigration to Canada, Brazil, and Paraguay, perhaps as many as 75,000 Mennonites remained in Russia. These have now been scattered throughout the Russian empire and partly destroyed. It is questionable whether 50,000 are left. They have been silenced and are slowly going to their graves. The young people for the most part have been poisoned by the Bolshevik system. . . . Over there they are longing for the time "when the Lord will redeem the prisoners of Zion." We too are longing for this time whenever we think of our brethren in Russia.[6]

While the problem was one of overwhelming proportion, initiatives could still be taken but this would require a united effort by Mennonite people of faith everywhere. Some unity had been achieved, as exemplified by joint action taken at Amsterdam. It had been decided to set aside a day on the annual calendar of Mennonite churches internationally on which to gather offerings for the outstanding *Reiseschuld* in Canada. Assistance in paying the transportation debt would be offered to persons who found themselves unable to pay. The Board would prepare lists of widows who needed help because the father had died and the mother was left with small children. Individuals and congregations would be asked to take on specific cases.[7] The Conference at Amsterdam also affirmed Benjamin H. Unruh as church worker in Germany on behalf of immigration.[8] Toews was greatly encouraged by these signs of solidarity.

At the Holland gathering, the tense world situation was on the minds of delegates. It seemed like the appropriate moment to reaffirm historic peace teachings. A document was presented to the delegates, entitled, "Mennonite Peace Manifesto."[9] The statement called on "all Mennonites everywhere to fulfil the task of propagating the Gospel of peace which God has entrusted to us in the history of our Mennonite forefathers." It also called on them to promote peace through service in the world, and to be prepared to "give spiritual and material help to our brethren who are convinced that God has called them to refuse military service or . . . to suffer for their peace convictions." Toews and C.F. Klassen were among 20 Mennonite world leaders who attached their names to the "Manifesto." It became a source of encouragement and guidance to Toews when he returned to Canada to face the question of conscientious objection in a renewed way at the onset of World War II.

From Amsterdam, Toews travelled to Berlin for meetings on questions of relief and immigration. C.F. Klassen and B.H. Unruh were also there. From Berlin he motored with Unruh to Karlsruhe and stayed at the Unruh residence for several days. His time there was filled with further meetings. In a letter to Margarete from there he reported that he felt quite satisfied with his accomplishments thus far, but that he was already looking forward to returning home. However, he was still planning to join Margarete in the Danzig area for a while. Then they would depart from London on August 1.[10]

Back home, Toews took some time to share his impressions of Germany with the readership of *Der Bote*.[11] He noted with some surprise that he found no one who was critical of Hitler. Indeed, the people, especially the young people, appeared to be supportive of him. He was impressed that in Germany it was not permissible to speak in heated antagonistic ways against other nations while, for example in Canada, one heard considerable negative public criticism of Germany. On the question of whether or not Germany wanted war, Toews thought not, and yet Germany was being pressed on every side, for example by Russia. It appears that he had a somewhat naïve, or at least shortsighted, picture of what was transpiring in Germany and of its political stance.

But Toews also expressed doubts about the German situation. What he did not like was that everywhere the masses were being co-opted on behalf of the state—even on Sundays when youth should be in church. He reflected critically on the way Hitler was counted as a Christian—reading his New Testament daily—yet this commitment did not seem to be borne out in the government. Toews was unhappy there was no freedom of the press in Germany. He noted that Jews in Germany had lost their citizenship rights and their businesses were curtailed and controlled. But, he thought they were still being treated better than Mennonites in Russia. Obviously, Toews did not have the advantage of the full picture. A disclaimer on his part, that he would not want to pose as an expert after such a short visit, preceded the article in *Der Bote*.

The 34th Annual CMC Sessions

While their chairman was in Europe in the summer of 1936, the Conference of Mennonites still held its sessions on July 5–7 in Drake, Saskatchewan. This was the first and only conference that Toews missed in his extensive tenure as chairman. He, together with J.J. Thiessen, had been active in arranging a place for the meetings and planning the program, but it was up to Benjamin Ewert of Winnipeg, vice-chairman, to lead the sessions. The meetings began with a Ministers Conference on Saturday, July 5, which the vice-chairman led as well.

Two questions discussed at the Ministers' Conference had to do with exceptions to "the rule," an indication of what Mennonite churches would face increasingly as the twentieth century progressed. First, could a Mennonite public official ask or require that someone take an oath? Discussion brought to light that there were many opinions on this question. The final decision was left to the *Komitee für Aufklärung, Lehre und Wandel* (Committee on Faith and Life) to decide. The second issue was the question of whether the minister of a congregation, even though not ordained as an *Ältester*, might officiate at baptism and the Lord's Supper where the situation warranted, that is, where and when an *Ältester* was not available. The group decided this would be permissible, provided the local congregation and the senior minister, who normally served the congregation, agreed to this. It is significant that questions such as this could be discussed and resolved without the presence of David Toews.

Following the *Missionsfest* on Sunday, a standard pattern by now, the delegates gathered for three days of deliberations. The first item on the program was reading greetings from the Mennonite World Conference which had just ended its session in Amsterdam. In the absence of David Toews, Jacob H. Janzen, resident in Vancouver at that time, preached the conference sermon. He addressed the conference theme, "To know Christ is to follow him in life," on the basis of Matthew 16: 24–25. The delegate body had David and Margarete Toews much on their minds and in their prayers during the sessions. At the time, the Conference of Mennonites in Canada was comprised of 35 congregations, with 285 votes represented by 89 delegates. David Toews was again elected as chairman for the following year.

Back in Canada

Upon his return from Europe, he had immediate matters to attend to. Correspondence had piled up in his absence. There were reports of his trip to prepare for the church papers and constant invitations to speak in the churches, in particular to report on his trip abroad. While Toews was

The wedding of Margaret Toews and Jacob Sawatzky on August 21, 1936.

in Europe, First Mennonite Church in Saskatoon had completed its building project. The dedication service took place on October 18, 1936 with David Toews as the keynote speaker. Shortly after that he embarked on an extensive trip to eastern Canada and the eastern United States. He began with a stopover in Winnipeg for meetings and for reporting in the churches. From there he proceeded to Toronto, then to New Hamburg, Kitchener, Waterloo, and Leamington, where he reported on the Amsterdam Conference and on relief and immigration concerns. At Leamington, an area settled by Mennonites only 12 years earlier, about 500 persons attended the church service where Toews reported. From there he took the train to Ottawa and Montreal, where he met with officials concerning ongoing immigration issues, some of which had been clarified for him in discussions in Europe.

An interesting aside shows itself in a letter that Toews wrote from Montreal to Margarete and the children.[12] At the CPR offices he had spoken with Mr. McAllister who was in charge of Toews' monthly stipend. He had asked McAllister for permission to receive his November and December allowance in advance, to which the official had readily agreed. In his letter to the family back in Rosthern, Toews gave instructions for dispensing the funds they should shortly be receiving. Benno was instructed to pay the taxes and the bill for coal, wood, and electricity. Margarete was to take what she needed for household sustenance and not to "forget to keep a record of everything spent."

From Montreal, Toews took the overnight train to Vineland where he not only reported on the World Conference but also participated at the service of dedication of a new church building. From Ontario, he embarked on an extensive seven-week itineration journey to the United States. Meetings there involved contact with Mennonite relief and mission agencies as well as reports in churches where he followed up with fundraising for various causes such as Russia relief, transportation debt, curriculum materials for Canadian congregational development, relief for poor Mennonite families in Canada, and more.

Weariness

Now 67 years of age, the pace and the burdens were showing their "wear and tear" on David Toews and, increasingly, weariness showed itself. In his birthday greeting to Toews on February 8, 1937, J.J. Thiessen expressed his congratulations and tried to be encouraging, although with a note of concern:

> Again a year of hard work lies behind you. God has given you the necessary strength to work with success in the various areas of our church life. With God's help, your spirit and your body have been able to endure all the difficult and unpleasant aspects that came with your work.[13]

A few months earlier, on his nine-week trip to Ontario and eastern United States, Toews had written to his family that he was concerned about his health in relation to his work load: "So far I am in reasonably good health. But my further assignment (on this trip) gives me some concern. Hopefully, with God's help things will work out. I'll be glad when this trip is over. . . . If only my trip and my work will not be futile."[14]

By the fall of 1937, David Toews found himself in St. Paul's Hospital in Saskatoon. There the surgeon removed a large stone from his gall bladder. While in hospital, Toews also received medical help for his diabetes which had shown up as a problem in the early 1930s. Since he had not been able to control his blood sugar through diet, his treatment was now converted to injections. After a 38-day stay in the hospital, Toews was taken home for a period of convalescence. During that time, a nurse from the Rosthern hospital administered the daily injections and taught daughter Anna the procedure.

A touching greeting from Toews to the Mennonite constituency appeared in *Der Bote* three days before Christmas in 1937. In the article, written while recuperating in bed at home, Toews gave thanks for all the prayers offered on his behalf during his recent illness. Evidently he had done much reflecting on his own dispensability, as he wrote:

No one should surmise that things would not get done without me. I believe the Lord would have found willing workers to succeed me, workers who would have concerned themselves with our problems. The Lord surely would have dealt with our problems without my help.[15]

Apparently while in hospital Toews had some struggles of the soul. But he had seen his way through, helped by one particular stanza of a poem by Karl Gerok, to which he often referred in later life:

Viel reut mich einst an meines Grabes Pforte
Beim Blick auf meinen irren Pilgerpfad.
In Scharen stehn Gedanken, Werke, Worte
Als Kläger wider meine Seele auf.
Mein Flehn, wenn mich des Richters Blick durchflammt
Ist: Herr, geh' mit dem Knecht nicht ins Gericht.

There is much that I will regret when I stand at my grave's portal
And look back upon the errors of my way.
Thoughts, works, and words crowd in upon me
Bringing accusations against my soul.
My plea, when the judge's eye pierces my being
Is this: Do not subject your servant to judgment.

Toews closed his Christmas message with a stanza of the hymn: "Nur mit Jesu will ich Pilger wandeln." This popular hymn, sung frequently in Mennonite worship services, expressed the desire: "With Jesus only do I wish to walk as a pilgrim on life's way."

By this time our sometimes weary pilgrim was bearing a three-fold physical burden: a hearing problem, digestive-urinary ailments, and diabetes. For the first few months of 1938 he found himself in a mode of recuperation from his hospital stay. The local constituency of the Conference of Mennonites in Canada followed the illness and recovery of their leader with concern. At the 36th sessions in Eigenheim in July 1938, the delegates expressed thanksgiving to God for sustaining the chairman of the Conference and the Board of Colonization during his serious illness and for answering the many prayers for his well being.[16]

Ältester J.J. Thiessen

Lest we get the impression that life for David Toews was one constant struggle, good things also befell him. This was particularly so in the period from May to September of 1938. One source of satisfaction for him was the privilege of officiating at ordination services. A particular highlight in this regard was the ordination of J.J. Thiessen as *Ältester* of the Rosenorter Church, in particular of First Mennonite Church of

David Toews and J.J. Thiessen who, despite their 23-year age difference, remained close friends and colleagues in their work with immigration, relief, church, and conference concerns. Photo: Frank H. Epp, *Mennonite Exodus*

Saskatoon. Toews had been intimately involved in nurturing and encouraging Thiessen ever since he had arrived from Russia in 1926. He had recognized in Thiessen a potential future leader of the church. Even though Toews was 23 years his senior, they had developed a close friendship from the beginning and related to one another as brothers and mutual confidantes. On May 28, 1938, Toews saw his hopes and aspirations for Thiessen's ministry come to fruition when he officiated at his ordination as elder of First Mennonite Church in Saskatoon. In 1931, Toews had ordained Thiessen as a "minister," meaning that he could do pastoral duties short of the official functions of baptizing and conducting the Lord's Supper. With his ordination as *Ältester,* Thiessen could provide leadership in all aspects of church life, including the ordinances.

David Toews, D.D.

Immediately after the ordination service, David Toews left for Newton, Kansas, to take part in an event in which he personally would be recognized for his ministry. In December of 1937 he had received a letter from the president of Bethel College in North Newton announcing that the Board of the College had, on the recommendation of the faculty, voted in favour of granting him the honourary Doctor of Divinity degree at its forthcoming commencement on June 2, 1938. Since this would be

Bethel's 45th commencement, the College was trying to make it something of a special occasion and would like to bestow this honour on Reverend Toews at that time. The letter made clear that the degree was "given in recognition of your efficient and sacrificial services rendered to the Mennonite church."[17] Toews was assured there would be no expenses for him except his travel fare to Kansas.

Evidently David Toews was quite taken aback by this invitation. His response to President Kaufman a week later stated: ". . . your letter almost stunned me by the offer you are making."[18] Then in a self-deprecating manner he proceeded to excuse himself from accepting the offer and tried to talk Kaufman and his faculty out of this gesture. His response is worth quoting at length, as it reveals something about Toews' self-assessment:

> I cannot conceive that you would have made such an offer if you and your faculty knew me as to my attainment and so forth more intimately. For that reason I consider it my duty to make you acquainted with my achievements, which are not at all academic. As to my education, I must say that I have only what was offered to me at Halstead in four years. I intended to continue my studies at Bethel College but, as I had no money, I took a position in Manitoba. . . . After two years at that school, I attended the Collegiate and Normal Schools at Winnipeg for two years. When I had finished as far as was necessary for teaching, I taught for several years in public schools until I was called to the Academy, where I think I taught for about 15 years until the movement of Mennonites from Russia started. Now there are a number of people who give me more credit than I think I should have in this movement. I did what I could to help my brethren who were in distress. We made the necessary connections, and others cooperated in doing the work. From the above you can easily understand that I feel entirely unworthy of the honour intended for me, and I would thank you very much if you would kindly go into this matter [sic] with your faculty once more. I can assure you that if you would retract your offer of bestowing the honour on me on account of lack of scholarly attainments, which I think is verified by this letter, I would feel that you have done the right thing. I may be able to do a little work in my simple way, but I am afraid that you would feel disappointed with me, if the honour really should be bestowed.[19]

Not surprisingly, the president wrote back, virtually ignoring the excuses offered by Toews. His brief rejoinder read as follows:

> Thank you for your letter. I was surprised that you think the Bethel College faculty would not look carefully into the case before offering anyone an honourary degree. Let me assure you that they as well as the

Board have done so and unanimously came to the conclusion that you should have one. We appreciate very much your willingness to accept and will be looking for you during the commencement week.[20]

Some time between January and the end of April, Toews must have written to Bethel College to indicate that he would be present to receive the degree. At the end of April, President Kaufman wrote a letter of confirmation in which he said, in part:

Your very humility about this honourary degree already indicates that you are a great soul and really deserve it. Let me assure you again that we have looked into this problem very carefully and that it was voted on by the faculty and the Board. . . . We don't go into this unless we know what we are doing.[21]

Toews was present on June 2, 1938 for the conferral of the honourary Doctor of Divinity degree. The diploma was signed by P.K. Regier, president of the Board, Ed G. Kaufman, president of the College, A.E. Funk, secretary of the Board, and P.J. Wedel, secretary of the Faculty.

The *Saskatchewan Valley News* printed the citation that was afforded Dr. David Toews by Bethel College on this formal occasion:

We present a man with an enviable record of achievement in ministering to fundamental needs of humanity, a pioneer of the north. His field of service is in the Mennonite settlements of western Canada. In scope his work includes pioneer as well as recent work in education, religion, organization, and colonization. As president and, more recently, as member of the Board of Directors of the German-English Academy at Rosthern, Saskatchewan, he ministered to the educational needs of Mennonite youth and exerted a direct influence on higher education among the Mennonites in the Canadian northwest.

As pastor of the Rosenorter Church since 1901, as organizer and chairman of the Canadian Mennonite General Conference, and for 27 years as member of the Home Mission Board of the General Conference of Mennonites in America, he ministered to spiritual needs and exerted a guiding influence on the religious life among Mennonites. He performed the most heroic and sacrificial task when in 1922 he organized the Canadian Mennonite Board of Colonization and as chairman of this Board was instrumental in helping 21,000 Mennonites escape from religious intolerance and physical suffering in Russia and establish homes in Canada where they could exercise religious freedom and look forward to economic and social welfare. All the services of this educator, religious leader, organizer, and colonizer were motivated by the cardinal virtues of faith, hope, and charity.[22]

Appropriately, this citation does not claim that David Toews made contributions single-handedly. It recognizes that many others worked along in the tasks named. At the same time, it speaks with integrity of his role as a key leader in major projects of his day.

At the Rosenorter Ministers Conference on May 23, 1938, Dr. Toews' colleagues applauded this well-deserved recognition. J.J. Thiessen added his personal commendation with the words:

> You did not invite such a recognition, nor did you expect it. It was given through an objective gesture. This gives us great joy. Your thankful friends feel obligated to the College that its faculty cherishes your contributions and knows how to appreciate them in a non-partisan way.[23]

Jacob H. Janzen reiterated this sentiment in a note sent to Toews that summer:

> [Brother Toews] did not gain his doctorate on the basis of a learned dissertation, but on the basis of his practical accomplishments, and we believe that if anyone has earned such an honour, it is David Toews, D.D. h.c., and we respect Bethel College highly for recognizing this and for taking action accordingly.[24]

The initials, "D.D.h.c." stand for "Doctoris in Divinitas honoris causa:" "honourary degree of Doctor of Divinity." Despite his initial protestation, David Toews was now a "man of letters." The degree was conferred over his head and against his own better judgment, so to speak.

Vision for Theological Education

While one can agree that David Toews did not have the necessary theological education to lead his people beyond the common wisdom of the ministers of his day, it is noteworthy that he articulated a vision for education beyond what he himself had attained. At the Ministers Conference preceding the 1937 conference sessions in Rosemary, Alberta, Toews presented a paper entitled, "Is it time to begin to think about a minister-preparation school?" After making a case for such a school, the ministers passed a resolution:

> The assembled ministers are agreed that there is need for such an institution [as Brother Toews has outlined]. The current situation in the world: unbelief, false teachings, materialism, as well as the need for a higher level of education in the church, makes it necessary that there be well-trained ministerial leadership to lead the church. If the enemies of Christianity prepare themselves for the fight, how much more should we do so.[25]

Several years earlier, Toews had promoted the idea of a four-year theological course under the auspices of "eine höhere Bibelschule" (an advanced Bible school). The Bible schools, which were arising in every province, were seen as the precursors to such a school. The idea became the forerunner to Canadian Mennonite Bible College, founded by the Conference of Mennonites in Canada in 1947, the year of David Toews' death.

Benno Commissioned

An encouraging event for David Toews was the commissioning service for his son Benno, held on Sunday, July 24, 1938 in Rosthern.[26] In May, Toews had shared with the ministers of the Rosenorter Church that Benno was going to the General Conference mission field in Oklahoma to work among the Cheyenne and Arapaho Indian tribes. The decision was significant in light of the fact that Benno was having some difficulty deciding on his life's calling. No doubt both his father and his father-in-law contributed to his difficulties in their own way. His high-profile father held out high expectations for his son as a worker in and for the church. While these expectations were, for the most part, subtle, they appear to have had a not-so-subtle influence on Benno who wanted to please and yet was destined to live under the shadow of his father. Meanwhile, Benno received little encouragement from his father-in-law, Isaak P. Friesen, who had his own issues with David Toews. Two years earlier, in a lengthy paragraph about Benno, J.J. Thiessen reported to Toews a conversation in which Benno complained that he received little encouragement from his father-in-law and, while he was searching for God's will, the process had its ups and downs.[27] Thiessen did his part to draw Benno into church ministry and to encourage him.

Now it appeared that Benno had set his course, and his father was proud of him. He would become the first Canadian commissioned to participate in a General Conference mission project. At the service, P.P. Wedel was the keynote speaker. He and others from south of the border had come to Saskatchewan for the triennial General Conference sessions to be held in Saskatoon the following week. During the act of commissioning, David Toews, whose hearing was by then quite weak, had bent forward intently to follow the words of commissioning spoken by Wedel. In his report of the event, J. G. Rempel comments: "If David Toews had a big heart for other people, his heart beat no less strongly for his own family."[28]

As it happened, Benno did not stay long on the mission field. Upon his return he had remarked to J.G. Rempel: "It is probably my calling from God to be a teacher."[29] Benno taught in the public schools of

Saskatchewan for several years, then at Rosthern Bible School and
Freeman Junior College in South Dakota. After that he enrolled at
Seminary in Chicago to complete his Bachelor of Divinity studies which
he had begun in 1934 in Dallas, Texas.

25th Anniversary as *Ältester*
    On Sunday afternoon, September 14, 1938, 900 persons gathered in
Rosthern to mark 25 years of service rendered by David Toews as
Ältester of the Rosenorter Mennonite Church. Anticipating the size of the
gathering, the local hockey arena was utilized for the celebration. The
occasion provided opportunity for offering praise and thanksgiving to
God, for addressing Toews with words of recognition for his service, and
for wishing him many more years of fruitful leadership. According to the
editor of *Der Bote*, it was rare for leading ministers in that day to
celebrate 25 years of service since they were not often chosen from
among the young. Toews' ordination to eldership had occurred when he
was 43 years of age.
    The service was marked by speeches, choir songs, poems, and
expressions of thanksgiving from the immigrant representatives. The
church choirs from Rosthern and Laird sang several anthems of praise.
The poem by Freilingrath, "Der Auswanderer" (The Immigrant), was
recited by Helen Dyck, and Karl Gerok's "Es reut mich nicht" (I have no
regrets) was presented by Miss Schellenberg. J.J. Klassen of Dundurn
spoke on behalf of the immigrant community when he said:

> The immigrants thank God . . . for David Toews who, as God's instru-
> ment, was called out and given wisdom and energy for the task. The task
> at which he worked afforded him much difficulty, annoyance, and
> unthankfulness, but it has also given him genuine joy in the knowledge
> that he has been of help in rescuing perishing souls. Thousands of hearts
> beat in thanksgiving for what he has done.[30]

The editor of *Der Bote* identified six contributions of Toews that were
expressed on the occasion: his energetic advocacy on behalf of young
people during wartime, his compassionate heart for the poor and for those
needing pastoral care in the church, his lengthy term of service as
chairman of the Conference of Mennonites in Canada, his leadership of
the German-English Academy at Rosthern, his faithful work as chairman
of the Board of Colonization, and his work for immigrants. Margarete
Toews was also recognized for the faithfulness with which she stood by
her husband and helped to lighten his load.
    To conclude the program, David Toews stepped to the podium. He
thanked the gathering with all his heart for the love shown him. Looking

Margarete and David Toews in 1938, the year David marked his 25th year as Ältester *of the Rosenorter Mennonite Church.*

back over the years, he had to say with Jacob that he was too unworthy to receive all the mercy and faithfulness that the Lord had shown him. He was engaged in humble work and was only a small instrument in the hand of an almighty God. These many expressions of love had strengthened him, he said, and he would now take up his work with new courage and enthusiasm. The celebration was a source of encouragement for both David and Margarete Toews.

In the weeks before and after the anniversary celebration, letters of congratulations and encouragement from near and far arrived in the Toews' mailbox.[31] The essence of these letters is exemplified in a tribute from "The Mennonite Provincial Committee of British Columbia," dated September 12, 1938, and signed by an inter-Mennonite group of 13 persons. The letter drew attention to the way in which Mennonites combined spiritual and church life with material and everyday activity. David Toews was named as an example of a person who, in his work as elder of the church and as director of the Board of Colonization, combined these two aspects. By working in both realms, Toews helped the Mennonite people in Canada to "know ourselves as members of a 'gemeinsame mennonitische Kette' (communal Mennonite chain) that we are constructing together." It was good that David Toews could hear these affirmations while he was still among the living.

Our Vulnerable Reputation
By the fall of 1938, controversy was again brewing over questions of peace and war. During and after the First World War, David Toews had been active in upholding the nonresistant stance of Mennonites. With increasing antagonism between nations in Europe in the 1930s, the issue surfaced once more. In an article entitled, "The controversy in our papers regarding nonresistance," Toews took the opportunity to address the issue. He had been asked whether he was certain that the commitment made earlier by Ottawa to the Mennonite people regarding exemption from the military on the basis of conscientious objection would stand today.

Toews reported that the Prime Minister had assured him that this was the case. The government based its stance on the laws of the land which allowed persons who were religiously COs (conscientious objectors) to absent themselves from military service. But Toews reminded his readers that this exemption was contingent on the Confession of Faith (*Glaubensbekenntnis*) of our people. And if we debated this matter in our papers, he argued, stating that some did not believe anymore in the principle of pacifism, we might put ourselves in a difficult position. The government and the public would read our papers and conclude that Mennonites no longer held to nonresistance. "Keep this in mind as you air your views," said Toews.[32] He knew whereof he spoke since it was Toews himself who, again and again, had to stand in high places as advocate for his people.

Always Fundraising
Toews must have had the Mennonite public reputation on his mind in the fall of 1938, and probably for good reasons. Following the article on the Mennonite peace witness, he again wrote about "Our transportation debt."[33] He was critical of his people for not keeping faith with their forebears. They stood by their word and kept their promises, he wrote, while we made debts and let them slide. Many were conscientious, but some made excuses or simply ignored their obligations. Others were evil-minded, arguing outrightly against any sense of obligation. There were always some who could not pay because of personal difficulties such as the death of the family's breadwinner. Toews recalled the signing of the loan when they had to pacify the critics by saying they surely would not burden the government, nor would any person be drawn into obligations unduly. And yet with the signing, he noted, we did place a burden upon our people collectively, since our reputation as a total people was at stake. The point of the article was: Let's not let up, but push on now to fulfil our promised obligations.

Although the subject of fundraising has been mentioned frequently in our story of the life of David Toews, this topic continued to recur. He was a persistent and unrelenting fundraiser, constantly seeking new sources for funding. On a recent trip to the western United States, he had obtained the names of well-to-do Mennonites so he sent off letters to Oregon and to California. The projects he presented were not necessarily of particular interest to these potential benefactors. His approach was to name the cause and describe the need, whether it was for the German-English Academy at Rosthern, or for the city homes for working women, or for poor suffering Mennonites in Russia, or for the retirement of the *Reiseschuld.* His appeals met with some success, especially where relief appeals were concerned. On other matters, such as the support of institutions and the conquest of the transportation debt, it sometimes amounted to a nickel-and-dime struggle.

David Toews made full use of his many contacts and acquaintances for financial solicitation. One church agency that Toews approached again and again was the Home Mission Board of the General Conference. Being a member of the Board, he had continuing access to its circle of decision-makers. With his broad understanding of home missions, he thought of numerous projects for which the Mission Board could offer assistance. Thus, when a Bible school was begun in Rosthern, as a sister institution of the German-English Academy, he asked the Mission Board for a $60 subsidy for the Bible School teacher. His rationale was that Bible school education was home mission work too. The Mission Board decided to contribute $50 a month.

Toews did not limit his requests to Mennonites only. He included such persons as the Minister of Public Health for the Province of Saskatchewan, Canadian Members of Parliament, and the German Consulate in Winnipeg.[34] He approached the wider public without apology, convinced that the Mennonite people intended to contribute to Canadian life as good citizens.

At times the lingering transportation debt appeared to be an all-consuming concern for David Toews but apparently that was not always the case. His coworker, Johann G. Rempel, once commented to Toews that at times he had his doubts whether the *Reiseschuld* would ever be retired. Toews, on the other hand, had said that it did not worry him unduly; it would be paid in time. He was much more worried about the survival of the school.[35] Above all else, the German-English Academy required a long-range, never-ending commitment. While the retirement of the transportation debt would contribute to the reputation and witness of the Mennonite people, the school was much more crucial in that regard.

Two Unique Fundraising Projects

In 1938, two rather unique fundraising projects were initiated in support of the German-English Academy. The Board of the school felt they could capitalize on the dedication of their dauntless leader. So they commissioned Jacob H. Janzen of Waterloo, who was serving the churches in Vancouver at the time, to write a biographical sketch of the life of David Toews. Janzen produced a 19-page booklet, entitled simply, *David Töws, Vorsitzender der Kolonisationsbehörde der Mennoniten in Canada: Biographische Skizze*. The publisher, D.H. Epp of Rosthern, embellished the contents with a dignified photo of David Toews and advertised the product for 60 cents a copy. The proceeds would go to the German-English Academy, and reprint without permission was forbidden. Every household was encouraged to own a copy. We do not know how much money the original 1938 printing generated, but we do know that the publishers did a second printing in May of 1939.

A second project initiated in 1938 involved a book sale as well. About the time of the 25th anniversary of his service as elder of the church, David Toews and Isaak P. Friesen took a significant step forward in their troublesome relationship as they put their differences behind them and made peace. As a gesture of good will, I.P Friesen, who had gifts as a poet and an evangelist, made an offer to Toews from his winter home at Long Beach, California. He would contribute the proceeds of the second volume of his book of poems, *Im Dienste des Meisters* (In the Master's Service), to the Academy if Toews would write a promotional article. This would be symbolic of the ability of these two to work together harmoniously. The book sold for $1.00 a copy. Records do not show how much this cooperative project yielded in donations.[36]

One might think that fundraising contributed substantially to Toews' emotional and physical weariness, and perhaps it did. On the other hand, he seemed to thrive on the challenge, even in his late sixties. And challenges there were! A letter written by a "Brother B." in the Mennonite Brethren paper, *Die Rundschau*, sought to put the entire immigration project in a bad light, seeing it as a politically-engineered people-movement with financial motives. In the letter the Board of Colonization was criticized for such false motives and for bad administration. Toews saw this as an attack on himself, but he did not become defensive. Rather he took the letter, point by point, and once again stated the honourable motives for immigration and recounted the history of the initiative. He admitted that if the project was in trouble financially, it may well be because he himself had been too soft on those who still owed money. The letter exuded a patient and pastoral spirit, even as he answered forthrightly to criticism.[37]

From time to time schemes were brought forward to change the approach to fundraising that was now so much a part of the personality of David Toews. He was growing older and the work was not decreasing. What would happen once he passed from the scene? Perhaps it was time for a change in strategy. And so a good friend of Toews, a member of the Board, suggested that the Board of Colonization should concern itself only with the *Reiseschuld* while the work of relief, both at home and abroad, could be left to the individual conferences who would need to organize themselves for this work and were quite capable of doing so. To this idea, Daniel P. Enns, manager of the Board is reported to have said: "To separate Ältester David Toews from the matter of relief is an impossibility, for if you take this away from him, you take everything away."[38] It seemed the immigration project had served to make Toews compassionate about suffering humanity so that "wherever there was need in the world, David Toews was there with his thoughts and his concerns." This included not only the world abroad but also the world close to home. As those who attended ministers and deacons meetings of the Rosenorter Mennonite Church over the years knew, the needs of the widows, the sick, and the poor in the community were always on his agenda. According to Rosenorter Mennonite Church historian, J.G. Rempel, the membership of that church stood faithfully behind their leader in the causes and the concerns he promoted.

Community Minded
In principle, David Toews strongly promoted the idea that in the end responsibility lay with the body of believers and not finally with the individual. Yes, the individual should consider him/herself accountable but the congregation as such should bear the final responsibility. In stating this principle Toews had to be careful, since at one time he had strongly upheld the hope and the promise that immigrants would come across with their share of the transportation debt. While he did not want to take the individual "off the hook," theologically he believed in the concept of peoplehood. Furthermore, he may well have realized that the congregation was indeed his last hope for conquering the debt. Thus, at the yearly meeting of the Rosenorter church on June 1, 1937, he proposed that the church should urge its individual members to pay their outstanding travel debt but, if they could not do so, the church should provide the necessary assistance. One immigrant objected, saying that they as direct benefactors wanted to do this themselves and not burden the church. At the end of a vigorous discussion, a resolution was passed which urged the immigrants to pay their individual debts and promised help from the church for the most difficult cases. Toews was not quite

satisfied with this way of stating it; he would have preferred a much stronger commitment from the church—the church would look at the debt in total and would settle it once and for all lest it linger on indefinitely. The best way to conquer the problem was to be strong in the face of the odds and to pull together and help one another as a church body.[39] Yet on that occasion he backed off, with the words: "Wenn ich nicht kann, wie ich will, dann will ich, wie ich kann" (If it is not possible to do as I desire, then I desire what is possible).[40] While we have seen an insistent Toews at times, he was also able and willing to accommodate to the wishes of the group.

Death of J.S. Dennis

Not long after this discussion, the Mennonite community heard the news that their benefactor at the CPR office, Colonel J.S. Dennis, had died at the age of 82. His was one of the few non-Mennonite obituaries that made it into *Der Bote*.[41] In his tribute in the same issue, David Toews stated that the Mennonite people owed Col. Dennis a great deal of respect. In the article Toews told of how, from his retirement home in Victoria, Dennis recently had come to Coaldale where he was invited to visit the Coaldale-Lethbridge Mennonite settlement with his successor. On that occasion a group of teenage girls ceremoniously laid bouquets of flowers at his feet, with the words: "You saved our lives, thank you." Tears had come to Col. Dennis' eyes. Toews continued:

> How we would have wished that this gracious gentleman had seen the fulfilment of the promise made years ago. But the adverse years of the 1930s have militated against that realization. I have had much to do with him concerning the debt, and I must say that I have never heard him utter a harsh word.[42]

Col. Dennis had been true to the word he spoke to Toews back in 1922 when he assured him that the contract was based on trust ("eine Vertrauungssache"), and this was the way it should stay.

16
War and Death
1939–1941

By the beginning of 1939 it was becoming apparent that a large-scale war was looming in Europe. If and when England would become engaged in the encounter, there was the distinct possibility that, given her allegiance to the British Commonwealth, Canada would become involved as well. In this milieu, the primary concern of Mennonite church leaders was the question of their status with respect to military service. If the government should implement the compulsory draft, would Mennonite young adults be exempt? Historically this had been the case. As early as 1808, a government statute had exempted those "Swiss" Mennonite immigrants, who had come to Upper Canada from the United States, from serving in the militia.[1] A follow-up statute of 1868 had reaffirmed the earlier one of 1808 but had also served notice that the government reserved the right to put conditions on this exemption if it so chose.

The second wave of Mennonite immigrants, who came from tsarist Russia between 1874 and 1880 (referred to as the *Kanadier*), were granted exemption from military service by a special Order-in-Council in 1873.[2] The assurances given these two immigrant groups protected them and their offspring against conscription during the First World War (1914–1918). Even those who had come by various other routes in the meantime, such as the Prussian immigrants of the 1890s or immigrants from America, were not prevailed upon to enlist in the army during World War I.[3]

For those Mennonite immigrants who came to Canada between 1923 and 1930 (referred to as the *Russländer*), the arrangement was not quite as clear. They had been given the assurance that the same laws relating to military exemptions would apply equally to them as to those Mennonites who had come earlier.[4] But apparently the government did not mean that they would be given complete military exemption as had been promised in 1873 to the earlier immigrants.[5] The Canadian government was acting cautiously since there had been considerable public animosity against the privileged Mennonites during the First World War. This had led to an Order-in-Council in 1919 which placed a ban on further immigration of Mennonites from central and eastern Europe, a ban that was lifted on June 2, 1923. At the time, a delegation led by David Toews had been assured in Ottawa that the laws applying to Mennonites already in Canada would apply equally to the new immigrants.[6] But even in the case of earlier immigrants, the government claimed the right to set conditions from time to time.

Reaffirming Nonresistance

In March of 1939, the Mennonite Central Committee convened a meeting in Chicago to seek agreement on a common statement of principle and a common approach in the face of the prospect of war.[7] Canadian representatives at the meeting were J.B. Martin, B.B. Janz, C.F. Klassen, and David Toews. The Canadian attendees were impressed with the urgency of arriving at a unity of conviction and taking a united approach to alternative forms of service. They decided it was necessary to have a similar all-Mennonite meeting in Canada. David Toews issued the invitation which read, in part, that "in case a war breaks out, we would do well if we could be united in our response to the various questions that would arise."[8] Toews was afraid that if Mennonite groups appeared disunited with respect to service and nonresistance, it would not only weaken but also damage their cause. On May 15, 1939, about 500 delegates and observers representing eight Mennonite groups and a ninth group, the Hutterites, met for the day in Winkler, to test their unity on the question of the principle of nonresistance and on the question of alternative service.[9] Some Americans, including Harold S. Bender, were present at Winkler and hoped that Canadians would subscribe to the (Old) Mennonite style of nonresistance, which was characterized by an attitude of separation from any involvement with government.

David Toews led the meetings. In his extended remarks on the common quest for a united voice, he called attention to the dangerous political situation, then stated his deep desire that all the groups present would agree on the principle of nonresistance.[10] He pointed to two obstacles that made it hard to negotiate special status for Mennonites. First, it was difficult to claim a position of nonresistance on behalf of Mennonite young people if and when they were seen as troublemakers in the community. In other words, there was a credibility gap between witness and action. Secondly, as long as the various groups of Mennonite churches were not united among themselves on their position and their proposals regarding alternative service, the government would find it difficult to take them seriously. While there was agreement in principle on peace and nonresistance, the discussion revealed sharp differences on questions of alternative service. Three distinct approaches became evident at the Winkler meeting, in accordance with the three immigrant groups.[11] The earliest (Old) Mennonite "Swiss" immigrants were willing to accept some form of alternate service, provided it would not be military. The *Kanadier* immigrants of the 1870s assumed they had been exempted from any form of state service whatsoever. The recent *Russländer* immigrants of the 1920s were open to a wide range of options, including medical and ambulance service under military command. The delegates did not come to a decision, partly because of these divisions, partly because alternative service was not yet a pressing issue. They did appoint a committee to work in the interim and to call a meeting at some future date when the matter might be more urgent. The committee members represented the three largest Mennonite groups present: David Toews of the Conference of Mennonites in Canada, Benjamin B. Janz of the Mennonite Brethren, Samuel F. Coffman of the (Old) Mennonites.[12]

At first it seemed that the Canadian government would require neither compulsory military service nor alternative service.[13] But by June of 1940, ten months after the outbreak of war, the National Resource Mobilization Act mandated compulsory conscription. This meant, in short, that all men between the ages of 16 and 60 must be registered, thus consider themselves as potential recruits. At the same time, the Mennonites were assured that they would be exempted from bearing arms. Toews' hope for a united response among all Mennonite groups received a major setback when, in September of 1940, the churches in Manitoba that considered themselves under the exemption assured in 1873, organized independently of the *Russländer* groups.[14] The *Kanadier* were confident they could negotiate an exemption, whereas the *Russländer* group felt they needed to be proactive by presenting a proposal for alternative service to the government. Toews thought the necessity for such action would come only when there was a demand for alternative service. In the months following the May 15 meeting, Toews went out of his way to assure the conservative element that the peace principle would not be compromised.[15]

In December 1939, David Toews and B.B. Janz travelled to the home of S.F. Coffman in Vineland, Ontario, for a meeting of the interim committee formed at Winkler. Orie O. Miller of Mennonite Central Committee was also present. Toews and Janz also sat in on the Executive Committee meeting of Ontario's Non-Resistant Relief Organization (NRRO) which had been in existence since 1918. Within the interim committee, discussion centred on seeking common mutual understanding and exploring possible initiatives in case there would be pressure on Mennonites to get involved in national service. The meetings in Vineland gave Toews and Janz encouragement to seek the formation of an organization in western Canada, similar to the NRRO in Ontario.[16]

244 David Toews Was Here

David Toews and B.B. Janz on a Reiseschuld *collection trip in Leamington, Ontario. The two men were instrumental in fhe formation of the Mennonite Central Relief Committee in 1940, Toews as its first chairman, Janz as secretary.* Photo: Frank H. Epp, *Mennonite Exodus*

Mennonite Central Committee Canada

The urgency of the situation internationally, as well as the desire to develop some semblance of inter-Mennonite unity, led Toews and Janz to act immediately on the idea of a western relief committee. Between January 12 and February 5 of 1940, David Toews chaired a series of four meetings—in Altona, Manitoba; in Saskatoon, Saskatchewan; in Coaldale, Alberta; and in Yarrow, British Columbia. At each of these gatherings, Toews made a significant contribution in setting the tone and direction. His introductory words at Altona, with which he addressed the 136 persons representing seven groups from the inter-Mennonite community, were summarized in the minutes as follows:

> Since the meeting in Winkler on March 15, 1939 concerning the military question, the world situation has changed. Our country has added itself to those ready to engage in war, hence new tasks await us also. Resulting from the war, will again be renewed suffering and misery. Thus it becomes our responsibility to be prepared to help alleviate the suffering. For this task we need to organize ourselves. Our brethren in Ontario have already done so. . . . We want to do the same in western Canada.[17]

At the conclusion of the meeting, Toews was quoted as saying:

> Today we have offered one another the brotherly handshake for the sake of helping those in need. If our inner attitude is right today, then future generations will speak of this as an important day. Brothers, let us do

good to all people. Today we have founded an organization and made decisions. But will the work proceed? Let us not disappoint the Committee we have elected today. Will we make the necessary sacrifices? Let's do it. May God help us.[18]

At the Saskatoon meeting, held a week later, Toews was again asked to preside. Representatives from the various congregations and church groups agreed that they wanted to do relief work together. In the course of the meeting, Brother Moses Schmidt of the (Old) Mennonite congregation at Guernsey felt moved to offer a statement of encouragement to Toews: "I want to take this opportunity to thank David Toews most heartily for his untiring work on behalf of our people. May God reward him for his efforts."[19] The meeting resulted in the founding of a Saskatchewan chapter of the larger Mennonite Central Relief Committee.

On January 30, David Toews was in Coaldale chairing the organizational meeting. There he was led to offer reflections on the call to suffering. According to the minutes, he spoke as follows:

We live in serious times. Whatever transpires here or across the ocean, there will be suffering. Of that we can be sure. We should not assume that we can be free from it. We want to suffer with those who suffer and we want to be active in doing good. We want to allow the Lord to prepare us for times of suffering. We want to remain steadfast in our convictions and not allow ourselves to be tossed to and fro by opinions. Let us stand firm and immovable, always increasing in the work of the Lord.[20]

The Coaldale folk raised questions beyond the relief issue as well. One asked: Who would qualify for exemption from military service: only baptized youth or the unbaptized as well? Toews expressed his view that we should not differentiate between baptized and unbaptized young men on this question, but we should vouch for all our Mennonite youth.

The last in this sequence of four provincial meetings was held in Yarrow, British Columbia, on February 5. The meeting proceeded in a fashion similar to the others, with Toews as chair and with the result that the inter-Mennonite community in British Columbia organized a relief committee through which to participate in the work of the Mennonite Central Relief Committee. Toward the close of the meeting, someone drew attention to the forthcoming 70th birthday of David Toews; Rev. Jacob B. Wiens read a prepared statement for the occasion:

Dear Brother Toews: We count ourselves fortunate that here today we have such an unexpected opportunity to thank the Lord together with you for his gift to you of 70 years. When Moses, the man of God, assumed his task, he did not give it up until God called him to do so. Only when God led him to Mt. Nebo, did he lay down his work and take his leave from his people and from his life. You are still leading us and you have been a rich blessing to us, Brother Toews. You are still spry, while others of your age are breaking down. God has been especially gracious to you and has kept you strong. We thank you for your work and wish you God's rich blessings also for your further work.

To this, David Toews responded:

I am thankful for all your love toward me. Looking up to God I must say: I am much too insignificant to deserve such mercy and faithfulness. Often times I have not been satisfied with my work, and I have much reason to humble myself and even at times to feel ashamed. I owe the Lord thanksgiving for what I was able to accomplish, and the honour is due God alone for that which could be done. I will convey your thank-you to my family at home. When I think back of my recent serious operation, at the time I was fearful this might be my last journey. God was gracious and answered the supplications of brothers and sisters. I want to continue to serve my people, and at the end of my days my prayer shall be, "Lord, do not subject your servant to judgment."[21]

Toews was still very much engaged in ventures that addressed the issues of the present and the future. At the same time, he was mindful of the tentative nature of his own physical person. His expression of humility and his reference to the sustaining grace of God were genuine reflections of his inner soul.

The four provincial chapters were rounded off with a central committee. At a meeting in Winnipeg in March of that same year, an overarching inter-provincial organization, called the Mennonite Central Relief Committee (MCRC), was organized. David Toews was elected as its chairman, with B.B. Janz as vice-chairman, and C.F. Klassen as secretary-treasurer. The MCRC, together with its sister organization in Ontario, formed the prelude to the eventual Mennonite Central Committee Canada. Later that spring, David Toews could report with some satisfaction to the Canadian Mennonite constituency on the initiatives taken across western Canada.[22] The meetings in Altona, Saskatoon, Coaldale, and Yarrow had given hope that Mennonites in the west could work together, at least when it came to alleviating human need.

Unity Not Achieved

Yet David Toews was to suffer a disappointment. It was one thing to cooperate on relief but quite another to work together on peace and nonresistance. The conservative elements in Manitoba could not bring themselves to join hands with those who favoured alternative service in cooperation with the government. They had formed their own committee of elders (*Ältestenkomitee*) and chose to make their own representations to government rather than work with their mainly *Russländer* counterparts. Toews had felt he was in a good position to bridge the gap between the two groups. As immigrant from the United States in 1893, he viewed himself as non-partisan, but the *Kanadier* viewed him as allied with the more liberal *Russländer*. After all, he was spokesperson for the largely *Russländer* Conference of Mennonites in Canada and had aided the *Russländer* in immigrating to Canada. Toews suggested a meeting of representatives from all groups in the four western provinces to be held on May 24, 1941. But within the newly formed Mennonite Central Relief Committee, B.B. Janz had little interest in such an effort; C.F. Klassen was also skeptical of any results.[23] However, through the efforts of J.H. Enns of Winnipeg, a meeting of western representatives was held on May 28 but little was accomplished. A debate ensued between those who advocated first-aid alternative service on the military front and those who agreed to alternative service in national parks and other government projects.[24] Toews and others wanted agreement on the latter, with those who favoured the former given permission to pursue that course if they chose. A vote revealed that the majority supported alternative service in non-military related projects, but a vocal minority were aggressive and determined in their bid for non-combatant first-aid service.[25] While David Toews felt defeated, he also thought he had done the right thing in his attempt to set the stage for a united approach.

While these efforts served to reveal disunity in the Mennonite ranks, they did little to ensure that each group would have its way. On December 24, 1940, the government of Canada passed an Order-in-Council that amended the National War Services Regulations.[26] In it the government prescribed three possible types of training as alternatives to military training: non-combatant military training at a military camp; first-aid training at a non-military facility; or civilian labour service. It should be noted that this new regulation focused only on training and not yet on assignments as such.

German Pride

For various reasons, Mennonites in Canada were in a particularly vulnerable position at the outbreak of the war. Their use of the German language in everyday conversation and in worship, together with their stance of nonresistance, made them suspect. In the later 1930s, as animosity intensified internationally between England and Germany, Mennonites were coming under increased scrutiny. Why was it, *really*, that Mennonites did not want to join the war against the Germans? A person who had no sympathy for the pacifist position would be prone to attribute ulterior motives to anyone who held to a nonresistant stance and spoke mainly German. Were the Mennonites perchance on the side of the enemy?

In the face of these biases, David Toews would not hear of withdrawing from the issues in the hope that they might go away. Some in the Mennonite constituency were embarrassed by their identity with German language and culture and tried in various ways to deny this connection. In Toews' view, it was better to be "up front" on the matter. His characteristic forthrightness required that the issues be faced. In any case, Mennonites would not be able to convince the public that they were not German. Their customs and their language belied them. Better to be up front and truthful, and then to urge the Canadian citizenry to respect even those Canadian citizens in their midst who were German, than to steer around the issue in some other way.[27]

In the spring of 1939, Toews outlined these concerns in a lengthy letter addressed to the editor of the *Saskatoon Star-Phoenix*, the city's main public daily paper.[28] The paper had recently reported on a meeting in Saskatoon at which it had been said that in Rosthern some 35 percent of voters were members of the Nazi party. Toews denied this statement, saying he doubted there was even one such person in the Rosthern area. At the same time, said Toews, if he himself was a member, he would not be afraid to say it publicly, since "I consider National Socialism to be a political party that has at least as much right in any free country as, for instance, Communism has, toward which many of our Canadian papers are so very tolerant." He went on to state emphatically:

> We Mennonites are German, our services in the churches are mostly German, the Sunday schools are being kept in the German language, and we are trying to have our children learn German. We are in no way trying to hide the fact that we are teaching our children the mother tongue, and I do not believe that we do anything contrary to law if we instruct them in German in their free hours on Saturdays and Sundays.[29]

While Toews was speaking on behalf of Mennonites, he pointed to the German Catholics, German Baptists, and German Lutherans who would claim the same convictions as Mennonites. Toews conceded that "there is a good deal of sympathy with Germany among the German people," and that one reason for this was the "most horrible persecution" that German people now living in Canada had suffered under the Communist system in Russia.

People in that country were murdered in untold numbers; . . . in many cases parents were taken away from their children and exiled. All the property was confiscated. People were starving and people are still starving now; untold numbers are homeless. Ministers have been shot or exiled; all their churches have been seized. . . . And still there was no word of protest on the part of any government and no protest in the press of this country. Germany stopped the spread of Bolshevism into other countries with no bloodshed and we as a people are very thankful to Germany for having done so.[30]

If there was sympathy for Germany among people of German background, that would be the reason for it, said Toews.

In the letter, Toews took on a number of formidable personages. He challenged the Prime Minister of Great Britain for stating that there was nothing objectionable about Communism. He advised a certain Rabbi Eisendrat of Toronto not to worry about alleged sinister plots by Nazis in this country. Tongue in cheek, he wondered aloud whether it was our government that had been training a Nazi core. As for those anonymous persons who fabricated lies about Rosthern's supposed Nazis, "a fairly good walking stick will keep men like that at a distance." Upon reading the letter in the paper, J.J. Thiessen wrote to Toews to say that his letter was a bit too biting. But Toews justified his approach, insisting that Mennonites had a right to counteract anti-German letters appearing across Canada and had an obligation to explain that they were against war because of historic convictions, not because of German attachments.[31]

Yet Toews was more flexible on the German question than one might have thought. When in July 1940 he placed an announcement in the papers, advising Mennonites on how to identify themselves in the upcoming census, he instructed that they should answer German (or Dutch or Russian) Mennonite to the question of "Racial Origin."[32] He received this advice from Ottawa. In a subsequent note, he added wisely that, of course, "Swiss Mennonite" was also an option.[33]

In the larger scheme of things, German language and German culture played a significant role in the life of those Canadian Mennonites who immigrated from Russia and Prussia beginning in the 1870s. David Toews entered the milieu some 25 years after the first migrants arrived in 1874. He brought with him his own experiences which included almost a decade of exposure to the situation among Mennonites in Kansas. As already noted, in the period between the two world wars, and particularly in the later 1930s, Mennonite attention to things German took on political and nationalistic overtones.[34] By the end of World War II, these elements had largely disappeared. In this respect, David Toews was a product of his times.

Meeting the King

With the prospect of war brewing in Europe, England wanted to ensure that its allies were on her side and would assist her. With this in mind, the English royal couple, King George VI and Queen Elizabeth, made a tour of Canada in the spring of 1939. Their main purpose was to test and strengthen Canada's loyalty to British military plans. Knowing that the royal entourage would be stopping in Saskatoon, the Board of Colonization asked a committee of three men—David Toews, B.B. Janz, and S.F. Coffman—to draft a message to the king. The letter assured the "King of Canada" and the Canadian government of the "deepest devotion and unwavering loyalty"[35] of Mennonites in Canada.

David Toews had conferred with Thiessen as to an appropriate way to convey the letter to the British visitors when they came to Saskatoon.[36] Imagine Toews' surprise when a few days before the king's visit, on June 2, in the course of a Ministers Conference in Laird, he received a phone call from Saskatoon asking that he, together with Margarete, be present the next day in Saskatoon, to be presented and introduced to the king and queen. Thus it was that on June 3, 1939, David and Margarete Toews met the royal couple. Toews reported later that as he shook hands with the king, he said, "God bless you!" To this the king had replied: "I thank you!" Some may have thought that David Toews would have been driven out of town because of his strongly worded letter in the recent May 6 issue of the *Saskatoon Star-Phoenix*. Instead, he was invited to a place of high honour. Does this perhaps bear a hint of the point Toews made, from time to time, that we only make gains when we present ourselves with integrity?

Remain Calm

With the outbreak of war in September 1939, the agenda for David Toews and the Mennonite churches came into clear focus. Officially, there was little preoccupation with the war as such, with who was at fault, or how things might turn out. The concerns focused rather on how a historic peace church, devoted in principle to nonresistance and nonparticipation in military enterprise, should respond internally. In the context of the Rosenorter Church, a spirit of calm prevailed. The young people would need to be instructed in the biblical peace position and on an appropriate procedure in case of compulsory draft, but this should not be done with much fanfare. Ottawa would be consulted to find out what kinds of forms were required for those who might be asked to enlist. For the next few years, the ministerial meetings were preoccupied with matters related to nonresistance: with acquiring and distributing peace literature, with registration, and with alternative service.

On the public level, David Toews was concerned about animosity against the Mennonites. During the fall of 1939, he and J.J. Thiessen sought direction and encouragement from one another with respect to a peaceful Mennonite stance. Writing to Thiessen on October 2, 1939, Toews noted that in Manitoba the citizenry was stirred up against the Mennonites. This led Toews to suggest that "we should be extremely cautious and wise in our actions so that we do not unduly agitate the English people."[37] Thiessen replied promptly, with the words: "Let's remain calm. I am not afraid. . . . I have had the thought that careless persons will hurt our cause. May our dear God give us grace to conduct ourselves as the quiet in the land, and give no one occasion for offence and anger."[38] When Toews complained that he was being called upon often to assist parents whose youth had too hastily signed up with the military, Thiessen spoke words of encouragement and comfort: "And there you [Toews] are, the one who is always expected to jump in when others have messed things up. I feel sorry for you in your position of responsibility. May God give you an abundance of wisdom and grace. We are praying for you."[39]

In the months following the outbreak of the war, the demands on Toews' time and wisdom did not cease. In a public article early in 1941, he gave instructions to those who had to appear before the conscription board in which he reminded the young people to be truthful about their stance and situation, and to uphold the reputation of the Mennonite church in their deportment.[40] He also reminded the young people that, if and when they received their conscription notice, they must present themselves for registration, albeit they should register as conscientious objectors. Some young people, particularly in Manitoba, were misguided in thinking they could simply ignore the summons which was not a wise alternative choice.[41]

Toews and others had a meeting with military officials in Saskatoon who wanted to persuade the Mennonites to allow their youth to undergo two months of military training, after which they were free to decide whether they would join the military or opt for alternate service.[42] The military officials argued that Mennonite young people would surely feel better if they did something substantial for their country, and they would surely feel badly if they knew their peers were fighting on their behalf. Toews assured the officials that Mennonites were not asking youth to go to war on their behalf: "The story of our people shows that we would rather face martyrdom unto death than to require of others that they should protect us and contribute in that way to the defense of our faith." One of the officials had remarked that Jesus had put his nonresistance on hold when he said that if his kingdom were of this world his disciples would fight. To this the Mennonite delegation (probably Toews) replied: "But our Lord Jesus went to the cross and did not fight with weapons in order to protect himself." One of the officials was overheard to say later: "Gentlemen, I must say I respect your conviction."[43]

Another question arose: should university students participate in military drill exercises? There was the case of a young Mennonite student from Eyebrow, Saskatchewan, who desired baptism. J.J. Thiessen was hesitant because the man was taking part in the university's compulsory military drill. When Thiessen asked for the advice of Toews in this case, Toews answered that he knew too little about what such drill entailed. Since Thiessen was better informed because he had first-hand information and since he knew the young man quite well, he would be able to make the right decision.[44]

On a related issue, Thiessen drew Toews' attention to the news, or perhaps the rumour, that in the coming year the University of Saskatchewan would not accept any students who took the CO position. That is, all male and female students must participate in military drill. What should he tell the young people? He urged Toews to state a position.[45] Toews advised that we should explain our stance to the president of the University, and it might be expected that the regulation would not be enforced strictly. If, however, the University remained firm, then we would need to advise our students to go elsewhere than to the University. Toews promised to look into this matter more carefully.[46]

But Toews and Thiessen did not always agree in their approach as representatives of "the quiet in the land," as the following incident shows. A member of First Mennonite Church in Saskatoon, A. Schellenberg, owned a grocery store where he employed Mennonites, in some cases members of the very congregation he himself attended. During the course of 1939, and particularly with the outbreak of the war, he had become nervous when his employees conversed publicly in German. Eventually he forbade them to do so and even went a step further: he asked them not to attend church services conducted in the German language. David Toews heard of this and became irate. It went against his principle of insisting that one could present oneself as a loyal citizen of Canada and also as German speaking. He formulated a letter that he intended to send to Schellenberg, but first checked it with Thiessen. The letter chastised Schellenberg for coming down hard on his employees.

Thiessen's assessment of Toews' approach was that he sounded hard, even angry ("böse"), and he wished that Schellenberg would not have to experience Toews in this way. Let's overcome evil with good, he wrote to Toews. Yet Thiessen conceded that the letter told the truth, so he advised him to send it. In a follow-up visit, Schellenberg had confided to

Thiessen that he had nothing against the church, only against the German language. Meanwhile, wrote Thiessen to Toews, there was great fear, with tears and anguish, in his church over this matter. It had unsettled many people.[47] We see the pastoral Thiessen in contrast to the principled Toews, taking a somewhat different approach to a "dicey" issue.

Respecting Differences

While David Toews was quite capable of defensive argumentation, such as he displayed in his letter to the editor of the *Star Phoenix*, in the main he expressed himself in less emotional and in substantial ways on issues that surfaced during the war years. We see this in an article on upholding Mennonite distinctives published in 1941.[48] Anyone who has visited other countries and cultures, wrote Toews, will have noted that people differ noticeably in their way of life. Society is comprised of a variety of peoples, each with a distinct culture, as for example, the difference between Quebec and the rest of Canada, or between Catholics and Protestants. Mennonite people also have their particular ways ("Eigenart"), shaped and inherited through history, nurture, habit, or conviction. Many of these ways are worth preserving and passing on to future generations; at the same time we learn from the ways of those who are different from us. Toews identified three main teachings that differentiate Mennonites from other religious groups: the teaching and practice of nonresistance, baptism upon confession of faith, and non-swearing of oaths. If we wish to preserve these particularities, he continued, we must teach them to our children in their younger years. According to Scripture, this has been the proven method. If we desire to respect these teachings as worthwhile, as our forebears did, then we need to convey to our youth, through word and example, that they have great value for their future.

In doing this we do not despise the approaches of other schools, Toews commented. We have respect for good accomplishments among those who take a different approach than we do. At the same time, we claim that our insights are of great value since our forebears forsook house and land for the sake of preserving these insights for their children.[49] Toews ended the article by making a brief case for Mennonite schools where young men and women had the opportunity to imbibe Mennonite distinctives and where they became inspired to influence society for the good.

Ongoing Board Agenda

During this time in which he gave leadership in matters of peace and nonresistance, the ongoing work of the Board of Colonization also needed attention. In February 1940 the transportation debt stood at

$558,000 plus interest. There was a constant round of counselling that needed to be done with Mennonites in transition. That is, Mennonites in Mexico wanted to return to Canada; families in Germany wanted to come to Canada; some Mennonites in Canada wanted to resettle in Germany, possibly to escape their debt. Because of the lingering Depression, some were declaring bankruptcy. Support needed to continue for B.H. Unruh who was still working among the immigrants in Germany. Cultural and educational issues needed to be addressed with book distributions. The work of *Reiseschuld* collectors in each district needed to be supported. And now issues of war and peace needed concerted attention. There was enough to do and to worry about![50]

Relief Work in England
In the spring of 1940, when the Mennonite Central Committee decided to focus its relief efforts on England, Canadian Mennonites were organized to swing into action. In May David Toews announced, by way of Canadian Mennonite church papers, that the purpose of the effort in England was to alleviate suffering among the civilians, especially women and children.[51] In the fall of that same year, he wrote to women's groups in the churches to give instructions on preparation of clothing articles for poor children in England.[52] In the same issue Toews and C.F. Klassen published an article informing the congregations of their obligations in support of MCC and MCRC relief work.[53] A few months later Toews again appealed for donations for the MCC project in England which, he emphasized, was providing assistance to Polish and English children.[54] The appeal showed that response to suffering was not limited only to the Mennonite people but to all people in need. It could be surmised that Toews cherished the opportunity to bear testimony to this broad ministry, particularly in light of the criticism of English Canada against the perceived, and sometimes justified, isolationist tendencies of the Mennonite people.

The relief work in England extended from forwarding material aid to sending relief workers. In 1940, the Non-Resistant Relief Organization of Ontario sent John Coffman, son of S.F. Coffman of Vineland. Then, Edna Hunsberger of Kitchener, followed the call to England. In 1941, the newly organized Canadian MCRC commissioned two persons—Peter J. Dyck, son of Johannes J. Dyck of Laird, Saskatchewan, and Elfrieda Klassen, a sister of C.F. Klassen—to work among children and old people in Birmingham and Manchester. It gave David Toews particular satisfaction to see that the Canadian churches, through their relief organizations, were beginning to send personnel to places of distress on the international front.

Meeting Another King
In May of 1940 David Toews was on his way to the Peace River area
by way of Edmonton when he was intercepted by B.B. Janz and C.F.
Klassen. They urged him to go to Ottawa once more to intercede on
behalf of Mennonites concerning their stance toward military service and
wartime activities. So he went on the spur of the moment and with no
prearranged appointments.[55]

Toews made his presence known at the parliament buildings, but it
seemed he would be unable to make significant contacts there. He got the
attention of Walter Tucker, parliamentary representative for the Rosthern
area, but Toews had hoped to speak with the Prime Minister himself
since, of all people in Ottawa, William Lyon Mackenzie King would
have an understanding for the Mennonite people. At the end of one of the
house sessions, Tucker approached the Prime Minister and informed him
of David Toews' presence. Immediately King motioned for Toews to
come to them. The two greeted one another warmly. Then Toews informed the Prime Minister of recent decisions to broaden the relief work
of Mennonites in Canada with particular focus on England. King
commended the Mennonites for this initiative and encouraged them,
through Toews, to continue in this way. Toews presented King with the
Mennonites' dilemma regarding war bonds, saying that he wished the
bonds would not be urged upon the Mennonites. It was as though they
were buying actual guns and doing battle with them. The Prime Minister
had understanding for Toews' point and said he thought a compromise
could be reached concerning bonds. He would refer the matter to the
deputy finance minister, Mr. Clark.

Toews also met with Mr. Crerar, the immigration minister, on the
question of whether English orphan children could be hosted among
Mennonites in Canada. Crerar said this kind of action was not yet in the
plans but he would keep the possibility in mind. Next he met with Mr.
Bexter and Mr. Carnegie, representatives of the Canadian press. He
registered his concerns with them regarding the frequent unfair press
given the Mennonites.

Before leaving Ottawa, Toews had opportunity to discuss the
worrisome issue of conscription with Walter Tucker. Tucker was of the
mind that conscription would not be introduced in Canada. One major
factor would be opposition of the French Canadian people who were set
against it. There was potential for unrest in the land if conscription were
imposed. Toews was quite satisfied with his trip to Ottawa. The
conversations he had there confirmed in his mind that, even during
wartime, Mennonites could not hide their heads in the sand but must
become engaged in the issues and stand up for their point of view and for

their course of action. If Mennonites were against killing, then they must work to promote life.

Over the years, David Toews had developed a relationship with Prime Minister Mackenzie King that could be characterized as "mutual appreciation." Toews liked to tell how, on one occasion when he was in Ottawa, he was invited to dine at the home of Prime Minister King.[56] When Toews had remarked about the many heavy duties that befell the Prime Minister, King took him into the room adjoining the dining room, and showed him a cabinet in which was a Bible. "The Bible was given to me by my mother," said King. "It is not only a precious keepsake and remembrance of my mother, but in times when the affairs of state weigh particularly heavily I take refuge in this book. I read from its pages and gain strength." Apparently King once considered becoming a minister of the gospel. He told Toews that if he had done so, his main text would have been: "Let the same mind be in you that was in Christ Jesus" (Philippians 2:5). Back at the office in Rosthern, Toews received personal notes of encouragement from the Prime Minister from time to time.

A Conference Milestone

The 38th annual sessions of the Conference of Mennonites in Canada, held at Waldheim, Saskatchewan, July 3–5, 1940, were important for several reasons. This was the first conference since the outbreak of war a year earlier. Much of the discussion focused on matters of nonresistance and relief, with reports by David Toews on his discussion with officials in Ottawa and on relief efforts in Europe setting the agenda.

At the close of the sessions, Chairman Toews took the initiative, apparently without consultation, to state that he would no longer let his name stand as chairman of the Conference.[57] Apparently this came as something as a surprise to the delegates and, in the name of the Conference, J.J. Klassen expressed regrets. With that Toews closed the sessions with prayer. He had chaired the Conference for 26 years, from 1914 to 1935 and from 1937 to 1940. In July of 1936 David and Margarete Toews had been in Europe for the Mennonite World Conference. Before 1914 he had served on the executive committee as secretary for six years, from 1906 to 1911. He had been part of the group that originally met in Tiefengrund in 1902 to begin the Conference. Toews would have sensed that it was time to make way for younger and more energetic leadership. At the same time, his opening conference sermon at these sessions was not about preserving the past but focused on the need for the power of the Holy Spirit to carry out the work of mission in a needy world. His text was Luke 24:49 and Acts. 1:4, which speak of awaiting divine power from on high and anticipating the promise of the Father.

Wedding of Anna Toews and Sylvester Funk on July 27, 1940.

The move on the part of Toews to bring his long-standing service as chairman to an end did not go unnoticed. In a letter to Toews the next day, J. J. Thiessen wrote: "I am still preoccupied with thoughts about what you said at the conclusion to our conference in Waldheim. You knew what you were doing and why you did what you did, but I must say that your action stirred me deeply."[58] Then he concluded with a note of appreciation for Toews' work:

> I want to thank you once again in the name of many for the huge service that you have offered to our people in general and to our immigrants in particular. May God richly reward you. Most surely, history will know how to offer appropriate appreciation for your work.

He ended his letter by expressing his pleasure that Toews' hearing aid was of great assistance in helping him understand the discussion.

Doing What I Can!
In the midst of a rather hectic fall schedule in 1940, Toews found himself having to answer to the criticism that Mennonite leaders were not doing enough to deal with the issue of military conscription. Toews took this personally and replied to the letter.[59] "Since the date mentioned in the criticism," he wrote, "I have been in Ottawa five times, in Chicago two times, in Regina many times, have appeared at many meetings in the provinces, have sent written reports to meetings in the east, and also

visited some meetings there." Back home in the office, he continued, "I have had to deal with a huge pile of correspondence on this issue. . . . Then I travelled with B.B. Janz and Jacob Gerbrandt to Regina, upon the wishes of the Committee in Saskatoon, to speak with Judge Embury, Chairman of the National War Services Board." Besides these activities, Toews explained, he was collecting money in the Drake area on behalf of the school. There his work was cut short because, as he said, "my dear wife who was staying with our youngest daughter suddenly became ill and had to be taken to the hospital in Saskatoon." The letter sounded defensive, and it appeared as though Toews was trying to do everything himself. This was not the case, as there were others who were also working with issues of conscription. Yet it was typical of David Toews to feel the weight of responsibility for the affairs of his people.

Margarete Seriously Ill

From the beginning of their marriage, David and Margarete had carried concerns about Margarete's health. The eye problem of 40 years earlier never did clear up entirely, even though Margarete was able to carry on with a full range of domestic duties and with church obligations besides. Then in the fall of 1940 things took a turn for the worse when extreme pain in the lower abdomen would not go away. She was admitted to the hospital in Saskatoon where she underwent examination. Hospital care and rest helped her considerably so she was able to go home in mid-November. At the same time the doctor advised that, if her condition worsened, she would need to return to the hospital. At home she was surrounded by the children and by David—except when he was off on one of his trips.

On one of them at the end of November, J.J. Thiessen, with whom Toews was travelling, wrote back to Margarete in Rosthern with a note of encouragement.

> I noticed that while underway [your husband] was very concerned about his "Liebe Grete." We immigrants feel very obligated to you. How often has our agenda taken him away from your side and sent him away from home so that he could represent us and work for us. That has left you all alone with raising the children. Because you have brought up your children so well, they have become industrious, useful persons of faith. I assume that in this task, God has been especially gracious to you. . . . And although you are not entirely well yet, you already think of others. Benno comes and brings us a chicken. What are we to do? Argue with you about it? That would not be appropriate. And so we will simply thank you heartily and enjoy a tasty treat.[60]

The Toews Christmas letter, appearing annually for a number of years in *Der Bote*, had a sombre note that year. The letter, dated December 20, 1940, said:

> The Lord has spoken very seriously and then again in a very friendly way to us and our family. When my dear wife, the mother of our children, became so seriously ill that we feared for her life, this was an earnest message to us. But the Lord helped here also, and today the doctor says that an operation will not be necessary. For that we as a family want to thank the Lord that he has spoken to us in such a friendly way.[61]

Margarete's condition seemed to improve for a time. In February 1941, she travelled to Saskatoon, Regina, and Drake to visit children. In April, David wrote to J.J. Thiessen that "at home we are all spirited (*munter*) and going about our work."[62] But then there was a set-back. Just before Easter, she had visited her children in Drake where she had a severe attack of internal pain. She was taken directly to the hospital for a brief stay but then was sent home. The doctors were not able to establish the problem. At home she attempted to carry on with household duties but soon found this impossible. On Easter Sunday she attended the worship service for the last time.

Right after Easter, Margarete was back to the hospital for investigative surgery. After a time of recovery, she was brought home where her daughters cared for her. This was a very difficult period as her pain continued with intensity. Although she was a patient sufferer, to this day the daughters remember her agony. She and the family prayed and hoped for her recovery. In early May, Toews wrote to Thiessen that Margarete was again in great pain, a pain that came and went.[63]

At the beginning of June, Toews reported that his dear wife was somewhat better, even to the extent that she could bake the communion bread for the service on Pentecost Sunday. But she was too ill to attend the service which evoked some tears.[64] Meanwhile, Toews had been going about his duties which included officiating at the baptism of 18 young people in Hague and 19 in Rosthern on that particular weekend. After Pentecost Sunday, he was off to Winnipeg for a meeting. It was cut short as he was called home to find Margarete back in the hospital in Saskatoon. Surgery was performed, and it was established that she was infested with cancer. After a hospital stay of 16 days, she was brought home and cared for there. Her condition worsened to the extent that she was admitted to the Rosthern hospital. There she died on Friday, July 11, 1941 at the age of 59.[65]

Burial of a Saint

The funeral service was held the following Monday, July 14, in the Rosthern Mennonite Church. A large tent had been erected just east of the church building. The church and the tent together did not offer adequate space for all who came to express their sympathy and respect. Six of Margarete's brothers served as pall bearers: John, Robert, Emil, Albert, Ernest, and Richard Friesen. The church choir was on hand to sing. Speakers at the service were J.G. Rempel of Rosthern, J. Klassen of Eigenheim, J.J. Thiessen of Saskatoon, J. Regier of Tiefengrund, and J. Schmidt of Waldheim who spoke in English. Besides many beautiful flowers sent by relatives, friends, and congregations of the Mennonite community, J.N.K. McAllister of the CPR office in Montreal and the Department of Immigration and Colonization also sent a bouquet.

At the time of her death, four of the eight living Toews children were already married. Most of the others were pursuing their professions, some at home and others away from home. The death of Margarete left a huge gap in the Toews family circle. Some years later daughter Louise (Toews) Friesen wrote:

The Toews family at the funeral of Margarete Toews on July 14, 1941. From left, adults: Jake Sawatzky, Sylvester and Anna (Toews) Funk, Elma Toews, Elsie (Toews) and Abe Hooge, Father David Toews, Louise Toews, Margaret (Toews) Sawatzky, Benno Toews, Dora Toews, Catherine (Friesen) Toews, Marie (Toews) and Herman Riesen; children: Donald Sawatzky, Margaret Hooge, Irene Riesen, Theodore Toews, David Riesen.

Mother had a major influence on our lives. . . . She was a strong support at home and she played her role with dedication and love. Her life was one of service to the family, relatives, friends, and community. When she passed away in July 1941, our life was never the same again. It seemed as though heart and soul were gone from our home.[66]

One has the distinct impression that Margarete Toews excelled in her devotion to her family, to her church, to the cause for which her husband stood, and to her Saviour and Lord. If the Mennonites would ever consider nominees for sainthood, Margarete Toews should be on the list.

Time of Silence
From the middle of June to the middle of August 1941, David Toews had other things on his mind than church affairs: attending to the last days of Margarete's suffering and then to the funeral arrangements. Following this time, he remained at home in a state of personal grief. During this two-month period, there is little in his personal files and nothing in the church papers from him. That summer, the Canadian Conference met as usual on the first weekend of July, but without Toews. Since he had resigned from his seemingly perpetual chairmanship a year previously, that was not an issue. Benjamin Ewert provided good leadership, and everyone understood why Ältester Toews was not present. At the end of July, Thiessen wrote to Toews about various matters, then added a note: "I commit you to the care of God during your time of loneliness and I want you to know that we remember you prayerfully."[67] Several days later, Thiessen reported to Toews on his recent visit to Herschel, and told

David Toews with daughter Marie (Toews) Riesen and his grandchildren in summer 1941, a year after Margarete died. Grandchildren from left: *Don Sawatzky with Margie, Eleanor Hooge, Bob Sawatzky, Margaret Hooge, Irene Riesen, Lois Riesen.*

Toews that someone there had expressed regret that Toews had not been able to come as he was such a "good speaker."[68]

On the Road Again

It did not take long for David Toews to re-enter his world of obligations. The General Conference sessions of 1941 took place from August 17 to 22 in Souderton, Pennsylvania. David Toews was there! Thiessen had also intended to go but was stopped at the Niagara Falls border because he did not have the required clearance. Because of the war, the United States was applying restrictions on border crossings. In his report on the General Conference sessions, Toews reflected something of his physical difficulties. He was unable to report on the content of J.N. Smucker's opening address because of his poor hearing. This drawback also affected his ability to follow the discussions. A high point for Toews was the musical presentation of the cantata, "The Holy City," by a mass choir comprised of Eastern District churches. The music called to mind the many who were already dwelling in that place where there is no pain or suffering. Surely David held his beloved Margarete in remembrance at that moment.

At the sessions, Toews reported on home missions in Canada. He noted that the General Conference gave four times as much to overseas missions as to home missions. He was not particularly pleased with this imbalance since "the work of home missions is very dear to my heart." Somewhat disconcerting was talk in the halls that United States churches wanted to cease contributing to the Canadians' transportation debt. Despite these criticisms, Toews concluded that it had been a wonderful conference and he could not have imagined a more blessed time.[69]

Going Downhill

Not all was well with David Toews at this time. In a note to Thiessen after his return from Souderton Toews confided, "I seem to be going downhill, and I am pleased when I see that other persons are prepared to serve, persons who, one can assume, still have a number of years of ministry to contribute."[70] No doubt, his friend Thiessen was counted among those stronger persons. At the beginning of October, Thiessen wrote to Toews that he had heard Toews was not feeling well and was downcast about his condition.[71] But nothing in their correspondence gives indication that Toews admitted to this, or even that he acknowledged Thiessen's expression of concern. Perhaps they discussed the question person-to-person.

17
Winding Down
1942–1944

By 1942, the situation of Mennonite churches in Canada with respect to conscientious objector status and alternative service had been somewhat clarified. As early as the spring of 1941, the government had approved service programs at designated national parks and on highway construction.[1] The following spring, forest fire service was added to the list of projects. Men were also assigned to seasonal farm work and labour in industries affected by the war. Not until September 1943 was the way clear for conscientious objectors to enlist in the medical or dental corps. The stipulations were that persons joining under this arrangement were to perform all the duties of a regular soldier except that they were not required to bear arms.[2] Where COs were paid regular wages, they were allowed to keep a small monthly allowance and contribute the remainder to the Red Cross. Over two and a half years, from May 1943 to December 1945, contributions to the Red Cross amounted to $2,222,802.70.[3] At first, the term of service was proscribed as three or four months, but by the beginning of 1942 it was understood that alternative service work would be required for the duration of the war. In the end, approximately 7500 Mennonites served as COs. This represented about 75 percent of conscientious objectors in Canada. In comparison, about 4500 men and women of ethnic Mennonite background joined the Canadian armed forces during the Second World War.

Still at the Helm
During this time, David Toews remained at the helm of the Canadian Mennonite Board of Colonization. There was much to do because of the war. Negotiations with the government had been complicated by difficult internal differences among the various Mennonite groups. Then, too, individual young people who realized they had made the wrong decisions sought help from Toews. Sometimes it was the parents, not the young people, who needed Toews' assistance in persuading their children not to enter the military or to reverse their decision once they already enlisted. A wrong decision was not always the fault of the enlistee. Young Mennonite men were often treated harshly when they appeared

before military draft boards, which caused some to enlist under the pressure of convincing military counsellors.

While David Toews was certainly not the only one giving pastoral attention to these matters, as elder of the Rosenorter Church and as director of the Board of Colonization, he remained centrally involved and took on many of the cases himself. Despite his years, his physical ailments, and his recent setback at home, he still carried on. However, it was becoming evident that he could no longer keep up with all the expectations of his office.

Seventy-second Birthday

On February 8, 1942, David Toews turned 72 years of age. J.J. Thiessen's birthday greeting on this occasion spoke to the momentum of his life: "Your last year was rich in experiences. You carried your loved one to her grave. God gave you strength to bear even that. To him be praise and thanksgiving."[4] Toews not only carried his own loved one to her grave, he continued to assist others in the church to carry their heaviest burdens as well. Just before his birthday, he had been in Yarrow, British Columbia, where he participated in the funeral service of Rev. J. J. Klassen who was fatally injured in an automobile accident while travelling home from Vancouver.

In the months that followed, Toews let go of his work a little at a time. This was difficult to do, not only because ministry had been his life and his passion, but also because others kept urging him to continue. It appeared there were few people, if any, who would openly advise him to retire. Left to himself, he had to come to grips, on the one hand, with his longstanding sense of obligation, and, on the other hand, with his diminishing physical strength and emotional fortitude.

1942 Conference in Winkler

In 1940, David Toews had given notice that he would no longer chair the annual sessions of the Conference of Mennonites in Canada. Because of his wife's imminent death, he was absent from the sessions in 1941, but at the 1942 sessions in Winkler, Toews was again able to be present. No doubt his colleagues in congregational and conference work were pleased to see him in their midst. As the Conference sessions progressed under the capable leadership of Benjamin Ewert, Toews was called on at various times for input. Thus he was still very much involved. He reported on relief work in England, on the status of the transportation debt, and on the alternative service camps.

The report on the travel debt was a source of encouragement to the delegates. Speaking on behalf of the Board of Colonization, Toews indicated that only about $350,000 of the *Reiseschuld* remained to be paid. He stated his optimism that the goal of debt elimination was within reach. In a resolution the Conference delegates stated their appreciation for the "tireless, unselfish, and spiritually prosperous activity" of the Board and its chairman, and they wished their leader "much faith and strength to move forward, until the work that God has given to the Board is accomplished."[5] Toews was elected as one of the Conference of Mennonites in Canada representatives to the Colonization Board for a further three-year term. Since he allowed his name to stand for election, we can assume he planned to continue his executive position on the Board.

While Toews was involved in the reports noted above, others now represented projects and institutions for which he would have been responsible in an earlier day. Notable examples were the reports on home missions and on the Rosthern school. While he still had an active role to play in Conference work, it was becoming increasingly evident that he needed to take a back seat.

The optimistic tone with respect to debt retirement evidenced at the Winkler sessions may have inspired Toews to pick up fresh courage. The following month he reported to readers of *Der Bote* that "it now appears possible that we can retire the debt in the next two years."[6] In the article he urged everyone to make every effort to bring this long and drawn-out situation to a good conclusion. As a result, "we will have a good feeling about our accomplishments, and our people's good reputation will not suffer." Toews surmised that not only the general populace but also the business community would view Mennonites in a positive light once the *Reiseschuld* would be conquered. But would two years be enough time to retire the debt?

Work Piling Up

As the fall of 1942 approached, there was no thought of a slow-down for David Toews. The pastoral visitation programs of the CO camps for alternative service needed to be organized and monitored. Mennonite pastors were reminded not to preach their sermons there in German but to use the English language.[7] There was the 25th anniversary of Mr. and Mrs. J.J. Thiessen on September 16 with David Toews as the main speaker. Gathering funds for the Rosthern school was always on the agenda. And there were the many trips to negotiate questions concerning military registration and conscientious objection.

For an aging man who had expressed the desire to step back, this was a demanding agenda, and in time Toews himself came to this realization. Toward the end of September of 1942 he appealed to J.J. Thiessen in something of a panic: "My work is piling up so much that I cannot see my way through to doing it all and I must arrange for assistance."[8] He asked Thiessen to please help him with collecting money for the school. Thiessen's initial assignment would be to visit every family in the areas of Dundurn, Hanley, Superb, Fiske, Glidden, and Herschel. Toews' plan was to assign collectors to other churches as well and he would cover the rest. Meanwhile, he requested that Thiessen not give him any assignment for the next Ministers Conference of the Rosenorter Church. He simply had no time to prepare. Besides, Toews was experiencing increased difficulties because of his hearing and his health. When he was asked to come to Ottawa to represent the Mennonites in a peace delegation, he declined, saying that because of his hearing he was not able to catch much of what was said at such meetings. He recommended that C.F. Klassen go instead.[9] While Toews was quite engaged in work, he was also declining some assignments he would eagerly have undertaken in an earlier day.

Hospitalized for Ten Weeks
On the evening of November 19, 1942, David Toews was admitted to the hospital in Saskatoon. As it turned out, he would be there for ten weeks. The doctor had urged that something be done to regulate his diabetic condition and to address his prostate problem surgically. The surgery would be possible only if his diabetic condition could be improved. After six days of waiting, Toews wrote to his children:

> Sunday was a lonely day for me. I read practically the whole day. Good thing that I supplied myself with good books. That has helped to pass the time. . . . I am doing quite well. Actually I shouldn't be here. The food is good, and at night I sleep reasonably well. The care is good. They want to operate as soon as my diabetic condition will allow it. I have been thoroughly examined already, blood tests, etc. I place myself in God's hands. Whatever happens to me has been ordained by God, and whatever God does is done according to his good pleasure.[10]

After 11 days of medical tests and imposed rest, the doctors performed exploratory surgery to determine what the next steps might be.

While in hospital, Toews received many visits as well as cards and letters from appreciative constituents. One particularly significant letter came from D. Hausknecht of Sardis, British Columbia[11] Written on behalf of the Mennonite congregation at Sardis, it assured Rev. Toews that the congregation had prayed to God that he might become well again. He assured Toews that he was still indispensable for the cause of the Mennonite people: "We all need you so badly (since) so much still rests on your shoulders, and so many of us still expect so much from you." In the view of the congregation, he lamented, "we would feel ourselves orphaned and forsaken if you were suddenly not among us anymore." The letter thanked Toews that he had "fought untiringly and in selfless service and self-sacrifice for our cause and our needs," and that in his approach he had "taken care of the older ones and the younger ones." The writer then proceeded to lay the responsibility for Toews' ill health at the feet of the churches. "We are guilty," he stated apologetically, "because we have caused you to become tired, depressed, and discouraged." This kind of encouragement, coming to Toews at the age of 72, may also explain why he sometimes had difficulty laying down his work and resting from his labours. Well-meaning efforts to express their gratitude to Toews in the manner reflected in the Sardis letter may have diverted him from dealing with the need to face retirement. As long as he was needed, he would bend every effort to carry on.

However, Toews' condition did not show improvement which meant that he had to exercise great patience while the doctors continued testing. Because of his diabetic condition, the wound left by the exploratory surgery became infected and he suffered severely. Sometimes visitors could do little but stand by and hear his groaning when the painful attacks came on. For periods of time Toews spoke little and only shed a tear or two in response to a comforting word. After one of his visits to Toews' bedside, J. J. Thiessen reported that he had said: "I would have preferred not to die until the *Reiseschuld* was completely cleaned up."[12] On another occasion he commented on the amount of nursing care surrounding him, at one time as many as three special nurses. Bothered by what this might cost, he said: "I don't want anyone to go begging on my behalf. God has helped until now, and God will help in the future." And on the same issue, he added: "Tell people in the churches that if they have poor and ill servants of the word in their midst, they should not leave them without help. Help must be sought and found for them." On the matter of his own hospital bills, Thiessen comforted Toews that everything would be taken care of. He assumed that a person who had helped so many others would receive the same kind of treatment when he was in need. Commenting on the thoughts that preoccupied Toews on his sickbed, Thiessen concluded his article: "I have the impression that Brother Toews expects to go [to his heavenly] home rather than to get well soon."

During the next two weeks, the patient grew gradually stronger. Soon he was sitting up in bed for periods of time and becoming somewhat animated again in conversations. This led the doctor to schedule surgery. The operation, which took place on January 22, 1942, proved to be quite successful. There was some anticipation that a tumour would be discovered, but this was not the case. Toews stayed in the hospital two more weeks for recuperation.

He came home from the hospital on February 10, one day after his 73rd birthday. The trip home on that wintry day, with a thermometer reading of minus 40 degrees Centigrade, was something of a dramatic event. J.J. Thiessen, who accompanied him on this sojourn, described the trip in great detail to A.J. Neuenschwander of Quakertown, Pennsylvania, Toews' colleague on the General Conference Home Missions Committee:

> Wednesday morning I was at the hospital at 8:30 a.m. Rev. Toews' room was the busiest on the floor. I had called the barber, who was in the process of shaving him. The nurses were packing his belongings. Others were describing his diet and how to use insulin. Many of the staff dropped by just to say good-bye. Everyone was happy, but no one was happier than our good brother Toews. You should have seen him! But he was quite surprised to see the stretcher-bearers enter the room. He did not argue this time, and in a few minutes he was "tucked in" and the ambulance took us to the train. On our arrival in Rosthern, the bed was quickly placed on the sleigh and in a few minutes he was in his study where his loving daughters had made his bed for him. When we asked him how he felt after the trip, he replied that it could not have been arranged more appropriately and that he felt fine. Soon the famous Mennonite chicken noodle soup (*Hühnersuppe*), which was a favourite of his, was ready. While in the hospital, brother Toews had frequently expressed the desire to celebrate his recovery with a short thanksgiving service. He was too weak for a large assembly, so the children, the ministers, and a few friends gathered at his home to give thanks to the Lord. We sang, prayed, and spoke of the days of suffering and agony in the hospital. The doctors say he has lost a great deal of his strength and it will take months for him to recuperate.[13]

Thus ended what Toews called a time of personal suffering and darkness. Now that he was home, he looked forward to the day when he would be able to resume his responsibilities. Daughters Elma and Dora took over the household tasks and the care of their father during the weeks of recuperation. Elma was the constant caregiver, while Dora came home on weekends to offer assistance and support. The sisters' care for their father was a sign of the affectionate love and respect that the Toews children had for their parents.

Almost immediately upon his arrival at home, he dealt with correspondence. His faithful and efficient secretary, Kaethe Hooge, came to the house to read his mail, after which he dictated his responses which

Daughter Elma was the main caregiver for the 72-year-old Toews after his surgery and 10-week stay in the hospital.

she then transcribed and mailed. Over a month later, on March 23, Toews was back in the office for the first time since coming home from the hospital. On March 28 he resumed his preaching duties at the Rosthern Church. Beginning in May, Toews was busy not only during the week, but was booked Sunday after Sunday. In the Rosenorter churches, he preached in various centres, instructed young people in catechism, conducted baptisms, officiated at weddings, and spoke at family anniversaries. His itinerary also included a ten-day trip to Winnipeg and Steinbach, May 4 to 13, where he preached and reported on Board activities in the churches. On May 15, he drove his car for the first time since hospitalization, making his way to Hague, just south of Rosthern, for a preaching assignment. David Toews was back on his feet again. In mid-April the doctor had determined that his blood sugar count was near normal, and Toews reported that he was feeling much better.[14]

It is understandable that, after a ten-week stay in the hospital and given the strains of his illness, Toews was out of touch with developments locally and in the wider church. So when on his return from the hospital he read a financial report prepared by J.J. Thiessen for the General Conference Home Mission Board, in which Thiessen revealed that the work in Saskatoon was running a $400 deficit and that he himself was far behind with his payment of bills, Toews chided him for not checking with the Rosthern office, that is, with Toews himself. Toews felt somewhat slighted that he did not know about the situation, and remarked that this was not the first time he had been left in the dark.[15] He was, after all, still a member of the General Conference Home Mission Board and felt himself responsible for the work in Saskatoon. Toews had not wanted a negative report to reach the Home Mission Board, as this could reflect badly on his ability to monitor mission work in Canada. Thus he would have preferred that the problem be worked out through the Rosthern office

Thiessen promptly explained that he had no intention of bypassing Toews. It was only that Toews had been ill and he did not want to bother him. He reminded Toews that they had spoken of this situation the past fall, and that Toews should have been informed on this matter, since he received all correspondence between Thiessen and the Mission Board. Furthermore, Thiessen added that he only reported what was matter-of-fact truth and there was nothing irregular about the situation. Toews himself had handled his finances honestly and with integrity.[16]

Toews answered with a hearty thank-you for Thiessen's response and an explanation that he did not want to be silent about something that bothered him.[17] He enclosed a sum of money from his personal savings to cover some of Thiessen's indebtedness. Thiessen promptly returned the cheque to Toews, whereupon Toews merely sent the cheque back to Thiessen again. This time Thiessen kept it and cashed it, but not without a lengthy letter of apology to Toews.

One can speculate on the meaning of this kind of sensitivity on the part of David Toews. Was he anxious about losing touch with a ministry in which he had been very much involved, knowing all the while that he would have to let go in the near future? Was he determined to maintain the respect of the General Conference Mission Board toward home mission work in Canada, which they had faithfully supported? Did he want Mission Board members from the United States to feel assured that their contributions were being deployed wisely and to good effect? Was Toews simply doing his duty as J.J. Thiessen's mentor, part of the task of grooming Thiessen as his successor? Or was it that Toews felt responsible, and perhaps embarrassed, that he could not build an adequate support base for the work in Saskatoon? Perhaps all of the above factors came into play to some extent in their relationship.

In any case, the two men remained faithful and mutually supportive colleagues and friends throughout their 22 years of association. Even when, in December of 1943, Toews wrote to Thiessen that "(he) has had the impression for some time now that (the two of them) are not as close to each other as in times past."[18] Thiessen passed off the comment with-

out a direct response. In his note Toews even added a request for forgiveness: "If the problem lies with me, I ask you to forgive me, and I promise
that henceforth I will not carry anything in my heart against you."
Perhaps the two of them had a discussion on this issue some time over
the Christmas recess, but nothing of this is found in the written record.

The next written communication from Thiessen to Toews came in the
form of a New Years greeting: "I wish you God's richest blessing in your
many-faceted work in the family, the church, and the community. May
God, the Giver of all good and perfect gifts, give you good health and
keep you from illness by his grace."[19] And on the occasion of Toews'
74th birthday, Thiessen sent his congratulations and a greeting with
Isaiah 46:4: "Even to your old age I am he, even when you turn grey I
will carry you." Thiessen lauded the fact that Toews had recuperated.
from surgery and illness, a sign that God still had a purpose for his life.[20]
At the 1943 sessions of the Canadian Conference in Langham, Thiessen
had been elected as chairman, a post he held for many years to come.

It could be expected that as the aging process became more notice-
able, sensitivities would continue and even increase. A letter from Toews
to Thiessen in the summer of 1945 sounded a rather sad but not unexpected note. Toews apologized to Thiessen for various things he had

*In his mid-seventies Toews
was beginning to let go of
his numerous involvements.*

messed up recently. He admitted that he was quite forgetful—even picking up his wrong set of false teeth, forgetting his glasses, and forgetting to use his hearing aid. He hoped brother Thiessen would forgive him and still be his friend. And he asked Thiessen to bear in mind "that by now I am reduced to a wreck (*ein Wrack*)."[21]

Admittedly Toews was aging and becoming less functional at his work. This was brought home to him, perhaps somewhat abruptly, when Thiessen wrote to Toews that he had heard someone in the constituency refer to Toews as "decoration" in his office and no longer a useful instrument.[22] When Toews criticized Thiessen for calling him "decoration," Thiessen explained he was only telling Toews what someone else had said, and that he himself had observed others "using" Toews for their own ends. It seems Thiessen wanted to help Toews come to a measure of self-awareness about his present lot in life. Perhaps this was Thiessen's way of helping Toews let go of some responsibilities. In any case, Thiessen apologized profusely and begged forgiveness for this miscommunication.[23] And so the relationship sometimes stumbled, but the friendship remained strong.

Should I Withdraw?

In the spring of 1944, Toews was again "testing the waters" with his friend Thiessen. Toews had felt strongly that he should withdraw completely from church obligations. The decision to discontinue as Conference chairman had been made rather abruptly so this time he was at least letting Thiessen know beforehand of his intentions. He wrote to Thiessen that in the future he would not accept any assignments at the ministers meetings or annual sessions of the Canadian Conference. He would be pleased if Thiessen would arrange things in such a way that he could just as well be absent from these events. Toews said he was finding there were too many schedule conflicts in his attempt to take care of his work.[24]

Thiessen was quick to respond. He regretted that Toews wanted to act hastily, saying that it seemed impetuous to do things in that way. Why not rather continue with reporting as energy allowed. Thiessen offered weighty words to Toews on that occasion:

> You, whom we regard as the most important person ("der grösste Mann") among Mennonites on the American continent because of your contributions over the past 25 years, should not vanish from the scene in that way. In Waldheim you withdrew with honour from one aspect of your work [chairmanship of the Conference]. If you feel that your energies are depleting and you wish to enter a quieter evening of life, you should take a further resolute step in your systematic withdrawal, but do not do so in haste. Choose successors for yourself. Distribute your

many-faceted work on the shoulders of various others and teach them to assume their tasks and responsibilities.[25]

It seems that Toews took the advice of his younger colleague this time. While he continued on his course of withdrawing, he did it gradually over the next years.

Letting Go of the School

Back in 1903, David Toews had chaired the meetings that led to the founding of the German-English Academy, which eventually became Rosthern Junior College. Now, 40 years later, he still carried the school on his shoulders as far as the "bottom line" of finances and policy was concerned. Toews was in discussion with President Kaufman of Bethel College in Newton, Kansas, on the possibility of pursuing an affiliate relationship between the two schools.[26] He was still collecting donations for the Academy and arranging for others to help. He again pressed Thiessen to collect in Saskatoon to the tune of $40, which would contribute to the elimination of the $3000 debt currently on the books.[27] Thereafter, Toews was on his way to Alberta to seek donations for the German-English Academy and to report on matters of relief, peace, and immigration. His plan was to hold evening meetings where he would speak and invite hearers to give money for the school. If not enough was gathered at the public meeting, he would need to do visitations in the community in the following days.

This venture took him on the road westward from April 12–27, 1944.[28] In his little black date book he entered his schedule and the amounts of money collected (see table next page).[29]

By the summer of 1944, Toews had decided in his own mind that he could not keep up this kind of personal investment in support of the school. He wrote to Thiessen on July 31, 1944 to say he had resigned from the Board of Directors of the school. His reason was simple: "It is my desire to spend the short time I have yet left to live in rest and peace."[30] Apparently there had been tensions between staff and the Board, some of which centred on Toews' close watch on finances, including salaries. In his view, the teachers did not understand the limited financial situation under which the school needed to operate, dependent as it was on constituency contributions and good will. As for Toews, he was the constant go-between. The tensions were becoming too great, and the load was too heavy. Thus it was that he resigned, but with a heavy heart. The matter had soured him to the extent that he spoke to Thiessen about selling his house and leaving Rosthern. Largely because of the school situation, he felt that this was no longer his home.

Schedule for Alberta trip, April 7–12, 1944

April 12 – Travel to Regina to visit children Marie (Toews) Riesen and Benno Toews
April 13 – Train travel from Regina to Bassano, Alberta
April 14 – To Countess, Alberta, for a service ($100)
April 16 – To Rosemary, Alberta. for two services
April 17 – Evening meeting in Gem, Alberta
April 18 – To Springridge, Alberta, two days of visitation and services ($100)
April 23 – Morning and afternoon services at Coaldale Mennonite Church ($249)
April 23 – Evening service in Coaldale Mennonite Brethren Church
April 24 – Train travel to Edmonton, Alberta
April 25 – To Tofield, Alberta, for visits in 11 homes and services in the church ($140)
April 27 – Depart from Tofield in the morning and arrive back home in the evening

An excerpt from David Toews' little black date book.

This time, Thiessen did not try to hold him back. Instead he offered a word of comfort and of commendation:

> That your resignation is accompanied by personal heavy-heartedness is understandable to me. With many worries and concerns, you have dragged ("schleppt") the school through its critical periods. It would have gone under long ago, if it had not been held together by your optimism, your faith in God, your willingness to serve. You often quote the wonderful poem by Karl Gerok: "Es reut mich nicht" (I have no regrets). I have sometimes become hot and cold when I heard this poem. I always felt that the poet, many years ago, brought to expression that which you yourself felt so deeply, so deeply; that which you carried forward in your own experience. O that even now, despite all malice, you would not become hateful toward people ("Werde auch jetzt, aller Bosheit zum Trotz, kein Menschenhasser"). No one will ever be able to erase the footprints of your work, rich in blessings. God will reward your efforts.[31]

Toews' actual resignation was submitted and accepted on July 29, 1944. On that day he was made an honourary life member of the Board. This presented no crisis as far as the school was concerned—over the past few years a widening circle of people, including above all J.G. Rempel of Rosthern and J.J. Thiessen of Saskatoon, had taken on major responsibilities for fundraising.[32] And as for the school's viability, by the year of Toews' death in 1947, the student population stood at a healthy 168 students. It should be mentioned that in 1945 the name had been changed from German-English Academy to Rosthern Junior College.

For a brief while, it seemed as though David Toews would have the opportunity to make a significant contribution of quite a different kind to Mennonite education. The Canadian Conference had formed a Committee to work on the idea, expressed in the mid-1930s by Toews among others, that an advanced Bible school, a Bible college, should be founded. When the Committee heard that Toews was thinking of moving away from Rosthern, they approached him informally to inquire whether he would consider selling his house for use by such an envisioned institution, should it be founded. It seems that Toews read the inquiry as an attempt to buy the house out from under him. His thoughts, expressed earlier, about moving out of town, were apparently not serious. Thiessen assured him that in asking him about the availability of his house, there was no intent to push him out. While he was sorry the Toews house was not available, the Committee would be exploring other directions.[33] The Committee's plans came to fruition in 1947 with the establishment of Canadian Mennonite Bible College in Winnipeg.

Offering Advice
In his position with the Board of Colonization and its Service Committee, Toews took it upon himself to advise the Mennonite constituency, from time to time, on political involvement. At one point he had advised Mennonites to refrain from voting on a referendum that was to determine whether the Prime Minister could be released from his promise not to implement a compulsory draft for overseas service. His reasoning had been that Mennonite participation in the decision would give the appearance of being self-serving. Some constituents had taken this to mean they should refrain from voting altogether. Upon hearing this, Toews encouraged people to exercise their vote if and when an election or a referendum did not involve a military matter. In his "Explanation," published in *Der Bote,* Toews went a step further by indirectly supporting the Liberal candidate of the Rosthern district, P.I. Hooge. He wrote of him: "He is known to us as a trustworthy and honest Mennonite who respects and honours his confession and his people and their sentiments; whereas the writer is less acquainted with the other

candidates." [34] No doubt many would have taken this as an endorsement of Mr. Hooge.

Toews also addressed the issue of supporting the Red Cross and of purchasing victory bonds. The government used these interest free loans from the public to finance the war. Should Mennonites participate? Do your research, use your discernment skills, and follow your conscience, said Toews. If the proceeds would go to alleviate suffering, we should be ready to help. If they support the war effort, we should refrain. In these ways he helped to guide politically inexperienced constituents through the political maze of the day. [35] As for supporting the Red Cross, Toews encouraged contributions since the funds helped to alleviate suffering during wartime. [36]

It is noteworthy that, while Toews had strong feelings on some issues, he was not persistently dogmatic. When it came to decisions on social and political matters, his advice often had a degree of flexibility. At one time, when Toews was asked by Thiessen to give counsel on an important question, his response was that he had no clear insights at this time and thus far had not heard the thoughts of others on the issue. If upon hearing other opinions he would sense a divine directive ("einen Wink Gottes"), then he would take that into consideration and possibly see a direction. [37] This statement reflected a wholesome communal process, linking the voice of others with the discernment of the Spirit. We see here a person who had mellowed in old age.

Planning a Family Wedding

Since Margarete Toews' death in 1941, David had had to adjust to his role as an aging widower. From the standpoint of parental duties, this was not a demanding task, as the children had all entered adulthood and had ensured that domestic duties did not become a burden for their father. There was at least one family occasion where David Toews was determined to fulfil his parental duty. [38] When daughter Louise announced her intention to marry Blake Friesen, a young man from Langham, father David determined that the wedding should transpire like mother Margarete would have done it. There would be many guests and the women of the church would serve a meal. After the wedding reception, the relatives would be invited to the house for a family gathering.

The wedding took place on Monday, October 9, 1944 in the Rosthern Mennonite Church. Besides ensuring that the physical arrangements were carried out, father Toews was the officiating minister at the ceremony. His text for the occasion was 1 Corinthians 13:13: "Now abideth faith,

*Wedding of Louise Toews &
Blake Friesen on October 9,
1944.*

hope, and charity, but the greatest of these is charity." In his reflections on the text, he emphasized that, while wedding gifts will wear out and even earthly friendships will wear thin, love will last forever. This is because love, a gift from God, is ever-present and eternal. If marriage partners would serve one another in love throughout all conditions of life, their earthly home would be a place of joy and contentment, and their relationship one to another would endure. On this occasion Toews preached in English.[39]

This was the only family wedding that occurred during the time that David Toews was a widower. Daughter Anna and Sylvester Funk were married in 1940, the year before mother Margarete died. There was to be one more wedding, that of daughter Dora to Peter Schellenberg on July 18, 1948, with J.J. Thiessen as the officiating minister.[40]

18
Bringing Closure
1945–1946

The Second World War ended in May of 1945 with the unconditional surrender of Germany. For Mennonites, the end of the war represented something of a transition from one era to another. Historian T.D. Regehr states that "the war forced Canadians, including Mennonites, to broaden their perceptions of the world."[1] In Canada, various of the Mennonite communities expanded their horizons beyond a narrow ethnic and immigrant perspective. For many, the war years had increased an awareness of what it meant to be Canadian, or at least what it meant to work out convictions and destiny in the Canadian context. Many grew in their sense of responsibility for people in need, whether in their own community or internationally. Young people who had served as conscientious objectors or on the war front came home ready to reorient their lives. Farming was no longer the primary option, as young people attended universities and moved to urban centres. The church was being prepared to face new opportunities in service and in mission.

While some stood at the brink of the new post-war age, David Toews was receding into the background. His strength was waning. He had made his contribution. He needed to bring closure to his assignments and, for that matter, to his life.

Final Report for the Board of Colonization
The Conference of Mennonites in Canada sessions, held in July 1945 in Eigenheim, Saskatchewan, provided the occasion for David Toews to represent the Canadian Mennonite Board of Colonization one last time. He had some help in preparing and presenting its work. In fact, Daniel P. Enns reported on the work of the Colonization Board[2] while David Toews, with the assistance of C.F. Klassen, presented the work of the Central Mennonite Relief Committee.[3] In the latter report, Toews pointed to the magnanimous and prolific work of God in feeding the children of Israel in their 38-year wilderness sojourn and in providing the miracle of the feeding of the 5000 through his Son, Jesus. Toews made the point that the latter event was a miracle, not only in the sense that the loaves and fishes were multiplied so that there was enough for all, but that the

Lord chose to enlist the service of the lad who supplied the food and the disciples who organized the multitude for its orderly distribution. This is a lesson for our times, continued Toews. In our relief work, we need to trust the Lord for a miracle and we need to involve ourselves in God's miraculous work. Against the background of this biblical reference, Toews then proceeded to give an account of the wide-ranging international relief work of the Mennonites—in England, France, Holland, Switzerland, Germany, Russia, Paraguay, Egypt, India, China, Puerto Rico, and the Philippians. He noted that, while there had been many difficulties, much had been accomplished. He concluded on a positive note with Psalm 118:23: "This is the Lord's doing, and it is marvellous before our eyes." It is good that David Toews could delight in the understanding that by providing humanitarian aid the Mennonites were witnessing to their faith in this tangible and broad way.

In the following months, Toews came to the realization that he could no longer attend to the work of the Board. He made trips to Leamington, Coaldale, and other places on behalf of relief work and the peace witness, but these trips were becoming physically more difficult for him. On April 4, 1946, he submitted his resignation to the Board of Colonization. Toews had served as chairman and executive director from 1922 to 1946, a span of 24 years. The main reason given for this resignation was his deteriorating health. In announcing his own retirement in *Der Bote*, he wrote: "Because of my hearing difficulty and my deteriorating health in general, it is regrettably not possible for me to continue to lead the Board, since its work has certain demands which I cannot meet in my current state of health. For that reason I have resigned my position."[4] In the same article, he informed the constituency that "the Board has asked J.J. Thiessen to take on the work in the interim until the conference sessions, and he is willing to engage his 'younger strength' into service."

Toews assured his readers that he was not bowing out completely. Now all his energies would be deployed to pay off the remainder of the transportation debt so that the Mennonite people could continue to enjoy the trust they had held until then. He attributed any success in his work to the grace of God and concluded with a note of encouragement:

Let us forge ahead, looking to the Lord, until the debt is entirely removed, so we may come before the Lord with a good conscience and bring him our thanksgiving. The Lord will bless our honest effort, and make it possible for us to bring our responsibility to completion.[5]

Shortly after David Toews announced his resignation, Daniel P. Enns, office manager of the Board and Toews' coworker, died. Enns, who had

Meeting of the Canadian Board of Colonization on April 4, 1946 when David Toews resigned as chairman. From left, front row: B.B. Janz, Coaldale; C.F. Klassen, Winnipeg; David Toews, Rosthern; D.P. Enns, Rosthern (secretary-treasurer); Alva S. Bowman, Guernsey (vice-chairman); J.J. Thiessen, Saskatoon (elected as chairman at this meeting); second row: A.H. Harder, Beamsville; J.H. Enns, Winnipeg; C.A. DeFehr, Winnipeg; G.J. Derksen, Yarrow; D.H. Epp, Rosthern; J.G. Rempel, Rosthern; Jacob Gerbrandt, Drake; back row: William Hildebrandt, Jordan Station; D.J. Janzen, Gem (representative of the Alberta Provincial Relief Committee); D.D. Rempel, Hague (representative of the Saskatchewan Provincial Relief Committee); J.N. Heppner, Altona.

succeeded A.A. Friesen some 20 years earlier, had given dedicated service to the work. His death was a shock to the Board and a set-back for
cleaning up the *Reiseschuld*. John G. Rempel said of Daniel P. Enns that
he pulled in the right direction, unlike "other men, whose activity does
not belong within the circle of the history [of the immigration project]."[6]
Jacob Gerbrandt succeeded Enns on an interim basis.

Resignation from the Home Mission Board

In all the years that David Toews represented the Canadian congregations on the Home Mission Board of the General Conference, he stood
out as a strong advocate for Canadian programs. Especially with the
coming of Mennonites from Russia, there were plenty of projects that
needed help. The General Conference contributed as they could in support of itinerating ministers who travelled to outlying districts, the construction or purchase of church buildings on new frontiers, the establishing of urban centres where working Mennonite women could find a home
away from home, and financial support of pastoral staff in some places.
With the encouragement and endorsement of the General Conference
Mission Board, the congregations in the United States were also
considered as valid sources for solicitation of funds for the transportation
debt and for other financial needs brought about by the coming of
immigrants.

David Toews had been elected to the Home Mission Board in 1911
and served continuously for three decades until 1946. During that time
he grew in knowledge of and passion for missions, both international and
what is called home or inner missions. He was able to convey this
information and enthusiasm to the Canadian constituency. But he mainly
concentrated on identifying mission projects of General Conference
churches in Canada that required financial support and tabling requests
for assistance through the budget of the Mission Board. In this he was
quite successful, and the Mission Board was responsive. It is to the credit
of David Toews that he had an open mind and heart for new projects as
the need presented itself. Thus, in 1944 he responded supportively upon
hearing the case for an English-language congregation in Winnipeg. By
this time, a considerable number of young people preferred to worship in
English, especially once they moved to the city. Where would this lead
if they attended only the available English-speaking services of other
denominations? Where would they hear and learn about peace teaching
and other Mennonite distinctives?

Thus it happened that Toews appealed to congregations across
Canada to collect offerings and submit donations for "Bethel Mission
Church."[7] It is significant that Toews did not go first to the General

Conference Mission Board for funds but rather to the Canadian constituency. He felt that by now the Canadians were running too quickly to the General Conference for help. They had come of age and should try to help themselves before they looked south of the border. Toews was criticized for this shift by some of his own brothers. But he defended his standpoints, arguing that we should first strengthen our own network of support, lest we develop a habit of dependency.[8]

During the last year of membership on the Home Mission Board, David Toews was a reluctant participant. He was finding it more and more difficult to travel, particularly the long distance south to Chicago or to Newton. He was absent from the Mission Board meeting in February of 1945—neither his doctor nor his family wanted him to go. Nor did he have much joy in the prospect of travelling.[9]

During these months, his health was unsteady. This affected his mood, and he began to ask questions more frequently about whether to continue or discontinue the ministries in which he was still involved. In February he had written to Thiessen that he was actually feeling somewhat better and that, in his words, "perhaps I can patch myself together somewhat yet so I last a bit longer."[10] In May of that year he confided to Thiessen that he was thinking of carrying on if he could continue to find the strength. Several elderly missionaries from the General Conference had visited with him and had evoked in him the thought that one should serve the Lord as long as one is able.[11] With this as inspiration, Toews and Thiessen planned and carried out a trip to Newton, Kansas, for early June 1945. Thiessen was willing to try to administer insulin injections for Toews along the way. If this failed, the plan was to seek medical help. So Elma Toews, who had been giving her father the injections, instructed Thiessen in the art before they went on their way. It was not an easy trip, as the transition from one train to another in Kansas City and in St. Louis had been particularly difficult. But they returned home safely and without major incident, to the great relief of Elma.[12]

Back home Toews assessed the trip as not very significant. His attendance at the meeting had made little difference, mainly because he was not able to hear the proceedings. The experience led him to think that his time of usefulness had come to an end. He realized that he might have been a burden to his travel partner. Admitting to Thiessen that he was not sure anymore which way to go or to think, he mused:

> May the Lord lead me and guide me in accordance with his Word. May I heed the signs given me by the Lord, and then walk the way that he leads me. I know that without work I can hardly find satisfaction in life.

May each of us be ready to heed the call: "Return to me, O child of God." I perceive myself to be so unworthy and unprepared for the heavenly calling. And yet I find the words of the poet compelling when he says: "I don't want to remain on earth forever, where storm follows upon storm, and misery prevails."[13]

We see here a person torn between wanting to hang on and to let go. In February 1946, David Toews submitted his letter of resignation to the Mission Board. The letter was sent to J.J. Thiessen, chairman of the Conference of Mennonites in Canada, who was responsible for this appointment. Thiessen's word to Toews at this juncture amounted to another citation:

> There are few people who, like yourself, can look back upon such a rich life of service and are privileged to see the fruits of their labour. So many years you have preached the Gospel. You have represented the largest Mennonite church in the province. You have led the Conference into productive work. And you have led the entire Mennonite people in overcoming colossal hardships. What a rich life! You deserve a friendly evening of life. May the Lord grant you the same in his love and grace![14]

Thus David Toews brought closure to another of his long-term assignments. In his place, the officers of the General Conference appointed Rev. Gerhard G. Epp of Rosthern.[15] Epp had served as secretary and then as chairman of the Canadian Home Mission Committee.

Finally, the *Ältester* Office

According to his date book, David Toews gradually decreased his church duties in the early 1940s. In part this was out of physical necessity with his ailments increasing and his strength diminishing. His time in hospital broke the momentum of his work, and created the need for others to step in where he would have taken the lead in former times. Then too, things were not the same anymore once his Margarete passed from the scene. Gone was the home base that had provided solace from the ebb and flow of his routine. Officially, he was still the leading minister of the Rosenorter Church. But unofficially and realistically he and his responsibilities were carried more and more by others.

The moment had come when David Toews needed to take the initiative to announce his intention to resign as *Ältester* of his beloved church. He did so at the meeting of Rosenorter ministers on August 7, 1944. His main reason was that his hearing hindered his ministry. He stated his intent in the context of the question: Should the Rosenorter Church consider, as it had in the past, appointing an *Ältester* for each local congregation? At least as far as Toews was concerned, he could no longer attend to the round of duties that were required in a centralized leadership arrangement.[16] At the time Toews made his statement, he offered it as something to think about, but the matter was left there.

Half a year later, again at a ministers meeting, Toews asked the group: "What is it that you expect of me?" The ministers answered in a somewhat open-ended way: "We want you to do what you are able to do." Meanwhile, a committee had been formed to make a recommendation regarding the future of Rosenorter leadership. Presumably their assignment included two matters: the question of multiple leadership and the question of David Toews. The committee eventually submitted a proposal that implied an answer to both questions. Johannes Regier should take full responsibility for the ministerial leadership of the church. He had been ordained as assistant *Ältester* back in 1929. David Toews should continue to serve in accordance with his ability to do so which, in effect, made him an assistant to Regier. Each of the two would be assured a salary of $100 a month. For Toews, this meant that his current salary would be supplemented by the church, if necessary, to bring it up to $100. The church accepted this proposal.[17]

The arrangement lasted for about a year. On February 28, 1946, David Toews submitted a letter of resignation to Johannes Regier. Again, his main reason was his hearing, but he also added that there were various additional reasons he could no longer serve. If it was desired by the church, he would be willing to continue to support the work of the church with counsel and assistance, but "I realize full well that I must resign my work at this time."[18] In his letter he wished the ministers, and in particular Johannes Regier, much strength and wisdom in their work. Then he added a line indicating that his work was not over until it was over. Shortly he would be off to British Columbia for a celebration of the liquidation of the transportation debt there.

On that occasion the ministers passed a resolution in which Toews' resignation was accepted. The resolution stated in part:

> Ältester Toews has served the Rosenorter Church for many years, first as minister, then as *Ältester*. Even when his health began to fail, he served at his post. Even while he was fulfilling the many obligations that came from the outside, he spared no effort to carry out his duties as *Ältester* of the many-branched Rosenorter Church. That entailed much travel. We remember with thanksgiving the work of our *Ältester*, and we wish him God's richest blessings for the years that remain for him. May the promise be fulfilled for him: When evening comes, there will be light.[19]

The wedding of Dorothy Toews and Peter Schellenberg, July 18, 1948, a year after David Toews' death.

Toews had served the church as minister since 1901 (45 years) and as *Ältester* since 1913 (33 years).

He did make his way to British Columbia in the interest of the transportation debt. He was accompanied by his daughter Elma, for whom the British Columbia folk offered to pay fare as well. She went along to administer the daily insulin shots and to ensure that her father travelled safely. As it happened, the trip was quite difficult for Toews and probably contributed to his deteriorating health.

Some months later, in June of 1946, a Rosenorter congregational meeting was held at Osler but David Toews was absent. He had weakened considerably in the past few months, and was more and more confined to his home. At that meeting, Johannes Regier announced that because of his wife's health, he would be moving to British Columbia that summer, which would necessitate the election of a new leader. He also reported that, as a result of his meetings with all the local groups belonging to the Rosenorter Church, the recommendation came that they should remain together as one. Subsequently an election was carried through by the brotherhood with J.G. Rempel receiving the majority of votes. Among the four candidates nominated by congregational groups was Benno Toews, son of David, but he had withdrawn his name before the vote since he had accepted a teaching position at Freeman College in Freeman, South Dakota. J.G. Rempel was ordained to the leadership of the Rosenorter Church by Johannes Regier on September 15, 1946.

Almost *Reiseschuld* Closure

At the Canadian Conference sessions in 1944 in Winnipeg, Colonization Board administrator Daniel P. Enns had given the Board report. When it came to the item on the *Reiseschuld*, he said:

> If the *Reiseschuld* payments will continue to come in as in the recent past, then there will only be one more report of the Board, at most two. We are truly grateful for this. How thankful we will be when the debt is fully paid. God will help us if we place our trust in him.[20]

Following his comments, David Toews rose and raised a caution, noting that if too much was made of the little that still remained to be paid, those who had not yet paid would consider themselves off the hook. The Conference decided to ask for one dollar per church member to ensure that the debt would be eliminated.

At the next Conference in 1945 in Eigenheim, where David Toews gave his last Board report, he recalled the many difficulties that had to be overcome in collecting the transportation debt since the beginning. Yet he expressed gratitude for accomplishments and cited Psalm 118:43: "It is from the Lord, and it is a wonder before our eyes." At the conclusion of the discussion on the Board report, John J. Wichert proposed a resolution that every effort should be made to clear away the debt within the current year. This resolve was accepted, and it was decided to convey this request to the Mennonite Brethren as well. The resolution was also carried back to each province where it was discussed and it was agreed that the time had come to put the debt behind them. In September of that year, David Toews wrote one of his last articles on the theme of debt. Among other things he said:

> In this year we must conquer the debt. We are now receiving appeals for help from Germany. But our work will be hindered if we continue to be indebted to the CPR. We have heard it said: "To experience rescue gives us a desire to rescue others" ("Gerettet sein gibt Rettersinn"). Unfortunately this word does not count anymore with many people. People have lost their conscience concerning the obligation for 21,000 immigrants.[21]

In the article Toews noted some of the pathos that had come with the lingering debt. An immigrant, whom he did not name, had broken down over the burden of the immigration project. Col. Dennis died without seeing the debt repaid as did Mr. MacAllister, a friend of the Mennonites within the CPR organization, who had died a few days earlier. "Because of this," wrote Toews, "our conscience should plague us, and we urge each other to do all we possibly can to conquer the debt." Toews saw the great need of World War II refugees in Europe on the horizon. To meet that impending challenge, the burden assumed more than 20 years earlier needed to be lifted.

But to the disappointment of David Toews, there was still debt on the books at the end of 1945. So he submitted one more appeal in the spring of 1946. It could be conquered in this year, he urged, if each family would contribute 40 dollars and if each congregation would take offerings.[22] This was the last that was heard from David Toews concerning the *Reiseschuld*. The letter appeared in the papers 20 days after Toews had submitted his resignation from the Board of Colonization.

At the conference sessions in the summer of 1945 in Beamsville, Ontario, J.J. Thiessen, new chairman of the Board of Colonization, expressed hope that by the end of summer there should be enough funds to liquidate the *Reiseschuld*, but the final announcement could not yet be made. David Toews was not at the Conference—by this time he was not been able to endure the trip nor the strain of the sessions. In his report on the Canadian Mennonite Board of Colonization, Thiessen offered the following public reflection on David Toews and the travel debt:

> When the unbiased historian will write the chapter on the *Reiseschuld*, he will find things worthy of praise but also deserving of blame. There will be stories of faithfulness unto death, of tears shed by widows and orphans yet faithfully fulfilling their obligations. Stories will be told to the world of how people, who had already paid their own debt with sacrifice and privation, made further sacrifices by contributing small and large sums on behalf of the poor, the unfortunate, and others. The record will show that some fought and quarrelled before they were persuaded to pay their debt. It will be shown that such and such a person, and so and so many, have not had their names removed from their debt and have let others pay. They bought houses and farms and inventory, but let others pay their dues. They have intentionally been a burden to their communities. . . . I pity the fathers and mothers, the sons and daughters, who showed themselves unthankful and despised their rescue from the land of terror. . . . Ältester David Toews always stood for the principle that the moral influence upon the debtor should be sufficient; there is no need to take people to the worldly court to settle their account. The work was started as a work of faith and should not be concluded in a worldly fashion. His deep, deep wish was to experience the full payment of the travel debt. He will experience it, even though not in the prime of his life and while still actively involved. He has retired and he observes the progress of the work from the side.[23]

Some may judge that David Toews was too preoccupied with the transportation debt. Did he neglect other matters because of it? Would it have taken care of itself even without the great amount of attention given to its repayment? Certainly the evidence shows that the *Reiseschuld* was constantly on his mind; and the fact remains that he felt keenly responsible for the original agreement with the CPR. Furthermore, he felt that the reputation of the Mennonite people hung in the balance as long as the debt was outstanding.

Someone Else Will Lead You

By the summer of 1946, the elderly and weakened David Toews had resigned from all obligations. He was still taking a daily walk to the office. There he sat in his padded chair, read the church papers, and dictated letters to friends and relatives. The staff welcomed him out of a sense of love and respect for their former chief. In his comments on this stage of life, J.J. Thiessen paraphrased the words of Jesus: "When you were younger you girded yourself and travelled where you wanted to; but when you become old you will stretch out your hands and someone else will gird you and lead you where you do not want to go." Thiessen saw it as his obligation to help his former mentor carry the burdens of old age. It was the least he could do in appreciation for all that Toews had sacrificed for the Mennonite people in general and for the immigrants in particular.[24]

19
Rest at Last
1947

As the days and weeks of 1946 slipped away, David Toews gradually weakened physically. Eventually he became confined to his home where he was cared for by his daughters. His thoughts moved away from concern with the outside world. He turned inward and spoke little. Because of pain, he was restless and had trouble sleeping. Because of deafness, communication even with those near to him was difficult.

One bright spot among others in David Toews' diminishing world of comprehension and awareness was his relationship with J.J. Thiessen. Just as Thiessen had cultivated a relationship with Toews in their working years, so now he devoted himself to Toews in his last days. In an article published in December 1946, Thiessen described their current level of interchange:[1] "To my question, what he [Toews] thought about in his quiet hours, he answered: 'A question, for which there is no easy answer.'" Thiessen knew that Toews was preoccupied with the past, so he focused on pleasant memories and relationships in days gone by: "We talk about trips we have taken together, particular events and experiences on those trips, at conferences, and in our work together." But Thiessen had an agenda in mind. He wanted to talk with him about the transportation debt:

> I notice that an opportune moment has come where I can get to him with the news that the transportation debt has been conquered. Somewhat skeptically he objects: "Hasn't that been said before?" I repeat the fact very emphatically that the *Reiseschuld* had been paid. He stares at me with a wide-eyed gaze. I look straight back at him and repeat loudly and clearly: "Brother Toews, it has happened. You have not been disgraced with your guarantees. Malice has not won the day. This important chapter of our history has come to a satisfying conclusion."

Thiessen noticed that Toews was staring at him, and wondered what Toews was thinking:

> His gaze is still fixed on me. Doesn't he believe me? Is he thinking of sleepless nights when he lay upon his bed weeping? Is he thinking of

difficult unfounded accusations? Of heartless criticism? I know his motto, that he often cited in his talks. So I call out loudly to him: "Es reut mich nicht!" (I have no regrets.) He continues to look at me, but now pearly tears run down his cheeks. He is weeping. I weep too. We pray to God. His demeanour changes. His face becomes mild and soft. He rejoices. God be praised! Faith is the victory.

Then the conversation turned to Advent and Christmas. Thiessen asked permission to convey a Christmas greeting from Toews to his dear Menno folk. Although by this time hardly a gesture was forthcoming from Toews, Thiessen assumed Toews had given his approval. Here is the greeting:

> And so, dear people, wherever you are, in Canada, United States, Holland, Germany, Denmark, Poland, Austria, Switzerland, under normal circumstances or as refugees or as exiles in the forests and icefields of Siberia—Ältester David Toews, grown old through service to our people, greets all of you, all, from his sickroom, and wishes you a festive day richly blessed by our loving God.

All readers of *Der Bote* and of *Die mennonitische Rundschau* received this Christmas greeting.

The suffering continued for almost two months into the new year but so did the tender loving care of his family and friends. Johann G. Rempel saw to it that his hospital bills were covered. In early January he placed a note in *Der Bote*, inviting contributions from Rosenorter churches, and other congregations as well, to help pay for all-night nursing assistance at the bedside of Toews, and also to cover eventual hospital bills that might yet arise.[2] During this time, many prayed that Brother Toews' faith and endurance would be sustained as he moved closer and closer to death. On February 25, 1947, David Toews breathed his last and died. His earthly pilgrimage had come to its end.

Release from Suffering

What do we make of David Toews' difficult sojourn toward death? He suffered much in the last months of his time on earth. B.J. Schellenberg observes that some people who have lived a life pleasing to God are granted the gift of a peaceful closure, even if their life has been fraught with much struggle. Humanly speaking, that would be desirable, but there is no guarantee that life will end in this way. Some of God's children enter a valley of great suffering, even martyrdom, on their way to their heavenly home. While David Toews did not die a martyr's death, he bore much physical suffering in the last months before he took his last breath.[3] Given the many struggles he endured in his active time of service, we would not have wished this for him. And yet against the background of his suffering, we cherish all the more his release from the cares of this life and his entrance into eternal rest. The text taken from 2 Timothy 4: 7–8 expresses a fitting closure to the life of David Toews: "I have fought the good fight, I have finished my course, I have kept the faith; henceforth there is laid up for me a crown of righteousness, which the Lord, the righteous judge, shall give me at that day; and not to me only, but to all those also that love his appearing."[4]

Largest Funeral in Rosthern

The funeral was held on Friday, February 28. According to newspaper reports, this was the largest funeral ever to take place in the town of Rosthern. About one thousand people were in attendance. They came from near and far. The church could never have held all the guests, so extra space was provided. A loudspeaker system was set up in the basement of the church, and sound was conducted to three other venues as well: the auditorium of Rosthern Junior College and the churches at Eigenheim and Laird. The service was also broadcast over a Saskatchewan radio station.

The memorial service consisted mainly of songs and addresses. The students of Rosthern Junior College and the Bible School combined with members of the Rosthern Mennonite Church to form a choir. A male quartet from the Bible School also sang. The funeral sermon was delivered by J.J. Thiessen with a roster of additional speakers: J.G. Rempel, J.C. Schmidt, J. Nickel, and H.C.P. Cresswell, chief commissioner of the CPR. On the same day, memorial services were held in various churches across Canada. That following Sunday the death was announced in all Mennonite congregations across Canada and in other countries. Prayers of thanksgiving for his work as well as support for his family were offered in many places.

A Prince and a Great Man

At the service in Rosthern, J.J. Thiessen gave the main address in the German language.[5] He spoke as brother, as friend, and in part as successor to the deceased. Thiessen read 2 Samuel 3:38: "Do you not know that a prince and a great man has fallen this day in Israel?" He began his address by drawing attention to what everybody knew: that David Toews bore many responsibilities in life and that it would take at least five persons to carry on what he had done by himself. Turning to the text, Thiessen conceded that, given its context, it did not really fit the spirit of this burial service. Ältester Toews would hardly have wanted to

The funeral of David Toews on February, 28, 1947 at the Rosthern Menno-nite Church. That same day memorial services were held in Mennonite churches across Canada.

be referred to as a prince and a great man. But, insisted Thiessen, historians would surely give him a place of honour among the great persons of our people's history, even while our chief concern should be to regard him as a faithful and loyal servant of God who has been invited to share in the eternal Kingdom.

Leaders do not become great overnight, continued Thiessen. So too with Ältester Toews. Whether as teacher, father, minister, *Ältester,* Conference leader, Colonization Board chairman, advocate before government, representative at the Mennonite World Conference, etc., he was enrolled always in the school of the Master. His pathway to maturity went by way of the difficult journey to America via central Asia, the pioneer years in Kansas, the years as teacher and as architect of a new school, the assignment as minister then as *Ältester* in the church, the 26 years of leadership in the Conference, the 35 years of service on the Mission Board, the 24 years of leadership in the inter-Mennonite work of immigration and settlement, the 23 years of wrestling with the transportation debt, and the list went on. These accomplishments qualified him to be designated as a prince and a great man, said Thiessen.

After recounting his life in this way, J.J. Thiessen disclosed that Brother Toews had asked him to convey a parting wish to his Mennonite constituency: "Give them all my greetings and tell them to live a life that will make it possible for us to meet in heaven." The speaker then addressed the children of David and Margarete Toews. He recognized the loving care they had provided to ease their father's suffering, and he encouraged them to continue to live in the spirit of hospitality and Christian faith they had learned in their parental home. Thiessen's address included a reference to David Toews' favourite watchword: "Es reut mich nicht" (I have no regrets). If Toews could address us once more, Thiessen surmised, he would surely quote this poem by Karl Gerok in its entirety.

Thiessen's address had a three-fold ending. It included a statement of release, a blessing, and a Christian confession of what Christians believe about life after death.

Release: And so brother Toews now rests from all his worries, his labours, his sorrows, his disappointments, and many joys of life which were given him to train him for eternity. We greatly feel the loss of this great man and yet we grant him his rest.

Blessing: Blessed are the dead who die in the Lord from henceforth; yea, says the Spirit, that they may rest from their labours; and their works do follow them.

Confession: As Christians we believe that we will meet our loved ones in heaven.

> There is a land of sweet delight
> Beyond the vale of tears,
> Where saints are robed in lily-white,
> And free from all their fears;
> Where Jesus sits upon the throne,
> The Lord of King and Love,
> And where He gathers all His own,
> To reign with them above.

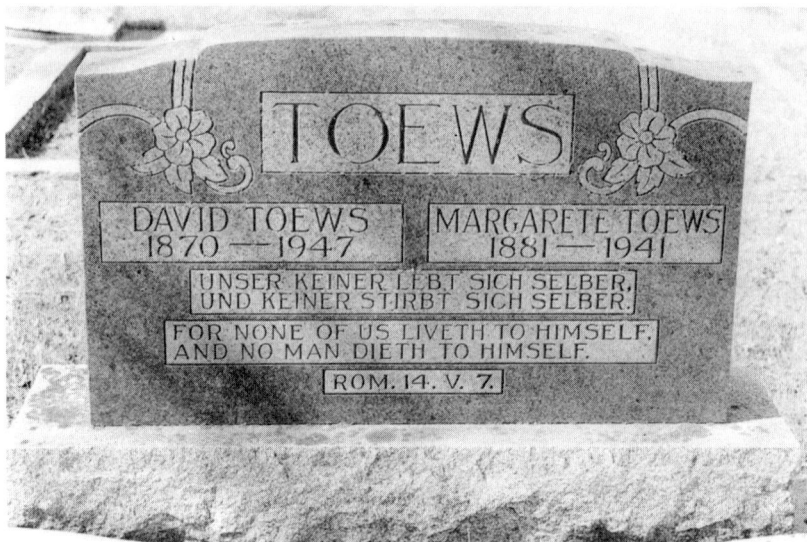

Photo: Dick Epp

David Toews (1870–1947) was buried in the Rosthern cemetery next to the grave of his beloved Margarete (1881–1941) and the burial site of their daughter Irene (1921–1926). The parents' memorial stone bears the inscription in German and in English:

UNSER KEINER LEBT SICH SELBER,
UND KEINER STIRBT SICH SELBER.

FOR NONE OF US LIVETH TO HIMSELF,
AND NO MAN DIETH TO HIMSELF

Romans 14:7

20

Legacy

By the end of the twentieth century, there were concrete signs in abundance to tell the coming generations that David Toews had been here. In 1957, a new administration and classroom building on the campus of Rosthern Junior College was dedicated "to the memory of Rev. David Toews." In 1964, a body of water in northern Saskatchewan was named Toews Lake in honour of Bishop David Toews who "gave dedicated service to fellow citizens."[1] In 1973, on the occasion of the 50th anniversary of the beginning of migration of Mennonites from Russia, immigrants and their descendants erected a cairn on the grounds of Rosthern Mennonite Church in memory of David Toews and B. B. Janz. A month-long "David Toews Memorial Festival of Sacred Music" was organized in association with the University of Saskatchewan in the summer of 1976. In 1988, the Rosthern community recognized the historic legacy of David Toews by commissioning a bronze bust of his likeness and giving it a place of prominence in the former German-English Academy schoolhouse, now the home of the Rosthern Mennonite Historical Museum. In 1991 a plaque was mounted on a cairn on the grounds of Canadian Mennonite Bible College in Winnipeg "in memory of a dedicated Christian teacher, minister and conference servant."

Such tangible memorials evoke the question among future generations: "What is the meaning of these stones?" Mothers and fathers wise in history will answer by telling of the significant presence of David Toews among his people. What have been the enduring contributions of David Toews? After he was laid to rest, what remains? Where and how is the presence of David Toews ingrained in the life and thought of the people with whom he intermingled and whom he sought to serve? Much of what can be said about Toews' legacy does not stand out as an individual contribution but as service rendered in company with others. He was a leader among leaders and among his people. What he contributed is best identified within the context of projects and initiatives he undertook together with others.

Opening the Way to Canada

Any attempt to highlight the enduring legacy of David Toews must begin in the latter half of his adult life. Toews was 52 in 1922 when he became the executive leader of the Canadian Mennonite Board of Colonization. Over the next six years he made his most notable contribution to Mennonite life: the transportation and settlement of over 20,000 Mennonite immigrants from Soviet Russia to Canada. Obviously, Toews did not do this single-handedly, yet it is doubtful that the "exodus from Egypt" and the "entry into the promised land" would have occurred on the scale that it did if Toews had not been at the helm of the ship that guided the project. While others prepared the ground for requesting advance credit to transport the migrants over sea and land to their destination in Canada, it was Toews who finally negotiated the arrangements with the CPR. He then led the Canadian Mennonite Board of Colonization in convincing a sometimes reluctant Mennonite constituency that his plan was feasible. Toews led the Board and staff in removing obstacle after obstacle throughout the immigration process. He stood out as the one person among all those who contributed to this achievement, without whom the project would conceivably not have happened at all, or would have happened in quite a different way and quite possibly to a much lesser degree. Today, when *Russländer* immigrants recall their coming to Canada, or when their children speak of that event, the name of David Toews comes to mind first.

In 1991 the David Toews plaque was mounted on the cairn commemorating Mennonite educators at Canadian Mennonite Bible College (now Canadian Mennonite University). It honoured Toews as "a dedicated Christian teacher, minister and conference servant." Photo: MHC Archives

IN MEMORY OF
REV DAVID TOEWS
ERECTED SEPT 29 1957

PROVINCE OF SASKATCHEWAN
DEPARTMENT OF NATURAL RESOURCES

"Saskatchewan's finest resource is the character and
quality of her peoples: It is appropriate that her
geographical features perpetuate the names and
honour the work of those prominent in development
of the Province, and those who gave dedicated service
to fellow citizens."

Toews Lake

is named after

BISHOP DAVID TOEWS

TOEWS
CANADIAN MENNOITES, ON THE
FIFTIETH ANNIVERSARY OF THE
MIGRATION OF MENNONITES
FROM RUSSIA TO CANADA AFTER
WORLD WAR I, GRATEFULLY
REMEMBER THEIR GREAT LEADER,
REV. DAVID TOEWS
ROSTHERN, SASKATCHEWAN, WHO,
WAS USED IN CANADA BY THE LORD
TO BRING 21,000 MENNONITE
IMMIGRANTS FROM RUSSIA TO
CANADA IN THE YEARS 1923 TO 1930.

1923 JULY 21 1973

Bishop
David To

*A sample of the tangible memorials which have been created in honour of
David Toews, as listed at the beginning of this chapter.* Photos: Dick Epp;
design: Roberta Fast

Those who know more than the basic facts are aware that the immigration project was laced with formidable troubles and trials. They know that, while Toews received the credit for much of what was accomplished, he also came under criticism for things he did and for things he left undone. What is more, rumours—often unfounded—abounded about things he was to have done. Sometimes it was a matter of a hard-pressed or disgruntled immigrant looking for someone to blame. Sometimes the occasion was a promise made, but understood differently by the guarantor than by the recipient of the promise. Looking back at what transpired, and given the largeness of the immigration program, it is inevitable that there would have been mistakes and disappointments. Nor can Toews be exonerated completely; he was by no means perfect, and he did not have adequate preparation for some of the tasks that needed doing.[2] Yet, above everything else that has been and can be said critically, he will be remembered with great appreciation as the Mennonite "Moses."[3]

David Toews did more than simply arrange for transportation and provide an appropriate welcome for the newcomers upon their arrival. He was concerned for their welfare as they settled into a new homeland. While this was part of the mandate of the Board of Colonization, Toews went beyond the call of duty in his pastoral concern for the immigrants and in his endeavour to nurture family and church life among them. It is widely recognized that he was better at providing a word of spiritual counsel than giving financial advice. But then, with the onset of the Depression in the late 1920s and early 1930s, good financial advice was hard to find anywhere. Frank H. Epp's depiction of the years from 1920 to 1940 as "a people's struggle for survival" was particularly applicable to the *Russländer* who found themselves facing drought and economic depression just when they were beginning life all over again, so to speak. It can be said to the credit of David Toews that he did not abandon the immigrants once they had Canadian soil under their feet. He engaged in their struggle with pastoral empathy, and he did what he could to draw them together into a community of mutual support. In turn, Toews was greatly encouraged and energized by the renewed vision and insight that ministerial and educational leaders from among the immigrant populace brought with them to their new environment.

New Educational Directions

A second place where we look for the enduring influence of David Toews is in the area of education. He began his vocational life as a teacher, and continued in this profession for quite some time. He taught in nine different locations—three schools in Kansas, two in Manitoba, and four in Saskatchewan. His accumulated time in the classroom amounted to 24 school years. He completed his last teaching assignment at the age of 52 in a one-room country school. His contribution as teacher extended beyond the school classroom to the church where he taught Sunday school classes and provided catechism instruction for young people until well into the 1940s.

While Toews was a good teacher, his enduring contribution lay not in modelling classroom teaching. Rather, he left his mark on what continues to be a significant Mennonite educational institution in western Canada: Rosthern Junior College (formerly German-English Academy). Many contributed in one way or another to the founding, the survival, and the growth of this school. But it is highly unlikely that without David Toews it would have survived the first decade or two of its fragile life. He not only articulated the worth of the school but was its chief fundraiser.

As for the founding principles of the German-English Academy, it was David Toews who, on the basis of his experiences and observations at Halstead Seminary in Kansas and at Mennonite Collegiate Institute in Gretna, was able to envision a similar educational venture on the western frontier. He gave leadership to the formulation of the philosophy of education for the Academy, and he promoted its educational vision among the school's prospective constituents. Furthermore, Toews deserves much of the credit for the philosophy of Rosthern Junior College over time. He encouraged a certain liberality of learning within the framework of biblical faith and Mennonite values. In the same spirit of liberality, he affirmed students in their potential service to God and to the community.

Today Mennonites in Canada have a flourishing network of private high schools and colleges. Toews was a significant early contributor to this current situation in that he placed matters of higher education on the agenda of the Conference of Mennonites in Canada. Together with Heinrich H. Ewert of Gretna, he ensured that Mennonite schools gained wide coverage in the church papers of the day. These two leaders in educational development among Canadian Mennonites in western Canada promoted their conviction that Mennonite-sponsored educational institutions were crucial for the formation of a sense of Mennonite peoplehood and for building the Mennonite church.

Faithful Church Minister

In 1901 David Toews was ordained as one of the ministers of the Rosenorter Mennonite Church. This was followed in 1913 by his ordination as *Ältester* of the Rosenorter Gemeinde. Toews served this church as minister and then as elder for an accumulation of 45 years until, in 1946, he became too ill to function publicly. During these years his pastoral ministry extended far beyond the boundaries of his home church. He preached in churches throughout the Mennonite constituency in Canada, and he counselled young and old wherever he went. J.G. Rempel, his coworker and eventual successor as elder of the Rosenorter Church, said of Toews that, like Ältester Regier, he continued to build the congregation "on a Christian-Mennonite foundation, entirely in the spirit of Menno Simons, whose watchword was 1 Corinthians 3:11: 'No other foundation can anyone lay than that is laid, which is Jesus Christ'."[4] To minister "in the spirit of Menno Simons" is to continue a legacy inherited from the past.

Toews was a role model for ministers and elders of his day in the way he served his church congregation with dedication and with determination. Due in part to his seemingly boundless energy and his focused dedication to ministry, he set a high standard for pastoral ministry among his ministerial colleagues in Saskatchewan and also in the wider sphere of his influence. However, there were also distractions. The added burdens he assumed once he took on the immigration project meant that he gave less time and energy to the congregation than was expected of him. Like most church ministers in his day, he suffered under time constraints and pressures. Yet because of the wider circle of assistant ministers who served in the local settings and beyond, the church for which he was responsible did not suffer unduly from neglect, although there was concern in this regard from time to time.

In the decades following Toews' death, the model for pastoral ministry among Mennonites changed significantly from the way Toews knew it. The *Ältester* system, which was the practice of having one person take responsibility for a number of congregations, was largely replaced by the arrangement whereby one pastor took charge of all functions in one specific congregation. Furthermore, today pastors are paid a fair wage for their services to the church. While the pastoral structure has undergone changes, Toews and his colleagues have left future generations of leaders with a sense of the continuing importance of ministerial leadership.

Durable Conference Chairman

David Toews was involved in the work of the Conference of Mennonites in Canada from its very beginning in 1902 until his final attendance at the sessions in Eigenheim, Saskatchewan, in 1945. There he gave final reports on his work with the Canadian Mennonite Board of Colonization and with the General Conference Home Mission Board. He attended all but three annual sessions during that time, being absent in 1903, 1936, and 1941. Toews served on the Conference executive for 31 years: six as secretary (1906–1911); 25 as chairman (1914–1935, 1937–1940). He holds the distinction of having been the longest-serving chairman of the Canadian conference in the twentieth century.

Why did David Toews remain as Conference leader for so many years? Was this by design or by default? Was it upon his insistence or at the urging of others? Were there not others who could have done it? Or was it that longevity in leadership was valued above frequent change? In simplest terms, one can say that, being nominated, he allowed his name to stand for election. Having done so, he was elected, whereupon he took up his duties. Why was he nominated? In the early years of the Conference, he was chosen because he stood out as a person who had the gifts of listening and leading. With the office of "elder" added to his name, he was regarded as a person who had the confidence and blessing of a substantial sector of the Conference constituency. In time, the expanding presence of *Russländer* immigrant leaders at Conference sessions made a difference. The newcomers gave Toews their vote since he was someone they knew from his work on the Board of Colonization. Then, too, in the first half of the twentieth century the passion for change had not yet gripped the mood of the people. Longevity was the order of the day. This would change only after J.J. Thiessen's subsequent tenure of 17 years as Conference chairman from 1943 to 1959.[5]

What has been the enduring significance of David Toews with respect to Conference leadership? He offered a presence that can be characterized as both charismatic and dignified. He had a way of using words and intonations that had a centring effect upon his hearers. His conference sermons and his way of chairing the discussions commanded attention and created community among those present. Toews had the effect of drawing the ministers together so that they developed a team spirit, an inclusive circle of collegial concern and of ministry. He was egalitarian in his respect for large congregations as well as for the ever widening circle of smaller congregations that was developing as new settlements emerged on the western frontier. In this way he contributed to the strong familial foundation that has characterized the Conference of Mennonites in Canada throughout most of the remainder of the twentieth century. Again, it should be emphasized that David Toews did not do this alone. But it is significant that he, as primary leader of the Conference, encouraged this spirit of oneness. It is conceivable that a leader could have introduced a contrary and divisive direction, particularly since in the 1920s and 1930s both fundamentalist and liberal movements were exerting their influence in the broader church scene. David Toews helped to keep the Conference focused on its faith and its mission.

Resolute Selfless Leader

David Toews did not claim fame. If he was considered a famous personage, it was because others said this of him. At heart, he was a humble man, preoccupied with matters at hand. He learned early in life to face opportunities and problems in a straightforward way, seeking to grasp situations realistically and with common sense. His advice to persons overcome with the complexities of life would have been: Keep life manageable. Don't inquire after things that are too difficult for you, and don't attempt to investigate what is beyond your reach. Try to understand what lies before you. Life has a mysterious edge that is beyond our understanding. Concentrate on what you can grasp and manage. Toews not only gave this advice to others, but he practised this approach as well. In the face of seemingly insurmountable problems, he would pace the floor or confer with others until he could foresee a reasonable and possible course of action. Then he would make every effort to respond to the situation in the hope of finding a way through the maze.

Some are inclined to view strong leaders with the assumption that they were driven by a passion for power. Some may have wanted to see Toews in this way. But one would be hard-pressed to prove this in his case. It is true that he was strong-minded, with definite ideas on how certain matters should be resolved. He tended to promote and even press his own ideas if and when, in his view, no wiser directions were forthcoming. In his case this was probably not the sign of an egotist or a person hungry for power, but of someone who had the interests of his people in mind and who thought he knew what was best for them. It is not that he did not listen to others, but that, in the face of conflicting opinions or perhaps no opinions, he wanted to move things forward. One might have faulted Toews for hasty action due to impatience, or for stubborn insistence on what he thought was best in a particular situation, but not for a self-serving spirit. His passion was to help others.

Toews knew full well that he was strong-minded. There were moments in his life when he regretted that he was too insistent. To his credit, he did not justify this trait, but readily confessed that this was part and parcel of his sinful nature. When he made mistakes, he was not prone to blame others, but bore the mistakes of his own doing as best he could. We must respect his own expressions of unworthiness and his claim that he was able to do what he did only by the grace of God. Toews understood himself to be a sinner saved by grace.

Forging Inter-Mennonite Relations

David Toews was a pioneer in Mennonite inter-church relations. Formally, his involvement in the wider church began in 1902 when he

participated in the organizational meeting of the Conference of Mennonites in Central Canada. He also worked on the inter-Mennonite scene,
mainly through the Canadian Mennonite Board of Colonization. Board
members were appointed not only from his own conference, but also
from the Mennonite Brethren, the (Old) Mennonites of Ontario and of
the Alberta-Saskatchewan Conference, the Brethren in Christ, the
Reinländer Mennonite Church, and the Church of God in Christ
Mennonite. Toews represented the work of the Board of Colonization
among Mennonite churches in the United States with the idea that all
Mennonite churches in North America should work together. The work
of immigration and relief connected Toews with Mennonites from
western Europe and from Russia. While he never revisited Russia, he
travelled to Europe on three different occasions, two of which took him
to Mennonite World Conference assemblies. He returned from his
European trips with renewed enthusiasm for the worth of international
inter-Mennonite fellowship and service.

Toews kept in close contact with American Mennonites, especially
through the General Conference Mission Board and through Mennonite
Central Committee. During his chairmanship of the Conference of
Mennonites in Canada, most of the congregations of the Conference,
except the Bergthaler Mennonite Church of Manitoba, joined the General
Conference Mennonite Church. The close cooperation between and
among Mennonite and Brethren in Christ churches in Canada has continued to the present day, as has the close working relationship with
Mennonite churches in the United States. Toews had an understanding
for the historic roots of the Mennonite people in their common Anabaptist faith. His spirit of inclusivity and cooperation is evident to this day
in the churches he served and beyond. The story of inter-Mennonite
relations would have been quite different if Toews, together with his
colleagues, had taken an exclusivist approach.

Upholding the Peace Witness

David Toews was an advocate for peace. He upheld the confessional
peace position of Mennonite churches, and he carried in his heart the
conviction that Mennonite young men should not go to war. He taught
that people should be prepared to die for their faith rather than to kill
others in self-protection. He held that when an enemy threatens possessions and property, one must leave material things behind and seek a
place of refuge elsewhere. These principles led him to seek exemption
from the draft and alternate service for young Mennonite men. Alone and
together with other Mennonite leaders, he travelled to Ottawa often to
negotiate arrangements in keeping with historic Mennonite principles.

The principles of peace and nonresistance motivated Toews to do all he possibly could to offer a refuge in Canada for persecuted Mennonites in Russia. In the latter years of the First World War and in the early years of the Second World War, he gave time and energy to the agenda of peace and nonresistance. The stance and advocacy of David Toews did much to uphold and to nurture the peace witness of Mennonites.

On the Frontier of Home Missions
David Toews gave leadership to home mission work among those Mennonites from Russia who identified with the Conference of Mennonites in Canada. As chairman of the Conference and director of the Canadian Mennonite Board of Colonization, he found himself carrying major responsibility for the organization of churches and church life on the frontier of the Canadian west. His membership on the Board of Home Missions of the General Conference Mennonite Church augmented this role. In a tribute written in memory of David Toews, J.M. Regier of the Home Mission Board said: "The Board always sought his opinion, and always felt that he strove to be selfless and servile."[6]

With the influx of immigrants and the creation of new agricultural communities, Toews gave attention to the establishment of churches and the assignment of ministers in new communities. On the Board of Home Missions he became a persistent advocate for financial assistance in support of itinerant preachers, city residences for working women, and pastoral visits to hospitals and institutions. Toews had the conviction that mission begins at home with the building of strong local congregations. Undoubtedly his efforts in this regard contributed to the continuing conviction within the Conference (now Mennonite Church Canada) that the foundation of healthy Christian life within the Anabaptist-Mennonite tradition depends significantly on vigorous local congregational life.

Generosity in Giving
From the earliest beginnings of the German-English Academy, David Toews was a fundraiser. In today's terminology, he would have been called a "development officer" and "stewardship consultant." But in an earlier day, the person doing this task was named for what he was: a collector of money for important causes. It is not entirely clear why this task fell to Toews. He had other things to do, especially in pastoral ministry. Besides, by his own admission, he was not a particularly good manager of finances, whether his own or those of others. And yet, when funds were needed, whether for the German-English Academy, for suffering people in the world, for an individual in trouble, or for retiring the transportation debt, David Toews found himself at the centre of the

action. He advocated for worthwhile causes and he went door-to-door as collector. Perhaps the reason was simply that he was a willing worker. Perhaps he enjoyed relating to people pastorally where they lived and saw fundraising as an opportunity to do pastoral visitation. Perhaps he believed people needed to be prodded for contributions and was confident in his own ability to do the prodding. More than likely, Toews set himself to the task of fundraising because he believed in whatever project he represented and felt that, for it to succeed, he himself would have to see to it that the funds were raised.

Today the Mennonite people in Canada are comparatively generous contributors to church programs and humanitarian causes. It is reasonable to claim that David Toews helped significantly to lay the groundwork for this spirit of generosity. He was unabashed in asking people to part with a fair share of their money. He challenged individuals to be open-handed and open-hearted with their contributions, even when he knew, at times, that people could ill afford to give. Insofar as this spirit of liberality prevails in the Mennonite constituency today, Toews, and those together with him who pressed matters of stewardship in hard times, helped lay the basis for the spirit of giving that characterizes the Mennonite people in Canada.

New Vistas in Relief Work

David Toews was a humanitarian relief coordinator. This assignment belonged to his work as director of the Canadian Mennonite Board of Colonization. On the Canadian front, the need for relief became acute among recent immigrants during the Depression of the 1930s. The Board had obligated itself to help Mennonite immigrants get settled on the land. When the Depression hit, it stepped up its aid program. Meanwhile, the Board offices were receiving hundreds of letters on a monthly basis from suffering and persecuted Mennonites in the Soviet Union. Toews, who had a heart of compassion for suffering people, urged congregations to respond generously to this plea for help.

As a person of faith who believed in God and in God's work of salvation, he also believed in the practical implementation of the kingdom of God among all people on earth. Some would voice the question as to whether the help was deserved. Some wanted the assistance to be directed to Mennonite people only. But Toews discouraged this kind of thinking. Help should be offered wherever there was suffering, and it should be extended regardless of religion, race, or clan. With this attitude, David Toews contributed significantly to the spirit in which Mennonites do relief and development work in our time through Mennonite Central Committee, Mennonite Disaster Service, Mennonite

Es reut mich nicht

Viel reut mich einst an meines Grabes Pforte
Beim Blick auf meinen irren Pilgerlauf,
In Schaaren stehn Gedanken, Werke, Worte
Als Kläger wider meine Seele auf; / Mein
Flehn, wenn mich des Richters Blick durchflammet
Ist: Herr, geh mit dem Knecht nicht ins Gericht!
Doch manches, Freunde, was ihr streng verdammet,
—Es reut mich nicht.

Mich reut kein Spruch, den schonend ich gesprochen,
Wo man den Bruder auf der Wage wog,
Wenn ich gehofft, wo ihr den Stab gebrochen
Und Honig fand, wo Gift ein Andrer zog,
Und war zu mild mein Spruch, zu kühn mein Hoffen:
Im Himmel sitzt Er, der das Urtheil spricht,
Auch mir bleibt nur ein Gnadenpförtlein offen;
—Es reut mich nicht.

Mich reut kein Tag, den ich in Thal und Hügeln
Durch meines Gottes schöne Welt geschwärmt,
Umsaust in Sturm von seiner Allmacht Flügeln,
Im Sonnenschein von seiner Huld gewärmt;
Und war's kein Gottesdienst im Kirchenstuhle,
Und war's kein Tagewerk im Joch der Pflicht:
Auch auf den Bergen hält mein Heiland Schule;
—Es reut mich nicht.

Mich reut kein Scherflein, das am Weg der Arme,
Im Bett ein Kranker—ungeprüft—empfing,
Dass durch ein Antlitz, trüb und bleich von Harme,
Wie Sonnenblick ein flüchtig Lächeln ging,
Und warf ich manchmal auch mein Brod ins Wasser:
Gott selbst im Himmel füttert manchen Wicht; / Mich
macht ein Schelm noch nicht zum Menschenhasser;
—Es reut mich nicht.

Mich reut die Thräne nicht, die mir entflossen
Bei fremdem Schmerze wie be eignem Weh,
Wo Andre männlicher ihr Herz verschlossen
Und kühler standen auf des Glaubens Höh; / Und
ist's noch menschlich, dass der Menschheit Jammer
Mein Aug mir feuchtet und mein Herze bricht:
Auch Jesus weint' an einer Grabeskammer;
—Es reut mich nicht.

Dass ich den Herrn verkannt auf tausend Pfade,
Wo liebend mir sein Geist entgegenkam,
Dass ich vergrub so manches Pfund der Gnaden,
Das, Freunde, reuet mich und ist mein Gram;
Doch, dass ich auch als Christ ein Mensch geblieben,
Und keck, was menschlich, fasste ins Gesicht,
Ein Mensch im Dulden, Glauben, Hoffen, Lieben,
—Es reut mich nicht.

—Karl Gerok

I Have No Regrets

There is much that I'll regret when at death's portal
I look back upon my erring pilgrim way,
Myriads of thoughts, and deeds, and words
Arise to accuse my soul.
My supplication, as I face the scrutiny of my Judge
Is: "Lord, do not submit your servant to judgment."
Yet, my friends, concerning much that you condemn,
—I have no regrets.

I regret no statement, meant to protect the brother,
When he was being judged upon the scale;
When I kept hope, where another used the rod,
When honey flowed, where another drew poison;
If my statement was too mild, too zealous my hope,
He who judges aright dwells in the heavens,
And offers me a measure of his grace.
—I have no regrets.

I regret not the day spent in valleys and on heights
Revelling in God's beautiful and spacious world,
Covered by his protecting wings during the storm,
Warmed by the sunshine of his grace at noonday.
And though such worship was not in the sanctuary,
Nor while engaged in daily labour at my task,
Even on the hills my God conducts his class.
—I have no regrets.

I regret no penny that a poor man along the way
Or one sick in his bed was—unreservedly—given,
A countenance, saddened and paled by affliction,
Radiated with sunshine and momentary happiness,
Tho' I may have cast my bread upon the waters,
God in heaven feeds many a wretched soul.
Because of one rogue I do not hate all humankind.
—I have no regrets.

I do not regret the tears I have shed
Over the pains of strangers, as over those I loved,
As others in mannish fashion fortified their hearts
And stood undaunted on the heights of faith.
Is it not human to allow the plight of humanity
To dampen my eye and break my heart?
Even Jesus cried at the graveside of one deceased.
—I have no regrets.

That I failed to recognize God in a thousand places
Where lovingly his spirit came to me;
That I buried many treasures of his graces,
This I regret, my friend, and sorely grieve.
And yet, that as a Christian I remained a *Mensch*, And
boldly looked what's human in the eye,
A *Mensch* in suffering, believing, hoping, loving,
—I have no regrets.

—Translation by Helmut Harder

This poem, often quoted by David Toews, reflected his view of life and faith (stanzas 3 and 4 omitted).

Economic Development Associates, and through the church's mission and service agencies. Benjamin B. Janz wrote of his colleague: "David Toews was the ideal person for [the leadership of the Board of Colonization], and he has become the greatest Good Samaritan and philanthropist of his time."[7]

A Sense of Pilgrimage

The spirit of pilgrimage was integral to the life of David Toews. His settled and safe childhood in Lysanderhöhe was no foretaste of things to come. Before he reached adolescence, his parents uprooted him and took him on a dangerous journey into unknown territory. When the anticipated place of refuge eluded them, they set out on a voyage across the sea to America. After eight years in Kansas, Toews took matters into his own hands and embarked on his own pilgrimage in search of challenge and adventure in western Canada. After five years in Manitoba, he unsettled himself once more and trekked further west. There he concluded his own geographical quest for a home.

The experiences of the first three decades of Toews' life, in particular the trek to Turkestan, must have ingrained in his psyche and in his theological understanding a sense of life as a pilgrimage toward a place of safety. His passion for assisting his suffering kinsfolk in Russia may be explained at least in part by his own experiences early in life. While Toews' engagement in the work of immigration and relief came partly through circumstance, it was no mere coincidence that he became deeply involved in orchestrating the pilgrimage of his own people from a place of persecution and suffering to a new land of freedom and opportunity. He came to the task with a passion for moving people from places of trouble to places of safety. Often, in his later years, Toews would refer to Psalm 107 when reporting on immigration work or when motivating his hearers to contribute to the relief of the poor and the persecuted. This Psalm expresses thanksgiving to God for gathering his scattered people from east and west and from north and south, from places where they were threatened by hunger and thirst, by imprisonment and hard labour, by sickness and death, by stormy seas, and by the oppression of evil persons. The biblical theme of pilgrimage to a better land was central to the self-understanding of David Toews and to his ministry on behalf of others.

For some decades following his death, the theme of pilgrimage was prominent in sermons and hymns among Mennonites who came to Canada from Russia. The sense of being a pilgrim people was an essential component in Mennonite spiritual self-understanding and in motivation for mission and service. Through his life and ministry, David

Toews was among those in the first half of the twentieth century who fostered this understanding. The theme is not as prominent among the Mennonite people and in Mennonite churches as it once was. As Mennonites become settled and secure, the sense of being a people on a quest, along with the expression of faith and life in terms of Christian pilgrimage, loses its edge. We would do well to renew this aspect of the legacy of David Toews in our time.

In Conclusion

G.G. Neufeld of Boissevain, Manitoba, wrote several months after the death of David Toews: "To me he represents a great personage of our people. Yes, he made mistakes, but these fade away in the face of the many ways God used him. He accomplished a great deal because he was driven by love for the Lord and for his people. We thankfully accept his completed service and we hold his memory in respect."[8] By the grace of God, David Toews was here!

Appendix 1
Last Conference Sermon

David Toews was a focused and engaging preacher. He knew at the beginning of a sermon what point he wanted to make, and he remained on theme throughout. Theologically, he grounded his proclamation in a chosen biblical text and in related biblical references. His preaching style was dramatic and charismatic, yet thoughtful and orderly. It was standard practice for the chairman of the Conference of Mennonites in Canada to preach an introductory sermon at the opening session of the annual conference. Over the decades Toews preached many of these conference sermons. Here is his last one, presented at the sessions in Waldheim, Saskatchewan, July 2, 1940.[*]

"Go Into All the World"

The text that has been laid on my heart this morning is found in Matthew 28:18–20: "Then Jesus came to them and said: 'All authority in heaven and earth has been given to me. Therefore go and make disciples of all nations, baptizing them in the name of the Father and of the Son and of the Holy Spirit, and teaching them to obey everything I have commanded you. And surely I will be with you always, to the end of the age'" (Matthew 28:18–20).

The disciples of Jesus were given a huge assignment when their master said to them: "Go into all the world and teach all nations, baptizing them in the name of the Father, and of the Son, and of the Holy Spirit." After all, they had sensed their weaknesses at times, and they had on occasion been reproved for their little faith and their hardness of heart. How often they had wanted to be great, one greater than the other. Yet Thomas had succumbed to unbelief; Peter denied his Lord; and the other disciples had time and again become aware of their failures.

Now they were given a major responsibility: Go into all the world! Go to the Jews and proclaim to them the message concerning the cross. This was no easy assignment. They knew all too well that the word of the

[*]David Toews, "Konferenzpredigt," in Johann G. Rempel, ed., *Jahrbuch der Allgemeinen Konferenz der Mennoniten in Canada,* 1940 (Rosthern: Dietrich H. Epp, 1940), 3–4. Translated from the German by Helmut Harder.

cross was a stumbling stone to the Jews. They knew about the Greeks with their philosophy and their ability to make speeches. The Romans too, with their military might, were no strangers to the disciples. And against these powers they were now to take up the fight! The Jews had been given the law at Sinai, which apparently was sufficient for them. The Greeks had their philosophy. How could a company of poor fishermen present the message of the cross to these people in such a way that they would accept the word about the cross? According to human perception and prediction, the disciples would accomplish nothing against these mighty bulwarks.

That's why the Lord Jesus told them to remain and wait in Jerusalem until they had received power from on high. According to our thinking, they might have needed more education, more knowledge, some instruction in the art of speaking, or at least become financially independent to the extent that material worries would not hinder their work.

But wait, they had been with the Lord, their master teacher, for three years. That already gave them some resources so they could relate to others what they had seen and heard. They could say: "What we have seen with our eyes, what we have heard with our ears, what our hands have touched." But how often we read of them that they did not understand what the Lord was saying! They needed another kind of power, one which the Lord said they should await in Jerusalem where, in time, they would receive from on high. The Apostle Paul says in Ephesians 6: "We do not wage war against flesh and blood but against kings and mighty ones, namely, the lords of the world, those who rule in the darkness of this world with the evil spirits under the heavens." The Apostle Paul had felt the pangs in his flesh when Satan's angel attacked him, and in that same way he was often attacked by weariness and lack of faith.

The other disciples too had frailties which hindered them in the battle to which they were called. Peter showed a weakness in Antioch when he derided the Jews who had come from Jerusalem. The Apostle Paul had to draw his attention to what he was doing and had to discipline him for his actions. Peter found the grace to accept this reproof, and we do not hear again about differences between these two primary witnesses. Paul and Barnabas had serious confrontations with one another at one time, and yet we see that their differences of opinion were overridden. Paul could say about John Mark: "He is a valuable servant to me."

Too often our weaknesses become our most formidable enemies. There is so much self-love, so much selfishness, so much self-justification, so much pride, even though we know that if we desire to proclaim the message of the cross, we are to take our own knowledge and possessions captive in obedience to Christ (2 Corinthians 10:5). Workers in the kingdom of God will find themselves engaging in a great struggle when it comes to letting go of self and of the things they love. Thus we understand the poet when he writes: "Extricate my very heart from my heart, be it ever so painful." How can I live in such a way that my life is a sign that the power of God is active in and through me? The times will come when we will be called on to do battle, as is the lot of every one of God's workers. But there will also be times when we are to wait until we receive the needed power from on high. The Lord supplied the disciples with the necessary power when he endowed them with the Holy Spirit. And we are assured that the Lord has said: "I will send my Spirit upon all who ask." On Pentecost Sunday we gladly sing: "O Holy Spirit, come to us, and abide with us." But when we examine the results of our labours, perhaps we need to admit that our hearts and our lives do not yet give evidence of the potential power that the Holy Spirit should have in our ministry. That is probably a sign that we do not plead as passionately as we should for the presence of the Spirit.

When the Lord gives us assignments, he also supplies the necessary power to fulfil them. May the Lord give each one of us the magnanimous grace to learn to overcome that which is evil in us. And may we pray with sincerity for the gift of the Holy Spirit. Then the fruits of the Spirit, will reside in us: love, joy, peace, patience, kindness, goodness, faithfulness, gentleness, and self-control (Galatians 5: 22). Thus through our feelings, our speaking, and our actions, we will show forth that which we preach. A godly garden would grow and flourish in which all of these beautiful attributes will decorate and beautify our human life. These blessing are promised to us through faith and obedience. The apostle John could say: "Our faith is the victory that overcomes the world" (1 John 5:4).

May our conference discussions prove fruitful. May we seek to fulfil the will of God in our deliberations and in the assignments given to us. May we, through the power of the Holy Spirit and through our relationship to the Lord, be able to say with the Apostle Paul: "In all these things we are more than conquerors through him who loved us" (Romans 8:37).

> Did we in our own strength confide,
> Our striving would be losing;
> Were not the right man on our side,
> The man of God's own choosing:
> Dost ask who that may be? Christ Jesus, is is He!
> Lord Sabaoth, His name, From age to age the same;
> And He must win the battle.
> "A mighty fortress is our God," stanza 2

Appendix 2
Children, Grandchildren, and Memories

Parents
David Toews (1870–1947) and *Margarete Friesen* (1881–1941), married September 20, 1900

Children and Grandchildren

1. **Maria Toews** (1901–1964) and Herman G. Riesen (1905–1999), married October 11, 1930. *Grandchildren*: Irene Margarete (Riesen) Gifford (b. 1932), David Herman Riesen (b. 1934), Lois Katherine (Riesen) Wiens (b.1940)

2. **Benno Toews** (1903–1986) and Catherine Friesen (1903–1997), married June 7, 1928. *Grandchildren:* Theodore David Isaac Toews (b.1929), Lorene Toews (b.1938), Glendon Toews (b.1945)

3. **Margaret Toews** (1906–1985) and Jacob Sawatzky (1902–1996), married August 21, 1936. *Grandchildren:* David Donald Sawatzky (b.1938), Robert Jacob Sawatzky (b.1940), Margaret Helen (Sawatzky), Arnold (b.1942), Eileen Louise (Sawatzky) Funk/Gratrix (b.1945), Dorothy Ann (Sawatzky) Woodley (b.1949)

4. **Elsie Toews** (1908–2000) and Abram Peter Hooge (1905–1973), married July 11, 1935. *Grandchildren:* Margaret Katherine (Hooge) Jantzen (b.1936), Eleanor Irene (Hooge) Ens (b.1938), Evelyn Marie (Hooge) Schlosser (b.1945)

5. **Dorothy (Dora) Toews** (1910–1974) and Peter Schellenberg (1910–1977), married July 18, 1948. *Grandchildren:* Allan (Schellenberg) Gyatso (b.1953), Carolyn Ann (Schellenberg) Regier (b.1955)

6. **Louise Emma Toews** (1912–) and C. Blake Friesen (1918–), married October 9, 1944. *Grandchildren:* Gary Wayne Friesen (b.1946), Alan Dale Friesen (b.1948), Howard Blake Friesen (b.1951)

7. **Elma Toews** (1915–1994)

8. Anna Ruth Toews (1918–) and Sylvester L. Funk (1917–), married July 27, 1940. *Grandchildren:* Marilyn Joan (Funk) Janzen (b.1942), Ann Doreen (Funk) Reynolds (b.1945), Gwenyth Louise (Funk) Epp (b.1950), John Ray Funk (b.1956)

9. Irene Toews (1921–1926)

Children and Grandchildren Remember**

When father was elder of the Mennonite Church in Rosthern and the singing began to drag, he would get up and conduct with a loud resonant voice. This hearty singing livened up the congregation.—Elsie Hooge and Anna Funk, daughters

One memory I have is when there was an interruption in the electrical power in the Rosthern church. This happened repeatedly with the lights coming on and then going off. Grandpa built this into his sermon using the lights going on and off as a metaphor for aspects of life. I recall the congregation laughing appreciatively as he turned a potential problem into an advantage.—D. Donald Sawatzky, grandson

Father loved music and many times he would gather us around him and teach us beautiful children's hymns. Some of them I clearly remember, such as "Weil ich Jesu Schäflein bin" and "Guter Mond, du gehst so stille." Since he had such a busy schedule we accepted these periods as exceptionally good quality times.—Louise Friesen, daughter

Our evenings at home were always cozy. Father would be sitting at the dining room table reading the newspapers and mother would be crocheting. Shortly before ten o'clock mother would get up and make hot chocolate for us all. After that father would conduct our evening devotions.—Elsie Hooge and Anna Funk, daughters

During my pre-school years, I was a frequent visitor in my grandparents' home when father was teaching at the German-English Academy. I remember lots of love and laughter in the house. The aunties would be busy in the kitchen preparing for the Christmas celebrations. The family had great respect for their father David. I can still hear my grandfather's beautiful, strong voice as he led the singing of hymns in church.—Theodore Toews, oldest grandson

---

** Some quotations are taken from "Toews Family Reflects," *Saskatchewan Mennonite Historian* 2 (December 1997): 15–20, and used by permission.

Then at last came Christmas Day. Plates had been set out the night before and, as we entered the room the next morning, we sang carols and father read the Christmas story. There were always a few small gifts—gifts of love which had been bought with a sacrifice.—Louise Friesen, daughter

At Christmas, as I recall, we grandchildren were kept out of the parlour until the crucial moment when the Christmas tree was revealed in all its glory: candles burning on the Weihnachtsbaum *and gifts in sparkly wrapping paper covering its base. The Christmas story, the prayers, the carols, and all the accoutrements that made Christmas special for a child were there. But I also remember the little ritual which was special, at least for me. Every Christmas for a number of years my grandfather would call me into his study and ask me in German: "Na David, bist du in diesem Jahr artig gewesen?" (Were you good this year?), whereupon I would invariably answer, "Yes," and get my reward, a one-dollar bill."*—David Riesen, grandson

Mother played a major role in our lives. She was a strong support at home and played her role with dedication and love. Her life was one of service to the family, to relatives, to friends, and to the community. When she passed away in July 1941, our life was never the same. It seemed as though heart and soul were gone from our home.—Louise Friesen, daughter

One of my cherished possessions is a simple brass lamp which belonged to my grandfather. I remember it always being on the oak desk in his study. Often when I look at this lamp I'm reminded of his study, his home, and about my relationship with him. Grandpa's study, in particular, has deep memories for me. This room, near the front of the house, seemed austere with its high-backed brown leather chairs, a bookcase with horizontal glass doors, and the oak desk. As a child, the room always seemed somewhat mysterious. Men in dark suits walked in and out for what, I was told, were important meetings.—D. Donald Sawatzky, grandson

I remember grandfather when he was very ill and greeting us with his hugs as we leaned over his bed, which was soon to become his death bed. I remember feeling very hurt and tearful when my mother informed me that grandfather had died.—D. Donald Sawatzky

Finally, in his last sad years, I remember him having to have insulin injections for diabetes, his trembling hands when he couldn't straighten

up the ketchup bottle, and his swollen feet soaking in the tub of cold water. I also remember the enormous respect that people had for him, be it the family catering to his every whim, be it the train conductors' extraordinary deference bringing him home from Saskatoon, or the barber who gave me a haircut on the day of his funeral and noting in a hushed voice what a huge gathering there would be in the town that day to pay their last respects to Bishop Toews.—David Riesen, grandson

Some might have had grandfathers who were more available to them. Others might have had grandfathers who were more playful with them. What I had was a grandfather who had become a role model for me of courage, integrity, and persistence in the face of adversity.—D. Donald Sawatzky, grandson

Notes

Chapter 1. Lysanderhöhe 1870–1880

[1] For an account of the origins and early development of the Am Trakt settlement, see Johannes J. Dyck and W.E. Surukin, *Am Trakt: Eine mennonitische Kolonie im mittleren Wolgagebiet* (North Kildonan: Echo Verlag, 1948); translated as, *Am Trakt: A Mennonite Settlement in the Central Volga Region*, trans. Hermina Joldersma and Peter J. Dyck (Winnipeg: CMBC Publications, 1995).

[2] Jacob Toews, "A Short Sketch of My Life," trans. and ed., Frank and Anna (Toevs) Wenger (Aberdeen, Idaho, 1963). David Toews Project files, Mennonite Heritage Centre Archives (henceforth, MHC Archives), Winnipeg, 9.

[3] Ibid., 6.

[4] Ibid., 7.

[5] For historical background to the Anabaptist movement and to Mennonite history, see C. Henry Smith, *The Story of the Mennonites*, 4th ed., rev. and enl. (Newton: Mennonite Publishing Office, 1957).

[6] For a statement of differentiation between the Anabaptists, on the one hand, and Protestants and Catholics, on the other hand, see Walter Klaassen, *Anabaptism: Neither Catholic nor Protestant* (Waterloo: Conrad Grebel Press, 1973, 1981; third edition: Pandora Press, 2001).

[7] C. Henry Smith, *Story of the Mennonites*, 384–403.

[8] Ibid., 396ff.

[9] Fred Richard Belk, *The Great Trek of the Russian Mennonites to Central Asia, 1880–1884* (Kitchener and Scottdale: Herald Press, 1976), 53ff.

[10] Mennonite history is no stranger to millennialist and chiliastic tendencies. The attempts of the radical Münsterites to set up a millennial kingdom (1534) and the theology of Melchior Hofmann (1495–1543) in the sixteenth century are but two examples.

[11] Jacob Toews, "A Short Sketch," 10.

[12] Ibid.

[13] J. Dyck and W.E. Surukin, *Am Trakt*, 3, note 8; F.R. Belk, *The Great Trek*, 40ff.

[14] J. Dyck and W.E. Surukin, *Am Trakt*, 5.

[15] Ibid., 28.

[16] B.J. Schellenberg, "Ältester David Toews, D.D. c.c.: Sein Leben und Wirken," unpublished 84-page manuscript dated May 1949, 15. See original manuscript in MHC Archives, vol. 1184, file 139. Bernhard J. Schellenberg (1879–1966) emigrated to Canada from southern Russia in 1923. In Canada he was teacher for a time, then served as the first archivist for the Conference of Mennonites in Canada. His manuscript of David Toews' life and work, prepared shortly after the death of Toews in 1947, was never published.

[17] Jacob H. Janzen, *David Toews, Vorsitzender der Kolonisationsbehörde der Mennoniten in Canada: Biographische Skizze* (Rosthern: D.H. Epp, 1938), 6ff. In this pamphlet, Janzen describes the work and personality of David Toews as it came to expression

from the time he began as chairman and executive director of the Canadian Mennonite Board of Colonization in the early 1920s until the mid-1930s.

[18] Jacob Toews, "A Short Sketch," 11.

[19] Ibid., 12.

[20] Ibid. See also F.R. Belk, *The Great Trek*, chapter 3.

[21] F.R. Belk, *The Great Trek*, 60ff., 75ff.

[22] Jacob Toews, "A Short Sketch," 13; F.R. Belk, *The Great Trek*, 76ff.

[23] Jacob Toews, "A Short Sketch," 15.

Chapter 2. Turkestan 1880–1884

[1] B.J. Schellenberg, "Ältester David Toews," 14.

[2] For a biographical sketch of Klaas Epp, Jr., see Franz Bartsch, "Epp, Claasz, Jr.," in *Mennonite Encyclopedia*, vol. II (Scottdale: Mennonite Publishing House, 1956), 234.

[3] Reservations about the interpretations of Klaas Epp were not uncommon among those who joined the trek. For example, in his "Diary of the Trek to Central Asia, 1880–81," Martin Klaassen has an entry dated Sunday, August 17, 1880, in which he ends his report on the three services at which Epp preached on Ezekiel 43 and 44, with the words: "The day proved to be a blessing in the end, but I had an inner struggle with many of the interpretations of scripture by Cl. Epp, so that especially in the morning service the blessing was lost to me" (1). MHC Archives, vol. 4221, file 2.

[4] Jacob Toews, "A Short Sketch of My Life," 15.

[5] Ibid.

[6] Ibid.

[7] Franz Bartsch, *Unser Auszug nach Mittelasien* (North Kildonan: Echo Verlag, 1948); translated as *Our Trek to Central Asia*, trans. Elisabeth Peters and Gerhard Ens (Winnipeg: CMBC Publications, 1993; 2002).

[8] Ibid., xiv.

[9] Jacob Toews, "A Short Sketch," 15ff.

[10] F.R. Belk, *The Great Trek*, 90.

[11] Jacob Toews, "A Short Sketch," 15.

[12] F.R. Belk, *The Great Trek*, 91.

[13] Dallas Wiebe, *Our Asian Journey: A Novel* (Waterloo: Wilfrid Laurier University, Department of English, 1997).

[14] Ibid., 158f.

[15] F.R. Belk, *The Great Trek*, 109.

[16] Jacob Toews, "A Short Sketch," 20.

[17] Ibid., 21.

[18] While in the Samarkand area, Jacob Toews wrote and sent to the newly established paper of the General Conference Mennonite Church in North America, the first of a series of accounts of the trek. Cf., "Asien," in *Christlicher Bundes-Bote* 1 (5 January 1882), 7. Evidently North American Mennonites followed the Asian journey with great interest. See further, five bi-monthly articles submitted by Jacob Toews in ibid. (15 January 1882–15 March 1882). One can surmise that, even before he arrived in the Newton, Kansas area, Jacob Toews will have become a familiar name to General Conference Mennonites through these submissions.

[19] Jacob Toews, "A Short Sketch," 26.

[20] F.R. Belk, *The Great Trek*, 120.

[21] Ibid., 123.

[22] Ibid., 223.

[23] Jacob Toews, "A Short Sketch," 16.

[24] F.R. Belk, *The Great Trek*, 124f., 143f.

[25] Ibid., 148ff.

[26] Ibid., 152ff.

[27] Ibid., 154.

[28] Ibid., 156.

[29] Ibid., 165ff.

[30] Ibid., 177. The idea of heading for America was not new to the group, even as they were underway. For example, when in Orsk in September 1880, Jacob Toews and several of the other leaders met with a representative of Governor General Kaufmann, who advised them that, given the meagre prospects for finding suitable land and given the demands of military conscription in the region, it would be better for the group to consider going to America. Cf., Walter Klaassen, *Anabaptism: Neither Catholic nor Protestant*, 7.

[31] F.R. Belk, *The Great Trek*, 180.

[32] Ibid., 186.

[33] Jacob H. Janzen, *David Toews, Vorsitzender*, 12.

[34] Waldemar Janzen, "The Great Trek: Episode or Paradigm?" *Mennonite Quarterly Review* 51 (April 1977): 130.

[35] Ibid., 133.

[36] B.J. Schellenberg, "Ältester David Toews," 15.

[37] The same biographer observed that Toews talked very little about the trek in his adult years. Ibid. David's brother-in-law, Jacob Klaassen, was a minister at Eigenheim, Saskatchewan, when David was living in Rosthern. Klaassen had also been on the Asian journey. One can presume the two of them would have discussed their common experience on the trek, since, according to the children of David Toews, Klaassen regularly came to the Toews home for lengthy, somewhat private, discussions. But, again, we do not know what thoughts their common experience kindled half a century later.

[38] Jacob H. Janzen, *David Toews, Vorsitzender*, 9.

Chapter 3. Kansas 1884–1893

[1] Cornelius Krahn, "Kansas," *Mennonite Encyclopedia*, vol. III (Scottdale: Mennonite Publishing House, 1957), 143–148.

[2] John D. Thiesen, *Prussian Roots, Kansas Branches: A History of First Mennonite Church in Newton*, ed. and rev. Menno Schrag (Newton: Historical Committee, First Mennonite Church, 1986), 4ff.

[3] Ibid., 17.

[4] Cornelius Krahn, "Kansas," 147f.

[5] John D. Thiesen, *Prussian Roots, Kansas Branches*, 32. According to Thiesen, some discussion arose when the two children of Jacob and Anna Toews asked to become members of First Mennonite Church. They had been baptized by Klaas Epp, Jr., who was not an ordained minister. The two were accepted into membership by the laying on of hands and were required to affirm their commitment to the teachings of the Bible and to a correct understanding of baptism.

[6] Jacob Toews, "A Short Sketch," 18.

[7] John D. Thiesen, *Prussian Roots, Kansas Branches*, 38ff.

[8] Dallas Wiebe, *Our Asian Journey*, 434ff.; Jacob Toews, "A Short Sketch," 1ff.

[9] Johann G. Rempel, *Die Rosenorter Gemeinde in Saskatchewan* (Rosthern: D.H. Epp, 1950), 33.

[10] Cornelius J. Dyck, "David Toews 1870–1947," chapter in *Twelve Becoming: Biographies of Mennonite Disciples from the Sixteenth to the Twentieth Century* (Newton: Faith and Life Press, 1973), 52.

[11] Jacob H. Janzen, *David Toews, Vorsitzender*, 15.

[12] For historical background on Halstead Seminary, see E.G. Kaufmann, "Halstead Seminary," in *Mennonite Encyclopedia*, vol. II, 638.

[13] For background to the life and thought of Heinrich H. Ewert prior to his coming to the Mennonite Collegiate Institute in Gretna, Manitoba, see Gerhard J. Ens, *"Die Schule muss sein": A History of the Mennonite Collegiate Institute, 1889–1989* (Gretna: Mennonite Collegiate Institute, 1990), 32ff.

[14] B.J. Schellenberg, "Ältester David Toews," 21.

[15] Gerhard J. Ens, *Die Schule muss sein*, 35.

[16] Ibid., 37.

[17] Frank H. Epp, *Mennonite Exodus: The Rescue and Resettlement of the Russian Mennonites since the Communist Revolution* (Altona: D.W. Friesen & Sons, Ltd., 1962), 86.

[18] Dennis D. Engbrecht, "The Americanization of a Rural Immigrant Church: The General Conference Mennonites in Central Kansas, 1874–1939" (PhD dissertation, The University of Nebraska, 1990), 144ff.

[19] B.J. Schellenberg, "Ältester David Toews," 21.

[20] Jacob H. Janzen, *David Toews, Vorsitzender*, 13.

Chapter 4. Manitoba 1893–1898

[1] Gerhard J. Ens, *Die Schule muss sein*, 20.

[2] Ibid., 15f.

[3] B.J. Schellenberg, "Ältester David Toews," 21.

[4] For a basic biographical sketch of Heinrich H. Ewert, see Paul J. Schaefer, *Heinrich H. Ewert: Lehrer, Erzieher und Prediger der Mennoniten* (Gretna: Verlag der Manitoba Jugendorganization der Mennoniten-Konferenz von Canada, 1945); translated as, *Heinrich H. Ewert: Teacher, Educator and Minister of the Mennonites*, trans. Ida Toews (Winnipeg: CMBC Publications, 1990).

[5] Paul J. Schaefer, "Mennonite Collegiate Institute," in *Mennonite Encyclopedia*, vol. III, 617.

[6] Lawrence Klippenstein, "Western Local Mennonite Teachers' Conference—An Early Minute Book," *Manitoba Pageant* (Winter 1977): 9. The information in this article is drawn from about 1894.

[7] David Toews to Ed G. Kaufman, 24 December 1937, MHC Archives, vol. 4387.

[8] B.J. Schellenberg, "Ältester David Toews," 22.

[9] Jacob H. Janzen, *David Toews, Vorsitzender*, 13f.

[10] Paul W. Riegert, *Deep Earth: A Short History of the Tiefengrund School District, No. 431 in Saskatchewan* (Regina: Rampeck Publishers, 1996), 17f.

[11] Lawrence Klippenstein, "Peter Regier: Churchman-farmer (1851–1925)," *Mennonite Historian* 2 (December 1976): 2.

[12] Peter Regier, "Kurze Geschichte unserer Rosenorter-Mennoniten-Gemeinde bei Rosthern, Sask.," *Der Mitarbeiter* 1 (October 1906): 7.

[13] Walter Klaassen, *The Days of Our Years: A History of the Eigenheim Mennonite Church Community, 1892–1992* (Rosthern: Eigenheim Mennonite Church, 1992), 23.

[14] Paul Riegert, *Deep Earth*, 12.

Chapter 5. Tiefengrund 1898–1903

[1] Frank H. Epp, *Education with a Plus: The Story of Rosthern Junior College* (Waterloo: Conrad Press, 1975), 25.

[2] Paul Riegert, *Deep Earth*, 1.

[3] Ibid., 17f.

[4] *Hague-Osler Mennonite Reserve, 1895–1995* (Saskatoon: Hague-Osler Reserve Committee, 1995), 19–20.

[5] Ibid., 39ff.; Helene (Dyck) Funk, "The Rosenort Mennonite Church of Saskatchewan, 1890–2000," *Saskatchewan Mennonite Historian* 5 (March 2000): 16f.

[6] Paul Riegert, *Deep Earth*, 46ff.

[7] Ibid., 22.

[8] Leonard Doell, *Mennonite Homesteaders on the Hague-Osler Reserve* (Saskatoon: Mennonite Historical Society of Saskatchewan, 1999), 271. On background to Mennonite homesteading in Saskatchewan, see *Hague-Osler Mennonite Reserve, 1895–1995*, 21–23.

[9] Ibid.

[10] Paul Riegert, *Deep Earth*, 18.

[11] B.J. Schellenberg, "Ältester David Toews," 24.

[12] Ibid.

[13] Ibid., 68.

[14] Jacob H. Janzen, *David Toews, Vorsitzender*, 15.

[15] Paul Riegert, *Deep Earth*, 68ff.

[16] Christian Hege and Ernest Regehr, "Rosenort Mennonite Church," in *Mennonite Encyclopedia*, vol. IV, 360.

[17] Walter Klaassen, *The Days of Our Years*, 36.

[18] David Toews, "Familiennachricht," *Der Bote* 18 (16 July 1941), 4.

[19] J.G. Rempel, ed., *Fünfzig Jahre Konferenzbestrebungen, 1902–1952, Erster Teil* (Rosthern: Konferenz der Mennoniten in Canada, 1952), 7–9. For a more extensive English article on the origins of the Conference of Mennonites in Canada, see Lawrence Klippenstein and Peter Paetkau, "The Conference of Mennonites in Canada: Background and Origin," *Mennonite Life* 34 (December 1979): 4–10.

[20] For an account of the proceedings of the first formal sessions of the Conference of Mennonites in Central Canada and a brief biography of the leading persons involved there, see J.G. Rempel, *Fünfzig Jahre Konferenzbestrebungen*, 13–25. In July of 1978 a cairn commemorating the 1903 conference was erected at the site of the former Hochstadt Bergthaler Church near Altona, Manitoba.

[21] Ibid., 18.

[22] *Hague-Osler Mennonite Reserve*, 579f.

[23] Ibid., 603ff.; Frank H. Epp, *Mennonites in Canada, 1786–1920: The History of a Separate People* (Toronto: Macmillan of Canada, 1974), 312f.

[24] See the chart in Frank H. Epp, ibid., 317.

[25] Paul Riegert, *Deep Earth*, 20.

[26] Information from Verner Friesen, Saskatoon, nephew of Margarete (Friesen) Toews.

[27] Paul Riegert, *Deep Earth*, 74.

[28] Ibid., 74–76.

Chapter 6. Eigenheim 1903–1906

[1] Walter Klaassen, *The Days of Our Years*, 9.

[2] Ibid., 22.

[3] Ibid., 24.

[4] Ibid., 34ff.

[5] Ibid., 41.

[6] J.G. Rempel, *Die Rosenorter Gemeinde*, 18.

[7] Walter Klaassen, *The Days of Our Years*, 26ff.

[8] Ibid., 27.

[9] B.J. Schellenberg, "Ältester David Toews," 23.

[10] Paul Riegert, *Deep Earth*, 68ff.

[11] Frank H. Epp, *Education with a Plus*, 14ff.

[12] Ibid., 24.

[13] Ibid., 27.

[14] Ibid.

[15] Ibid., 29.

[16] David Toews' biographers do not agree on how long he lived and taught at Tiefengrund and Eigenheim, and when he began as teacher at the German-English Academy. J.G. Rempel stated incorrectly that Toews taught at Tiefengrund for three years (1898–1901), then at Eigenheim for three years (1901–1904), after which he moved to Rosthern in 1904 where he worked to establish the school and became its first teacher in 1905 (J.G. Rempel, *Fünfzig Jahre Konferenzbestrebungen, Erster Teil*, 31f.). B.J. Schellenberg is also incorrect when he states that Toews taught in Tiefengrund from 1898 to 1904, after which he moved to Rosthern to become principal of the Academy in 1905 (B.J. Schellenberg, "Ältester David Toews," 36). Frank H. Epp appears not to be correct when he suggests that Toews may have spent the school year, 1905–1906, in Gretna, Manitoba, taking a refresher course or teaching there (Frank H. Epp, *Education with a Plus*, 29). Rather, the overwhelming evidence bears out that Toews taught at Tiefengrund for five years from 1898 to 1903, then moved to Eigenheim where he stayed

for another three years from 1903 to 1906 before moving to Rosthern to take up teaching duties at the newly founded school. The Tiefengrund years are established by Paul Riegert (*Deep Earth*, 160). The Eigenheim years are established by the Eigenheim District 502 N.W.T. attendance registry which shows that David Toews was the teacher up until and including the month of June 1906.

[17] B.J. Schellenberg, "Ältester David Toews," 25.

[18] J.G. Rempel, *Fünfzig Jahre Konferenzbestrebungen*, 31.

[19] Ibid., 35.

[20] Ibid., 27.

[21] Ibid., 28.

[22] Ibid., 37.

[23] Frank H. Epp, *Education wtih a Plus*, 33f.

Chapter 7. Rosthern 1906–1912

[1] Frank H. Epp, *Mennonites in Canada, 1786–1920*, 311.

[2] "Schule und Erziehung," *Der Mitarbeiter* 1 (October 1906): 2–3.

[3] Frank H. Epp, *Education with a Plus*, 33.

[4] David Toews, "Mitteilungen aus Saskatchewan," *Der Mitarbeiter* 1 (December 1906): 21.

[5] Frank H. Epp, *Education with a Plus*, 33.

[6] Ibid.

[7] Ibid., 42.

[8] J.G. Rempel, *Die Rosenorter Gemeinde in Saskatchewan*, 41.

[9] Ibid., 40ff.

[10] Ibid.

[11] Ibid., 42.

[12] Ibid.

[13] Ibid., 42f.

[14] David Toews, "An unsere geschätzten Schulfreunde in Saskatchewan," *Der Mitarbeiter* 3 (April 1909): 50.

[15] Frank H. Epp, *Education with a Plus*, 27 and 45.

[16] Ibid., 44.

[17] Ibid., 47f.

[18] Ibid., 51.

[19] J.G. Rempel, *Die Rosenorter Gemeinde in Saskatchewan*, 25f.

[20] Isaak J. Penner, "Bericht der Sonntagschulkonvention . . . ," *Der Mitarbeiter* 6 (November 1911): 9f.

[21] Walter Klaassen, *The Days of Our Years*, 38f.

[22] Frank H. Epp, *Education with a Plus*, 37.

[23] J.G. Rempel, *Fünfzig Jahre Konferenzbestrebungen*, 40f.

[24] J.G. Rempel, *Die Rosenorter Gemeinde in Saskatchewan*, 43f.

[25] J.G. Rempel, *Fünfzig Jahre Konferenzbestrebungen*, 47.

[26] Ibid., 52.

[27] Ibid., 85f.

[28] Ibid., 87.

[29] David Toews, "Reisebericht," *Der Mitarbeiter* 2 (October 1907): 3ff.

[30] David Toews, "Reiseerinnerungen," *Der Mitarbeiter* 5 (November 1910): 9ff.

Chapter 8. Elder Toews 1913–1918

[1] Walter Klaassen, *The Days of Our Years*, 43.

[2] Walter Klaassen suggests David Toews was chosen because he was better educated than the other candidates, and that he was more charismatic and energetic than some of them. Ibid., 39.

[3] W. Rempel, "Ein Gemeindefest," *Der Mitarbeiter* 8 (October 1913): 2ff.

[4] Ibid., 4.

[5] Cornelius Krahn, "Elder," in *Mennonite Encyclopedia*, vol. II, 178–181.

[6] David Toews, "Mitteilung aus der Rosenorter Gemeinde," *Der Mitarbeiter* 8 (March 1914): 46ff.

[7] Frank H. Epp, *Education with a Plus*, 63.

[8] J.G. Rempel, *Die Rosenorter Gemeinde in Saskatchewan*, 38.

[9] Ibid., 95. Rempel provides no information about the fire.

[10] David Toews, "Wo fehlt es?" *Der Mitarbeiter* 5 (July 1911): 73f.

[11] Ibid., 74.

[12] Walter Klaassen, *The Days of Our Years*, 68ff.

[13] David Toews, "Innere Mission," *Der Mitarbeiter* 4 (March 1910): 139f.

[14] David Toews, "Die Kinder der Welt sind klüger als die Kinder des Lichts," *Der Mitarbeiter* 6 (March 1912): 42f.

[15] Ibid., 43.

[16] J.G. Rempel, *Fünfzig Jahre Konferenzbestrebungen*, 96.

[17] David Toews, "Konferenznachklänge," *Der Mitarbeiter* 8 (July 1914): 73.

[18] J.G. Rempel, *Fünfzig Jahre Konferenzbestrebungen*, 96.

[19] David Toews, "Konferenzanzeige," *Der Mitarbeiter* 10 (May 1916): 1.

[20] For a detailed account of the interchange between the Mennonites and the Canadian government on this issue, see Frank H. Epp, *Mennonites in Canada, 1920–1940: A People's Struggle for Survival* (Toronto: Macmillan of Canada, 1982), 365–389.

[21] J.G. Rempel, *Fünfzig Jahre Konferenzbestrebungen*, 113.

[22] Ibid., 120.

[23] Walter Klaassen, *The Days of Our Years*, 62.

[24] David Toews, "Aus der Fortbildungsschule in Rosthern," *Der Mitarbeiter* 7 (September 1913): 93.

[25] Ibid.

[26] David Toews, "Etwas über Schulverhältnisse in Saskatchewan," *Der Mitarbeiter* 8 (February 1914): 36f.

[27] For the text of this address, see David Toews, "Wie können wir versuchen durch unsere höheren Schulen den Bedürfnissen unseres Volkes mehr zu entsprechen," *Der Mitarbeiter* 8 (August 1914): 83ff.

[28] Frank H. Epp, *Education with a Plus*, 68.

[29] Walter Klaassen, *The Days of Our Years*, 52.

[30] Frank H. Epp, *Education with a Plus*, 39.

[31] Frank H. Epp, *Mennonites in Canada, 1920–1940*, 366.

[32] Ibid.

[33] Ibid., 370.

[34] Ibid., 371.

[35] Ibid.

[36] Quoted in ibid., 381.

[37] See Donald F. Durnbaugh and Charles W. Brockwell, Jr., "The Historic Peace Churches: From Sectarian Origins to Ecumenical Witness," in *The Church's Peace Witness*, ed. Marlin E. Miller and Barbara Nelson Gingerich (Grand Rapids: Eerdmans, 1994), 191–195. Durnbaugh and Brockwell state that "the experiences of conscientious objection during World War I were as a rule unsatisfactory, in some cases intolerable, because of wartime hysteria and the Wilson administration's delay in defining acceptable noncombatant military pursuits. Peace church leaders determined to pursue better arrangements, a resolution that acquired urgency in the 1930s as the rise of totalitarianism in Europe made the outbreak of the war probable. At a meeting in Newton, Kansas, in the fall of 1935, peace church leaders made plans to work together to prevent war and, failing that, to secure the best possible service for conscientious objectors" (191). While the foregoing comments pertain mainly to the United States, it appears they are applicable to Canada as well.

[38] J.G. Rempel, *Die Rosenorter Gemeinde in Saskatchewan*, 34f. For the record, we must correct Rempel. According to a Friesen family historian, Verner Friesen, Margarete was the fifth child of Abraham Friesen's second marriage.

Chapter 9. Advocate for His People 1919–1922

[1] Frank H. Epp, *Mennonite Exodus*, 94.

[2] Frank H. Epp, *Mennonites in Canada, 1920–1940*, 152ff.

[3] Frank H. Epp, *Mennonite Exodus*, 94.

[4] Ibid., 98.

[5] Heinrich H. Ewert, "Welche Aufgabe haben wir jetzt nach dem Kriege unserem Land gegenüber?" *Der Mitarbeiter* 13 (February 1920): 9ff.

[6] J.G. Rempel, *Die Rosenorter Gemeinde in Saskatchewan*, 37.

[7] Ibid.

[8] David Toews, "Erinnerungen aus der Zeit der Russlandhilfe und Immigrationsarbeit," 5. These memoirs, beginning in 1919, were completed August 10, 1934. For a copy of the original manuscript see the David Toews research file at MHC Archives. A complete and slightly edited version appeared in a series entitled, "Tagebuechern des David Toews," in *Mennonite Mirror*, beginning in 2 (February 1973): 17.

[9] J.G. Rempel, *Die Rosenorter Gemeinde in Saskatchewan*, 37.

[10] J.G. Rempel, *Fünfzig Jahre Konferenzbestrebungen*, 124f.

[11] David Toews, "Erinnerungen," 7.

[12] Ibid.

[13] J.G. Rempel, *Fünfzig Jahre Konferenzbestrebungen*, 56f.

[14] David Toews, "Nachrichten aus den Gemeinden," *Der Mitarbeiter* 14 (March 1921): 21.

[15] Frank H. Epp, *Education with a Plus*, 70.

[16] David Toews, "Erinnerungen," 1.

[17] Gerhard Ens, born in Russia in 1863, had migrated to Canada in 1891, being one of the first Mennonite settlers to come to the Rosthern area. There he occupied a homestead, opened a store and a post office, and began dealing in land and promoting immigration. Together with Peter Janzen of Nebraska, he formed the Saskatchewan-Manitoba Land Company. In 1905 Ens became an elected member of the first Saskatchewan legislature, representing the Rosthern area. No one can understand why David Toews considered Ens a useful person in the immigration project. The fact that Ens was a leader in "The Church of the New Jerusalem," sometimes referred to as the Swedenborgian Church, did not deter Toews from working together with him. See Frank H. Epp, *Mennonites in Canada, 1786–1920*, 311f.

[18] J.G. Rempel, *Die Rosenorter Gemeinde in Saskatchewan*, 55ff.

[19] Ibid., 55.

[20] David Toews, "Erinnerungen," 1.

[21] J.G. Rempel, *Fünfzig Jahre Konferenzbestrebungen*, 124ff.

[22] Ibid., 130ff.

[23] For a historical overview of the origin and development of Mennonite Central Committee in the early years, see Harold S. Bender, "Mennonite Central Committee," in *Mennonite Encyclopedia*, vol. III, 605–609.

[24] For a summary of the origin and development of the Nonresistant Relief Organization of Ontario, see Samuel F. Coffman, "Nonresistant Relief Organization (NRRO)," in *Mennonite Encyclopedia*, vol. III, 907–908.

[25] For a note on the formation and role of the Canadian Central Committee, see J. Gerbrandt, "Canadian Mennonite Board of Colonization," in *Mennonite Encyclopedia*, vol. I, 507. See also Peter H. Rempel, "The First Canadian Mennonite Central Committee, 1920–1924," *Mennonite Historian* 21 (December 1995): 1f.

[26] Harold S. Bender, "Mennonnite Central Committee," 609.

[27] John B. Toews, *With Courage to Spare: The Life of B.B. Janz* (Winnipeg: The Christian Press, 1978), 23–35.

[28] Frank H. Epp, *Mennonite Exodus*, 44ff.

[29] J.G. Rempel, *Fünfzig Jahre Konferenzbestrebungen*, 145.

[30] Frank H. Epp, *Mennonites in Canada, 1920–1940*, 156.

[31] Frank H. Epp, *Mennonite Exodus*, 103f.

[32] Ibid., 105.

[33] Ibid., 73.

[34] Interestingly, the minutes of the organizing meeting of the Canadian Mennonite Board of Colonization were included in the biography of Heinrich H. Ewert. See, Paul J. Schaefer, *Heinrich H. Ewert*, 129–131.

[35] Ibid., 74f.

[36] The organization of the Canadian Mennonite Board of Colonization at this point in time should be distinguished from its official incorporation which occurred at a meeting of the executive committee on January 27, 1926, in Regina, Saskatchewan. See documents in MHC Archives, vol. 1164, file 11.

[37] Frank H. Epp, *Mennonite Exodus*, 75.

[38] Ibid.

[39] J.G. Rempel, *Die Rosenorter Gemeinde in Saskatchewan*, 56.

[40] For a report of the service, see ibid., 46f.

[41] Frank H. Epp, *Mennonite Exodus*, 44.

[42] Paul J. Schaefer, *Heinrich H. Ewert*, 130f.

[43] Frank H. Epp, *Mennonites in Canada, 1920–1940*, 159.

[44] For correspondence related to this transportation, see MHC Archives, vol.1079, file 8.

[45] David Toews, "Erinnerungen," 11.

[46] Ibid.

[47] Ibid., 12.

[48] Frank H. Epp, *Mennonites in Canada, 1920–1940*, 160f.

[49] Ibid., 162f.

[50] David Toews, "Erinnerungen," 12.

[51] Ibid.

[52] Ibid. See also, Frank H. Epp, *Mennonites in Canada, 1920–1940*, 161.

[53] J.G. Rempel, *Fünfzig Jahre Konferenzbestrebungen*, 149.

[54] For correspondence on this issue, see MHC Archives, vol.1163, file 3.

[55] David Toews, "Erinnerungen," 13.

[56] Ibid., 15.

[57] Ibid.

[58] Ibid., 16.

[59] Ibid.

[60] Ibid., 17.

[61] Ibid., 18.

[62] David Toews to C.J. Andres, 19 January 1923, MHC Archives, vol.1163, file 3.

[63] Cited in a lay sermon preached by J.A. Funk on January 4, 1987 at Grace Mennonite Church, Regina, Saskatchewan. Personal files of Louise (Toews) Friesen.

[64] See MHC Archives, vol.1163, file 5.

[65] David Toews, "Erinnerungen," 19.

[66] Ibid., 21.

[67] Ibid., 22.

[68] Frank H. Epp, *Mennonites in Canada, 1920–1940*, 163.

[69] Ibid., 161.

[70] J.G. Rempel, *Die Rosenorter Gemeinde in Saskatchewan*, 57f.

[71] Ibid., 58.

[72] Ibid., 96.

[73] Frank H. Epp, *Mennonite Exodus*, 82ff. This is the title of the chapter in which Epp introduced David Toews to his readers.

[74] John B. Toews, *Lost Fatherland: The Story of the Mennonite Emigration from Soviet Russia, 1921–1927* (Scottdale: Herald Press, 1967).

[75] See John B. Toews, *With Courage to Spare*, 108.

[76] Ibid., 108f.

Chapter 10. A Mennonite Moses 1923–1925

[1] Frank H. Epp, *Mennonite Exodus*, 139ff.

[2] The matter of persons kept back in Germany and in England because of disease is a sad chapter in the immigration story of the 1920s. During the first year of the immigration movement, 700 persons were held back. Some were allowed to proceed to Canada after a few weeks while others were detained for months, even years. A few remained in Germany for the rest of their lives.

[3] Frank H. Epp, *Mennonite Exodus*, 146.

[4] Ibid., 145.

[5] David Toews, "Erinnerungen," 25.

[6] Ibid., 26.

[7] Ibid., 26f.

[8] B.J. Schellenberg, "Ältester David Toews," 55.

[9] David Toews, "Erinnerungen," 27.

[10] David Toews to D.H. Bender, 21 September 1923, MHC Archives, vol.1163, file 4.

[11] In total, 124 Mennonite families comprised of 600 persons immigrated to Mexico from Russia between 1924 and 1929. Why did they go? The Mexican government had no medical restrictions and they had an open immigration policy, even when Canada's doors were closing. Eventually a considerable number came to Canada via Mexico. See Marianne Janzen, "Notes on the Emigration of Russian Mennonites to Mexico, 1924–1929," *Mennonite Historian* 16 (March 1990): 1f.

[12] Cornelius Krahn, "Central Mennonite Immigration Committee (Das zentrale mennonitische Immigrantenkomitee)" in *Mennonite Encyclopedia*, vol. I, 542–543.

[13] David Toews, "Ein Geleitwort," *Der mennonitische Immigranten-Bote* 1 (14 January 1924), 3.

[14] David Toews, "Erinnerungen," 28. See, further, David Toews to C.J. Andres, 4 October 1923, MHC Archives, vol.1163, file 5.

[15] J.G. Rempel, *Die Rosenorter Gemeinde in Saskatchewan*, 122f. Kaethe Hooge is one of only two women church workers featured in Rempel's history. The other is Clara Schellenberg of Hague, MCC worker in Mexico (ibid., 168).

[16] Esther Epp-Tiessen, *J.J. Thiessen: A Leader for His Time* (Winnipeg: CMBC Publications, 2001), 179f.

[17] J.G. Rempel, *Die Rosenorter Gemeinde in Saskatchewan*, 59.

[18] Ibid., 66.

[19] Hallman was bishop of the Alberta-Saskatchewan (Old) Mennonite Conference (later named the Northwest Mennonite Conference) and pastor of the Sharon Mennonite congregation at Guernsey, Saskatchewan.

[20] Throughout the work of the Canadian Mennonite Board of Colonization, it appears the (Old) Mennonites were involved in critical decisions of the Board. See Frank H. Epp, *Mennonite Exodus*, 154. This was the case again in June 1925 when Eli S. Hallman moved that the Board should incorporate.

[21] David Toews, "Erinnerungen," 29.

[22] Ibid.

[23] David Toews to S.F. Coffman (19 March 1924), MHC Archives, vol. 1165, file 13.

[24] J.G. Rempel, *Fünfzig Jahre Konferenzbestrebungen*, 164.

[25] Ibid.

[26] Frank H. Epp, *Education with a Plus*, 70.

[27] David Toews, "Willkommen in Canada!" *Der mennonitische Immigranten-Bote* 1 (13 August 1924), 2.

[28] David Toews, untitled, ibid., 1 (15 October 1924), 2.

[29] David Toews, "Nachklänge," *Der Bote* 2 (13 May 1925), 1ff.

[30] David Toews, "An die 1923–24 Eingewanderten," *Der Bote* 2 (18 March 1925), 3.

[31] David Toews, "Erneueter Aufruf," *Der Bote* 2 (8 July 1925), 2.

[32] David Toews, "Danke und Bitte," *Der Bote* 2 (9 September 1925), 1f.

[33] David Toews, "Erinnerungen," 38.

[34] Ibid.

[35] Ibid., 38f.

[36] David and Margarete Toews, untitled, *Der Bote* 2 (14 October 1925), 1.

[37] David Toews, "Kurzer Arbeitsbericht der Canadian Mennonite Board of Colonization," *Der Bote* 3 (10 February 1926), 1f.

[38] Ibid.

[39] The full statement of gratitude was printed in *Der Bote* 3 (27 January 1926), 3. A similar expression of gratitude was forwarded to A.A. Friesen, secretary of the Board (ibid., 3f.).

Chapter 11. Travel and Trouble 1926

[1] Three volumes of correspondence, mostly between Jacob H. Janzen and David Toews, bear testimony to the close association of these two men from the time that Janzen came to Canada in 1924 to the mid-1940s. See MHC Archives, volumes 1171–1173.

[2] David Toews, "Zur Veröffentlichung," *Der Bote* 3 (3 March 1926), 2.

[3] Jacob H. Janzen, "Mehrzahlbildung," *Der Bote* 3 (31 March, 1926), 2f. Janzen provided the date of February 24 for the meeting in the CPR offices, but it is more likely that the meeting occurred a week earlier, on February 17. This would correspond with Toews' travel schedule. The article carried the date of February 19, the day after Janzen would have returned home to Waterloo.

[4] David Toews, "Zur Veröffentlichung," 2.

[5] David Toews, "Erinnerungen," 40.

[6] Ibid.

[7] David Toews, "Kurzer Reisebericht," *Der Bote* 3 (5 May 1926), 2.

[8] Frank H. Epp, *Mennonite Exodus,* 39ff.

[9] Ibid., 41ff.

[10] David Toews, "Kurzer Reisebericht," *Der Bote* 3 (12 May 1926), 3.

[11] David Toews, "Erinnerungen," 42.

[12] David Toews, "Kurzer Reisebericht," *Der Bote* 3 (5 May 1926), 2.

[13] David Toews, "Erinnerungen," 44.

[14] Ibid., 46.

[15] David Toews, "Kurzer Reisebericht," *Der Bote* 3 (12 May 1926), 2ff.

[16] For an explanation of such incidents, see David Toews, "Erinnerungen," 48.

[17] Ibid., 46.

[18] Ibid., 47.

[19] Ibid.

[20] George P. Friesen, *The Fangs of Bolshevism or Friesen-Braun Trials in Saskatchewan, 1924–1929* (Saskatoon: George P. Friesen, 1930), 14ff.

[21] Ibid., 18.

[22] Frank H. Epp, *Mennonite Exodus*, 215.

[23] Ibid.

[24] Ibid.

[25] Ibid., 215f.

[26] David Toews, "Eine Erklärung," *Der Bote* 3 (17 November 1926), 3f.

[27] Ibid.

[28] David Toews, "Erinnerungen," 32.

[29] David Toews, "Aufruf und Erklärung," *Der Bote* 3 (30 June 1926), 3.

[30] Ibid.

[31] "Eine Erklärung," *Der Bote* 3 (30 June 1926), 4.

[32] J.G. Rempel, *Fünfzig Jahre Konferenzbestrebungen*, 187.

[33] Ibid.

[34] David Toews, "Weiteres zur Erklärung," *Der Bote* 3 (1 December 1926), 1f.

[35] David Toews, "Die Auswanderung aus Russland in der Vergangenheit und in der Zukunft," *Der Bote* 3 (15 December 1926), 2.

[36] Based on a personal conversation with Mary Harder, Fall 1999.

[37] David Toews, "Erinnerungen," 50. See also D.P. Enns, "Feuersbrunst in Rosthern," *Der Bote* 3 (22 December 1926), 5ff.

[38] Interview with Kaethe Hooge, August 2000, Eston, Saskatchewan.

[39] David Toews, "Erinnerungen," 5.

[40] Ibid.

Chapter 12. Immigration Ends 1927–1929

[1] "Aufruf an alle Immigrantenkinder," *Der Bote* 3 (15 December 1926), 5.

[2] Col. Dennis to David Toews, 14 December 1926, MHC Archives, vol.1183, file 135c.

[3] See file of letters in ibid., file 135.

[4] David Toews, "Margarete Toews," *Der Bote* 18 (16 July 1941), 4.

[5] David Toews to Franz Albrecht, Beatrice, Nebraska, 24 February 1927, MHC Archives, vol.1183, file 135a.

[6] David Toews to Johann Bueckert, 12 January 1927, ibid.

[7] David Toews to Franz Albrecht, 24 February 1927, ibid., file 135a.

[8] David Toews to B.S. Borneman, 11 March 1927, ibid., file 135b.

[9] F. Enns to David Toews, 26 December 1926, David Toews Project file.

[10] David Toews to John Epp, Whitewater, 27 April 1927, MHC Archives, file 135e.

[11] David Toews to C.F. Claassen, 11 March 1927, ibid., file 135c.

[12] David Toews, "Erinnerungen," 52.

[13] David Toews to John F. Dick, 20 January 1927, MHC Archives, vol.1183, file 135d.

[14] David Toews to Heinrich Ediger, Germany, 1 February 1927, ibid., file 135e.

[15] David Toews to John Epp, 27 February 1927, ibid.

[16] David Toews to Heinrich Ediger, 1 February 1927, ibid., file 135c.

[17] Frank H. Epp, *Mennonite Exodus*, 228.

[18] Ibid., 227f.

[19] Henry Paetkau, "Separation or Integration?: The Russian Mennonite Immigrant Community in Ontario, 1924–1945" (PhD dissertation, University of Western Ontario, 1986), 159ff.

[20] David Toews to his family, 2 April 1927 and 5 April 1927, personal files of Louise (Toews) Friesen.

[21] J.G. Rempel, *Fünfzig Jahre Konferenzbestrebungen*, 195f.

[22] Ibid., 200.

[23] David Toews, "Probleme und Bedürfnisse in unserer Immigrantenarbeit," *Der Bote* 4 (24 August 1927), 1.

[24] David Toews, "Erinnerungen," 52.

[25] David Toews, "Probleme und Bedürfnisse," 1.

[26] For letters, see MHC Archives, vol. 4673, file 61.

[27] David Toews, "Aus den Gemeinden für die Gemeinden," *Der Bote* 4 (21 December 1927), 1.

[28] David Toews, "Herzlichen Dank," *Der Bote* 5 (14 March 1928), 2.

[29] J.G. Rempel, *Die Rosenorter Gemeinde in Saskatchewan*, 99.

[30] As told to the author by Justina (Pankratz) Heese.

[31] J.G. Rempel, *Fünfzig Jahre Konferenzbestrebungen, Zweiter Teil* (Rosthern: Konferenz der Mennoniten in Canada, 1952), 244f. This second volume gives an account of the Conference of Mennonites in Canada annual sessions 26 to 50, 1928–1952.

[32] David Toews, "Einladung zur Konferenz," *Der Bote* 5 (20 June 1928), 2.

[33] David Toews, "Bericht über die Immigration," *Der Bote* 5 (5 September 1928), 1.

[34] *Konferenz-Bericht der 26. Konferenz der Mennoniten im mittleren Canada*, Rosthern, Saskatchewan, July 2–4, 1928, 8.

[35] David Toews to H.J. Braun, 20 September 1928, MHC Archives, vol. 1183.

[36] Frank H. Epp, *Mennonite Exodus*, 216. Epp quotes a letter from David Toews to John C. Miller, 3 October 1927: "I can say with an honest conscience that we have neither in private or as a Board had anything to do with [the case] or now have, except that A.A. Friesen and I were called to witness. . . . I have emphasized again and again that only God and these two [Braun and Friesen] know how this situation is" (216, footnote 34).

[37] J.G. Rempel, *Fünfzig Jahre Konferenzbestrebungen, Zweiter Teil*, 222.

[38] Ibid., 215.

[39] For a full report of this GC session, see *The Mennonite* 44 (29 August 1929).

[40] David Toews, "Mennonite Immigration to Canada in the Future," ibid., 3.

[41] Ibid., *The Mennonite* 44 (5 September 1929), 4.

[42] Ibid.

[43] David Toews, "Gedanken und Erinnerungen," *Der Bote* 6 (9 October 1929), 2.

[44] J.G. Rempel, *Die Rosenorter Gemeinde in Saskatchewan*, 62.

[45] Ibid., 63f.

[46] Ibid., 64f.

[47] Ibid., 65.

[48] Ibid., 66.

[49] Ibid., 66. For a detailed account of the relationships and dynamics involved, see Walter Klaassen, *The Days of Our Years*, 77–82.

[50] Esther Epp-Tiessen, *J.J. Thiessen: A Leader for His Time*, 82ff.

[51] Ibid., 88ff.

[52] Ibid., 91f.

[53] Ibid., 105f.

[54] J.J. Thiessen to David Toews, 2 September 1929, MHC Archives, vol. 30, file 30.

[55] Ein Zuhörer, "Ein Besuch beim Premierminister," *Der Bote* 6 (11 April, 1929), 2. This article was submitted by an unnamed person identified as "a listener" to David Toews' report.

[56] David Toews to his family, 10 March 1929, personal files of Louise (Toews) Friesen.

[57] David Toews, "Dringender Aufruf und Bitte," *Der Bote* 6 (4 November 1929), 2.

[58] For a detailed account of this unfortunate episode in Mennonite refugee history, see Frank H. Epp, *Mennonite Exodus,* 221–277.

Chapter 13. Relief Work Begins 1930–1931

[1] David Toews, et al., "An alle Mennonitengemeinden Canadas!" *Der Bote* 7 (5 March 1930), 1.

[2] David Toews to Thomas B. Appleget, 24 March 1930, MHC Archives, vol. 1163, file 1.

[3] *Konferenz-Bericht der 20. Konferenz der Mennoniten im mittleren Canada*, Winkler, Manitoba, Juli 7–9, 1930 (Winnipeg: Rundschau Publishing House, 1930), 28f.

[4] David Toews, "Reise- und Konferenzbericht," *Der Bote* 7 (29 October 1930), 1.

[5] Ibid.

[6] David Toews to his family, Toronto, Ontario, 12 August 1930, personal files of Louise (Toews) Friesen.

[7] Idem., Quebec City, Quebec, 19 August 1930, ibid.

[8] Idem., on the high seas, 24 August 1930, ibid.

[9] Ibid.

[10] Ibid.

[11] David Toews to his family, Hamburg, Germany, 29 August 1930, ibid.

[12] Ibid.

[13] B.J. Schellenberg, "Ältester David Toews," 70.

[14] David Toews to his family, Berlin, Germany, 4 September 1930, personal files of Louise (Toews) Friesen.

[15] David Toews, "An alle Gemeinden," *Der Bote* 7 (22 October 1930), 1.

[16] David Toews to his family, Berlin, Germany.

[17] David Toews, "Reise- und Konferenzbericht," *Der Bote* 7 (5 November 1930), 2.

[18] Idem., *Der Bote* 7 (19 November 1930), 1.

[19] Idem., *Der Bote* 7 (29 October 1930), 2.

[20] David Toews to Rev. Dr. J. Chisholm, Rosthern, Saskatchewan, 4 October 1930, MHC Archives, vol. 1164, file 8.

[21] David Toews to William Borak, Rosthern, Saskatchewan, 8 May 1931, MHC Archives, vol. 1163, file 4.

[22] "Protokoll der Provinzialen Versammlung der seit 1923 eingewanderten Mennoniten," Hague, Saskatchewan, July 15–16, 1931, *Der Bote* 8 (2 September 1931), 3.

[23] David Toews to John P. Andres, Elbing, Kansas, 19 October 1931, MHC Archives, vol. 1163, file 1.

[24] David Toews, "Nicht müde werden," *Der Bote* 9 (13 January 1932), 1.

[25] David Toews, "Etwas über unsere Flüchtlinge," *Der Bote* 8 (27 May 1931), 1.

[26] David Toews to Alvah Bowman, 4 December 1930, MHC Archives, vol. 1164, file 7.

[27] David Toews, "Bitte um Hilfe," *Der Bote* 7 (10 December 1930), 1.

[28] David Toews to Alvah Bowman, 22 October 1931, MHC Archives, vol. 1164, file 7.

[29] J.G. Rempel, *Die Rosenorter Gemeinde in Saskatchewan*, 90.

[30] David Toews to W.S. Gottschalk, 25 October 1930, MHC Archives, vol. 896, file 252.

[31] Idem., 29 December 1930, ibid.

[32] Idem., 31 January 1931, ibid., file 253. Obviously, "cenjure" is a misspelling of "censure."

[33] W.S. Gottschalk to David Toews, 6 February 1931, ibid.

[34] See, for example, J.J. Thiessen to David Toews, 12 June 1931, ibid.

[35] Frank H. Epp, *Education with a Plus*, 102.

[36] David Toews to J.J. Thiessen, 30 May 1931, MHC Archives, vol. 896, file 253.

[37] Idem., 3 September 1931, ibid.

[38] David Toews to his family, Ottawa, Ontario, 7 March 1931, personal files of Louise (Toews) Friesen.

[39] Ibid.

[40] Ibid.

[41] A substantial volume of correspondence between David Toews and Jacob H. Janzen bears evidence of the supportive relationship these two ministers enjoyed. See MHC Archives, vol. 1172, files 62–63 and vol. 1173, files 64–66.

[42] Frank H. Epp, *Mennonite Exodus*, 57.

[43] David Toews to his family, Philadelphia, Pennsylvania, 17 March 1931, personal files of Louise (Toews) Friesen.

[44] J.G. Rempel, *Fünfzig Jahre Konferenzbestrebungen, Zweiter Teil*, 254.

[45] David Toews to J.J. Thiessen, 20 July 1931, MHC Archives, vol. 896, file 253.

[46] David Toews to his family, 11 August 1931, personal files of Louise (Toews) Friesen.

[47] David Toews to J.J. Thiessen, 7 October 1931, ibid.

[48] B.J. Schellenberg, "Ältester David Toews," 72.

[49] J.J. Thiessen to Isaak P. Friesen, 11 May 1932, MHC Archives, vol. 896, file 254.

[50] David Toews to J.J. Thiessen, 3 February 1932, ibid.

[51] Idem., 9 February 1932, ibid.

Chapter 14. Some Laurels But No Rest 1932–1935

[1] B.J. Schellenberg, "Ältester David Toews," 72.

[2] *Bericht über die 30. Allgemeine Konferenz der Mennoniten in Canada,* Laird Saskatchewan, July 11–13, 1932 (Rosthern: D.H. Epp, 1932), 19.

[3] B.J. Schellenberg, "Ältester David Toews," 72.

[4] David Toews, "Die neuesten Wanderungen unseres Volkes und die Hilfe in Russland," *Der Bote* 9 (20 July 1932), 3.

[5] Ibid.

[6] David Toews, "Etwas Weiteres zum Nachdenken," *Der Bote* 9 (13 April 1932), 1.

[7] Provincial Committee of Manitoba, "Wer ist nun mein Nächster?" *Der Bote* 10 (1 March 1933), 1. Here, David Toews is quoted with respect to this information.

[8] David Toews, "Aufmunterung zur Mithilfe für unsere Nervenkranke," *Der Bote* 10 (13 December 1933), 2.

[9] David Toews to his family, 22 February 1932, personal files of Louise (Toews) Friesen.

[10] David Toews to his family, 1 March 1932, ibid.

[11] Idem., 7 June 1934, ibid.

[12] David Toews to John Becker, 27 December 1932, MHC Archives, vol. 1163, file 4.

[13] J.J. Thiessen to David Toews, 17 August, 1932, MHC Archives, vol. 896, file 254; David Toews, "Paketversand in der Sovietunion," *Der Bote* 9 (1 June 1932), 1.

[14] David Toews, "Brüder in Not," *Der Bote* 9 (5 October 1932), 1.

[15] David Toews, "Ein Neujahrsgruss," *Der Bote* 10 (4 January 1933), 1.

[16] David Toews, "Notizen über das Hilfswerk in Russland," *Der Bote* 10 (17 May 1933), 1.

[17] David Toews, "Russlandshilfe," *Der Bote* 12 (2 October 1935), 3.

[18] J.G. Rempel, *Die Rosenorter Gemeinde in Saskatchewan,* 95ff.

[19] David Toews, "Unser Problem," *Der Bote* 10 (24 May 1933), 1.

[20] J.G. Rempel, *Die Rosenorter Gemeinde in Saskatchewan,* 96.

[21] David Toews, "Zur freundlichen Beachtung unserer canadischen Gemeinden," *Der Bote* 11 (3 October 1934), 1.

[22] David Toews to Mrs. Brett-Perring, 1 September 1934, MHC Archives, vol. 1163, file 4.

[23] Quoted by Jacob H. Janzen, *David Toews: Vorsitzender,* 16.

[24] J.J. Thiessen to David Toews, 3 October 1932, MHC Archives, vol. 896, file 254.

[25] David Toews to J.J. Thiessen, 6 October 1932, ibid.

[26] J.J. Thiessen to David Toews, 26 September 1933, ibid., file 255.

[27] Idem., 5 January 1934, ibid., file 256.

[28] David Toews to J.J. Thiessen, 6 January 1934, ibid.

[29] Idem., 7 July 1934., ibid.

[30] *Mädchenheim* residents to David Toews, 20 December 1934, ibid.

[31] David Toews, "Weiteres zum Nachdenken," *Der Bote* 10 (27 September 1933), 2.

[32] J.J. Thiessen to David Toews, 8 February 1933, MHC Archives, vol. 896, file 255.

[33] David Toews to J.J. Thiessen, 9 February 1933, ibid.

[34] David Toews to Henry Fieguth, 5 December 1933, personal files of Louise (Toews) Friesen.

[35] J.J. Thiessen to David Toews, 5 September 1934, MHC Archives, vol. 896, file 256.

[36] David Toews to J.J. Thiessen, 6 June 1932, ibid., file 254.

[37] Frank H. Epp, *Education with a Plus*, 104.

[38] David Toews to J.J. Thiessen, 2 May 1934, MHC Archives, vol. 896, file 256.

[39] David Toews, "Unsere Deutsche-Englische Fortbildungsschule," *Der Bote* 12 (18 December 1935), 2.

[40] David Toews, "Unsere Schule," *Der Bote* 13 (22 January 1936), 1.

[41] David Toews, "Eine Erklärung und Bitte," *Der Bote* 10 (7 June 1933), 1.

[42] David Toews, "Zur Beachtung," *Der Bote* 11 (24 October 1934), 3.

[43] David Toews, "Über unsere Reiseschuld," *Der Bote* 12 (11 December 1935), 4.

[44] Helena Goossen Friesen is the author of *Daydreams and Nightmares: Life on the Wintergruen Estate* (Winnipeg: CMBC Publications, 1990).

[45] A.A. Friesen to David Toews, Rabbit Lake, Saskatchewan, April 1935, MHC Archives, vol. 1168, file 34a.

[46] Dietrich H. Epp, "Sitzung der Canadian Mennonite Board of Colonization," *Der Bote* 11 (8 August 1934), 1f. Editor D.H. Epp commented on the issue in this report.

[47] A.A. Friesen to David Toews, 18 September 1935, MHC Archives, vol. 1168, file 34a.

[48] David Toews to A.A. Friesen, 6 November 1935, ibid.

[49] J.H. Janzen, "Erinnerungen an A.A. Friesen und David Toews," *Mennonitisches Jahrbuch* 65 (1950): 18–24.

[50] David Toews, "Bericht über die 27. allgemeine Konferenz," *Der Bote* 12 (11 September 1935), 1f.

[51] Ibid., 2.

[52] David Toews to his family, 7 August 1935, personal files of Louise (Toews) Friesen.

[53] Kaethe Hooge to J.J. Thiessen, 17 July 1933, MHC Archives, vol. 896, file 255.

[54] David Toews to J.J. Thiessen, 10 February 1936, ibid., file 258.

Chapter 15. Third Trip to Europe 1936–1938

[1] For a report on this trip and on the conference in Amsterdam, see a series of articles by David Toews, "Reisebericht," *Der Bote* 13 (2, 9, 16, 30 September 1936).

[2] Frank H. Epp, *Mennonites in Canada, 1920–1940*, 240.

[3] David Toews, "Reisebericht," *Der Bote* 13 (2 September 1936), 2.

[4] Ibid., 3.

[5] David Toews, "Reisebericht," *Der Bote* 13 (9 September 1936), 2.

[6] Quoted in Frank H. Epp, *Mennonites in Canada, 1920–1940*, 331.

[7] David Toews, "Eine Bitte," *Der Bote* 13 (28 October 1936), 4.

[8] David Toews, "Erneuter Ruf," *Der Bote* 14 (3 February 1937), 4.

[9] J.A. Toews, *Alternative Service in Canada during World War II* (Winnipeg: The Christian Press, 1979), 28f.

[10] David Toews to Margarete Toews, 9 July 1936, personal files of Louise (Toews) Friesen.

[11] David Toews, "Einige Reiseeindrücke," *Der Bote* 13 (30 September 1936), 1ff.

[12] David Toews to his family, 30 October 1936, personal files of Louise (Toews) Friesen.

[13] J.J. Thiessen to David Toews, 8 February 1937, MHC Archives, vol. 896, file 259.

[14] David Toews to his family, 30 October 1936.

[15] David Toews, "Ein Weihnachtsgruss," *Der Bote* 14 (22 December 1937), 3.

[16] *Jahrbuch 1938 der Allgemeinen Konferenz der Mennoniten in Canada*, Eigenheim, Saskatchewan, July 29, 1938 (Rosthern: D.H. Epp, 1938), 36.

[17] Ed G. Kaufman to David Toews, 16 December 1937, MHC Archives, vol. 4387.

[18] David Toews to Ed G. Kaufman, 24 December 1937, ibid.

[19] Ibid.

[20] Ed G. Kaufman to David Toews, 7 January 1938, ibid.

[21] Idem., 27 April 1938, ibid.

[22] Quoted in Frank H. Epp, *Education with a Plus*, 114f.

[23] J.J. Thiessen to David Toews, 6 June 1938, MHC Archives, vol. 896, file 260.

[24] Jacob H. Janzen, *David Toews, Vorsitzender*, 17.

[25] J.G. Rempel, *Fünfzig Jahre Konferenzbestrebungen, Zweiter Teil*, 299.

[26] J.G. Rempel, *Die Rosenorter Gemeinde in Saskatchewan*, 99f.

[27] J.J. Thiessen to David Toews, 13 July 1936, MHC Archives, vol. 896, file 258.

[28] J.G. Rempel, *Die Rosenorter Gemeinde in Saskatchewan*, 100.

[29] Ibid.

[30] D.H. Epp, "Festtag der Rosenorter Gemeinde," *Der Bote* 15 (28 September 1938), 1.

[31] See the collection of letters and telegrams in the album, "Ältester David Toews zum Jubiläum von Freunden nah und fern," MHC Archives, vol. 4387.

[32] David Toews, "Die Zeitungskontraverse wegen der Wehrlosigkeit," *Der Bote* 15 (21 September 1938), 1.

[33] David Toews, "Unsere Reiseschuld," *Der Bote* 15 (9 November 1938), 2.

[34] Frank H. Epp, *Education with a Plus*, 107.

[35] J.G. Rempel, *Die Rosenorter Gemeinde in Saskatchewan*, 113.

[36] Frank H. Epp, *Education with a Plus*, 115.

[37] David Toews, "Wir und die Reiseschuld," *Der Bote* 13 (13 May 1936), 1f.

[38] J.G. Rempel, *Die Rosenorter Gemeinde in Saskatchewan*, 94.

[39] David Toews, "Unsere Schuld," *Der Bote* 14 (2 June 1937), 1f.

[40] J.G. Rempel, *Die Rosenorter Gemeinde in Saskatchewan*, 118.

[41] David Toews, "Col. J.S. Dennis," *Der Bote* 15 (21 December 1938), 3f.

[42] Ibid. It is beyond the scope of this biography to provide an account and a critique of the role played by the CPR official Col. John Stoughton Dennis in his earlier years. Both he and his father of the same name were active in promoting the policies and strategies that evoked the Riel rebellions of 1869–1870 and 1885. The younger Dennis earned his rank as Colonel when he commanded the Dennis Scouts in the 1885 Rebellion (cf., Frank H. Epp, *Mennonite Exodus*, 109f.). On the context in which the senior J.S. Dennis was active, see, for example, Marcel Giraud, *The Metis in the Canadian West*, vol. II, trans. George Woodcock (Edmonton: The University of Alberta Press, 1986), 367ff.; and Gerald Friesen, *The Canadian Prairies: A History* (Toronto: University of Toronto Press, 1984), 91ff. An awareness of the respective roles played by father and son in Canadian-Metis history may well cause Mennonites to modify the unqualified accolades offered to Col. Dennis as their benefactor. In this connection, a general recounting of the

nineteenth- century history of the conflict over land in the Canadian west provides a sobering note to the story of the settlement of Mennonites in the Canadian West in the 1920s. There is little, if any, reference to this (pre-Mennonite) history in the writings of David Toews. See Walter Klaassen, *The Days of Our Years*, 3–7 for an excellent account of aboriginal and Metis history in the prairie region.

Chapter 16. War and Death 1939–1941

[1] J.A. Toews, *Alternate Service in Canada*, 14f.

[2] Ibid., 19.

[3] David Warren Fransen, "Canadian Mennonites and Conscientious Objection in World War II" (MA thesis, University of Waterloo, 1977), 23.

[4] Frank H. Epp, *Mennonites in Canada, 1920–1940*, 57.

[5] T.D. Regehr, *Mennonites in Canada, 1939–1970: A People Transformed* (Toronto: University of Toronto Press, 1996), 39. Regehr's book is the third volume of the trilogy, *Mennonites in Canada.*

[6] Frank H. Epp, *Mennonites in Canada, 1920–1940*, 157.

[7] David Fransen, "Canadian Mennonites and Conscientious Objection," 21ff.

[8] Ibid., 24.

[9] J.A. Toews, *Alternative Service in Canada*, 32f.

[10] Ibid., 33.

[11] T.D. Regehr, *Mennonites in Canada, 1939–1970*, 39.

[12] David P. Reimer, *Experiences of the Mennonites of Canada during the Second World War, 1939–1945* (Altona: D.W. Friesen & Sons., n.d.), 52.

[13] T.D. Regehr, *Mennonites in Canada, 1939–1970*, 40.

[14] J.A. Toews, *Alternative Service in Canada*, 34.

[15] See David Toews' letter addressed to Bishop Wilhelm Falk of the Rudnerweide Church in Altona (David Fransen, "Canadian Mennonites and Conscientious Objection," 38f.). See also Fransen's report of David Toews' attempt to persuade B.B. Janz to proceed slowly with his idea of non-combatant military service (ibid., 39f.).

[16] Ibid., 42f.

[17] "Protokoll der Mennonitischen Provinzialen Versammlung," Altona, Manitoba, 12 January 1940, 2, MHC Archives, vol. 606, file 6.

[18] Ibid., minute 17.

[19] "Kurzgefasstes Protokoll der Mennonitischen Versammlung," Saskatoon, Saskatchewan, 19 January 1940, 9, ibid.

[20] Ibid., Coaldale, Alberta, 30 January 1940, 12, ibid.

[21] Ibid., Yarrow, British Columbia, 5 February 1940, 16, ibid.

[22] David Toews, "Aufruf an alle Mennonitengemeinden im Westen Canadas," *Der Bote* 17 (3 April 1940), 2.

[23] David Fransen, "Canadian Mennonites and Conscientious Objection," 67.

[24] Ibid., 69.

[25] Ibid., 70.

[26] T.D. Regehr, *Mennonites in Canada, 1939–1970*, 49ff.

[27] David Toews to J.J. Thiessen, 24 April 1939, MHC Archives, vol. 896, file 261.

[28] Letter to the editor, *Saskatoon Star-Phoenix* (6 May 1939), 6

[29] Ibid.

[30] Ibid.

[31] J.J. Thiessen to David Toews, 9 May 1939, MHC Archives, vol. 896, file 261.

[32] David Toews, "Eine Bekanntmachung," *Der Bote* 17 (31 July 1940), 3.

[33] David Toews, "Zur Bekanntmachung," *Der Bote* 17 (14 August 1940), 3.

[34] See, for example, Benjamin Wall Redekop, "The German Identity of Mennonite Brethren Immigrants in Canada, 1930–1960" (MA (History) thesis, University of British Columbia, 1990), 36.

[35] Frank H. Epp, *Mennonite Exodus*, 327f.

[36] David Toews to J.J. Thiessen, 31 May 1939, MHC Archives, vol. 896, file 261.

[37] Idem., 2 October 1939, ibid.

[38] J.J. Thiessen to David Toews, 4 October 1939, ibid.

[39] Ibid.

[40] David Toews, "Offener Brief an unsere Jünglinge," *Der Bote* 18 (12 February 1941), 1.

[41] David Toews, "An unsere Jünglinge," *Der Bote* 18 (19 March 1941), 3.

[42] David Toews, "Eine Erklärung in Bezug auf militärische Übungen," *Der Bote* 18 (3 December 1941), 3.

[43] Ibid.

[44] J.J. Thiessen to David Toews, 17 April 1942; David Toews to J.J. Thiessen, 18 April 1942, MHC Archives, vol. 896, file 264.

[45] J.J. Thiessen to David Toews, 12 May 1942, ibid.

[46] David Toews to J.J. Thiessen, 13 May 1942, ibid.

[47] J.J. Thiessen to David Toews, 14 September 1939, ibid., file 261.

[48] David Toews, "Unsere Fortbildungsschule zu Rosthern—ein Faktor im Kampf für unsere Eigenart," *Der Bote* 18 (18 June 1941), 1.

[49] It may be noted parenthetically, that here Toews may well have been expressing profound appreciation for his upbringing and for the hardships his parents suffered in their effort to find a "place of refuge" where they could practise their convictions for the sake of their children.

[50] David Toews, "Bericht der CMBC," *Der Bote* 17 (21 February 1940), 5.

[51] David Toews, "Zu unserer Hilfssache," *Der Bote* 17 (29 May 1940), 1.

[52] David Toews, "An unsere Nähvereine," *Der Bote* 17 (4 September 1940), 1f.

[53] David Toews and C.F. Klassen, "An alle Mennonitengemeinden in Westcanada," ibid., 2.

[54] David Toews, "Zu unsrem Hilfswerk," *Der Bote* 18 (29 January 1941), 3.

[55] J.G. Rempel, *Fünfzig Jahre Konferenzbestrebungen, Zweiter Teil*, 324; J.G. Rempel, *Die Rosenorter Gemeinde in Saskatchewan*, 105ff.

[56] MHC Archives, David Toews biography research file.

[57] J.G. Rempel, *Fünfzig Jahre Konferenzbestrebungen, Zweiter Teil*, 325.

[58] J.J. Thiessen to David Toews, 6 June 1940, MHC Archives, vol. 896, file 262.

[59] David Toews, "Zur Kenntnisnahme," *Der Bote* 17 (16 October 1940), 3.

[60] J.J. Thiessen to Margarete Toews, 26 November 1940, MHC Archives, vol. 896, file 262.

[61] David and Margarete Toews, "An alle lieben Freunde nah und fern," *Der Bote* 17 (25 December 1940), 3.

[62] David Toews to J.J. Thiessen, 2 April 1941, MHC Archives, vol. 896, file 263.

[63] Idem., 5 May 1941, ibid.

[64] Idem., 3 June 1941, ibid.

[65] The obituary can be found in *Der Bote* 18 (16 July 1941), 4.

[66] Louise (Toews) Friesen, "Mother Strong Pillar in Family," *Saskatchewan Mennonite Historian* 2 (December 1997): 16.

[67] J.J. Thiessen to David Toews, 29 July 1941, MHC Archives, vol. 896, file 263.

[68] Idem., 5 August 1941, ibid.

[69] David Toews, "Bericht," *Der Bote* 18 (24 September 1941), 1f.

[70] David Toews to J.J. Thiessen, 6 September 1941, MHC Archives, vol. 896, file 263.

[71] J.J. Thiessen to David Toews, 1 October 1941, ibid.

Chapter 17. Winding Down 1942–1944

[1] J.A. Toews, *Alternative Service in Canada*, 51.

[2] Ibid., 54.

[3] Ibid., 52f.

[4] J.J. Thiessen to David Toews, 9 February 1942, MHC Archives, vol. 897, file 264.

[5] J.G. Rempel, *Fünfzig Jahre Konferenzbestrebungen, Zweiter Teil*, 340.

[6] David Toews, "In Gelegenheit unserer Reiseschuld," *Der Bote* 19 (19 August 1942), 3.

[7] David Toews, "Ein offenes Wort an die Gemeinde," *Der Bote* 19 (26 August 1942), 4.

[8] David Toews to J.J. Thiessen, 22 September 1942, MHC Archives, vol. 897, file 264.

[9] David Toews, "In Angelegenheit der Dienstfrage," *Der Bote* 19 (25 November 1942), 1.

[10] David Toews to his family, 24 November 1942, personal files of Louise (Toews) Friesen.

[11] D. Hausknecht to David Toews, 8 December 1942, MHC Archives, vol. 897, file 264.

[12] J.J. Thiessen, "Wie befindet sich Ältester Töws, Rosthern?" *Der Bote* 19 (23 December 1942), 2f.

[13] J.J. Thiessen to A.J. Neuenschwander, 16 February 1943, MHC Archives, vol. 897, file 265.

[14] David Toews to J.J. Thiessen, 17 April 1943, ibid.

[15] Idem., 4 March 1943, ibid.

[16] J.J. Thiessen to David Toews, 6 March 1943, ibid.

[17] David Toews to J.J. Thiessen, 23 March 1943, ibid.

[18] Idem., 21 December 1943, ibid.

[19] J.J. Thiessen to David Toews, 3 January 1944, ibid., file 266.

[20] Idem., 8 February 1944, ibid.

[21] David Toews to J.J. Thiessen, 19 July 1945, ibid., file 267.

[22] J.J. Thiessen to David Toews, 29 November 1945, ibid.

[23] Idem., 1 December 1945, ibid.

[24] David Toews to J.J. Thiessen, 13 May 1944, ibid., file 266.

[25] J.J. Thiessen to David Toews, 15 May 1944, ibid.

[26] David Toews to J.J. Thiessen, 1 November 1943, ibid., file 265.

[27] Idem., 21 February 1944, ibid., file 266.

[28] Idem., 5 April 1944, ibid.

[29] David Toews, "Tagebuch, 1942–1944," MHC Archives, vol. 300.

[30] David Toews to J.J. Thiessen, 31 July 1944, MHC Archives, vol. 897, file 266.

[31] J.J. Thiessen to David Toews, 2 August 1944, ibid.

[32] Frank H. Epp, *Education with a Plus*, 143.

[33] J.J. Thiessen to David Toews, 16 July 1945; 27 August 1945, MHC Archives, vol. 897, file 267.

[34] David Toews, "Erklärung," *Der Bote* 21 (7 June 1944), 4.

[35] David Toews, "Zur Kenntnisnahme," *Der Bote* 22 (2 May 1945), 3.

[36] David Toews, "Ein Aufruf an unser Volk," *Der Bote* 22 (7 March 1945), 4.

[37] David Toews to J.J. Thiessen, 6 August 1945, MHC Archives, vol. 897, file 267.

[38] Interview with Louise (Toews) and Blake Friesen, Calgary, Alberta.

[39] The wedding sermon is contained in a collection of mostly undated sermons of the 1940s, contained in two notebooks, and belonging to the personal family collection of Louise (Toews) Friesen.

[40] At the time of writing, two Toews daughters, Louise and Anna, together with their husbands, Blake Friesen and Sylvester Funk, respectively, are the surviving children and sons-in-law of David and Margarete Toews.

Chapter 18. Bringing Closure 1945–1946

[1] T.D. Regehr, *Mennonites in Canada, 1939–1970*, 60.

[2] *Jahrbuch der Konferenz der Mennoniten in Canada,* 1945 (Rosthern, 1945), 110ff.

[3] Ibid., 91ff.

[4] David Toews, "Zur Kenntnisnahme," *Der Bote* 23 (17 April 1946), 1.

[5] Ibid.

[6] J.G. Rempel, *Die Rosenorter Gemeinde in Saskatchewan*, 120.

[7] David Toews, "Erinnerung an einen Konferenzbeschluss," *Der Bote* 21 (26 July 1944), 2. For an account of the emergence of Bethel Mission Church within the General Conference context, see Lois Barrett, *The Vision and the Reality: The Story of Home Missions in the General Conference Mennonite Church* (Newton: Faith and Life Press, 1983), 133–135.

[8] David Toews to J.J. Thiessen, 4 August 1944, MHC Archives, vol. 897, file 266.

[9] Idem., 27 February 1945, ibid., file 267.

[10] Ibid.

[11] David Toews to J.J. Thiessen, 22 May 1945, ibid.

[12] Idem., 18 June 1945, ibid.

[13] Ibid.

[14] J.J. Thiessen to David Toews, 25 February 1946, ibid., file 268.

[15] "Rev. David Toews Resigns," *The Mennonite* 61 (3 September 1946), 4.

[16] J.G. Rempel, *Die Rosenorter Gemeinde in Saskatchewan*, 147f.

[17] Ibid., 133.

[18] Ibid., 148.

[19] Ibid., 149f.

[20] *Jahrbuch der Konferenz der Mennoniten in Canada,* 1944 (Rosthern: D.H. Epp, 1944), 18.

[21] David Toews, "Unsere Reiseschuld," *Der Bote* 22 (12 September 1945), 3.

[22] David Toews, "Eine Bitte an alle mennonitischen Gemeinden," *Der Bote* 23 (24 April 1946), 1.

[23] J.J. Thiessen, "Bericht der Canadian Mennonite Board of Colonization," in *Jahrbuch der Konferenz der Mennoniten in Canada,* 1946 (Rosthern: D.H. Epp, 1946), 131f.

[24] Ibid.

Chapter 19. Rest at Last 1947

[1] J.J. Thiessen, "Fröhliche Weihnachten und ein glückliches Neujahr," *Der Bote* 23 (18 December 1946), 2f.

[2] J.G. Rempel, "Eine Bitte," *Der Bote* 24 (1 January 1947), 2.

[3] B.J. Schellenberg, "Ältester David Toews," 77f.

[4] The quotation of 2 Timothy 4:7–8 is from the King James Version, which is the English version of the Scriptures that would have been familiar to David Toews.

[5] J.J. Thiessen, "Funeral Sermon," *Saskatchewan Valley News* (5 March 1947). See original "Leichenrede" manuscript in MHC Archives, vol. 895, file 251.

Chapter 20. Legacy

[1] Toews Lake, about two and a half miles long, is located in the Geiko River area 256 kilometres north of La Ronge in northern Saskatchewan. The Department of Natural Resources of the Province of Saskatchewan took the initiative in making this gesture.

[2] The main criticisms of Toews with respect to his work as chairman and director of the Canadian Mennonite Board of Colonization were that he was not an exacting administrator and was at times too defensive when the Board came under criticism.

[3] Whether totally justified or not, it is a fact that accolades abound among *Russländer* Mennonites for the work of David Toews. See, for example the statement of B.J. Schellenberg: "This simple man of faith has carried out a rescue operation where men of politics, of finances, of intelligence would have faltered." B.J. Schellenberg, "Ältester David Toews," 74.

[4] J.G. Rempel, "Die Rosenorter Gemeinde unter Ältesten David Töws," *Der Bote* 27 (24 May 1950), 5.

[5] This sense of historic continuity extended into the second half of the twentieth century by way of the long tenure of J.J. Thiessen as subsequent chairman of the Conference (1943–1959). But in the late 1950s constitutional stipulations had been introduced that limited the terms of office for elected conference officials. See Esther Epp-Tiessen, *J.J. Thiessen: A Leader for His Time,* 252ff. There was the feeling among some that the earlier practice of extended terms of office was no longer appropriate.

[6] J.M. Regier, "David Toews—Nachruf und Erinnerungen," *Der Bote* 24 (9 April 1947), 2.

[7] B. B. Janz, "Die Grundlage der groszen Auswanderung aus Russland in den 20ger Jahren," *Mennonitische Rundschau* 84 (30 August 1961), 2.

[8] G.G. Neufeld, "Nachruf," *Der Bote* 24 (4 June 1947), 2.

Bibliography and Resources

Books

Barrett, Lois. *The Vision and the Reality: The Story of Home Missions in the General Conference Mennonite Church*. Newton: Faith and Life Press, 1983.

Bartsch, Franz. *Our Trek to Central Asia*, trans. Elisabeth Peters and Gerhard Ens. Winnipeg: CMBC Publications, 1993. Translation of *Unser Ausgang nach Mittelasien*. Halbstadt: H.J.Braun, 1907.

Belk, Fred Richard. *The Great Trek of the Russian Mennonites to Central Asia, 1880–1884*. Studies in Anabaptist and Mennonite History, no. 18. Scottdale and Kitchener: Herald Press, 1976.

Doell, Leonard. *Mennonite Homesteaders on the Hague-Osler Reserve*. Saskatoon: Mennonite Historical Society of Saskatchewan, 1999.

Dyck, Cornelius J. *Twelve Becoming: Biographies of Mennonite Disciples from the Sixteenth to the Twentieth Century*. Newton: Faith and Life Press, 1973.

Dyck, Johannes J. and W.E. Surukin, trans. Hermina Joldersma and Peter J. Dyck. *Am Trakt: A Mennonite Settlement in the Central Volga Region*. Winnipeg: CMBC Publications, 1995. Translation of *Am Trakt: Eine mennonitische Kolonie im mittleren Wolgagebiet*. North Kildonan, Echo Verlag, 1948.

Ens, Gerhard J. *"Die Schule muss sein": A History of the Mennonite Collegiate Institute, 1889–1989*. Gretna: Mennonite Collegiate Institute, 1990.

Epp, Frank H. *Education with a Plus: The Story of Rosthern Junior College*. Waterloo: Conrad Press, 1975.

Epp, Frank H. *Mennonite Exodus: The Rescue and Resettlement of the Russian Mennonites since the Communist Revolution*. Altona: D.W. Friesen & Sons, Ltd., 1962.

Epp, Frank H. *Mennonites in Canada, 1786–1920: The History of a Separate People*. Toronto: Macmillan of Canada, 1974.

Epp, Frank H. *Mennonites in Canada, 1920–1940: A People's Struggle for Survival*. Toronto: Macmillan of Canada, 1982.

Epp-Tiessen, Esther. *J.J. Thiessen: A Leader for His Time*. Winnipeg: CMBC Publications, 2001.

Francis, E.K. *In Search of Utopia: The Mennonites in Manitoba*. Altona: D.W. Friesen and Sons Ltd., 1955.

Friesen, George P. *The Fangs of Bolshevism, or Friesen-Braun Trials in Saskatchewan, 1924–1929.* Saskatoon: George P. Friesen, 1930.

Friesen, Gerald. *The Canadian Prairies: A History.* Toronto: University of Toronto Press, 1984.

Friesen, Helena Goossen. *Daydreams and Nightmares: Life on the Wintergruen Estate.* Winnipeg: CMBC Publications, 1990.

Friesen, Helene Sarah. *David Toews: A Brief Sketch of his Life and Work, 1870–1947.* Winnipeg: Mennonite Heritage Centre, 1997.

Gerbrandt, Henry J. *Adventure in Faith: The Background in Europe and the Development in Canada of the Bergthaler Mennonite Church of Manitoba.* Altona: D.W. Friesen & Sons, 1970.

Giraud, Marcel. *The Metis in the Canadian West,* vol. II, trans. George Woodcock. Edmonton: The University of Alberta Press, 1986.

Hague-Osler Mennonite Reserve, 1895–1995. Saskatoon: Hague-Osler Reserve Book Committee, 1995.

Janzen, Jacob H. *David Toews: Vorsitzender der Kolonisations-behoerde der Mennoniten in Canada: Biographische Skizze.* Rosthern: D.H. Epp, 1939.

Klaassen, H.T. *Birth and Growth of the Eigenheim Mennonite Church, 1892–1974.* Rosthern: Valley Printers, 1974.

Klaassen, Walter. *Anabaptism: Neither Catholic nor Protestant.* Waterloo: Conrad Grebel Press, 1973, 1981; third edition: Pandora Press, 2002.

Klaassen, Walter. *The Days of Our Years: A History of the Eigenheim Mennonite Church Community, 1892–1992.* Rosthern: Eigenheim Mennonite Church, 1992.

Klassen, Herbert & Maureen. *Ambassador to His People: C.F. Klassen and the Russian Mennonite Refugees.* Winnipeg and Hillsboro: Kindred Press, 1990.

Neff, Christian, ed. *Bericht über die Mennonitische Welt-Hilfs-Konferenz vom 31. August bis 3. September 1930 in Danzig.* Karlsruhe: Verlag Heinrich Schneider, 1930.

Peters, Gerhard I. *Remember Our Leaders: Conference of Mennonites in Canada, 1902–1977.* Clearbrook: Mennonite Historical Society of British Columbia, 1982.

Poettcker, Henry, and Rudy A. Regehr, eds. *Call to Faithfulness: Essays in Canadian Mennonite Studies.* Winnipeg: CMBC Publications, 1972.

Regehr, T. D. *Mennonites in Canada 1939–1970: A People Transformed.* Toronto: University of Toronto Press, 1996.

Reimer, David P. *Experiences of the Mennonites of Canada during the Second World War, 1939–1945.* Altona: D.W. Friesen & Sons, n.d.

Rempel, Johann G. *Die Rosenorter Gemeinde in Saskatchewan.* Rosthern: D.H.Epp, 1950.

Rempel, Johann G., ed. *Fuenfzig Jahre Konferenzbestrebungen, 1902–1952.* Erster Teil (1902–1927), Zweiter Teil (1928–1952). Rosthern: Konferenz der Mennoniten in Canada, 1952.

Riegert, Paul W. *Deep Earth: A Short History of the Tiefengrund School District, No. 431 in Saskatchewan.* Regina: Rampeck Publishers, 1996.

Schaefer, Paul J. *Heinrich H. Ewert: Lehrer, Erzieher und Prediger der Mennoniten.* Gretna: Verlag der Manitoba Jugendorganization der Mennoniten-Konferenz von Canada, 1945. Translated as *Heinrich H. Ewert: Teacher, Educator and Minister of the Mennonites,* trans. Ida Toews. Winnipeg: CMBC Publications, 1990.

Smith, C. Henry. *Smith's Story of the Mennonites,* 4th ed., revised and enlarged. Newton: Mennonite Publishing Office, 1957.

Thiesen, John D. *Prussian Roots, Kansas Branches: A History of First Mennonite Church of Newton,* ed. and rev. Menno Schrag. Newton: Historical Committee of First Mennonite Church, 1986.

Toews, J.A. *Alternative Service in Canada during World War II.* Winnipeg: The Christian Press, 1959.

Toews, John B. *Czars, Soviets & Mennonites.* Newton: Faith and Life Press, 1982.

Toews, John B. *Lost Fatherland: The Story of the Mennonite Emigration from Soviet Russia, 1921–1927.* Scottdale: Herald Press, 1967.

Toews, John B. *With Courage to Spare: The Life of B.B. Janz.* Winnipeg: The Christian Press, 1978.

Wiebe, Dallas E. *Our Asian Journey: A Novel.* Waterloo: Department of English, Wilfred Laurier University, 1977.

Articles

Bartsch, Franz. "Epp, Claasz, Jr.," *Mennonite Encyclopedia,* vol. II. Scottdale: Mennonite Publishing House, 1956.

Bender, Harold S. "Mennonite Central Committee," *Mennonite Encyclopedia,* vol. III. Scottdale: Mennonite Publishing House, 1957.

Coffman, Samuel F. "Nonresistant Relief Organization (NRRO)," *Mennonite Encyclopedia,* vol. III. Scottdale: Mennonite Publishing House, 1957.

Doerksen, Ben. "*Kanadier* and *Russländer*: Tensions on the Prairies," *Mennonite Historian* 19 (June 1993): 1–2.

Dueck, Abe. "Canadian Mennonites and the Anabaptist Vision," *Mennonite Historian* 19 (December 1993): 1–2.

Funk, Helene (Dyck). "The Rosenort Mennonite Church of Saskatchewan, 1890–2000," *Saskatchewan Mennonite Historian* 5 (March 2000): 14–21.

Gerbrandt, J. "Canadian Mennonite Board of Colonization," *Mennonite Encyclopedia*, vol. I. Scottdale: Mennonite Publishing House, 1955.

Hege, Christian and Ernst Regehr. "Rosenort Mennonite Church," *Mennonite Encyclopedia*, vol. IV. Scottdale: Mennonite Publishing House, 1959.

Janzen, J.H. "Erinnerungen an A.A.Friesen und David Toews," *Mennonitisches Jahrbuch* 65 (1950): 18–24.

Janzen, Marianne. "Notes on the Emigration of Russian Mennonites to Mexico, 1924–1929," *Mennonite Historian* 16 (March 1990): 1–2.

Janzen, Waldemar. "The Great Trek: Episode or Paradigm?" *Mennonite Quarterly Review* 51 (April 1977): 282–289.

Kaufmann, E.G. "Halstead Seminary," *Mennonite Encyclopedia*, vol. II. Scottdale: Mennonite Publishing House, 1956.

Klippenstein, Lawrence "Strengthening Mennonite Ties: Letters by S.F. Coffman and H.H. Ewert," *Mennonite Historian* 21 (June 1995): 1–2, and 21 (September 1995): 4–5.

Klippenstein, Lawrence. "Peter Regier—Churchman-farmer (1851–1925)," *Mennonite Historian* 2 (December 1976): 1–2.

Klippenstein, Lawrence. "Western Local Mennonite Teachers' Conference—An Early Minute Book," *Manitoba Pageant* (Winter 1977): 9–10.

Krahn, Cornelius. "Central Mennonite Immigration Committee (Das zentrale mennonitische Immigrantenkomitee)," *Mennonite Encyclopedia*, vol. I. Scottdale: Mennonite Publishing House, 1955.

Krahn, Cornelius. "Kansas," *Mennonite Encyclopedia*, vol. III. Scottdale: Mennonite Publishing House, 1957.

Letkemann, Peter. "Mennonite Victims of Revolution, Anarchy, Civil War, Disease and Famine, 1917–1923," *Mennonite Historian* 24 (June 1998): 1ff.

Paetkau, Peter and Lawrence Klippenstein. "The Conference of Mennonites in Canada: Background and Origin," *Mennonite Life* 34 (December 1979): 4–10.

Redekop, Benjamin. "German Nationalism among Canadian Mennonites during the Early 1930s," *Mennonite Historian* 19 (September 1993): 1–2, 9–10.

Rempel, D.D. "From Russia to Canada, Twenty-Five Years Ago," *Mennonite Life* 3 (July 1948): 42–44.

Rempel, Johann G. "David Toews," *Mennonite Encyclopedia*, vol. IV. Scottdale: Mennonite Publishing House, 1959.

Rempel, J.G. "Rosenort Mennonite Church (GCM)," *Mennonite Ency-*

clopedia, vol. IV. Scottdale: Mennonite Publishing House, 1959.

Rempel, Peter H. "Inter-Mennonite Cooperation and Promises to Government in the Repeal of the Ban on Mennonite Immigration to Canada 1919–1922," *Mennonite Historian* 19 (March 1993): 1, 7.

Rempel, Peter H. "The First Canadian Mennonite Central Committee, 1920–1924," *Mennonite Historian* 21 (December 1995): 1–2.

Schaefer, Paul J. "Mennonite Collegiate Institute," *Mennonite Encyclopedia*, vol. III. Scottdale: Mennonite Publishing House, 1957.

Toews, David. "Die Auswanderung aus Russland bis Herbst, 1928," *Mennonitische Welt-Hilfs-Konferenz von 31. August bis 3. September 1930 in Danzig (1930)*: 73–79.

Toews, David. "Die Einwanderung nach Kanada vom Herbst 1928 bis jetzt," *Mennonitische Welt-Hilfs-Konferenz (1930)*: 94–99.

Toews, David. "The Mennonites of Canada," *Mennonite Quarterly Review* 11 (January 1937): 83–91.

Toews, Jacob. "A Short Sketch of my Life," with forward by the translators Frank L. and Anna (Toevs) Wenger. Aberdeen, Idaho, 1963. David Toews project files, MHC Archives, Winnipeg.

Wedel, P.G. and E.G. Kaufman. "Halstead Seminary," *Mennonite Encyclopedia*, vol. II. Scottdale: Mennonite Publishing House, 1956.

Unpublished Sources

"Aus den ersten Tagen der Ansiedler um Rosthern herum." MHC Archives, vol. 1079, file 8, n.d.

Engbrecht, Dennis D. "The Americanization of a Rural Immigrant Church: The General Conference Mennonites in Central Kansas, 1874–1939." PhD dissertation, University of Nebraska Press, 1990.

Epp, Frank H. "An Analysis of Germanism and National Socialism in the Immigrant Newspaper of a Canadian Minority Group, the Mennonites, in the 1930s." PhD dissertation, University of Minnesota, 1965.

Fransen, David Warren. "Canadian Mennonites and Conscientious Objection in World War II." MA thesis, University of Waterloo, 1977.

Klaassen, Martin, "Martin Klaassen Diary of the Trek to Central Asia, 1880–81." MHC Archives, vol. 4221, file 2.

Paetkau, Henry. "Separation or Integration?: The Russian Mennonite Immigrant Community in Ontario, 1924–1945." PhD dissertation, University of Western Ontario, 1986.

Peters, Jacob. "Organizational Change within a Religious Denomination: A Case Study of the Conference of Mennonites in Canada, 1902–1978." PhD dissertation, University of Waterloo, 1986.

Redekop, Benjamin Wall, "The German Identity of Mennonite Brethren Immigrants in Canada, 1930–1960." MA (History) thesis, University of British Columbia, 1990.

Rempel, Johann G. "Ältester David Toews' Lebensgeschichte bis zur Einwanderung der Russländer." Manuscript in archives of the Canadian Mennonite Board of Colonization.

Schellenberg, B.J., "Ältester David Toews, D.D.c.c.: Sein Leben und Wirken," May, 1949. MHC Archives, vol. 1184.

Toews, David, "Erinnerungen aus der Zeit der Russlandhilfe und Immigrationsarbeit." Unpublished manuscript, 1934. Mennonite Heritage Centre Archives, Winnipeg..

Periodicals, Church Papers, and Yearbooks

Conference of Mennonites in Canada Yearbooks, 1903 to 1947
*Der Bote
Der Herold
Der Immigranten-Bote
The Mennonite
Der Mitarbeiter
Die Mennonitische Rundschau
Mennonite Mirror
Mennonite Historian
Saskatchewan Mennonite Historian
Saskatchewan Valley News

*Der Bote contains more than 150 articles, reports, and notes by David Toews. References to many of these appear in the footnotes.

Archival Collections

David Toews files on the Board of Missions of the General Conference Mennonite Church, MHC Archives, Winnipeg

Canadian Mennonite Board of Colonization files, MHC Archives, Winnipeg

A.A. Friesen holdings on microfilm at MHC Archives; originals Mennonite Library and Archives, North Newton, Kansas

Katherine Hooge papers, Mennonite Historical Society of Saskatchewan, Saskatoon

Private collection of Louise (Toews) Friesen

Personal files of David Toews, MHC Archives, Winnipeg

Rosenort Mennonite Church files, MHC Archives, Winnipeg

Interviews and Conversations

Henry Bartel, Saskatoon – 29 July 2000

Leo Driedger, Winnipeg – 16 December 2001
Otto and Florence Driedger, Regina – 14 February 2000
Louise (Toews) and C. Blake Friesen, Calgary – 2 August 2000
Verner Friesen, Saskatoon – 29 July 2000
Anna (Toews) and Sylvester Funk, Saskatoon – 29 July 2000
Henry and Elfrieda Harder, Saskatoon – 29 July 2000
Elsie (Toews) Hooge, Saskatoon – 29 July 2000
Katherine (Kaethe) Hooge, Eston (formerly of Rosthern and Saskatoon)
    – 1 August 2000
Tina Hooge, Rosthern – 31 July 2000
Margaret (Hooge) and Henry Jantzen, Regina – 14 February 2000
Paul Schroeder, Abbotsford, British Columbia – 14 July 2001
Group conversation in Rosthern, with Cornelius J. and Wilma Dyck,
    Helen Dyck, Rita Enns, Tina Isaac, Sarah Krause, Helena Lesser,
    Anne Martens, Elise Quiring, Ed Schmidt – 30 July 2000

Helmut Harder, professor emeritus of Canadian Mennonite University, was born in Manitoba to immigrant parents. In 1934, the year of his birth, they moved from Arnaud, Manitoba, to Beamsville, Ontario. Helmut studied at Eden Christian College, Niagara-on-the-Lake, at the Normal School and McMaster University in Hamilton, at Mennonite Biblical Seminary in Elkhart, Indiana, and graduated from the Toronto School of Theology with a ThD in theology. In 1962 he moved to Winnipeg where he served as professor of theology at Canadian Mennonite Bible College until 1990. He was general secretary of the Conference of Mennonites in Canada from 1990 until his retirement in 1999.

Helmut is the author of numerous books, including *Guide to Faith* (1980), *The Biblical Way of Peace* (1982), *Accountability in the Church* (1985), and *Understanding the Faith in a Mennonite Perspective* (1997). He has travelled and worked internationally on behalf of the Mennonite church, and served for a year in Taiwan under the Commission on Overseas Mission of the General Conference Mennonite Church.

Helmut and his wife Irma live in Winnipeg where Irma is a teacher of voice and piano. Their family circle includes two sons Bryan (daughter-in-law Cheryl Pauls) and Randall, a daughter Marilee, and two grandsons Jonathan and Nicholas.